Family Matters in the British
and American Novel

Family Matters in the British and American Novel

editors

Andrea O'Reilly Herrera
Elizabeth Mahn Nollen
Sheila Reitzel Foor

Bowling Green State University Popular Press
Bowling Green, OH 43403

Copyright © 1997 Bowling Green State University Popular Press

Library of Congress Cataloging-in-Publication Data
Family matters in the British and American novel / Andrea O'Reilly
   Herrera, Elizabeth Mahn Nollen, and Sheila Reitzel Foor, editors.
      p.   cm.
   Includes bibliographical references (p.   ) and index.
   ISBN 0-87972-745-4 (cloth). -- ISBN 0-87972-746-2 (pbk.)
   1. Domestic fiction, English--History and criticism. 2. Domestic
fiction, American--History and criticism. 3. Family in literature.
I. Herrera, Andrea O'Reilly. II. Nollen, Elizabeth Mahn. III. Foor,
Sheila M. (Sheila Marie), 1949- .
PR830.D65F36   1997
823.009'355--dc21
                                                            97-10064
                                                              CIP

Cover design by Dumm Art

We dedicate this book

to all those

who make our family circles complete

A. O. H.

E. M. N.

S. R. F.

Contents

Preface

Family Matters is the product of what has indeed been a truly collaborative effort evidencing academe working at its very best. We editors and contributors have crossed paths, mentored one another, and genuinely broadened our horizons through meetings at conferences such as those of the Popular Culture Association, Mid-Atlantic Popular Culture, MLA, NEMLA, SAMLA, CCCC's, NCTE, New York College English Association, Pennsylvania College English Association, the American Women of Color conference, and many more. Most of us have served as area chairs, have chaired panels and have delivered dozens of papers in such venues. This book should reflect the value of universities' continuing to fund such faculty activities.

We coeditors have exchanged numerous ideas for papers/panels over several years, discovering in the process that we had very similar takes on particular issues outside the norm. At one women's conference we were, in fact, the only panel addressing a full-time female faculty member's ability to juggle—successfully—family, home, and academe. Long-time spouses and parents all, the audience discussants generated breaths of fresh air; many appreciated our having addressed the topic at an academic conference and expressed the notion that they had heretofore felt marginalized while wearing several hats simultaneously. However, we noted both there and elsewhere numerous other familial patterns and configurations equally successful, equally worthy of study. These patterns, it seemed to us, had always been varied and prominent in the novel. Thus began our sojourn into matters of family.

Interestingly, this project brings together three editors who, in other writing, are quite diverse. My book, *Dickens' Rhetoric* (1993); Andrea's novel, *The Pearl of the Antilles* (1997); and Elizabeth's composition text, *Cultural Connections: Explorations in Popular Culture* (1997) indicate the breadth of our own interests enriched further by those authors whose essays have been included in the collection. A glance at the contributors' section reveals their wealth of academic pursuit, background, and expertise. The theme obviously strikes a chord.

While the collection contains essays by both Andrea and Elizabeth, my main contribution has been in editing/proofreading—the close, detail work that in part is what makes English teachers English teachers. It has been a privilege to work with such outstanding scholars.

Andrea, Elizabeth, and I wish particularly to thank our English Departments—SUNY at Fredonia, West Chester University, and Lincoln University, respectively—for their support of conference activities which leads to such productive networking and friendships beyond the borders of our individual campuses and interests. It is always a joy to work with Pat Browne and her staff at Popular Press, who are as task-oriented as we are. And, finally, our spouses and children need to be recognized for their shouldering of those extra family matters while we forged a little more room of our own.

Sheila Reitzel Foor

Introduction

Andrea O'Reilly Herrera

"The family," writes Ian Robertson, "is the most basic and ancient of all social institutions, and it remains the fundamental social unit in every society."[1] It is, in other words, the primary unit of social organization. Though it was not entirely self-sufficient, the preindustrial household in Britain and colonial America—often consisting of more than two generations of a kinship line, servants, and sometimes boarders living together either in the same home or in adjacent dwellings—was a "unit of production which largely depended upon goods that were produced within the home."[2] As a result, there was little distinction between the private and public spheres, and women's work was, for the most part, valued equally to men's. During the latter half of the eighteenth and early nineteenth centuries, however, fundamental changes in the nature and the configuration of the household and the family occurred, due in part to industrial capitalism, scientific advancements, and improvements in methods of production and modes of transportation. Both Britain and the United States moved away from a "home" or "family" economy and entered an expanding foreign market, and cottage industries moved outside of the domestic sphere.

As both countries became increasingly urbanized and industrialized throughout the eighteenth and nineteenth centuries, visible shifts began to occur not only between the classes but in gender roles and relations as well. In effect, personal achievement and economic success came to be based upon merit, rather than birth or inheritance. By the end of the eighteenth century, aspects of courting practices rapidly began to transform as well. Not only were unions being forged between the classes, but marriages were frequently founded on love, rather than being arranged according to heredity or economic status.[3] As Robertson observes, the concept or phenomenon of marriage based on romantic love, rather than on pragmatic considerations, was a "cultural trait found primarily in industrialized" capitalist societies. Although the extended, multi-generational household continued to exist within the ranks of the urban elite and middle class, it was gradually replaced by a smaller,

1

often geographically isolated, nuclear family (consisting of a monogamous couple and their dependent children), which resided apart from
other relatives and thus established a neolocal pattern.

Although the family continued to function as an institution based on
"economic dependence," the middle-class nuclear family gradually
became a "privitized affectionate unit" and women were ensconced at
the center of that order. Largely excluded from the public realm of cultural and economic production, middle- to upper-class women and children were relegated to the domestic sphere. As a result, the nineteenth
century simultaneously witnessed an increasingly sentimentalized view
of children and developed rigorous codes of female deportment. "Home
idealism," combined with the "cult" or "ideology" of "true womanhood," not only promoted female chastity and envisioned marriage and,
consequently, motherhood as the fulfillment of a woman's destiny, but it
confirmed a gendered division of labor. In effect, a woman's social significance was defined in terms of her physiological functions and her
activities within the domestic sphere, and a man's to his success in the
public economic arena.

Up until the last few decades, the nuclear familial "norm" that
British and American society publicly advocated and, moreover, characterized as being representative was monogamous, patriarchal, heterosexual, middle to upper class, and Caucasian. In reality, however, many sub-
cultural variations in the organization of the family have always existed
and coexisted in Britain and the United States. Often, these configurations are not solely based on kinship ties, nor are they always heterosexual, patriarchal, and/or nuclear. Nevertheless these alternative familial
patterns had until recently gone largely unacknowledged in popular culture or were perceived as being aberrant, unacceptable, and inferior
simply because they did not conform to the public norm.

In recent years, however, phrases such as "the traditional family" or
"the ideal family" have, for all intents and purposes, become obsolete.
As early as the 1970s, anthropologists and sociologists began to predict
the total disappearance of the nuclear familial system. Many pointed to
statistical evidence, such as the rising rates of divorce and illegitimacy,
whereas others emphasized the changing role of women and, consequently, men, the increasing secularization of society, the spread of
sexual permissiveness, the perceived sense that society at large had low-
ered its values and moral standards, and the growing acceptance or
"political correctness" of alternatives to traditional marriages and family
structures. Nowadays, as the title of a recent critical study suggests,
many perceive that "family history" is "at the crossroads."[4] As the
divorce rate continues to soar and single-parenting increasingly becomes

the norm, the British ideal of family life, which is purportedly represented (however illusory it may be) by the royal family, or the Ozzie and Harriet image of middle-class family life portrayed in the media in the 1950s and 1960s has not only virtually ceased to exist but for the most part has been acknowledged to be an impossible ideal for most to measure up to. Increasingly, in both the media and society at large, there seems to be a growing recognition and acceptance of diversity and an acknowledgement of alternative lifestyles and alternative time allocations—a direct result of the changed conditions of contemporary social and economic life—and a tendency to be more outspoken about (familial) dysfunction.[5]

* * *

The gradually shifting practices and perceptions regarding courtship and the institutions of marriage and the family can be traced in literature as well as in life. During the nineteenth century, for example, as British and American society moved toward a more democratic mode of governance and away from a stratified class system based on heredity, and women slowly gained a legal identity, novels gradually ceased to conclude with what has come to be known as the "marriage solution." And thus, in scarcely over a century, novels such as Francis Burney's and Jane Austen's, in which the themes of marriage and love are of central thematic significance and supply continuity and cohesion to the plot, were replaced by works that either treated the theme of the failed marriage, divorce, and disillusioned love or posed radical solutions and alternatives such as bigamy, free love, open marriages, or utopian communities of independent women that thrive without male protection or guardianship.[6] More contemporary writers have acknowledged that although the nuclear family continues to exist in modern society, it often suffers from dysfunction.[7] In their works, they tend to deromanticize marriage and child rearing and treat taboo subjects such as incest, adultery, and child abuse. In addition, the burgeoning of multicultural literature has introduced into the canon a wide variety of works that portray not only alternative familial configurations but culturally and economically diverse paradigms as well.

Family Matters examines a body of literature that challenges and alters widely held assumptions about the form of the family, familial authority patterns, and the function of courtship, marriage, and family life from the late eighteenth century to the present time in Britain and the United States. The essays in this collection are arranged in roughly chronological order to reflect broadly defined historical periods. Thus,

Family Matters opens with two essays that consider late eighteenth- and early nineteenth-century novelists who paralleled larger political and social movements with the struggles within the family unit. In the work of these writers, the family functions as a microcosm of the larger political sphere.

Comparable in geographical location and chronological period, Susan Allen Ford's and Charlene E. Bunnell's studies are based on the premise that from the late eighteenth through the nineteenth century in Britain the very notion that the family and the state were analogous bodies raised the issue of their constitution and suggested the centrality of women to both the body and the family politic. The result was an emerging identity that politicized the private, the domestic, and the feminine. The novel, a genre largely appropriated by women during this period, was implicated in this contest over definition perhaps more than any other literary form. Allen Ford and Bunnell thus argue that novelists such as Charlotte Smith, Jane West, Eliza Fenwick, Mrs. Opie, and Mary Shelley entered, either directly or indirectly, into the debate about family responsibilities and national duties.

In "Tales of the Times: Family and Nation in Charlotte Smith and Jane West," Susan Allen Ford reveals that Charlotte Smith's *Desmond* (1792) and Jane West's *A Tale of the Times* (1799) approached the debate about family responsibilities and national duties from quite different political perspectives. As these novelists depict a society facing the promise or the threat of change, both Smith and West use the family to register its destructive and destabilizing pressures. For both novelists, moreover, the family is also the source of restorative power, and each explores the means toward family reform. To embody these critiques, both Smith and West suggest a redefinition of family fictions themselves, partly through the form of the wedlock plot—or, as Joseph Allen Boone would have it, its countertradition—and through their experimentation with narrative modes. The definitions of family and nation that arise from these novels, however, are radically divergent: Smith suggests an egalitarian model, which disrupts the traditional lines of power and authority, while West demands submission to a hierarchical model that enforces those traditional relationships. As Charlotte Smith and Jane West engage in the struggle over what the family is or should be—what the nation is or should be—they provide a shape for the anxieties that haunt their culture and are implicated in the construction of what Benedict Anderson has termed the "imagined communities" that are Britain.

In a similar vein, Charlene E. Bunnell's "Breaking the Tie That Binds: Parents and Children in Romantic Fiction" suggests that when put into relief against the social upheavals of the late eighteenth and early nineteenth centuries, respectively, Fenwick, Opie, and Shelley expose the problematics resulting from filial dissidence and disobedience. In Fenwick's *Secresy: or, The Ruin on the Rock* (1795) the heroine, Caroline Ashburne, revolts against her mother's strict view of social manners and behavior and calls for a more principled and tolerant practice. In the same vein, Adeline, the namesake of Mrs. Opie's *Adeline Mowbray* (1806), incurs her mother's disfavor by living her life according to Mrs. Mowbray's staid theories regarding marriage and male-female relationships. In both of these works, the daughters discover that they must sacrifice the accepted notion of "duty to parent" and break the maternal tie to achieve independence and self-esteem. In contrast to these two earlier novelists, Mary Shelley, in her sixth novel, *Lodore* (1835), depicts the dangers when the bond between parent and child is broken. Although the separation threatens the mother rather than the daughter, Lady Lodore is eventually redeemed and made whole once again by Ethel's love and example and by the recognition of her duty as a mother.

During the Victorian period the idea of home—embodied by the white, patriarchal, middle-class household—came to represent social and political stability in both the British and the American imagination. Despite the sentimentalized public image of home and family preserved and perpetuated both in domestic fiction and in conduct books, the family was, by that time, undergoing dramatic transformations as a result of imperialism, industrialism, and women's changing roles and options in society. The next three essays in the collection, therefore, explore works that contest or posit alternatives to the rigorous image of the nuclear family. "Herself Beheld: Marriage, Motherhood, and Oppression in Brontë's *Villette* and Jacobs's *Incidents in the Life of a Slave Girl*," by Andrea O'Reilly Herrera, compares Charlotte Brontë's fictional, semi-autobiographical autobiography to Harriet Jacobs's celebrated account of her own experiences as a suffering slave mother. Although their "autobiographies" are ostensibly quite different, when compared it soon becomes apparent that Brontë's and Jacobs's works, written less than four years apart, mirror each other in surprising and extraordinary ways. Both contest the public vision of female deportment and female destiny—a vision that suggests that marriage and motherhood complete a woman's destiny. In *Villette* Charlotte Brontë depicts the plight of a genteel Victorian spinster seeking to carve out a space for herself, both economically and psychically, in a society in which female identity is largely dependent upon pedigree, personal appearance, and sexual integrity. In an attempt to address the issues of personal versus private identity, Brontë sends her heroine, Lucy Snowe, abroad on a quest to find personal fulfillment. In her foreign environment Lucy defies the traditional roles allotted to women and establishes herself as an independent agent, free of male guardianship and protection, without precluding the possibility of love.

Like Charlotte Brontë, Harriet Jacobs writes in response to her own painful circumstances, but she, unlike Brontë, must first establish her fundamental rights not simply as a woman but as a human being. Although she appeals for the chance to fulfill the very ideals of womanhood that Brontë rejects, the end result—from a contemporary vantage point—is that her autobiography becomes an exposé that reveals the shortcomings of what she characterizes as two combatant institutions— slavery and the black family—for both predetermine her destiny not only as a woman but as a human being. When paired together, Brontë's and Jacobs's works stand as powerful commentaries on women's positions and roles, particularly as they relate to the family, during the Victorian period. Ultimately, both reveal the limitations of Britain's and America's vision of women and the family.

Maureen Thum's "Breaking Loose From 'Chin-Bands of the Soul': Barrett Browning's Re-Visioning of the Patriarchal Family" argues that Elizabeth Barrett Browning's verse novel *Aurora Leigh* (1857) also presents a sustained, if not implicit, critique of bourgeois and patriarchal norms. Furthermore, Barrett Browning's work radically departs both from the doctrine of the nuclear family and from its corollary, the doctrine of separate spheres. Instead of depicting the bourgeois family as a static, self-enclosed unit, the author argues for a wider, more inclusive view of family as a flexible, dynamic network of relationships, capable of multiple transformations and even of drastic alterations. In exploring the relationship of her protagonist, Aurora Leigh, to a series of families depicted throughout the work, Barrett Browning not only emphasizes the potential instability and volatility of the nuclear family, but she also proposes alternative arrangements and support networks that violate the strict patterns of the bourgeois ideal of family life. These alternative, less strictly conceived familial groupings carry out functions that the nuclear family, with its prescriptive roles and static relationships, cannot fulfill.

In contrast to O'Reilly Herrera's and Thum's essays, Frank P. Riga examines the image of the patriarchal family in Victorian children's literature. In "(De)constructing the Patriarchal Family: Mary Louisa Molesworth and the Late Nineteenth-Century Children's Novel," Riga points out that contrary to some widely held assumptions about the inflexibility of the Victorian family structure, Mary Louisa Molesworth unobtrusively questioned the status quo of the rigorous, patriarchal image of the nuclear family. In her 1887 children's novel *The Palace in the Garden*, she uses the naive, unformed child narrator to provide an unusual view of a family mystery, the resolution of which leads to a reconstruction of the nuclear family on lines different from what a strict construction of patriarchal ideology would allow. Part of the "naive" narrator's strategy involves her mixing of "realism" or actual events with fairy tales. These two modes of perception result in a dialectic in which the information of the actual events is processed through the "magic subversion" of the fairy tale. Initially, fairy tales help the narrator make sense of her family reality and, by novel's end, they help reshape the reality of the family. Approaching the family from this angle allows the older forms and images of domestic life to contain new dimensions, thereby preserving a sense of familiarity and security while negotiating new terms for family vitality. In other words, though the family seems to have retained its traditional aspects, it maintains its integrity and stability by being transformed. A careful reading of Molesworth's book, therefore, reveals that many of our current assumptions about the Victorian family are probably too narrow and formulaic to describe the manner in which individuals adjusted the family structure to meet everyday realities.

Scott F. Stoddart rounds off the period in his treatment of the subject of the family in Henry James's *Portrait of a Lady* (1881) and E. M. Forster's *Howards End* (1910). In his essay, he takes a slightly different tack by focusing on the particular problems connected with step-parenting—a highly charged and equally ignored subject by composers of the domestic tradition in the nineteenth-century novel. "The 'Muddle' of Step-Parenting: Reconstructing Domestic Harmony in James and Forster" thus examines these two canonical works within the tradition of the American and British domestic novel, both long-understood to exist as women's traditions. Each writer focuses on the particular ordeals of their central heroines as they enter marriages with previously constructed families. James's heroine, Isabel Archer, is a woman who believes her destiny will produce a most "extraordinary" life. She finds that parenting satisfies her immediate needs; however, her relations with Pansy Osmond, the daughter of her foppish husband Osmond, creates a bond which threatens *his* position within this new family. In the same vein, Forster's Margaret Schlegel, who enters a marriage with Henry Wilcox, finds her new role as mother equally precarious, but for very different reasons. The Wilcox children, who are already grown up, conceive of their father's remarriage as a threat to their selfish notion of family, mainly because of Margaret's connection to their deceased mother. In both novels the women simultaneously represent threats to male control over the domestic sphere, and to the class system as a whole. Experimenting with the conventions of domestic fiction by focusing on the undervalued role of step-parents, James and Forster cast their female protagonists within roles that introduced their contemporary audiences to the changing definitions of the family; ultimately, they serve as a basis for the reexamination of men's literature through feminist revisionism.

At the close of the nineteenth century feminist thinkers initiated a rigorous investigation of female identity as it related to all aspects of a woman's life. A dialogue resulted among these women that incorporated radical as well as more conservative points of view. This dialogue becomes the complex subject of female authors such as Virginia Woolf and Edith Wharton. In "Virginia Woolf's Dialogues with the 'New Woman,'" Wendy Perkins suggests that the intricate narrative structure of Woolf's *To the Lighthouse* (1927) reveals fragmentary and contradictory images of female identity. Throughout the novel Lily Briscoe struggles to define Mrs. Ramsay and her relation to her world, and thus defines a role for herself. Lily's explorations create dialogues on several levels: between Lily and Mrs. Ramsay, between the text and Woolf's contemporaries, and between the text and the reader. Throughout the novel Lily struggles to achieve a concrete vision of self, to find the "essential thing" in Mrs. Ramsay, and to represent on canvas the latter's roles as mother and wife. Lily's task is complicated, though, by the shifting personal and cultural lenses through which her gaze is filtered— lenses that delineate Lily's own varied roles as artist, spinster, friend, and surrogate daughter. These diverse points of view and oppositional discourses regarding the nature of marriage and motherhood, which are framed by the novel's chapters, simultaneously suggest the difficulties inherent in a woman's quest for an authentic, nonrelational self, and create a fragmented narrative that functions as a critique of representation in general and a denial of any absolute vision of female identity in particular.

Taking up the same subject, Hildegard Hoeller's "Competing Mothers: Edith Wharton's Late Vision of Family Life" focuses on the late work of Edith Wharton which was, according to Elizabeth Ammons, "obsessed with the subject of motherhood." In her essay, Hoeller argues that in her novellas "The Old Maid" (1924) and "Her Son" (1933) Wharton offers strikingly complex and unconventional ways of looking at motherhood. Her stories, overtly dealing with motherhood, are driven by the secret force of "illegitimate" (meaning extramarital) female desire. Wharton's anarchic celebration of a particular, "illegitimate," passionate motherhood allows her to launch a devastating critique of "legitimate" family life within marriage and to reveal or allow the centrality of female sexual desire in her tales and in the lives of her characters. Wharton's heroines—the "real" mothers in these works—are willing to pay any price; they are driven by a sentimental passion for their children that is unrestrained and unconditional. Like the heroines of sentimental fiction, Wharton's protagonists stand in sharp contrast to the world around them—a world that calculates and schemes. But unlike sentimental fiction, marriage most forcefully symbolizes this world of calculation in Wharton's works. Therefore, all of her characters seek meaning in the space of illegitimacy, a space that dangerously mingles female sexual desire and motherhood. It is a space in which lovers, in the guise of "mothers," exploit and destroy the "true" mothers. Wharton's late vision of family life thus speaks most powerfully to the dangerous power of illegitimate female desire and the stifling oppression of the legitimate space of marriage.

Although her focus is more contemporary, Aleta F. Cane also explores the figure of the mother. "In Demythifying Motherhood in Three Novels by Fay Weldon," Cane suggests that in *Puffball* (1980), *The Lives and Loves of a She-Devil* (1983), and *Life Force* (1992) Weldon parodies the Freudian myths of motherhood and rejects patriarchal society's marginalization of women and of women's roles as mothers. In so doing, Weldon also explodes the prevailing notion that feminism and post modernism are mutually exclusive critical modalities. Relying upon theories of feminist critics such as Chodorow, Suleiman and Kristeva, Cane's essay isolates five Freudian myths and explores the ways in which Weldon shows them to be utterly false. The works of Freudians Helene Deutsch and Melanie Klein are cited to foreground the androcentric ideology that Weldon takes to task. In her use of parody, Weldon demonstrates throughout these three novels that poor mothering begets poor mothering. Moreover, Weldon's protagonist-mothers explore and embrace radical ideas about mothering, including selling one's own children to ensure them a better life. Such solutions create the necessary gaps in readers' minds in which questions develop and changes are begun. Thus, Weldon opens the way for speculation about other ways of seeing and other ways of being a mother.

Treating a theme which is frequently ignored or overlooked, the next three authors shift the focus from female to male parenting. Although it employs the same method as Allen Ford's and Bunnell's studies, D. Quentin Miller's "Updike's *Rabbit* Novels and the Tragedy of Parenthood" follows a slightly different trajectory, for not only does it focus on the developing relationship of a father and son but it treats novels that are set in the United States during the Cold War. In his work, Miller observes that during this period in history American novelists of social realism began to question whether social institutions such as the family were able to provide any stability in a chaotic world. John

Updike's *Rabbit* tetralogy (*Rabbit, Run* 1960, *Rabbit Redux* 1971, *Rabbit Is Rich* 1981, *Rabbit at Rest* 1990) provides a striking example of the fate of both the family and, consequently, parenthood during this period. The animosity and jealousy that arise between Harry "Rabbit" Angstrom and his son, Nelson, becomes the dominant concern of the last two novels in this tetralogy, though the breakdown of this father-son relationship has its roots in the first two. Both father and son feel as though they are deprived of the American Dream—a concept held especially precious during the Cold War—and each feels the other is to blame. Harry was clearly unprepared for parenthood when it surprised him in the 1950s; his consequent irresponsibility, which provokes Nelson's destructive reactions, sets into motion a tragic pattern that runs through the four novels, complete with the catharsis of Nelson's rehabilitation and commitment to his own family—a commitment that Harry never realizes.

Addressing the theme of male parenting from a different angle, Elizabeth Mahn Nollen, in "Fatherhood Lost and Regained in the Novels of Anne Tyler," examines Tyler's positive representation of the father figure. Mahn Nollen's essay opens with an examination (though not chronological) of three male protagonists who lie along a continuum of fatherly effectiveness in parenting: Jeremy Tull in *Celestial Navigation* (1974), Ian Bedloe in *Saint Maybe* (1991), and Macon Leary in *The Accidental Tourist* (1985). Although the sculptor Jeremy Tull is humanized by his experience with fatherhood, art wins out over life in the end as he reluctantly abandons his children to a squalid existence with their mother. Ian Bedloe, on the other hand, proves to be a quite effective, if reluctant, step-father to his dead brother's children. Moreover, he is given a "second chance" at parenting, as it were, with his own child, which promises to be a joyful, if worrisome, undertaking. The third protagonist Mahn Nollen treats, Macon Leary, is also given a "second chance" at parenting after the tragic death of his son, Ethan, when he accepts the role of step-parent to Alexander, the son of his female companion, Muriel. Thus, we move from Jeremy, who is neither allowed nor fully able to develop his budding parental instincts, to Ian, who has the potential to become an effective father to his own biological child after forcing himself to parent his brother's children as a penance. Finally, in Macon Leary, Tyler presents what is in her works the apogee of good fathering. Through a mutually regenerative process Macon transforms the sickly Alexander into the healthy, well-adjusted son that Ethan had been, and in the process the psychologically damaged Macon is transformed into the relaxed and successful father he could never be with his own child. In addition, Macon makes Muriel into a less obsessive, hence more effective, mother. It is Macon Leary, more than Jeremy Tull or Ian Bedloe, who learns to enjoy, and indeed joyfully embrace, father-hood.

The final studies in our collection—"Moynihan's 'Tangle of Pathol-ogy': Toni Morrison's Legacy of Motherhood," and "Pregnant with Pos-sibilites: Revisions in the Family Romance in Stephen McCauley's *The Object of My Affection*"—represent the most extreme challenges to widely held public assumptions about family and parenthood. In her essay, Michelle Pagni Stewart reads Toni Morrison's *Song of Solomon* (1977) and *Beloved* (1987) in light of the findings of the 1965 Moynihan Report—a study conducted at the behest of the United States Govern-ment. In his report, Daniel Moynihan argued that the deterioration and instability of the African American family, due to absent fathers and ille-gitimacy, among other things, was the major source of the social disad-vantages or "problems" faced by the black community, such as the exceptionally high rates of poverty. He suggested, moreover, that the matriarchal family system represented the main obstacle to racial equal-ity. Pagni Stewart then contrasts the different families represented in each of Morrison's novels. She suggests that Pilate's and Sethe's fami-lies, respectively, are typical of the ones depicted in Daniel Moynihan's report, whereas Macon's family in *Song of Solomon* more closely resem-bles what Moynihan would have characterized as a "normal" family—a father in charge of a financially secure household. Pagni Stewart points out, however, that when one examines the children in these households, it soon becomes apparent that the family structure is not responsible for the problems that the members of these younger generations experience. Instead, Morrison suggests that their problems stem from the institution-alized prejudice and discrimination in American society.

Focusing upon yet another alternative familial paradigm, Paul M. Puccio examines McCauley's *The Object of My Affection* (1987), a novel that explores the viability of reinventing the family according to dis-tinctly modern facts of life, such as the feminist value structure, gay lib-eration, AIDS, the obstacles (internal and external) to commitment in personal relationships, the necessity of double income households, and the need for child care. Yet the novel also investigates why its characters are not prepared for the very social and political changes that they embody—how alternatives to the nuclear family have not been success-fully assimilated into the economic structure and social fabric of modern American life; how our mythologies of the ideal family prevent us from envisioning more viable structures. This novel subverts narrative as well as social conventions, thus suggesting the need for a new family saga form that corresponds to the demands of contemporary life.

This study has taken as its directive the exploration of the multifarious ways in which a wide array of British and American writers have not only questioned the notion of a familial norm, but have, in some cases, redefined or refigured—and in the process posited alternative paradigms to—the patriarchal configuration of the nuclear family unit. The literary works treated in this volume were not chosen to constitute an all-inclusive treatment or a chronologically focused period. Rather, they represent a broad approach that demonstrates the diverse critical approaches that the subject of the family has elicited in a variety of British and American authors working within the domestic tradition. As these essays suggest, art does not merely imitate or comment upon life by pointing to the complexity of human relationships, it also paves the way to a different kind of life.

Notes

1. For more information on this subject see chapter 24 of Robertson's textbook *Sociology* (New York: Worth, 1977) 349-75, or chapter 13 of James W. Vander Zanden's *The Social Experience: An Introduction to Sociology* (New York: McGraw Hill, 1990) 368-97.

2. Much of the information on the family—particularly regarding men's and women's roles—was taken from Naomi Gerstel and Harriet Engel Gross's thorough examination of this subject in their essay "Gender and Families in the United States: The Reality of Economic Dependence," *Women, A Feminist Perspective*, ed. J. Freeman (Mountain View, CA: Mayfield, 1995, 92-127); and Lawrence Stone's *The Family, Sex, and Marriage in England*, 1500-1800 (New York: Harper, 1977). See also Martha Vicinus' *Independent Women, Work and Community for Single Women, 1850-1920* (Chicago: U of Chicago P, 1985), and Edward Shorter's *The Making of the Modern Family* (New York: Basic, 1975). I would also like to acknowledge the assistance of my colleague Peter Sinden.

3. Novels such as Samuel Richardson's *Pamela, or Virtue Rewarded* (1740-41), Jane Austen's *Persuasion* (1815-16), and Emily Brontë's *Wuthering Heights* (1847), respectively, treat these themes.

4. See Tamara Hareven and Andrejs Plakans's *Family History at the Crossroads* (New Jersey: Princeton UP, 1994).

5. Take, for example, the term "quality time," which signifies the way in which parents distinguish or divide the time that they spend directly interacting with their children. Also, consider the manner in which daycare centers and retirement homes—both of which are phenomena that can be attributed, in part, to men's and women's changing roles—have affected familial life.

6. Obvious examples of works that treat these themes are Henry James's *What Maisie Knew*, Mary Elizabeth Braddon's *Lady Audley's Secret*, George Gissing's *The Odd Women*, Thomas Hardy's *Jude the Obscure*, Kate Chopin's *The Awakening*, and Charlotte Perkins Gilman's *Herland* and "The Yellow Wallpaper."

7. See, for example, Jane Smiley's *A Thousand Acres*, Doris Lessing's *The Fifth Child*, and Toni Morrison's *The Bluest Eye*.

1

Tales of the Times:
Family and Nation in Charlotte Smith and Jane West

Susan Allen Ford

Anxiety about the family and women's roles within it dominates discursive and imaginative genres of the later part of the eighteenth century. Conduct books, political polemic, cartoons, novels, poetry, all focus on threats to the family, in the 1790s specifically connecting the danger that the domestic might disintegrate to the upheavals of revolution. The nature of the French Revolution, in its claim that the very defining structures of the society—social hierarchies, religious beliefs, political boundaries, even the calendar itself—might be subjected to the interrogations of Reason and so reinvented, raised for the British the possibility, the necessity, the danger of reform, if not of similar revolution. Further, as Linda Colley has argued, the participation of women in the Revolution, combined with the threat of a French invasion and the execution of Marie Antoinette and the French Royal family, increased anxiety about the boundaries of woman's sphere as well as the security of those boundaries.

Political writers of the 1790s make the link between family and nation explicit. Mary Wollstonecraft in 1792 writes:

A man has been termed a microcosm; and every family might also be called a state. . . . [M]orality, polluted in the national reservoir, sends off streams of vice to corrupt the constituent parts of the body politic. . . . The conclusion which I wish to draw is obvious; make women rational creatures, and free citizens, and they will quickly become good wives, and mothers; that is—if men do not neglect the duties of husbands and fathers. (177-78)

For Laetitia Matilda Hawkins in 1793, the link is equally explicit though differently significant:

I do not scruple to assert, that by diminishing the respect formerly paid to authority, the national female character is endangered. She who is taught the merit of resistance is taught to be obstinate; she who has early imbibed an aversion towards the kingly character, will easily be persuaded to consider her husband as an unauthorized tyrant, and fancying she has reason on her side, if he is not very easy to live with, she will applaud the spirit that turns inconvenience into misery. (1: 105-06)

As these critiques suggest, the very notion that the family and the state were analogous bodies raised the issue of their constitution and suggested the centrality of women to both the body and the family politic. The result was an emerging identity that politicized the private, the domestic, the feminine: "This was the period in which women first had to come to terms with the demands and meanings of Britishness" (Colley 281).

The novel, of course, perhaps more than any other genre, was implicated in this contest over definition. According to Gary Kelly, the circulating library had become, by the 1790s, "a controversial element in the world of fashionable consumption where class attitudes, values, and cultures met, came into conflict, and were worked out" (*English Fiction* 4). As the largest constituent both of what was owned by and borrowed from circulating libraries, the novel, then, was the genre of choice for the professional and middle classes. The novel's very identity as commodity, of course, made it sensitive to—to some extent even determined by—contemporary issues and public opinion (Butler 120). Moreover, its traditional concern with the relationship between the individual and society, its referentiality, and, as Marilyn Butler points out, its contemporary setting "more or less force[d] it into sensitive areas" (120). And as the novel privileged the idea of marriage (especially as it focused on courtship, seduction, or wedlock), it became a convenient and powerful site for the contest over the definition of the family.[1] As Jane Austen's narrator suggested at the end of *Northanger Abbey* (written during the 1790s), the reader would be interested in deciding "whether the tendency of this work be altogether to recommend parental tyranny, or reward filial disobedience" (228).

Two novels of the 1790s, Charlotte Smith's *Desmond* (1792) and Jane West's *A Tale of the Times* (1799), entered the debate about family responsibilities and national duties, though from quite different political perspectives. *Desmond*—to a large extent an answer to Edmund Burke's *Reflections on the Revolution in France*—is an epistolary novel set between June 1790 and February 1792. The principal correspondents—Lionel Desmond and his mentor Erasmus Bethel, Geraldine Verney and her sister Fanny Waverly—engage with the issues of the day as Desmond leaves England for revolutionary France in a hopeless attempt to conquer his virtuous passion for the unhappily married Geraldine. While Desmond occupies himself with social observation and political argument, Geraldine, whose husband grows increasingly degenerate, finds herself compelled to move with her children from one place to another as her husband entertains prostitutes in his ancestral home, gambles away his estate, and attempts to sell her to his friends. Finally, Verney's death from wounds sustained while fighting on the side of the displaced French aristocrats makes possible the marriage of Geraldine and Desmond, whose family will include the Verney children as well as Desmond's illegitimate daughter.

Jane West's conservative novel *A Tale of the Times*—written after the British declaration of war with France—appears to be a redaction of Smith's more radical fiction, adopting its basic plot structure and motifs. West's narrator, Prudentia Homespun, tells the story of the marriage of Geraldine Powerscourt to James, Earl of Monteith. Though urged by her father to marry her virtuous cousin Henry Powerscourt who loves her, Geraldine instead, in an excess of passion and sentiment, chooses the undisciplined and poorly educated Monteith. Relatively happy though mismatched, the couple falls prey to the evil Fitzosborne, who seduces Monteith into vice and Geraldine into dangerous opinions, ultimately kidnapping and raping Geraldine, whose only possible plot can be "seclusion, repentance, and death" (3: 329). As Monteith degenerates further, Henry and his wife, Geraldine's friend and "sister" Lucy Evans, are bequeathed the task of educating Geraldine's children.

Centering on thoughtful and virtuous heroines named Geraldine, *Desmond* and *A Tale of the Times*—often to very different purposes—use the basic wedlock structure of marriage threatened by disaffection and/or seduction (see Boone), raise the question of whether a "virtuous passion" for a married woman is possible, and critique the ideology and conventions of sentimentality. From their different political perspectives, they consider such politically charged issues as the role of the established church, the British constitution, natural rights and universal love, the nature of the revolution in France. As they depict a society facing the promise or the threat of change, both Charlotte Smith and Jane West use the family to register its destructive and destabilizing pressures. For both novelists, the family is likewise the source of restorative power, and both explore the means toward family reform. To embody these critiques, both Smith and West suggest a redefinition of family fictions themselves, partly through the form of the wedlock plot—or, as Joseph Allen Boone would have it, its counter-tradition—and through their experimentation with narrative modes. The definitions of family and nation that arise from these novels, however, are radically divergent: Smith suggests an egalitarian model that disrupts the traditional lines of power and authority while West demands submission to a hierarchical model that enforces those traditional relationships.

In entering the debate, both Charlotte Smith and Jane West significantly position themselves as writers—as women with a public voice—
with respect to their domesticity even as they problematize the very
notion of separate spheres. Smith's preface to *Desmond* protects her
novel from the charge that "women . . . have no business with politics"
by citing not only the "fathers, brothers, husbands, sons, or friends [so]
engaged" (1: iii) but also the need for knowledge of current history "in a
world where [women] are subject to mental degradation" (1: iv). But lest
it be suspected that such knowledge has come to her "by the sacrifice of
domestic virtues, or the neglect of domestic duties," she asserts that "it
was in the *observance*, not in the *breach* of duty, *I* became an Author"
(1: iv). For Charlotte Smith, the preservation of her threatened family
demands public action, a public voice.

Jane West presented herself to her reading public as a mother and a
farmer's wife responsible for the superintendence of a dairy and the
manage of a household, as a woman whose literary productions did not
interfere with her domestic ones. In an early poem, she notes that she
"wrote all kinds of verse with ease, / Made pies and puddings, frocks
and cheese."[2] Ironically, however, her narrator Prudentia Homespun
(also the narrator of *The Advantages of Education* [1793] and *A Gossip's
Story* [1796]) is a spinster and in this novel a traveller, a giver of domestic advice without domestic ties of her own. West's narrator, then, speaks
from a position that subjects her to no other—and, significantly, to no
male—voice even as she recommends to women an acceptance of their
subjection. Further, this domestic story which she has heard at Brighton
—one of the most fashionable public places of the 1790s—becomes "a
tale of the times," a vehicle of private "instruction, or even innocent
amusement" (1: 10), but one which has also a public face as it attempts
to "repel the enemy's insidious attacks" (3: 387). Here private and public
are again conflated.[3]

Out of the threats to her own domestic security and her own public
concerns, Charlotte Smith created a novel that puts the domestic at the
center of the drama of revolution. *Desmond* provides many versions of
disintegrating families. Bethel's cautionary narrative describes the
destruction of his family as his wife Louisa succumbed to the dissipations of London: her vanity led to her elopement, desertion of her husband and children, and death. Dissipation—drinking, gambling, promis-
cuity—also draws Verney from the circle of his family so that Geraldine
must face even the birth of her youngest child alone. The French widow
and children Desmond meets in the streets of Margate face poverty and
homelessness because of greed. But such vice is individually located,
even though it seems to be stimulated by the influences of London soci-

ety. The main cause for the disintegration of the family, however, seems to be the very grounds on which marriages are made: parental tyranny dictated by motives of interest, vanity, greed. Daughters are sacrificed while sons are favored and indulged. So the family of Desmond's friend, the *ci-devant* Marquis de Montfleuri, has consigned two daughters to convents and two to unhappy marriages in order to increase the estate of the son. Similarly, Geraldine's family, in order to secure her feckless brother Waverly's estate, has defined as duty her marriage to Verney— who married her because he "fancied it very knowing to marry a girl that all the young fellows of my acquaintance reckoned so confounded handsome" (2: 39).

Smith, following the dictates of the wedlock plot, highlights the turmoil of Geraldine's family situation. The effects of Geraldine's distresses and anxiety on her ability to nurse her newborn child (2: 228), her worries about the damage she might be causing to that child's constitution (2: 196), and the "fatigues" of travelling with three small children (3: 30) are realistic details that both help define her as mother and define that maternity as precarious—especially at a time when her husband seems determined to sell her to his friends. In contrast, Geraldine's own mother stands as a model of maternal insufficiency. With room in her heart only for her son (2: 184), she destroys Geraldine's hope that "she will not refuse some maternal kindness to her unfortunate child" (3: 21) by invoking Geraldine's duty to Verney: "I cannot let my daughter Frances see you, nor consent to receive you myself, till I find you have determined to embrace the proper conduct of going to your husband" (3: 39). (Mrs. Waverly also argues that since the infant has been weaned, Geraldine should "leave [the children] very properly with some careful person" [3: 40] while she travels with Verney's friend to France.)

Indeed such a traditional—and unthinking—patriarchal definition of family responsibilities seems to account for the domestic imbalance and disintegration that plagues Charlotte Smith's Britain. Verney's disregard of his wife and children is plainly due to his contempt for women: as Geraldine reports, he says "that we are good for nothing but to make a shew while we are young, and to become nurses when we are old" (2: 32). And Bethel recounts Verney's dismissal of his family from Geraldine's dressing-room: "away with ye all . . . get ye along to the nu[r]sery, that's the proper place for women and children" (2: 36). Indeed, Verney sees his "lovely and promising children" not only as "encumbrances" (2: 39) but as competitors, even usurpers: "I know nothing that they promise, but to grow up, to pull harder still, and find out that I am in their way before I have any mind to relinquish the enjoyments of this life" (2: 39). Indeed, the novel reveals Verney's attitudes as part of a life-destroying pattern of male behavior. While men such as Desmond, Bethel, and even Montfleuri regard women with a measure of respect, Verney's friends and, significantly, Geraldine's own father see women only as sexual ciphers. So Geraldine's trip to France, where she too gets a chance to see the effects of the revolution, inspires reflections not only on the question of democracy but also on the subject of her own education:

My father, indeed, would not condescend to suppose that our sentiments were worth forming or consulting; and with all my respect for his memory, I cannot help recollecting that he was a very Turk in principle, and hardly allowed women any pretentions to souls, or thought them worth more care than he bestowed on his horses, which were to look sleek, and do their paces well. (3: 133)

Smith's conviction, of course, is that this pattern of family disintegration has political implications. Geraldine imagines herself as akin to the oppressed French peasantry—"a miserable slave, returning with trembling and reluctant steps, to put on the most dreadful of all fetters" (3: 71)—and sees the upheavals of France through the filter of her own domestic travails:

We know, from daily experience, that even in a private family, a change in its oeconomy or its domestics, disturbs the tranquillity of its members for some time—It must surely then happen, to a much greater degree, in a great nation, whose government is suddenly dissolved by the resolution of the people; and which in taking a new form, has so many jarring interests to conciliate. (3: 124-25)

The question of one's obedience to government—whose business it is, according to one of Smith's cynical lawyers, "to enforce obedience" (2: 136)—is set against the question of one's obedience to one's husband and parents: Fanny conveys to Geraldine her skepticism about "what you think your duty—obedience!—unqualified obedience!" (2: 141). Revolution, indeed, is a family matter. To Montfleuri, the American Revolution, like the French Revolution a civil war between "men speaking the same language, and originally of the same country" (1: 153), was a family war and England, the "mother-country," an "unnatural parent" (1: 154). Traditional definitions of authority must be submitted to the inquiries of reason; as in much English Jacobin fiction, mutual responsibilities become the web holding families and nations together.

While for Charlotte Smith the pressures on the family—and indeed on the country itself—stem from their traditional patriarchal definitions, for Jane West the crisis springs from the perversion of those definitions by revolutionary ideas. Like Smith, West provides a range of fractured or disintegrating families. Neglect of the connubial tie and domestic duties always coincides with neglect of one's estate: family happiness and unity are connected with public responsibility. So the parents of Lord Monteith, absentee landlords resident in London, fall "victim to the demon of modern honour . . . and the pale orgies of dissipation" (1: 19): he dies in a duel with an officer paying court to his wife; she dies of disappointment, either at her husband's death or at "the necessity of seclusion and oeconomical retrenchment" (1: 20). Geraldine's parents have a similarly troubled relationship. The benevolent though simple Sir William Powerscourt, attached to his estate through "a generous philanthropy" (1: 27), marries "much on the wrong side of forty" (1: 30) when he's told by "[t]he wife of a neighbouring gentleman . . . that one of her daughters was so deeply in love with him, that death must be the inevitable consequence of his obduracy" (1: 31). Lady Powerscourt's vanity, selfishness, and acquisitiveness, however, lead her to insist on fashionable "improvements" to Powerscourt, residence in Bath and London, and then—once Geraldine is born—resumption of her social life. As a consequence of this "neglect of the first maternal duty" by "a too early appearance in public" (1: 73), Lady Powerscourt is condemned to life as an invalid followed by an early death. For West as for Smith, the vanity and dissimulation London represents erode domestic stability: as Lady Powerscourt quickly realizes, "of all places in the world a husband was least wanted at London. The late hours and perpetual routine of engagements left no leisure for domestic conversation" (1: 47).

But as Jane West depicts Geraldine's marriage, she examines both its limitations as well as the possibilities for its survival. Like Charlotte Smith's Geraldine, West's Geraldine marries unwisely; unlike Smith's heroine, West's Geraldine marries *against* the advice of her father and for qualities in Monteith that Geraldine "like Pygmalion" (1: 115) invents. The couple's essential incompatibility—Monteith's selfishness, irritability, need for entertainment, lack of intellectual interest—somewhat dims Geraldine's perfect happiness. (As in Smith's novel, London puts additional strains on the marriage.) However, these "fainter marks of the penalty of Adam" (2: 9) are balanced by Monteith's pride in and genuine respect and fondness for Geraldine and by West's insistence on "that depressing but infallible truth, that all the good of this world must be blended with evil" (2: 39). Further, their residence in Scotland provides an opportunity for Geraldine and vicariously for Monteith to solidify domestic ties, introduce "a spirit of order and improvement" (2: 31) to the newly established village of James-town, and assume their proper place as the landed family in the county.

The responsibility for the destruction of this marriage West lays to two principle causes: the vanity of Geraldine and the politically charged malignity of Fitzosborne. Fitzosborne—a somewhat unbelievable villain, as contemporary reviews suggested[4]—is a repository of Jacobin values as seen through highly-colored anti-Jacobin lenses. He arrives in London from Paris, "where he was just then contemplating the sublime spectacle of a great nation emancipating itself from the fetters of tyranny and superstition" (2: 97). Allied to literary circles, a deist whose "systematic" vice is "guided by sophistry" (2: 153), he envies the domestic happiness of the Monteiths and, "[h]abitually skeptical, . . . doubt[s]" its reality: "For it was utterly repugnant to all his received ideas, that affection could really subsist between persons of discordant habits, or that principle could supply the place of attachment, and give equal uniformity to the conduct" (2: 120). Geraldine's flaw is her desire for praise and her confidence in her intellectual powers. Fitzosborne's flattery, his critique of Dr. Johnson, his argument for "the abstract loveliness of virtue" rather than religion as a moral guide for "exalted minds" (2: 194), all distract her so that as she accompanies her husband on "Britons Strike Home," a stirring martial song, "her careless hand str[ikes] a false chord" (2: 197).[5]

The blow Fitzosborne strikes at the heart of this family is also, as West continually proclaims, a blow struck at the heart of the nation. Fitzosborne is merely a stand-in for the "sophists . . . falsely called enlightened" (2: 272) whom West blames for corrupting the principles of the age. "Should it therefore be told to future ages, that the capricious dissolubility (if not the absolute nullity) of the nuptial tie and the annihilation of parental authority are among the blasphemies uttered by the *moral* instructors of these times . . . they will not ascribe the annihilation of thrones and altars to the successful arms of France, but to those principles which, by dissolving domestic confidence and undermining private worth, paved the way for universal confusion" (2: 274-75). The dissolution of the family is a precursor to, a cause of the dissolution of the nation. When Monteith believes Geraldine has been seduced (rather than entrapped) by Fitzosborne, he immediately questions the paternity of his son and banishes the infant heir to his earldom. "Britons Strike Home," indeed.

Even while they chart the disintegration of the family, both Charlotte Smith and Jane West depict its potential as a source of restorative power. For each novelist, however, motherhood occupies a radically different relationship to authority. In *Desmond*, the maternal can be the means either to suppress or exert the claims of self. Geraldine's despair comprehends not only herself but her children as well: "there are moments, when I most sincerely wish that I and my babies were all dead together" (2: 159). But to the extent that Geraldine's despair can be mitigated, it is her children who are responsible: "my children and my duty must and shall teach me to submit unrepiningly to fulfil the latter, for the sake of the former—Their innocent smiles repay me for many hours of anxiety, and while they are well around me, I believe I can bear any thing" (2: 79).

The danger, however, is that Geraldine will use her children to reinforce her notions of duty, subordination, and self-denial.[6] Indeed, Geraldine's duties as wife and as mother here come into conflict. Although so ingrained are the habits of duty and obedience to spousal and parental authority that Geraldine takes her children to war-torn France, her maternal responsibilities are, as Desmond desires, able to rouse Geraldine to a resistance to the commands of her husband and mother that her own sense of self cannot: "My hope is, that the proposal—so cool a proposal too, that she should leave her children, will rouse that proper spirit of resistance against usurped and abused authority which, for herself, she would not, perhaps, exert" (3: 42). Maternal identity thus demands the response of revolution: in order to safeguard her children (and herself), wife must resist the commands of husband, daughter must resist the commands of mother. The lines of authority in the family are radically disrupted.[7]

For Smith, then, traditional definitions of the spousal and the maternal, thought to be complementary, come into conflict and are destabilized. For West, those definitions are complementary, the maternal rooted in the spousal so that destruction of one necessitates the eradication of the other. In *A Tale of the Times*, Geraldine expects to compensate for the limitations of her relationship with Monteith by "bending [her daughters'] ductile minds to such pursuits as would enable her to find those colloquial pleasures in her maternal character, which had been withheld from her connubial portion" (2: 78). Later, her despair at Monteith's involvement with "a venal wanton" (3: 10-11) is qualified by the necessity of exertion: "[M]y Heroine was a *mother*. . . . [S]he had more to do than lie down and die" (3: 11-12).

Motherhood, in fact, is the most significant female characteristic of this novel, the sole condition for female heroism. Even in the face of infidelity, "maternal feelings have frequently inspired such long-suffering quiet fortitude as would add lustre to the annals of a martyr" (3: 11-12). But after Geraldine's rape, she relinquishes all identity: "I have forfeited the name with which lord Monteith once honoured me, and I will not disgrace the unsullied purity of my father's." She can sign herself only "Geraldine" (3: 298). With this loss of identity as both wife and daughter, she loses also her maternal role: "Wherever my children appeared, the sad tale of their mother would still be whispered, and the blush of shame must dye their cheeks" (3: 304); "I have no right to the disposal of my children. I gave them being, but I have forfeited all pretensions to direct their education, or to dispose of their persons" (3: 325). This is the language of authority, and West suggests that maternal authority is dependent for its very existence on higher authority: that of husband, of father, even (as Monteith begins to pursue his divorce action in court and in the House of Lords) of the state.

In their depiction of the possibility of familial reform, Charlotte Smith and Jane West present sharply divergent models of the renewed domestic. As Pat Elliott argues, *Desmond*'s ending illustrates "the democratic principle of freedom of choice; mature, intelligent adults have a better chance at happiness when they have the power to choose their own destinies" (110-11). The novel ends with the projected marriage of Desmond and Geraldine and the incorporation of Geraldine's children and Desmond's natural daughter into the new domestic unit. This new family accepts the results of sexual transgression and reintegrates maternal and paternal affection rather than authority into the family. The pictures the correspondents provide emphasize the bonds of love rather than relationship characterized by hierarchy, duty or obedience: according to Montfleuri, "If [Desmond] knows [Geraldine] is engaged, or unwilling to be in company, he takes her children in his arms—he plays with, he caresses them; and still he is content" (3: 337). To Desmond, Geraldine's domestic exertions are equally striking: "were you to witness . . . her behaviour to a mother, who was once so harsh, so ungenerous, so cruel to her; . . . were you to behold the tender solicitude which she bestows equally on her own children, and on my little girl, you would love her a thousand—oh! a million times better than ever" (3: 344-45). Their projected retreat to the country will bring together a "circle of friends"— Desmond and Geraldine, Montfleuri and Fanny, Bethel and his daughter Louisa—a group diverse in age, disposition, and citizenship, but united by ties of affection. The pursuits Desmond imagines for them, including "studies," "amusements," "rural improvements," "a series of domestic and social happiness" (3: 348), promise domestic renovation with wider reverberations.

A Tale of the Times, with its apocalyptic overtones, presents a completely fragmented family in need of restoration. "The path of reconciliation," West's narrator intones, "is impeded by insurmountable barriers" (3: 359). After Geraldine's death, when Monteith finds "the prattle of childhood too mild an opiate to lull the tortures of corroding reflection," and his sister Lady Arabella discovers "that verbs and prepositions were very dull reading" (3: 377-78), Geraldine's children are committed to the education and care of the virtuous Henry and Lucy Powerscourt. West emphasizes the qualities of order and stability as familial values are restored.[8] Lucy, of course, is the daughter of Mrs. Evans, inspiration and guide to all the novel's virtuous characters; she inherits her mother's role as moral center of the novel. Henry is what both Fitzosborne and Monteith are not: self-disciplined, self-sacrificing, pious. Almost as important, he is also presented as "the true heir of the good sir William's virtues" (3: 380), "confer[ring] happiness" on the neighborhood, extending the domestic virtues outward.

Significantly, both novelists, even as they project the restoration of the family, convey an uncertainty, an ambivalence as to the success of that restoration. *Desmond* leaves the marriage of Geraldine and Desmond as a *projected* union; Josephine's marriage to her first love relies on at least two *if*-clauses and an assertion of probability for its achievement (3: 341); Montfleuri's tendency to libertinism and his description of himself as having been "tolerably in love, when I determined on an affair, so entirely out of my way, as marrying" (3: 337-38) provides an opening for the wedlock plot to play itself out yet again. For Stuart Curran, "Smith leaves the dénouement unacted, thereby ending the novel with a stress on the sexual exploitativeness of both male figures and the vulnerability of her women" (70).[9] And, although *A Tale of the Times* asserts with certainty the virtues of Henry and Lucy, the *success* of this new family is another matter: "The opening graces of the lovely children promise to reward [Lucy's] pious care, but who that recollects their mother's fate will dare to predict the event?" (3: 379-80).

Neither Charlotte Smith nor Jane West is able to achieve the kind of confidence in the conventional resolutions available to Henry Fielding, whose conclusion to *Amelia*'s wedlock plot both affirms marriage as an institution and rewards Booth and Amelia with perfect happiness. Indeed, the resolutions of *Desmond* and *A Tale of the Times* suggest what Vivien Jones identifies as a pattern of "ambivalent articulation of failed possibilities [that] reverberates through the novels of the revolutionary period" (197). But Smith and West wear their ambivalence with a difference. Charlotte Smith in choosing an epistolary form for *Desmond* insists on a negotiation of voices and a narrative that resists a monovocal, settled resolution. While at its worst—as in Smith's own case—marriage can lead to both emotional and literal imprisonment, even at best the fictional marriages she projects can only promise the *possibility* of respect, companionship, and love. The situation of the nation is similarly uncertain: how will France respond to the opportunity to remake itself? how will Britain respond to its opportunity for reform?

Jane West's choice of the omniscient and opinionated Prudentia Homespun as narrator in *A Tale of the Times* pleads a certainty about her novel's resolution and meaning.[10] Henry and Lucy Powerscourt represent the strength of mind, will and virtue necessary for that surety. But even as that certainty is mobilized to validate the institution of marriage as the strength of the nation, the novel's representation of its very fragility in the hands of fallen human nature undermines that confidence. West's martial conclusion—her depiction of herself as resisting "the delving mole" which "might undermine all the sacred edifice" (3: 385), the forces of skepticism which might subvert all the structures of British society—addresses a continual need for vigilance, a distrust of the very stability on which she wants to rely.

As Charlotte Smith and Jane West engage in the struggle over what the family is or should be, what the nation is or should be, they provide a shape for the anxieties that haunt their culture. Randolph Trumbach has suggested that Britain had no revolution in the 1790s in part because the rise of the egalitarian family naturalized patterns of behavior derived from an affectionate domestic ideal rather than from a patriarchal and authoritarian model (288). The novel, as it both reflects that change and makes it felt, is implicated in the construction of what Benedict Anderson has termed the "imagined community" that is Britain. In her introduction to her 1810 series *The British Novelists*, Anna Laetitia Barbauld measures the dignity of the novel partly by "the power exercised over the reader's heart" (4) and justifies her attention to a genre which some deem "frivolous" but which "every body reads" by suggesting its sly social efficacy: "It was said by Fletcher of Saltoun, 'Let me make the ballads of a nation, and I care not who makes the laws.' Might it not be said with as much propriety, Let me make the novels of a country, and let who will make the systems?" (62).

Notes

1. See Ellis on the implication of the Gothic novel in the argument over the ideology of separate spheres.

2. "To the Hon. Mrs C—e" from West's 1791 *Miscellaneous Poems* (Watson, "West, Jane" 706). See also Lloyd.

3. See also Gary Kelly's argument that Jane West "[p]aradoxically, in opposing women's novelistic interventions in the Revolution debate, . . . transgressed gendered canons of subject matter" ("Women Novelists" 380).

4. *The Analytical Review* described him as "drawn with equal inconsistency and improbability" (605), "a most incongruous nonentity" (606). For *The Monthly Review* Fitzosborne's "delineation . . . shews at least an honourable wish in the author to expose the selfish and dangerous principles of some modern ethics" (90).

5. "Britons Strike Home," the climactic song by Henry Purcell for George Powell's 1695 adaptation of John Fletcher's *Bonduca or, The British Heroine,* like "Rule Britannia" was popular throughout the eighteenth century. (The title also appears as a legend in political cartoons of the 1790s.) I am indebted to Charles A. Knight for identifying this song for me.

6. As Diana Bowstead points out, "the reader is finally not altogether certain that abjection is a heroic posture" (253). See also Eleanor Ty's *Unsexed Revolutionaries*: "Unlike the novels of West and More, Smith's *Desmond* challenges the beliefs of conservatives, which included suffering in silence, submission without question, and forgiveness at all costs" (139).

7. See also Bowstead, who argues that the reader's pity for Geraldine "is supposed to become indignation on her behalf and on behalf of all victims of institutionally authorized oppression" (252).

8. These noble qualities, however, remain somewhat abstract. Eleanor Ty helpfully analyzes how West's prescription of the feminine ideal which "can only be created through opposites to or differences from the negative 'other' . . . suggests the precarious basis of the exemplary" ("Jane West's" 139).

9. Again, Bowstead suggests a more politically charged ambivalence: "Smith intends her reader to see that the security of Geraldine's position in the household Desmond governs depends on his honest intention to translate his ideological opposition to political autonomy into reasonably democratic domestic policies" (261).

10. Indeed, Nicola J. Watson points to the "rapid disintegration of the epistolary novel in the late 1780s and 1790s . . . [as] intimately bound up with the problematic political resonances of its narrative mode in the revolutionary and post-revolutionary period" (*Revolution* 17). Mary Anne Schofield argues (with specific reference to *A Tale of the Times*) that by the end of the century "the thinly disguised author-narrator really becomes the chief protagonist of the piece, and the later-century novels become more critical examinations of the entire form than those before 1740" (187).

Works Cited

Anderson, Benedict. *Imagined Communities: Reflections on the Origin and Spread of Nationalism.* London: Routledge, 1983.

Austen, Jane. *Northanger Abbey*. Ed. Anne Henry Ehrenpreis. 1818. Harmondsworth: Penguin, 1972.

Barbauld, Anna L. "On the Origin and Progress of Novel-Writing." *The British Novelists*. Vol. 1. London, 1810. 1-62.

Boone, Joseph Allen. *Tradition Counter Tradition: Love and the Form of Fiction*. Chicago: U of Chicago P, 1987.

Bowstead, Diana. "Charlotte Smith's *Desmond*: The Epistolary Novel as Ideological Argument." *Fetter'd or Free? British Women Novelists, 1670-1815*. Ed. Mary Anne Schofield and Cecelia Macheski. Athens: Ohio UP, 1986. 237-63.

Butler, Marilyn. *Jane Austen and the War of Ideas*. Oxford: Oxford UP, 1975.

Colley, Linda. *Britons: Forging the Nation 1707-1837*. New Haven: Yale UP, 1992.

Curran, Stuart. "Charlotte Smith and British Romanticism." *South Central Review* 11.2 (1994): 66-78.

Elliott, Pat. "Charlotte Smith's Feminism: A Study of *Emmeline* and *Desmond.*" *Living By the Pen: Early British Women Writers*. Ed. Dale Spender. Athene Ser. New York: Teachers College P, 1992. 91-112.

Ellis, Kate Ferguson. *The Contested Castle: Gothic Novels and the Subversion of Domestic Ideology*. Urbana: U of Illinois P, 1989.

Hawkins, Laetitia Matilda. *Letters on the Female Mind, Its Powers and Pursuits*. 2 vols. London, 1793.

Jones, Vivien. "Women Writing Revolution: Narratives of History and Sexuality in Wollstonecraft and Williams." *Beyond Romanticism: New Approaches to Texts and Contexts, 1780-1832*. Ed. Stephen Copley and John Whale. London: Routledge, 1992. 178-99.

Kelly, Gary. *English Fiction of the Romantic Period 1789-1830*. London and New York: Longman, 1989.

——. "Women Novelists and the French Revolution Debate: Novelizing the Revolution/Revolutionizing the Novel." *Eighteenth-Century Fiction* 6 (1994): 369-88.

Lloyd, Pamela. "Some New Information on Jane West." *Notes and Queries* 229 (1984): 469-70.

Schofield, Mary Anne. *Masking and Unmasking the Female Mind: Disguising Romances in Feminine Fiction, 1713-1799*. Newark: U of Delaware P, 1990.

Smith, Charlotte. *Desmond*. 3 vols. London, 1792. Facsimile version. Intro. by Gina Luria. The Feminist Controversy in England 1788-1810. New York: Garland, 1974.

Trumbach, Randolph. *The Rise of the Egalitarian Family: Aristocratic Kinship and Domestic Relations in Eighteenth-Century England*. New York: Academic P, 1978.

Rev. of *A Tale of the Times. The Analytical Review* ns 1 (June 1799): 603-06.

——. *The Monthly Review*. 29 (May 1799): 90-91.

Ty, Eleanor. "Jane West's Feminine Ideals of the 1790s." *1650-1850: Ideas, Aesthetics and Inquiries in the Early Modern Era* 1 (1994): 137-55.

——. *Unsex'd Revolutionaries: Five Women Novelists of the 1790s.* Toronto: U of Toronto P, 1993.

Watson, Nicola J. *Revolution and the Form of the British Novel, 1790-1825: Intercepted Letters, Interrupted Seductions.* Oxford: Clarendon P, 1994.

——. "West, Jane." *British Women Writers: A Critical Reference Guide.* Ed. Janet Todd. New York: Continuum, 1989. 705-07.

West, Jane. *A Tale of the Times.* 3 vols. London, 1799. Facsimile version. Intro. by Gina Luria. The Feminist Controversy in England 1788-1810. New York: Garland, 1974.

Wollstonecraft, Mary. *A Vindication of the Rights of Woman.* 1792. Ed. Carol Poston. 2nd ed. New York: Norton, 1988.

2

Breaking the Tie That Binds:
Parents and Children in Romantic Fiction

Charlene E. Bunnell

Hotly debated topics in the eighteenth and nineteenth centuries, child-rearing practices and education of the young increasingly became a significant theme in various types of discourse, such as conduct books, tracts, poetry, and fiction. By the late eighteenth century, the issue of duty had gradually shifted from children's obligation to parental accountability. Indeed, the parent-child relationships depicted in Romantic literature not only offer an idealized portrayal of children's innocence, a marked departure from the prior original sin philosophy but also question parents' worthiness as guardians and exemplars. In her 1792 *A Vindication of the Rights of Woman*, Mary Wollstonecraft details the commitment of parents to their young, asserting that "the formation of the mind must be begun very early" (227). Although best known for its eloquent affirmation of women's rights, *Vindication* also highlights the issue of parental responsibility, as Wollstonecraft charges mothers and fathers to exhibit respectable behavior, to possess enlightened attitudes, and to follow the moral precepts they often preached to their offspring. Warning against a tyrannical demand for obedience, she persuasively argues that if children are expected to be dutiful and affectionate, parents must be responsible and loving in turn.

Wollstonecraft's philosophies regarding relationships between parents and children provide a common thread linking three Romantic novels that address these problematic issues: Eliza Fenwick's *Secresy: or, the Ruin on the Rock* (1795), Amelia Opie's *Adeline Mowbray: The Mother and Daughter* (1804), and Mary Shelley's *Lodore* (1837). Both Fenwick and Opie knew Wollstonecraft well and embraced her theories; Mary Shelley read and reread her mother's writings and incorporated many of Wollstonecraft's views in her own works.[1] In Fenwick's novel, Mrs. Ashburn is an ineffectual mentor to Caroline, and Mr. Valmont is nothing less than a dictator, to whom children are but pawns for social experiments. The reasonable, strong-willed Caroline Ashburn manages to survive her

31

mother's failings; however, Sibella Valmont and the weak Clement Montgomery become victims of Valmont's "systems." The adolescent Adeline
of Mrs. Opie's work incurs her mother's disfavor by living her life
according to Mrs. Mowbray's own theories, particularly with regard to
marriage and male-female relationships. Adeline's social failing, Opie
asserts, is the direct result of her mother's inability to recognize a reasonable connection between theory and practice. In a much later novel,
Lodore, Mary Shelley explores the disastrous results of parents who exert
too much control over their respective children and of those who do not
take an active part in their child's life. In this generational novel, Lord
Lodore and Lady Santerre manipulate the education of their children for
personal gain and twisted vindictiveness; Cornelia Santerre Lodore, herself a product of suspect childrearing philosophy, becomes in turn an inept
mother until through near tragedy her parental instinct awakens.

Although a central theme in these Romantic novels, parent-child
relationships had been part of social and literary discourse for several
hundred years, emerging, some critics argue, in conjunction with the
notion of childhood. In his study, *Centuries of Childhood: A Social History of Family Life*, Philippe Ariès explores the development of the concept of childhood and changing attitudes toward children themselves.
From early Renaissance on, writes Ariès, "a new sensibility granted
these fragile, threatened creatures a characteristic which the world had
hitherto failed to recognize in them" (43). By acknowledging childhood
as a stage of life, society became aware that children are distinct from
adults, deserving different treatment and care (Ariès 128).[2] A primary
reason for this recognition, writes Ariès, was "the growing influence of
Christianity on life and manners" as the church and moralists addressed
education of children (43; 132). Most of these conduct books, religious
tracts, and juvenile literature, however, focused on the child's duty to
parents. Lord Chesterfield's letters to his son, John Gregory's "A
Father's Legacy to his Daughters," and Reverend James Fordyce's "Ser-
mons to Young Women" are a few representative examples of eighteenth-century texts designed to instruct the child. However, not until
later would the parents' role in the instruction of their children become
an issue of debate (Grylls 16).[3]

Neil Postman credits this change of perspective in part to John
Locke and Jean-Jacques Rousseau. Locke's concept of tabula rasa, Postman argues, had a significant effect on the very notion of childhood as an
innocent phase of one's life, a phase that needed to be molded and shaped
carefully by parents (57). Also integral to this consideration of parental
duty was Rousseau's educational theories. Rousseau emphasized the
child's intellectual and emotional development and assumed that the child

was an individual deserving respect (Postman 58).[4] Just as influential, however, were the Romantic writers, who, taking their cue from Locke and Rousseau, offered an alternative view toward children and adults to that of Protestant moralists. Postman notes that Calvinistic theology labeled the child as "untamed," requiring the instruction of the "civilized adult" (59), and Grylls cites original sin doctrine as central to the belief that children must be saved from their innate evil as soon as possible (24-26). However, the Romantics, especially Blake and Wordsworth, viewed the adult as "deformed" and the children as innocents so often corrupted by their elders and society (Postman 59). From the late eighteenth century on, literature often featured children as natural beings, pure and inherently moral. In fact, Grylls notes, childhood became a significant literary symbol and theme of innocence and virtue (35).

In the early to mid-1700s, the notion of childhood and the depiction of children as complex characters remained largely unexplored, according to T.G.A. Nelson:

While children are no longer passed over in silence, and the positive connotations of childhood are thrown increasingly into relief, the challenge of exploring the child's inner life, and of portraying it as a separate being with an existence apart from that of its parents, is seldom confidently met. The child figure appears more often as an object than as a subject, and on those occasions when a first-person narrator is made to tell the story of her or his childhood the account is often tantalizingly brief. (27-28)

Consider, for example, Sarah Fielding's 1749 conduct tale, *The Governess*: the characters are two-dimensional representations rather than complex figures who invite analysis or vicarious response. Despite their reluctance to explore the notion of childhood, novelists often portrayed the bond (or lack thereof) between children and their parents. Nelson argues that parent-child relationships are significant components in fiction prior to Romanticism. Citing examples from *Moll Flanders, Roxana, Amelia, Pamela*, and *Tom Jones*, Nelson concludes that such relationships "are important and continuous themes in the early novel, and increase in importance as the eighteenth century advances" (27). Combining the Romantic conceptualization of the child as an innocent being with a vigorous re-evaluation of the parents' role in raising their young, Romantic novelists began charting new territory in depicting family matters. Writers such as Fenwick, Opie, and Shelley not only concentrated on the bond between children and parents, but also directed the spotlight to the parents' obligation to their children and, more significantly, their complicity in offsprings' destinies.

Guidelines regarding behavior and duty heretofore directed toward children were addressed to parents as well, although specific practices and theories were clearly distinguished along class lines, as Lawrence Stone has noted in his study, *Family, Sex and Marriage in England 1550-1800*. Nevertheless, regardless of social status, unworthy parents were chastised as society began to recognize that one is a product of environment, including the domestic one (Grylls 37). If children erred, the fault lay primarily with parents and society. Parents had an obligation not only to instruct their children in religious and social matters, but also to nurture their development into maturity: "Parenthood was seen as a sensitive art, with its own skilled methods and its own mystique; incompetence, even though well-meaning, could maim a developing mind" (Grylls 38). In *Vindication*, Mary Wollstonecraft asserts that "a right always includes a duty" and exhorts parents to be virtuous models: "the parent who sets a good example patiently lets that example work; and it seldom fails to produce its natural effect—filial reverence" (233). "If parents discharge their duty they have a strong hold and sacred claim on the gratitude of their children," writes Wollstonecraft; however, she adds, "few parents are willing to receive the respectful affection of their offspring on such terms. They demand blind obedience, because they do not merit a reasonable service" (229).

Wollstonecraft's remonstration regarding parental responsibility is echoed in Eliza Fenwick's epistolary novel, *Secresy*, published three years following *Vindication*. A close friend of the radical Jacobins that included not only Wollstonecraft, but also Elizabeth Inchbald, Mary Hays, and for a time Amelia Opie, Fenwick was interested in the welfare of both women and children. In addition to her work as novelist, editor, and translator, she wrote seven children's books (Rogers 262). In her introduction to the Pandora edition of *Secresy*, Janet Todd notes that Fenwick's text addresses the issue of how to educate children and whether girls should be given a comparable education to boys or "be raised 'innocently' in nature, out of reach of corrupting society" (viii). Integral to that issue is Fenwick's assertion that parents should be nurturing, moral examples to their children; if they are not, the children frequently suffer.

The novel presents the correspondence between two seemingly unlikely friends: the wise, worldly Caroline Ashburn and the innocent, sheltered child of nature, Sibella Valmont. Having met during Mrs. Ashburn's visit to her prior acquaintance, Mrs. Valmont (Sibella's aunt), the two young women form a strong bond of sisterhood, and Sibella, secluded at her uncle's castle, is ecstatic with having discovered a friend, particularly one who has experienced the world beyond the Valmont estate. In one of Caroline's early letters to Sibella, Fenwick introduces the theme of parental responsibility. Caroline outlines her history to her new friend, beginning with her mother's upbringing. Mrs. Ashburn, she writes, was "the very fashionable daughter of very fashionable parents" (10). A wealthy orphan at 23, Mrs. Ashburn married a well-to-do Englishman living in India and had one daughter, Caroline, whom she raised to be spoiled and insolent, just as she had been. A social climber absorbed in her unhappiness with living in India, Mrs. Ashburn is no model parent. Caroline confesses that her mother hates children, for "their noise and prattle and monkey tricks threw her into hysterics" (13). Admitted occasionally into her mother's dressing room for a perfunctory "kiss or a frown," Caroline lacks a nurturing environment.

Fenwick's portrayal of Mrs. Ashburn's relationship to Caroline reflects the attitudes that many aristocratic parents had regarding their offspring, what Lawrence Stone has termed the "negligent mode" of childrearing (451). In *Family Ties: English Families 1540-1920*, Mary Abbott notes that for many well-off parents, a child was merely a "decorative accessory" to represent a domestic image (63). Caroline confesses to Sibella that Mrs. Ashburn would periodically permit her to enter the dressing room or ride in the same carriage with her, but only when Caroline's presence suited her or satisfied a particular need: "on those occasions I reached the highest pinnacle of her confidence, and used to listen while she poured forth her longing desires to return to England" (13-14).

Eliza Fenwick's depiction of Mrs. Ashburn's attitude toward her daughter becomes significant when viewed in conjunction with contemporary discourse regarding family relationships. Aristocratic parents still tended to distance themselves from their children; however, Mrs. Ashburn, although first daughter and then wife of wealthy landowners, is not a member of that elite upper class. By emphasizing the woman's aristocratic approach to raising her daughter, Fenwick is able to criticize more effectively Mrs. Ashburn's pretensions, which affect her parental role throughout her daughter's childhood and adolescence. Fenwick's criticism becomes more obvious when we consider that the gentry and upper bourgeois class, to which Mrs. Ashburn belongs, were reevaluating childrearing practices and, under the influence of Rousseau, were gradually adopting what Lawrence Stone labels the "child-oriented, affectionate and permissive mode" (456). As Stone notes, "many wives and mothers, when faced with the choice of personally supervising their children, or leaving them to servants, nurses and governesses and accompanying their husbands on pleasure or business, unhesitatingly chose the former" (456). Mrs. Ashburn, intent on maintaining beneficial social connections, would never presume to refuse a visit or engagement to remain with her daughter. Nor does she consider Caroline's interests as she accepts invitations for month-long stays at acquaintances' estates and concerns herself with the latest fashion of manners and dress. Although an older adolescent at the time of her correspondence with Sibella, Caroline frequently complains about Mrs. Ashburn's behavior toward her as well as her self-serving conduct in society. She is not permitted to refer to her as "mother," only as "Mrs. Ashburn" (10), and they rarely enjoy any time together: "I very seldom breakfast with my mother, our hours of rising and morning avocations are so different" (141). Mrs. Ashburn was quite likely the type Hannah More had envisioned when she entreated well-off women to moderate their extravagant life (Pickering 101).

Caroline is frequently frustrated and appalled by her mother's sense of priorities, which are entirely opposite her own. Explaining how she came by some money to help a needy and misguided young man, Henry Davenport, Caroline discloses to Sibella that Mrs. Ashburn had settled an annual income on her, not to foster her independence or to encourage any philanthropic activities, but to purchase the necessary fashions associated with her class status:

That I do not employ this allowance in keeping pace with her elegance, that I do not blaze in jewels, and riot in the luxury of dress, displeases my mother; yet she continues me the stated income, flattering herself daily though daily disappointed that I will secure my own indulgences by overlooking the errors reason tells me I am to condemn in her. (115)

By relating Mrs. Ashburn's parenting practices to her social aspirations, Fenwick censures both.

How is it, one might ask, that Caroline, unlike many of her peers in this novel, chooses not to follow in her mother's path? Again, combining social commentary with depicting contemporary changes in the family and childrearing philosophies, Fenwick juxtaposes class differences regarding parental duties. Were it not for an incident when she was thirteen, Caroline confesses to Sibella, she should act as Mrs. Ashburn does. While the Ashburn family resides in India, the working-class English mother of a close playmate unexpectedly refuses to allow her daughter visits to the Ashburn estate. Upon Caroline's questioning the motive, the mother frankly explains:

"You, Miss, who are so high born and so rich, need not care if people do hate you; but my Nancy is a poor child . . . she never used to fleer, and flout, and stamp at her little brothers and sisters, as she does since she came to your house,

Miss. And so, Miss, as she will never be able to pay folks for saying she is good when she is bad, I, who am her mother, must make her as good as I can. You may be good enough for a great lady; but Nancy will never be a great lady; and, be as angry as you will, Miss, indeed she can't come to your fine house any more." (12-13)

Shocked, Caroline admits that the mother "had awakened in my mind a true sense of my situation" (13). Embarking on a course of self-reformation, Caroline soon thereafter rejects her parents' example of social behavior and self-centered attitudes. From this incident, Caroline experiences a lesson on how people judge others by manners. However, this scene also demonstrates an instruction for parents. As a member of the working class, Nancy's mother understands her role of preparing her daughter for an occupation and/or marriage. Nancy's imitating a spoiled upper-class girl's behavior would not serve her in the capacity of a house servant, nor would it likely attract a similarly-classed husband who could ill-afford a lazy or demanding wife. Considering her daughter's best interests, the mother recognizes that Nancy would not succeed without her intervention. Granted, the concern is an ambiguous one. As Lawrence Stone has noted, the working class, though often attentive to their children, also tended to exploit them for economic reasons (468-78). Nevertheless, for Fenwick's purpose, Nancy's mother represents a more astute and interested parent than Mrs. Ashburn, even if the concern generates from the necessities of class limitations.

Another example of ineffective parenting in Fenwick's novel is George Valmont, who, like Mrs. Ashburn, continues the tradition with which he was raised, in addition to incorporating some of his own philosophy—the result of his unfruitful experiences in life. Once again, Eliza Fenwick chastises upper-class attitudes toward children as well as their regressive customs, including that of primogeniture. As the elder son, George Valmont enjoyed privileges his younger brother (Sibella's father) did not: he was "the only hope, the only joy, the only object of the careful solitude of his anxious parents. . . . [and] received a stately education within the castle walls" (23-24). The decision by Valmont's parents to educate him at home was not an unusual one. Despite the reputation of highly regarded schools such as Eton, some upper-class parents chose at-home education to prevent their sons from contact with less desirable families (Stone 423).

However, by contrasting Valmont's experience with his younger brother's, Fenwick questions home schooling, especially given the narrow-mindedness of the upper-class family. Sibella's father was "happier because of less consequence [and] passed his early years with other young men of fashion at school and at college" (24). Having experienced some diversity, Sibella's father is better equipped to succeed profession- ally and personally in society; George Valmont is not. Explains Caroline, "no sooner was your uncle emancipated from the fetters of his minority, than he resolved to repair to court, where he expected to find only his equals, and those equals alive to and exact in the observance of all that haughty decorum, which Mr. Valmont deemed indispensably necessary to the well being of social institutions" (24). What he discovered, how- ever, was that his "high-born pretensions" failed to serve him among the "artful intrigues." After a humiliating experience with the coquettish Lady Margaret B———, George Valmont retreated to his family estate, bitter and reclusive. As Caroline astutely notes, "instead of attempting to reform mankind, he retires to rail at them" (25). His only other associa- tion with the "heterogeneous multitude" was to procure a wife, whom he "snatched . . . from the scenes where her existence was alone valuable to her, and buried her amidst obscurity and horror at Valmont castle" (25).

Upon the death of her parents, Sibella becomes George Valmont's ward, and he later adopts Clement Montgomery, the son of poor cot- tagers, whom we eventually learn is his own illegitimate child. Clement is instructed at home by a well-loved tutor, Bonneville, who also teaches Sibella secretly.[5] Although Sibella tells Caroline that Clement occasion- ally accompanied his father on business, the two children primarily spend their childhood and adolescence in seclusion at the Valmont estate. When Clement turns nineteen, Valmont then embarks upon his "project," as Caroline terms it. Gradually Caroline learns of his scheme and experiment regarding both Sibella and Clement, and all the charac- ters come to rue the results of his "secresy." Without adequate prepara- tion, Valmont unexpectedly sends Clement out into the world. "You shall mix with society," he instructs the young man, "but remember that you are not to be attracted by its specious appearances. Scrutinize into its fol- lies and enormities, as I have done; and let my precepts and instructions be your guide and law" (21). Although Valmont's advice is unarguably sound, the words fail to serve Clement because the young man is weak- willed not only by nature, but also by upbringing. "To be able to follow Mr. Locke's system . . . the parents must have subdued their own pas- sions," writes Wollstonecraft in *Thoughts on the Education of Daughters* (9). George Valmont has most decidedly not "subdued [his] own pas- sions," and a direct result is Clement's unresourcefulness and inexperi- ence.

A complication to the scenario is the growing attachment between Sibella and Clement. Yet when Valmont sends Clement away, he tells them they are to think of each other as siblings, nothing more, even though, as we later learn, Valmont has always planned that the two should marry. Caroline quickly guesses the situation and reassures the distraught Sibella: "Your uncle . . . I perceive, intended you for your lover, and your lover for you. His project, then, was to place a second Adam and Eve in the garden of Eden" (22). However, first Valmont must complete Clement's "education," indulging his own desire to observe his son develop as he wishes, and like Milton's Adam and Eve, Clement exercises free will and so falls from grace.

For nearly two years, Clement is given a carte blanche to do as he wants. The unexpected freedom is a boon for the good-natured but self-serving young man. Enjoying the benefits of high society, he temporarily forgets Sibella as well as Valmont's warnings, and Valmont, in turn, seems to take little heed of his ward's activities, merely observing from a distance. As suddenly as he previously dismissed Clement, Valmont summons him to return "to enjoy . . . the pleasant solitude of Valmont castle" (69). When asking for a report of his experiences and observations, Valmont is enraged that instead of despising society, Clement has embraced it: "It seems," Clement writes to his friend Arthur Murden, "I had not rancour enough for Mr. Valmont; I could not belie my feelings with sufficient warmth. I could not renounce enormities I had never known, and which have no existence but in his own inflated imagination" (75). Enjoying the dissipations that were so despicable to Valmont, Clement naturally cannot understand his benefactor's violent reaction.

As a result of both Clement's perception of society and Sibella's forthright plea that they be allowed to marry, Valmont once again sends Clement away, this time, however, without unlimited funds. As Clement complains to Murden, Valmont "had determined . . . that I should go to London; and there choose for myself a profession, hereafter to live by it; and that his friendship and assistance would always be mine, according to the decency and propriety of my deportment" (78). Raised to expect the privileges of an eldest (or only) son, Clement is even less-prepared to meet this new demand than he was the first. His situation reinforces Wollstonecraft's earlier observation that, "poverty . . . cannot be patiently borne by those who have lived on the vain applause of others" (*Thoughts* 48). Arthur Murden concurs: "Certainly Mr. Valmont managed his plan of making you a Hermit with wonderful ingenuity, to send you forth from your cave at that very age when the fancy runs gadding after novelty, and shadow passes for substance" (87). Yet he also urges Clement to make the most of the experience, what he labels an "unimportant circumstance"; if in such a situation, he (Murden) would undeniably survive. "Five hundred pound," he writes, "'Tis a mine. Ah, sigh not to be foremost of the throng! Independence, peace, and self approving reflection may be, if you will, the companions of your new destiny" (87). Clement, however, does not possess Murden's fortitude. He squanders his money, abandons Sibella, and ends up marrying Mrs. Ashburn so that he may continue the only way of life he has ever known.

Valmont fails his wards by not only being a poor example as an individual (though well-meaning), but also because he expects blind obedience from them and does not recognize his duty to foster their independence to mutual benefit. With no greater experience of the world and human nature than what she has learned from the tutor Bonneville and from her life within the walls of the estate, Sibella realizes her uncle's shortcomings as a parent figure:

He demands my obedience, too! What obedience? the grateful tribute to duty, authorised by reason, and sanctioned by the affections? No. Mr. Valmont, here at least, ceases to be inconsistent. He never enlightened my understanding, nor conciliated my affections; and he demands only the obedience of a fettered slave. I am held in the bondage of slavery. . . . Shall my uncle tell me that my actions are confined to the mechanical operations of the body, that I am an imbecile creature. . . . Blind to conviction, grown old in error, he would degrade me to the subordinate station he describes. He daringly asserts that I am born to the exercise of no will; to the exercise of no duties but submission; that wisdom owns me not, knows me not, could not find in me a resting place. (32-33)

Sibella's invective words have merit. Valmont has made it clear to her on several occasions that she is a mere puppet to his will: "I have chosen a part for you," he tells her, "nothing is required of you but obedience" (21). When she dares first to reason with him and then to challenge his authority, he responds, "Have I not a right over you?" (77). Her emphatic answer: "No right to the exercise of an *unjust* power over me" (77, emphasis added). This incident is yet another that reflects the novel's debt to *Vindication*. In the chapter entitled, "Parental Affection," Wollstonecraft writes, "obedience, unconditional obedience, is the catchword of tyrants of every description" (225). Because of Valmont's unjust tyranny, Sibella violates her uncle's directive that she and Clement remain friends only. She clandestinely comes to him before he departs, and they "wed." Although Sibella remains loyal to her "husband," even during her disastrous lie-in, Clement easily finds others to replace her in his affections.

In this novel, Eliza Fenwick reinforces Mary Wollstonecraft's conviction that parents can only demand children to obey when they themselves are both loving and reasonable in their expectations. Caroline Ashburn again voices Fenwick's concern in a final letter to George Valmont, and her effective commentary deserves the following lengthy quotation:

I know not of any opposing duties, and wherever the commands of parents are contrary to the justice due from being to being, I hold obedience to be vice. The perpetual hue and cry after obedience and obedience has almost driven virtue out of the world, for be it unlimited unexamined obedience to a sovereign, to a parent, or husband, the mind, yielding itself to implicit unexamined obedience, loses its individual dignity, and you can expect no more of a man than of a brute. What is to become of the child who is taught never to think or act for himself? . . . You send Clement into the world and you commanded him to hate, but you never told him why it merited this abhorrence, only he was to hate because it pleased you that he should hate the world. . . . Then you bid him make himself independent, and you had not given him one lesson of independence of mind, without which he must ever be a tool and dependent. Indeed, Sir, you have no right to withhold from him your forgiveness, for you taught him by your own example to say one thing and intend another; in your own mistakes, you trace the foundation of his vices. (290-91)

Despite Clement's own culpability in his fate, greater blame must be given to Mr. Valmont, whose failure to educate and monitor his son prompts Caroline's admonition. Indeed, the entire text illustrates Mary Wollstonecraft's warning: "Vicious or indolent people are always eager to profit by enforcing arbitrary privileges; and generally, in the same proportion as they neglect the discharge of the duties which alone render the privileges reasonable" (231). "A right always includes a duty," argued Wollstonecraft; George Valmont undeniably failed in his duty, thus having no claim to any right over either Sibella or Clement Montgomery.

The theme of "trac[ing] the foundation of [one's] vices" to one's parents appears in a later novel by Amelia Opie, *Adeline Mowbray: The Mother and Daughter*. A member of the Wollstonecraft and Godwin circle, Opie, wife of portrait painter John Opie, greatly admired Mary Wollstonecraft and her theories regarding childrearing and parental responsibility.[6] *Adeline Mowbray* was generally read as a veiled biography of Wollstonecraft, yet such a reading is both problematical and reductive, as Roxanne Eberle has effectively demonstrated.[7] Furthermore, the subtitle directs our attention to the parent-child theme. Approaching *Adeline Mowbray* as novel of ideas regarding parent-child relationships not only resolves the apparent disjunction between the text's end result and Wollstonecraft's views on marriage and women's rights, but also offers yet another voice on the parenting debate. As

Jeanette Winterson notes in her introduction to the Pandora edition, "Adeline's defeat is not at the hands of men, it's first and foremost at the feet of her mother" (vii).

Editha Mowbray, adored and spoiled by her parents, aspires to great intellectual and literary ambitions. An avid reader in her youth, she soon directs her energies to writing. However, as the narrator tells us, "she could not think of disgracing [an ancient] family by turning professed author; she therefore confined her little effusions to a society of admiring friends, secretly lamenting the loss which the literary world sustained in her being born a gentlewoman" (2). In addition to setting the scene for the parent-child conflict, Opie's attention to Mrs. Mowbray's "unfeminine" ambitions in this passage raises disturbing questions regarding society's reception of female authorship as well as the limited education and experience granted women. Restricted to the confines of close friends, Mrs. Mowbray is unable to achieve any understanding of the world at large or how her ideas relate to those debated in public. The result is an impractical view of life not unlike that of the Dickens' character Mrs. Jellyby in *Bleak House*: "Wrapt in philosophical abstraction . . . and imagining systems for the good of society . . . she allowed individual suffering in her neighbourhood to pass unobserved and unrelieved. While professing her unbounded love for the great family of the world, she suffered her own family to pine under the consciousness of her neglect" (2-3). Amelia Opie does not judge Mrs. Mowbray's views, on either social or family issues; she does, however, criticize both the mother's obsession with theoretical systems and her illogical distinction between theory and practice.

Since publication of philosophical treatises was disgraceful to a gentlewoman, Mrs. Mowbray discovered one acceptable publishing venture: the topic of children's education. Therefore, Mrs. Mowbray determines to research "rules on the subject, on which she might improve, anticipating with great satisfaction the moment when she should be held up as a pattern of imitation to mothers, and be prevailed upon, though with graceful reluctance, to publish her system, without a name, for the benefit of society" (3). As a result of her mother's obsession with her project, Adeline is victimized by the many experiments Mrs. Mowbray conducts: flannel, then no flannel; stays, then no stays; vegetarian diet, then meat diet. It is not until Adeline's feet bleed on a Turkish carpet even as her mother investigates the pros and cons of shoes, that Mrs. Mowbray questions whether "a little experience is better than a great deal of theory" (5).

In an effort to please her mother, Adeline eagerly reads literature on theory and philosophy. However, as the narrator notes, this selection of reading that "only served to amuse Mrs Mowbray's fancy, her more enthusiastic daughter resolved to make conscientiously the rules of her practice" (13). One such work was by a writer named Frederic Glenmurray, who had published a convincing argument against the institution of marriage, an argument that impresses Mrs. Mowbray as well, that is, until Adeline wishes to act on that theory and become Glenmurray's lover. Such a union shocks Mrs. Mowbray for two reasons: one, Glenmurray has dueled with Sir Patrick O'Carrol, who courts the mother to gain access to her daughter; and two, she cannot accept that one would actually put one's theory or system into practice. Referring to her daughter as a "kept mistress," Mrs. Mowbray tries to address Adeline's reasoned line of questioning regarding her opposition:

The poetical philosophy which I have so much delighted to study, has served me to ornament my conversation, and make persons less enlightened than myself wonder at the superior boldness of my fancy, and the acuteness of my reasoning powers;—but I should as soon have thought of making this little gold chain round my neck fasten the hall-door, as act upon the precepts laid down in those delightful books. No; though I think all they say are true, I believe the purity they inculcate too much for this world. (42)

Mrs. Mowbray's fault lies in the fact that "her practice was ever in opposition to her opinions" (3). Adeline, who has been seriously employed in her studies, cannot understand her mother's hypocrisy. Nor can she comprehend Glenmurray, whose genuine love for her prompts him to ask her to marry him. She refuses, resolving to stand by her convictions, *his* convictions as well, she reminds him. Although she loves him, Adeline resolves not to join with Glenmurray out of respect for her mother's wishes: "Be but the kind affectionate parent that you have ever been to me; and though I will never marry out of regard to my own principles, I will also never contract any other union" (42). Adeline makes it clear that as long as her mother recognizes parental duty, Adeline will in turn recognize filial duty. Therein lies Mrs. Mowbray's ultimate violation: she abandons her responsibility to her daughter, the indirect result of which is Adeline's eventual "elopement" with Glenmurray. Attracted to and flattered by Sir Patrick, Mrs. Mowbray marries him, and they and Adeline go to his remote Berkshire estate. Consumed by her own lust, Mrs. Mowbray cannot or will not believe Adeline's fears regarding Sir Patrick's advances to her. When he attempts to seduce her in her mother's absence, Adeline escapes, unexpectedly meets Glenmurray, who offers her protection, and flees with him, never dreaming that her mother would disown her.

Although Adeline violates social conventions, Amelia Opie clearly aligns the reader's sympathy with the young protagonist. Despite bearing the reputation as a "fallen woman," Adeline possesses genuine virtues that contrast with society's pretensions.[8] As Roxanne Eberle notes, "Even as Opie condemns the consequences of radical theory, she satirizes the hypocritical society which shuns the lovers" (135). What Opie also asserts, is that had Mrs. Mowbray been more realistic in her child-rearing theories, had made them consistent with practice, and had been less selfish about her own desires, Adeline would not have become the social outcast she is. As Dr. Norberry, a family friend, reminds Mrs. Mowbray, "though a parent does not, at a child's birth, solemnly make a vow to do all in his or her power to promote the happiness of that child—still, as he has given it birth, he has tacitly bound himself to make it happy. This tacit agreement you broke" (101). When Mrs. Mowbray asks if she should forgive her daughter, Dr. Norberry quickly replies, "Certainly; a fault which both your precepts and conduct occasioned" (101). Mrs. Pemberton criticizes Editha Mowbray's childrearing techniques, claiming that the faults of her daughter Adeline "originated" in the mother. When Mrs. Mowbray defensively protests that she had always been concerned about her parental duties by writing a "voluminous manuscript on the subject," Mrs. Pemberton counters: "But where was thy daughter; and how was she employed during the time that thou wert writing a book by which to educate her" (257). Mrs. Mowbray's contemplative silence indicates that she recognizes her culpability regarding the unfortunate state of her daughter. Offering her assessment of the situation, Mrs. Pemberton is forthright with the saddened and contrite Mrs. Mowbray:

A child's education begins almost from the hour of its birth; and the mother who understands her task, knows that the circumstances which every moment calls forth, are the tools with which she is to work in order to fashion her child's mind and character. What would you think of the farmer who was to let his fields lie fallow for years, while he was employed in contriving a method of cultivating land to increase his gains ten-fold? (257)

When Mrs. Mowbray protests that she could not possibly have realized Adeline's daring, Mrs. Pemberton resolutely lays the blame where it belongs: "thou didst not, as parents should do, inquire into the impressions made on thy daughter's mind" (258).

Gary Kelly has observed that *Adeline Mowbray* "shows women corrupting women" (8). Roxanne Eberle offers a different view by noting the healing and protective feminine powers of Mrs. Pemberton,

Savanna (Adeline's loyal Caribbean servant), and the penitent Mrs. Mowbray (144-45).[9] Both critics' conclusions are justified. Opie takes a broad-minded approach, criticizing not only Mrs. Mowbray's child-rearing practices and inability to reconcile theory with practice, but also society's hypocrisy. Eberle notes that Opie does not privilege one doctrine: "By situating the debate between 'radicals' and 'conservatives' directly over the heroine's desirable—and commodifiable—female form, Opie exposes the self interest implicit in both radical and conservative prescriptions about female education and citizenship. Ultimately, the novel critiques rather than proselytizes" (123-24). Opie also censures parents who, absorbed in the theory of raising their children, spend little time in doing so or in considering the effects that theory has on formative young minds.

In *Vindication*, Mary Wollstonecraft writes that "to be a good mother a woman must have sense, and that independence of mind which few women possess who are taught to depend entirely on their husbands. . . . [U]nless the understanding of woman be enlarged, and her character rendered more firm, by being allowed to govern her own conduct, she will never have sufficient sense of command of temper to manage her children properly" (227). Sense, independence, self-governance, Wollstonecraft argues, are essential for all women, be they parents or not; however, she makes her "radical" appeal more palatable to a late eighteenth-century audience by demonstrating how these attributes serve that most sacred of female duties—motherhood. Despite her untimely death in 1797, ten days after Mary Wollstonecraft Shelley was born, Wollstonecraft left a legacy in writing and philosophy that Shelley willingly inherited and reconfigured in her life and literary works.

Though less publicly outspoken than her mother, Mary Shelley demonstrates in her fiction her debt to Wollstonecraft's philosophy toward not only women's social, formal, and domestic education, but also parent-child relationships. From her first mature work, *Frankenstein* (1818) to her final novel, *Falkner* (1837), she examined the issue of parents' responsibility toward their children. *Lodore*, which contemporary critics highly praised and which was second only to *Frankenstein* in popularity, demonstrates how a generation of misguided child-rearing practices can end in near disaster, not only for the child, but also for the parent.

Cornelia Santerre Lodore must break free of both her husband's and mother's influence to reclaim her relationship with Ethel, her daughter. In fact, it is Cornelia's maternal instinct that empowers her to escape the imprisonment of social conventions and of a regressive upbringing. Shelley does not, however, present the stereotypical sentimental ending of mother and child reunited simply to moralize that motherhood is women's primary function and mode of fulfillment. Rather she presents Cornelia's history as a persuasive example to convince a conservative readership that women require a sound education to think rationally. In *Thoughts on the Education of Daughters* (1787), Wollstonecraft advocates education to develop children's intellect and morals: "I wish them to be taught to think," she writes, "thinking is indeed a severe exercise" (11). Implied in Wollstonecraft's words is that girls should be raised to act independently with the freedom to govern themselves under the supervision of caring adults.

Much of Cornelia's unhappiness is the direct result of the education she receives from her mother, Lady Santerre, who dominates and controls her life. Fashioned by her mother and married at sixteen, Cornelia has had little chance to experience life and to establish any sense of independence or self-esteem. Lady Santerre views her daughter not as a rational individual but as a commodity by which she herself can purchase a life of ease and social gain that her impoverished state cannot afford her. In *Moral Instruction and Fiction for Children: 1794-1820*, Samuel Pickering notes that eighteenth-century social critics felt parents "were misled by the promises inherent on Locke's educational views. Dazzled by the possibilities for advancement in society and then by the 'ornamental' surface of aristocratic life, they forgot the criticism of the aristocracy implied in Locke's educational views, and copying 'their betters,' provided children with educations which taught the 'show' rather than the 'useful'" (100). So it is with Lady Santerre. As the narrator remarks, she "was a clever though uneducated woman: perfectly selfish, soured with the world, yet clinging to it. To make good her second entrance on its stage, she believed it necessary to preserve unlimited sway over the plastic mind of her daughter" (31). Once she has manipulated the willing Lodore into marriage with Cornelia, she then sets herself up as a barrier to an intimate relationship between the couple, advising her daughter to sacrifice marital and parental responsibilities when those duties threaten her own selfish desires or her public image.

Cornelia receives few benefits from her mother's dictatorial demands. When circumstances dictate that Lodore flee to America, Cornelia listens to Lady Santerre's selfish arguments for why she should remain in England rather than follow her husband or fight for the custody of her young daughter.[10] As the narrator observes, age, inexperience, and poor education at this point excuse the decision that she was to regret for a long time:

Lady Lodore was nineteen; an age when youth is most arrogant, and most heedless of the feelings of others. . . . [T]hrough the bad education she had received, and her extreme youth, elevation of feeling degenerated into mere personal pride, and heroism was turned into obstinacy: she had been capable of the most admirable self-sacrifice, had she been taught the right shrine at which to devote herself; but her mind was narrowed by the mode of her bringing up, and her loftiest ideas were centred in worldly advantages the most worthless and pitiable. (52-53)

Cornelia is reluctant, quite understandably, to sever the ties with her mother which Lodore insists that she do. As she later confesses to a friend, "He [Lodore] asks but the trivial sacrifice of my duty to my mother—my poor mother! I am to tear away, and to trample upon the first of human ties, to render myself worthy of the guardianship of my child! I cannot do it—I should hold myself a parricide" (86). Cornelia's dependency upon her mother and desire for her approbation illustrates Wollstonecraft's observation that, "the early habit of relying almost implicitly on the opinion of a respected parent is not easily shook, even when matured reason convinces the child that his father [or mother] is not the wisest [person] in the world" (230). Cornelia, however, lacks "matured reason" to recognize the dangers of her mother's self-serving advice. Admirable though it may be, her love for her mother prevents Cornelia from realizing how readily Lady Santerre manipulates her each time she begins to exercise her own will and decides to take action. It also severs her relationship with her child, a relationship, Shelley suggests, that takes precedence over parental ties.

After the death of her mother and her husband, Cornelia is free to govern her life. However, having been raised to be dependent, she lacks the formative education to do so. Following her mother's example, she is reluctant to give up her opulent life. When she learns that Ethel has returned to England, Cornelia discovers that Lodore's outdated will dictates that she not establish any contact with her daughter if she wishes to maintain her jointure. This legal restriction coupled with the mistaken belief that Ethel despises her discourages the mother from pursuing the matter. The lonely young woman recognizes the emptiness of her life and assumes she is unable to alter its course. She has no motivation to be self-reliant and to escape the throes of self-pity, until she hears of Ethel's predicament. At that point, maternal instinct takes over and becomes the impetus for rejecting Lady Santerre's values.

Deciding to be the mother she has not been, Cornelia visits Ethel in a shabby apartment of London's prison section. Meeting her daughter for the first time in nearly fifteen years, Cornelia realizes how wrongly she has imagined her as a hateful, bitter child. Impressed by Ethel's bravery and devotion to her husband, Cornelia promises to help her, having finally realized what little happiness and personal fulfillment her own upbringing has generated. The catalyst for Cornelia's discovery of independence and self-esteem has been her love for her daughter: "Why was this change? She could not tell—memory could not inform her. She only knew that since she had seen Ethel in her adversity, the stoniness of her heart had dissolved within her, that her whole being was subdued to tenderness, and that the world was changed from what it had been in her eyes" (192-93). As Katherine Hill-Miller notes, motherhood frees Cornelia: "Cornelia's new life of devotion to her daughter, for all its conventionality, allows her to escape some of the configurations of traditional marriage—in particular the patterns of dominance and dependence involved in her relationship to Lodore" (159). One might also add that she has cast off the dominance and dependence of Lady Santerre as well. With her age and experience, Cornelia is ultimately able to do what Sibella, Clement, and Adeline are unable to: reject misguided and destructive parental influence and choose her own way.

Inspired by Ethel's example of disinterested love as well as by her very determined and independent spirit, Cornelia determines her course of action: "Latent maternal pride might increase her admiration, and maternal tenderness add to its warmth. Her nature had acknowledged its affinity to her child" (181). She discovers that she, not Ethel, is the unfortunate one: "Arrived at home, she found herself in prison within the walls of her chamber. She abhorred its gilding and luxury—she longed for Ethel's scant abode and glorious privations" (182). Despite regretting her past behavior, Cornelia is enchanted with the feeling of power that the role of mother grants her, a very different role from the dependent daughter and wife she had always been:

She was resolved to sacrifice every thing to her daughter—to liberate Villiers, and to establish her in ease and comfort. The image of self-sacrifice, and of the ruin of her own fortunes, was attended with a kind of rapture. She felt as if, in securing Ethel's happiness, she could never feel sorrow more. This was something worth living for: the burden of life was gone. . . . While indulging these reveries, she sunk into a balmy sleep—such a one she had not enjoyed for many months—nay, her whole past life had never afforded her so sweet a joy. (182)

The next day, Cornelia visits the solicitor who is helping Edward to arrange the sale of her jointure and to turn her London house over to Ethel.

Initially, Cornelia is motivated not only from the genuine love for her child, but also by the heroic aspect of her decision. She realizes that her actions save not only her daughter but also herself:

Her sensibility, awakened by the considerations forced on her by her new circumstances, caused her to make more progress in the knowledge of life, and in the philosophy of its laws, than love or ambition had ever done before. The last had rendered her proud from success, the first had caused her to feel dependent on one only; but now that she was about to abandon all, she found herself bound to all by stronger ties than she could have imagined.

Alone, friendless, unknown, and therefore despised, she must shift for herself, and rely on her own resources for prudence to ensure safety, and courage to endure the evils of her lot. (191)

Shelley does not offer the stereotypical sentimental ending of mother and child reunited to idealize motherhood. Rather, she presents Cornelia's history as a persuasive example to convince a conservative readership that to be effective parents themselves, children require models by which to imitate. The catalyst for Cornelia's discovery of independence and self-esteem has been her love for her daughter. Enacting the responsibilities of motherhood has not imprisoned Cornelia; rather it has liberated her.

Cornelia is not the only victim of a self-rewarding philosophy of rearing children. Her child, Ethel, is as well. Once Ethel and her father have settled in the Illinois frontier, Lodore embarks on his own educational system. Borrowing from literary stock images and archetypes, he molded the plastic Ethel so that "she grew into the image on which his eye doted" (10). The parallels to *Frankenstein* are evident: Lodore is as intent on creating a perfect specimen as Victor was, a being that would not only bless him as a father, but also represent his ideal image of woman, an image that neither Cornelia, given her excessive attachment to her mother, nor Theodora, the woman whose unrequited love prompted his alliance to Cornelia, could match. In an apparently heartening domestic scene by the hearth of their Illinois home, Lodore teaches Ethel, who sits at his feet on a stool as he instructs her: Lodore "drew his chief ideas from Milton's Eve, and adding to this the romance of chivalry, he satisfied himself that his daughter would be the imbodied [*sic*] ideal of all that is adorable and estimable in her sex" (12). Shelley undercuts the sentimentality of this scene by suggesting that Lodore's educational philosophy serves his purpose rather than benefits his daughter's future. Not one of the three figures that he draws upon as roles for Ethel—Eve the helpmate, the fair damsel of romance, and *The Tempest*'s Miranda, whose fate is completely dependent upon her benevolent father—teaches the young girl independence or selfhood. Instead, all three literary figures are designed to shape her into the type of woman Lodore has imagined is the ideal: submissive, pliable, and dependent.

Lodore decides to return to England when he recognizes that his daughter has become a young woman in a country that cannot provide the society he feels she would need:

[Lodore] had become aware that the village of the Illinois was not the scene fitted for the development of his daughter's first social feelings, and that he ought to take her among the educated and refined, to give her a chance for happiness. A Gertrude or an Haidèe, brought up in the wilds, innocent and free, and bestowing the treasure of their hearts on some accomplished stranger, brought on purpose to realize the ideal of their dreamy existences, is a picture of beauty, that requires a miracle to change in to an actual event in life. (54)

Lodore's desire to create Ethel into an obedient, ingenuous figure like Haidèe or Gertrude, both of whom have been raised in isolated, natural surroundings and were educated by their fathers, indicates what is his Rousseau-influenced perception of the ideal woman.[11] Bitter about his prior relationships, Lodore is determined that his daughter will be different than his lover and his wife; as the narrator observes, "white paper to be written upon at will is a favourite metaphor among those men who have described the ideal of a wife" (29). Like Caroline Ashburn, Ethel Lodore survives her childhood education, maturing into an independently thinking young woman. Despite her father's regressive educational philosophy, Lodore genuinely loved and respected his daughter, and he demonstrated that love and respect. Also integral is her natural spunkiness and willingness to disobey authority if obeying violates her reason or perceived duty. For example, Ethel determines to join her husband, Edward Villiers, in London, where he awaits a prison sentence, despite his and her aunt's dictates that she remain home.[12]

In *Lodore*, Mary Shelley exposes the artificiality of social roles and criticizes the reductive education that children, particularly girls, so often receive, an education that ill-prepares them for life's unexpected events. Like Opie, she chastises society for emphasizing public rather than private virtue, particularly for women. "To thine own self be true," Polonius tells Laertes, for "Thou canst not then be false to any man" (*Hamlet* I. iii. 82-84). In a world that privileges appearance over character and that encourages masked rather than sincere principles and morals, Polonius' advice is difficult to live by. It is even more difficult for women who are discouraged or prevented from discovering a self, let alone governing it independently.

Given the numerous publications instructing children to obey and honor their parents, these novels by Fenwick, Opie, and Shelley take their cue from Mary Wollstonecraft's principles to engage in the debate on parent-child relationships. These novelists' progressive stance on education and their charge to parents to be moral exemplars reflect the growing trend of reciprocal duty and responsibility within the family unit in their depiction of the often unfortunate results when parents fail to respect and honor their children. Wollstonecraft's conclusion to her chapter on "Parental Affection" epitomizes these writers' concern:

Yet, till esteem and love are blended together in the first affection, and reason made the foundation of the first duty, morality will stumble at the threshold. But, till society is very differently constituted, parents, I fear, will still insist on being obeyed, because they will be obeyed, and constantly endeavour to settle that power on a Divine right which will not bear the investigation of reason. (235)

Until parents adhere to reason, children, assert these writers, are fully entitled to disobey, even to "break the tie that binds."

Notes

1. Fenwick was with Wollstonecraft when she died ten days after the birth of her second daughter, Mary Wollstonecraft Shelley. According to some critics, Opie was the object of William Godwin's affection prior to (and perhaps during) his acquaintance with Mary Wollstonecraft. See Roxanne Eberle, "Amelia Opie's *Adeline Mowbray*: Diverting the Libertine Gaze; or, the Vindication of a Fallen Woman" and Jan Fergus and Janice Farrar Thaddeus, "Women, Publishers, and Money, 1790-1820."

2. See the Introduction in T.G.A. Nelson's *Children, Parents, and the Rise of the Novel* for an overview of other theories regarding the concept of childhood. Nelson particularly notes Linda Pollock's study, *Forgotten Children: Parent-Child Relations from 1500 to 1900*, which disputes some of Ariès' hypotheses regarding society's view of children.

3. Samuel Pickering chronicles a change in juvenile literature at this time; not only did authors construct tales and stories for moral instruction, they also emphasized their entertainment value.

4. Wollstonecraft takes Rousseau's theories regarding women's nature and their education to task in *Vindication*; see especially pages 128-48.

5. Valmont disapproves of Bonneville's teaching Sibella, and upon the first tutor's death, he instructs the second one to exclude her from the lessons (34). At this time, girls did not enjoy the same education that boys did. "Masculine" subjects, such as Greek, Latin, higher mathematics, and philosophy, were thought to defeminize females, whose education was designed to prepare them

to be suitable wives and mothers. See Katharine Rogers' *Feminism in Eighteenth-Century England*, Lawrence Stone's *Family, Sex and Marriage in England 1550-1800*, and Mary Abbott's *Family Ties: English Families 1540-1920*.

6. Opie published another novel, *Father and Daughter* (1801) that examines parent-child relationships.

7. See "Amelia Opie's *Adeline Mowbray*: Diverting the Libertine Gaze; or, the Vindication of a Fallen Woman."

8. For example, Glenmurray's cousins, who refuse to see Adeline as Glenmurray's lover, engage in extramarital affairs of their own (131).

9. Eberle does qualify this empowerment, noting that the women are able to effect it within the socially-isolated site of Rosevalley, the Mowbrays' maternal ancestral home.

10. Lord Lodore has been challenged to a duel by Casimir Lyzinski, his illegitimate son with Countess Lyzinski. Honor dictates that he accept the challenge, yet concern for Casimir forbids it. Casimir and others are unaware that Lodore is the young man's father. Unwillingly caught in such a predicament, Lodore determines to move to the States.

11. Haidèe refers to one of the characters from Lord Byron's *Don Juan* (1818-1824); Gertrude, from Thomas Campbell's *Gertrude of Wyoming (1809)*.

12. Edward is imprisoned because of his father's debts. The child of an irresponsible and morally corrupt parent, he also overcomes the detrimental influence, largely because of a worthy and helpful uncle who acts more the father to Edward than his own does.

Works Cited

Abbott, Mary. *Family Ties: English Families 1540-1920*. London: Routledge, 1993.

Ariès, Philippe. *Centuries of Childhood: A Social History of Family Life*. Trans. Robert Baldick. New York: Knopf, 1962.

Eberle, Roxanne. "Amelia Opie's *Adeline Mowbray*: Diverting the Libertine Gaze; or, the Vindication of a Fallen Woman." *Studies in the Novel* 26:2 (1994): 121-52.

Fenwick, Eliza. *Secresy: Or, the Ruin on the Rock*. Intro. Janet Todd. London: Pandora Press, 1989.

Fergus, Jan, and Janice Farrar Thaddeus. "Women, Publishers, and Money, 1790-1820." *Studies in Eighteenth-Century Culture* 17 (1987): 191-207.

Grylls, David. *Guardians and Angels: Parents and Children in Nineteenth-Century Literature*. London: Faber and Faber, 1978.

Hill-Miller, Katherine. *'My Hideous Progeny': Mary Shelley, William Godwin, and the Father-Daughter Relationship*. Newark: U of Delaware P, 1995.

Kelly, Gary. "Amelia Opie, Lady Caroline Lamb, and Maria Edgeworth: Official and Unofficial Idealogy." *Ariel* 12.4 (1981): 3-24.

Nelson, T.G.A. *Children, Parents, and the Rise of the Novel.* Newark: U of Delaware P, 1995.

Opie, Mrs Amelia. *Adeline Mowbray.* Intro. Jeanette Winterson. London: Pandora Press, 1986.

Pickering, Samuel F., Jr. *Moral Instruction and Fiction for Children: 1749-1820.* Athens: U of Georgia P, 1993.

Postman, Neil. *The Disappearance of Childhood.* New York: Delacorte, 1982.

Rogers, Katharine M. *Feminism in Eighteenth-Century England.* Urbana: U of Illinois P, 1982.

Shelley, Mary Wollstonecraft. *Lodore.* New York: Wallis, 1835.

Stone, Lawrence. *The Family, Sex and Marriage in England 1500-1800.* New York: Harper, 1977.

Wollstonecraft, Mary. "Thoughts on the Education of Daughters." *The Works of Mary Wollstonecraft.* Vol. 4. Ed. Janet Todd and Marilyn Butler. New York: New York UP, 1989. 1-50.

——. *A Vindication of the Rights of Woman.* Ed. Charles W. Hagelman, Jr. New York: Norton, 1967.

3

"Herself Beheld":
Marriage, Motherhood, and Oppression
in Brontë's *Villette* and Jacobs's
Incidents in the Life of a Slave Girl

Andrea O'Reilly Herrera

Some will object, that a comparison cannot fairly be made between
the government of the male sex and the forms of unjust power . . .
But was there ever any domination which did not appear natural to
those who possessed it? . . . Did not the slaveowners of the Southern
United States maintain the same doctrine, with all the fanaticism with
which men cling to the theories that justify their passions and legitimate their personal interests?
                    —John Stuart Mill, *The Subjection of Women* (1869)

In 1853 Charlotte Brontë published her last and perhaps her most
controversial novel, *Villette,* a semiautobiographical work written in the
form of an autobiography. Less than four years after the publication of
Villette, Harriet Jacobs, a woman born into slavery, completed her now
famous autobiography, *Incidents in the Life of a Slave Girl, Written by
Herself* (though it was not actually published until 1861). Although both
of their "autobiographies" are written out of clearly different circumstances and are, therefore, ostensibly distinct from one another, when
approached in a refracted light it soon becomes apparent that Brontë's
and Jacobs's works actually mirror one another in surprising and extraordinary ways, for both put into relief the issues of marriage, motherhood,
and oppression against the larger social attitude toward women. In short,
both Brontë's and Jacobs's works stand as powerful commentaries on
women's positions during the mid-nineteenth century.
    In order to pursue such a reading, one must first establish the pre-
vailing attitude toward middle-class white women's positions and female
deportment both in Britain and in the United States during the period in
which Brontë and Jacobs were writing, for this ideology provides the

undergirding for both of their works. As scores of historians and critics have pointed out, the middle-class ideal of domesticity and womanhood during the nineteenth century, often referred to as "home idealism" and the "cult of true womanhood" (respectively), enjoined females to be sexually and socially passive, modest, self-effacing, self-sacrificing, pious, and pure in body and mind.[1]

In addition, women were denied entrance into most universities and were barred from most professions, excluding teaching, acting as a governess, and nursing, all of which essentially were extensions of their domestic duties. Because they were not expected (or allowed in many cases) to earn wages outside of the home and frequently did not have any direct claim to property, the large majority of middle- to upper-class women were entirely dependent upon men both for economic support and for intellectual stimulus, a social reality that has prompted many students of the period to claim that white middle-class women were little more than chattel.

Perhaps Martha Vicinus best sums up middle-class women's positions during the period when she says, "In her most perfect form," the ideal woman was expected to "[combine] total sexual innocence, conspicuous consumption and the worship of the family hearth."[2] The female ideal that Vicinus refers to was advocated both in works of fiction and nonfiction. A good example is John Ruskin's essay "Of Queens Gardens" (1865).[3] In it Ruskin—dubbed by many as the Victorian "interpreter" of art and culture—sketches an idyllic portrait of the domestic sphere which figures home as an enclosed garden, a kind of prelapsarian asylum where women rear children and reform, or even redeem, irascible and bellicose men. Home, according to Ruskin, is the locus of peace, security, and morality, and woman is rooted at the center of that order.

Visions of home and womanhood such as Ruskin's helped typify nineteenth-century attitudes toward women's role within the domestic sphere and her position in British and American society. A great portion of the writing produced during the period carved out male and female spheres of activity and advocated in very specific terms modes of female deportment. Not only was female propriety and chastity emphasized, but both novels and conduct books alike were preoccupied with preparing women for the wedded state, for only in marriage could they fully assume their Ruskinian roles as ministering angels. However, despite the fact that wifehood and motherhood had come to be regarded—in the popular imagination at least—as quasi-religious vocations and marriage was viewed as the fulfillment of a woman's destiny, in reality economic and social circumstances precluded many females, such as Brontë and Jacobs, from realizing these ideals.

* * *

In some sense Brontë's *Villette* can be read as a rebuke against the narrowness and the limitations of the female domestic ideal Ruskin, among others, had laid out for women to emulate. During the time at which Brontë was writing, middle-class women such as herself were faced with the undeniable fact that British society was teeming with increasing numbers of "superfluous" or "redundant" women.[4] By mid-century nearly one out of every four English women was dependent upon her own resources; by 1850 there were over half a million more women than men in England. As a result, unmarried women who had passed their prime or lacked the economic, social, or physical attributes that would enable them to compete in the marriage market were forced to seek other ways to support themselves.

Though marriage was the preferred vocation for women, there were actually several alternative occupations to the wedded state. Often, "displaced" women either became governesses or companions to elderly widows. By the early 1840s single women were encouraged to pursue careers such as nursing or ministering to the poor. Aside from marriage, teaching, and social or charitable work, there was one other legitimate, though much disputed, alternative for middle-class Victorian spinsters during the period: entering the nunnery. However, the revival of the Roman Catholic religious orders and the establishment of Anglican nunneries during the 1840s stirred a furious debate that persisted nearly throughout the Victorian period, for female religious life represented, for many, a rejection of women's "natural" roles and functions as wives and mothers. In effect, the woman who willingly professed a vow of chastity and consciously abjured the "noisy" secular world of men not only failed to fulfill her (procreative) duty but, moreover, leveled a threat at the very underpinnings of British society: home and family.

Charlotte Brontë was well aware of the career options open to English women. Perhaps as a direct result of her own painful circumstances, she was extremely concerned with validating the solitary woman's experiences and activities and endowing her with a status comparable to that of the married woman. In an 1846 letter addressed to Miss Wooler, the headmistress of the boarding school where Brontë herself matriculated and later taught, she wrote:

. . . it seems that even a lone woman can be happy, as well as cherished wives and proud mothers. . . . I speculate much on the existence of unmarried and never-to-be married women nowadays; and I have already got to the point of considering that there is no more respectable character on this earth than an unmarried woman, who makes her own way through life quietly, perseveringly, without support of husband or brother; and who, having attained the age of forty-five or upwards, retains in her possession a well-regulated mind, a disposition to enjoy simple pleasures, and fortitude to support inevitable pains, sympathy with the suffering of others, and willingness to relieve want as far as means extend.[5]

In her final novel, *Villette,* Charlotte Brontë dramatizes the plight of the genteel Victorian spinster and orphan Lucy Snowe, a woman who seeks to define an independent identity for herself in a society that devalues unmarried or "displaced" women and virtually denies them visibility outside of a domestic context.[6] That *Villette* is centrally concerned with the subject of personal, as opposed to public, identity is suggested by its autobiographical form—a narrative form that implicitly and consciously entails the exploration and exposure of the self for public display. *Villette* is, more specifically, profoundly concerned with the idea of women's social identity, as opposed to private identity, and the novel "plays" with the idea of artifice or self-fashioning—allowing people to see what they want to see or what we want them to see—and its narrator, Lucy, is the queen of masking.[7] Lucy's narrative is not only filled with mysteries, conspiracies, and confusing relativities, but it is shot through with strategic omissions, silences, and concealments. Lucy repeatedly withholds important information from the reader, such as the identity of Dr. John, thus establishing and maintaining her authorial control both over her own narrative and over her audience. In effect, she presents for the reader's scrutiny only selective incidents in her life. Even those who appear to be closest to her do not really seem to know Lucy at all. Graham Bretton, for example, fails to perceive her painfully obvious romantic attraction to him. In addition to puzzling those around her, Lucy evades our gaze as well. Though she provides us with a relatively detailed, though highly subjective, portrait of her surroundings and the people whom she encounters in her travels, we are never given a clear description of her physical appearance, and we must continuously adjust and readjust our impression of her mental state. Lucy's shifting, fragmented identity is further underscored by her unreliable narrative and by the multiple nicknames the people whom she encounters in her travels give her, such as Ginevra Fanshawe, M. Paul, and Graham Bretton, among others. Her lack of identity is also emphasized by the fact that the first part of her autobiography chronicles the activities in the Bretton household and provides little to no insight into the inner life of Lucy herself. In the first part of her narrative, Lucy accounts for her own thoughts and actions only as they relate to others.

As many critics have observed, Lucy's social invisibility and displacement—her lack of identity—are highlighted at the very outset of

Brontë's novel. Unlike her foster family, the Brettons (a name that obviously suggests that they represent all of Britain), whose social identity is so firmly established that the house and the town that they live in is named after them, Lucy has no fixed identity. She not only lacks a physical home or family of her own, but she is neither at home in her native England, nor, as her agitated first person narrative suggests, at "home" with herself. She is, in other words, both physically and psychically homeless. In the first quarter of the novel she, like Jane Eyre, moves peripatetically from manor house to manor house, ever conscious of her marginalization and her comparative insignificance to those who take her in. In Lucy's own words, she is a "placeless person," who is as inconsequential and "unobtrusive" as a piece of "furniture" simply because she lacks all of the attributes that would establish her social identity, such as money, title, pedigree, and physical beauty (135).[8]

In each "foster" home that Lucy temporarily inhabits, she assumes many of the roles or careers available to single women such as herself. At the outset she is the Bretton's ward; after leaving their home she takes a post as a companion-nursemaid to the wealthy elderly spinster Miss Marchmont, who Sandra Gilbert and Susan Gubar describe as a "nun" who "lives in confinement, a perpetual virgin dedicated to the memory of the lover she lost."[9] When the latter dies, leaving her unexpectedly destitute, Lucy's physical and psychic alienation, coupled with her absolute penury, prompt her to abandon England and sail to Villette, the "great" capital of the imaginary kingdom of Labassecour, "the land of convents and confessionals."

In Villette the social displacement and alienation that Lucy experienced in England is temporarily magnified, for she is literally an alien on foreign turf. Not only is she friendless and without references, but she lacks even the most basic and essential tool to establish her identity: language. In desperation, Lucy seeks shelter in a girls' school located on the grounds of a former convent: Madame Beck's Pensionnat de Demoiselles on the Rue de Fossette. There she dons a dark *grissete*, like a kind of secular nun immured behind the high convent walls that surround the Pensionnat, and assumes the only other roles available to her, aside from marriage: governess and teacher.

At the outset the Pensionnat, like the newly established monasteries in England, functions for Lucy as a secular protective haven—a home away from home—for destitute females who share her plight. Madame Beck acts as her surrogate mother, and the demi-convent functions as her surrogate home, complete with an extended secular family. However, Madame Beck, who is often characterized as a kind of abbess, runs her boarding school like a monastery.[10] Much like a Mother Superior, she maintains constant surveillance over her community, wielding the arbitrary authority that the Protestant Brontë associated with the Catholic Church.[11] Her presence is ubiquitous. Calling for unquestioning obedience, she administers her school with absolute control; Lucy tells us, she kept all but her own children "in distrustful restraint, in blind ignorance, and under a surveillance that left no moment and no corner for retirement" (99). Despite its shortcomings, the demi-convent protects Lucy from "the perils of darkness" and the "new Gothic" world she depicts as being peopled with "dreaded [male] hunters" who pursue her through the streets (89, 86).[12] In effect, the demi-convent attracts and shelters those who, like Lucy, are unsuccessfully socialized and unable to regulate their own lives or cope in the outside world.

Cloistered within the convent walls, Lucy struggles to overcome her sense of alienation. There, she aspires toward an ideal of passionlessness that female religious life purportedly demanded, an ideal that was also enjoined upon women by the Victorian establishment.[13] It is at this point that Brontë yokes together her feminist concerns with the overarching theme of institutional restraint, for as one critic has noted, "the female monastery represented patriarchal institutional restraint on a large scale in the British imagination."[14] Mistakenly, Lucy perceives that the only way to establish an independent identity, without compromising or losing respectability or social integrity, is to remain completely detached from life, "cool" and "calm" and "stoical," she tells us, "about [her] future" (151). Clearly, Lucy is well-schooled in the Victorian notions that in order for a woman to preserve her intellectual and social integrity, she must suppress her natural sentiments and passions; unrestrained desire portends female ruin; and female sexuality is simply "an aspect of women's social function." In effect, Lucy struggles with an ideology which suggests that emotional capacity and desire in a woman are signs of weakness or inferiority, an ideology which functioned as a means of maintaining control over female sexuality and ambition, for it "kept" women in their "places."

In her struggle to exercise self-restraint and suppress her natural inclinations, Lucy measures herself against the potential female and male role models whom she encounters on her "journey." Although she represents an extreme, Modeste (modest?) Beck embodies the rational, reserved ideal toward which Lucy aspires, rather than the frivolous and self-indulgent Ginevra Fanshawe, who consents to play the role of the coquette, or the subservient and self-effacing Polly *Home* (my emphasis), who dedicates herself to domesticity and to pleasing men. In Lucy's view, not only is she morally and intellectually superior to women like Ginevra, but she regards the latter, along with Polly Home, as puppets or playthings for men who maintain absolute authority over them, though they claim to endow them with a morally superior or "angelic" status.

Just as Lucy systematically rejects the standards and ideals against which women were expected to measure themselves, so is her identity "tested" against two types of men: Dr. John, the embodiment of the Victorian ideal of manhood, and M. Paul, a foreigner and a Roman Catholic, who functions as the physical and emotional antithesis of the fair physician.[15] The passion and personal desire that she feels first for Graham Bretton, and then for M. Paul proves to be completely incompatible with her Victorian education and poses a very real threat to her beliefs regarding female behavior. Though Lucy has willingly cloistered herself within the old demi-convent and adopted the garb and the lifestyle of a nun, to her great dismay she discovers that more often than not her passionate and sometimes irrational inward sensibility is at odds with the dispassionate, rational social or external personage she believes she must be in order to establish an identity that is independent of the expectations placed upon her by her society.[16] The ability to conceal and suppress her emotions and disavow her natural inclinations toward both Graham Bretton and M. Paul become, simultaneously, the source of her power and her demise. The oppressive environment of the demi-convent, coupled with the emotional and physical isolation of the life Lucy has chosen to lead, cause her to undergo an identity crisis which pits her authentic or natural emotional self against her passionless social self, a crisis which leads her to the very brink of madness.[17]

Brontë carefully traces the steps Lucy takes to overcome both her psychic and emotional fragmentation and to get beyond the damaging, artificial notion of cultural and religious propriety; the images of the convent and the nun figure largely in this process. Lucy's various encounters in the demi-convent with the spectral nuns mark her progress toward independence and self-realization; both Graham Bretton and M. Paul are linked, either through direct experience or association, to a separate nun.

There are two deceased nuns in *Villette:* the phantom nun who haunts the Pensionnat on the Rue de Fossette and M. Paul's former lover, the "sainted nun" Justine Marie, who represents in the novel a kind of latter-day version of Miss Marchmont.[18] Both women have been victims of their passion; their marginalization is emphasized by the fact that they are ghosts, literally relegated to a state of virtual invisibility, which is akin to Lucy's insignificant status in Victorian society. The former, according to legend, was buried alive for committing some nameless "sin," presumably of passion, against her vow; and the latter opted to take a vow of poverty and chastity—as a sign of her fidelity—because she was forbidden to marry the then impecunious M. Paul. In effect, the nun of legend and Justine Marie embody the two combating aspects of Lucy Snowe: the first represents indulgence and unrestraint, and the second the renunciation and sublimation of worldly passion.

Lucy encounters the nuns, individually, on five separate occasions: the nun at the demi-convent haunts her three times as she struggles to suppress her feelings for Dr. John (Graham Bretton), and the spirit of Justine Marie torments her during her "courtship" with M. Paul. The first and second visitations take place in the *grenier* of the Rue de Fossette. There, the nameless phantom interrupts her while she is reading Dr. John's letter and frightens her as she searches for a dress to wear on an unchaperoned outing to the theater. Significantly, the second visitation takes place during the same evening that she witnesses Vashti's overtly passionate and (literally) inflammatory performance. Lucy is then confronted with the spectral nun a third time just after she has grown disillusioned with Dr. John and buries (an obvious metaphor for repression) his letters beneath the "dryad skelton" of the old pear tree (which she refers to in her narrative as Methuselah) where the young nun was purportedly interred (422). (The pear, with its curved, hour glass shape, suggests the female form.) Gathering her courage at this third meeting, Lucy attempts to determine the nun's identity. "Who are you? and why do you come to me?" she asks, but the shrouded figure remains silent (426). As the nun rushes past her, Lucy vainly stretches out her hand to determine whether the figure is real or illusory, since Dr. John had repeatedly assured her that the nun was merely a product of her overwrought imagination. She calls after it into the darkness, "If you have any real errand to me, come back and deliver it." Once again, Lucy receives no response.

Although Lucy has yet to decipher it, the spectral nun has a clearly defined errand in the novel; however, Brontë denies her heroine knowledge of the true identity of the specter at this juncture, for Lucy has yet to have fully undergone her "education." In other words, Lucy's disappointment with the physician—a man who clearly prefers a woman with domestic "talents," rather than one with intellectual aspirations, such as Polly Home(body?)—represents only the first stage of her development; she must also confront M. Paul and, by association, the second nun—Justine Marie—whom she encounters on two separate occasions.

The fourth visitation occurs shortly after Lucy's disillusionment with, and consequent rejection of, the English Dr. John and the onset of her emotional/intellectual attachment to M. Paul. The nun intrudes upon M. Paul and Lucy while they are sharing a relatively intimate moment in the *allée défendue* in the garden of the demi-convent. It is he who suggests that the phantom is not the nun of legend but, rather, his deceased lover, Justine Marie. He tells Lucy, "her business is as much with you as with me" (531). As they continue to discuss the "nature" of the apparition, the nun sweeps past them in the alley; Lucy proclaims, "never had [she] seen her so clearly" (534). Although Lucy is still deceived, for she has yet to "see" the nun for what she really is, it is at this point in her narrative that she first entertains the possibility that the ghost is something more than a "nervous malady," something that lies outside of herself.

Lucy's final encounter with a nun follows the incident in the park where she sees M. Paul with his young and beautiful ward, a woman whom Lucy mistakes for his lover. Upon discovering the couple, Lucy undergoes a severe nervous breakdown. It is this second disillusionment which prepares her for her last confrontation with the specter of the nun. Even though Lucy misreads the scene—thinking at the time that M. Paul was engaged to the girl—in retrospect she reflects upon the absurdity of her romantic "infatuation" with the professor, an infatuation that parallels her idealized vision of Graham Bretton. The revelation is liberating for her, and she suggests:

In my infatuation, I said, Truth, you are a good mistress to your faithful servants! While a lie pressed me, how I suffered! Even when the falsehood was still sweet, still flattering to the fancy, and warm to the feelings, it wasted me with hourly torment. The persuasion that affection was won could not be divorced from the dread that, by another turn of wheel, it might be lost. Truth stripped away Falsehood, and Flattery, and Expectancy, and here I stand—free!'

Nothing remained now but to take my freedom to my chamber, to carry it with me to my bed and see what I could make of it. The play was not yet indeed quite played out. . . . (677)

Indeed, Brontë's play was not yet played out. Having undergone this second disillusionment, despite the fact that it was prompted by her own misapprehension, Lucy is prepared to free herself of the romantic notion that the only way for a woman to find happiness is through love for a man—any man. Her final awakening takes place in two stages. Upon returning to the dormitory, the dark "nun's cell," to meditate upon her new-found freedom, Lucy encounters the specter of Justine Marie lying across her bed—the emotionally barren woman, who had sacrificed her self for love, that Lucy had almost allowed herself to become. Provoked by jealousy, rage, perhaps self-hatred and a sense of inexplicable guilt, she engages in a symbolic struggle with the nun.[19] In this final encounter, Brontë uses the ghost nun to signify the ambiguous, contradictory images of womanhood that have haunted Lucy. In one respect the supine nun represents the Victorian ideal of female passionlessness that Lucy has attempted to internalize, simply by virtue of the fact that Justine Marie is a nun. On the other hand, however, she is an amorous young woman who consciously buried her passion for her lover by entering the convent. In effect, she simultaneously functions as the very embodiment of the contradictory impulses with which Lucy is battling: passion vs. reason and restraint. However, because Brontë fails to identify which nun lies stretched across Lucy's bed in this episode, there resides the possibility that she may also be the phantom who haunts the demi-convent—the passionate woman who submitted to her desire and was punished. In the conflated figure of the nun, therefore, Brontë brings together and encapsulates a triad of conflicting cultural ideologies that have contributed to, or perhaps caused, Lucy's fragmented identity.

When she first finds the nun lying on her bed, Lucy perceives that she is a figment of her own imagination; then she quickly discovers that it is a "spectra" which has material form, something other than, or apart from, herself:

I defied the spectra. In a moment, without exclamation, I had rushed on the haunted couch; nothing leaped out or sprang, or stirred; all the movement was mine, so was all the life, the reality, the substance, the force; as my instinct felt. I tore her up—the incubus! I held her on high—the goblin! I shook her loose— the mystery! And down she fell—down all around me—down in shreds and fragments—and I trode upon her. (681)

In that moment Lucy discovers that the nun is neither illusory, nor is she a specter; rather, "the long nun proved a long bolster dressed in a long black stole, and artfully invested with a white veil." Moreover, she herself endows the black stole and the white veil with life, or so she thinks.

By allowing Lucy to struggle with the pillow-nun, which she believes is another woman, before discovering that it is a bolster covered with a stole and a veil, Brontë subtly suggests that the notion of the impropriety of female passion or desire to which Lucy adheres (and the nuns represent) is a sham, a myth. Her unconscious complicity in animating and perpetuating the ideology that the nuns represent, coupled with her realization that she has been deceived yet again, causes Lucy to ask two central questions: "*Whence* came these vestments? *Who* contrived this artifice?" (my emphasis). In framing these questions, Lucy reveals her sudden awareness of the fact that the specter is—beyond the "shadow" of a doubt—not the product of her own imagination but, rather, an illusion created by another. Only then can she, like a neo-

Radcliffian heroine, lift the "veil" that conceals the ultimate "mystery" in Villette and penetrate the "homely web of truth": the fact that the nun, in all of her manifestations, is nothing more than a male creation, contrived—in a spectacular act of spectral transvestism—by Ginevra Fanshawe's foppish lover, Alfred de Hamal, so that he might gain access to and possess the object of his affections. With this revelation Brontë brilliantly suggests that the stultifying notion of female propriety that Lucy perceives she has violated is a myth or illusion. And so, just as the struggle with the pillow-nun marks the moment at which Lucy acknowledges that her physical and emotional confinement is self-administered, the final demystification of the phantom represents the point at which she recognizes that she has been victimized or haunted by a perversely sentimental image of womanhood. In effect, the phantom nuns, with their multiple and conflated associations, are scarecrows set up by men in the "Queen's Garden."

The final sequence in Villette projects Lucy beyond the domestic sphere and the demi-convent into the wider world where she establishes herself as an independent agent. Despite her linguistic and cultural displacement in Villette, the foreign setting functions as a positive distancing factor which allows Lucy to acknowledge and overcome the seemingly insurmountable obstacles and limitations placed upon her by British patriarchal culture. In other words, her journey away from her native homeland ultimately serves as a catalyst for self-discovery. On foreign turf, her social invisibility becomes a source of power, rather than a debilitating attribute as it was in Britain. In some sense, however, Brontë subtly avoids a direct challenge to patriarchal ideology by allowing Lucy to remain abroad, at a safe distance from British shores; moreover, we learn that she has taken up a "respectable" career that does not disrupt traditional notions of woman's ministering role within the public domain: teaching. What remains notable, however, is the fact that Lucy struck out on her own, albeit with the assistance of M. Paul, and established herself outside the context of marriage and the convent. In so doing, she neither denied herself the experience of love, nor did she renounce her femininity.[20] That Lucy attained her economic and personal independence partly as a result of M. Paul's interventions seems to signify Brontë's recognition of the social reality that even under the most propitious circumstances most women remained reliant upon male esteem and, more often than not, male financial support for their success. However, M. Paul was for her only a temporary "savior." Not only does Lucy literally outlive him, but his death does not leave her helpless like Miss Marchmont, who confined herself to the domestic sphere after the loss of her lover, or without future ambitions like Justine Marie, who renounced the possibility of happiness and chose convent life because of her thwarted love. In the same vein, M. Paul was not solely responsible for Lucy's ultimate success. Though he established her in a "cot" with a small classroom, it was actually Miss Marchmont's legacy that enabled her to expand her *externat* (day school) into a *pensionnat* (boarding school) (594). At the conclusion of her narrative—which marks the passage of many years since the death of M. Paul—it becomes apparent that although Lucy had been enriched by their brief relationship, she had also managed to go on quite happily and successfully without him.

* * *

Like Charlotte Brontë, Harriet Jacobs also wrote in response to her own painful circumstances. Acutely conscious of her tenuous position in society, she employed a pseudonym (Linda Brent), like Charlotte Brontë (Currer Bell), to write about the unspeakables of her plight as a woman during the period; however, her story is complicated by the fact that she was a black woman born into slavery in the South during the pre-Civil War period.

Incidents in the Life of a Slave Girl, Written by Herself dramatizes the plight of a black female slave who is both genteel and educated. Unlike Lucy Snowe, Linda Brent (aka Harriet Jacobs) is a woman who seeks to define an identity for herself independent of her race but not necessarily independent of her gender, for as many critics have noted Jacobs portrays herself in her narrative as a "maternal icon" and a "heroic," "suffering," and "outraged" slave mother.[21] Unlike *Villette,* which aims to validate the life of the single woman, *Incidents* sets out to justify the life of the single slave mother. Though its final vision is different from *Villette*'s, *Incidents* also functions as a critique against the ideals of womanhood and domesticity that white patriarchal society institutionalized during the period—impossible ideals to which Linda Brent, like Lucy Snowe, could not conform.[22] In short, it too exposes the limitations and the narrowness of these ideals. As Jean Fagan Yellin states,

Like all slave narratives, *Incidents* was shaped by the empowering impulse that created the American Renaissance. Jacobs' book expressed democratic ideals and embodied a dual critique of nineteenth-century America: it challenged the institution of chattel slavery with its supporting ideology of white racism, as well as traditional patriarchal institutions and ideologies.[23]

Although the distinctions between their "plights" are self-evident, and the intention of this essay is not to suggest that the obstacles white middle-class spinsters faced were equivalent to or greater than those with which female slaves were confronted, Brontë's and Jacobs's accounts bear striking resemblances to one another. On the most obvious level both employ an autobiographical narrative form. In addition, *Villette* and *Incidents* are written in a "confessional mode" which, ironically, frees the narrators of their "social" guilt and sins, which neither one is responsible for having committed. Although she is openly emotional, Linda, like Lucy, maintains a controlled, rational tone as she recounts the horrors of slavery; her self-control is put into relief against the semi-hysterical ranting of Mrs. Flint. In the same vein, both narratives contain, to borrow Franny Nudelman's words, "strategic concealments" that insure the heroines' "authorial liberty" and control.[24] For Jacobs, the adoption of this form, coupled with the fact that she portrays herself as a fictional character, is especially significant, for she positions herself at the center of a narrative from which black women had traditionally been marginalized; like Lucy Snowe, Brent simultaneously assumes the role of an insider and an outsider in her own story and, as many critics have noted, she transforms herself from object to subject.[25] More important, as Nudelman has pointed out, by privileging both the voice and the experience of a female slave, Jacobs "radically alters the structure of a discourse that typically constructs the slave as a mute [and tragic] subject whose experience must be translated by an empathetic white observer" (924). Perhaps what is most noteworthy, however, is Jacobs's mastery of language itself, the most basic tool, as noted above, for shaping and controlling identity.

Although one should never lose sight of the very human story behind Jacobs's account, her autobiography is generally treated as a carefully crafted and edited abolitionist statement. As Fagan Yellin observes, Jacobs's narrator "utilizes standard abolitionist rhetoric to lament the inadequacy of her descriptions of slavery and to urge her audience to involve themselves in anti-slavery efforts" (xiv). Not only is *Incidents* filled with abolitionist "sentimentality" and rhetoric, but Jacobs draws upon and transforms a literary paradigm previously established in other slave narratives, such as Frederick Douglass's.[26] Like *Villette, Incidents* also manipulates the conventions of sentimental domestic fiction as well as overturns the traditional power relations in the seduction novel.

Linda Brent's narrative also follows a trajectory that is quite similar to Lucy Snowe's. At the outset of her narrative, Linda establishes her "communal identity."[27] Contrary to the plight of most slaves, she has a clear sense of her connections and her origins. Unlike the young Lucy Snowe, who is only a temporary ward in the Bretton's home, Linda grows up in the house that she was born in and gives birth to her own children in that same house. In some sense her grandmother's (Aunt Martha Horniblow) home can be likened to Mrs. Bretton's in that it functions, at least in Linda's memory, as a kind of safe haven which temporarily shelters her from the realities of the outside world. As Linda herself notes, she was "fondly shielded" in that house from the fact that she was a slave until six years of age, when she learned that in the eyes of white society she was little more than "a piece of merchandise" (5).[28]

In some sense the Brent/Horniblow household mirrors the white bourgeois ideal of domesticity, for it consists of an extended family which includes Linda's maternal grandmother and great aunt, her parents, and her brother. Though she is taken from her family prematurely, Linda's mother is characterized as being warm and loving; Martha Horniblow replaces her daughter after her death, thus functioning as a kind of wise surrogate mother. Unlike the typical slave father, who was robbed of his paternal authority and his role as protector and bread winner, Linda's father is an accomplished carpenter who maintains absolute authority over his household even after his wife's death. Although Linda's family embodies the vision of domesticity her bourgeois audience prized, it is soon undercut and robbed of its "status" by the harsh realities of slavery. As Linda repeatedly points out, slavery not only robs black Americans of the "right to family ties," but it prevents even the strongest men from "protecting their wives and children" and women from fulfilling their maternal duties, and denies her own children "lawful claim to their own name" (43, 38, 78). In her own words, families were sent to the auction block where "Husbands were torn from wives, parents from children, never to look upon each other again this side of the grave" (106). Paralleling the scene in which Lucy Snowe discovers that her recently deceased employer, Miss Marchmont, failed to leave her a (monetary) legacy—something which would have insured her independence in English society—Linda's happiness and future prospects are "blighted" when she discovers that her slave-mistress had broken her death-bed promise to free her and her brother, William (53). At the reading of the will she learns, moreover, that she is "bequeathed" to her mistress's five-year-old niece, Emily Flint. Like Lucy Snowe, Linda thus begins an odyssey in search of freedom and her own "hearthstone."

Linda's second "home"—the household of the physician Dr. Flint—is, theoretically, the "genuine" embodiment of the white Southern bourgeois ideal of domesticity. However, Linda reveals that in reality it is a "cage of obscene birds" (52). Though Dr. Flint maintains the outward appearance of a healer and a pious Christian, he embodies the very worst characteristics of a Southern slave holder. She states,

Reader, I draw no imaginary picture of Southern homes. I am telling you the
plain truth. . . . The young wife soon learns that the husband in whose hands she
has placed her happiness pays no regard to his marriage vows. Children of
every shade of complexion play with her own fair babes, and too well she
knows that they are born unto him of his own household. Jealousy and hatred
enter the flowery home, and it is ravaged of its loveliness. (36)

At a later juncture in her narrative she observes,

I can testify from my own experience and observation, that slavery is a curse to
whites as well as blacks. It makes the white fathers cruel and sensual; the sons
violent and licentious; it contaminates the daughters and makes the wives
wretched. (52)

In Hazel Carby's words, *Incidents* is a "sophisticated sustained narrative dissection of the conventions of true womanhood."[29] In Dr. Flint's
home, Linda is confronted with the irreconcilable incongruities between
the prevailing conception of female identity and "true womanhood" and
her own condition as a female slave. From the very outset it is made
clear that despite her lowly status she possesses many of the attributes
which would make her "marketable" in genteel society, such as piety and
beauty. But Linda quickly discovers that these very attributes make her
vulnerable to exploitation. In vain, she attempts to uphold the values
advocated by bourgeois society and model herself after the very same
ideals or virtues against which Lucy measured herself: modesty, chastity,
passionlessness, and domesticity. However, she soon discovers that slavery "deemed" it a "crime" for a black woman to "wish to be virtuous"
(31). Moreover beauty, a coveted attribute for a white woman, becomes
her "greatest curse," for it makes her the object of Dr. Flint's desire and
Mrs. Flint's jealousy and scorn. Rejecting her grandmother's form of
piety, which advocates passive acceptance and compliance with "God's
will," or one's "lot in life," Linda sidesteps the female ideals of silence
and submissiveness in order to combat her master-pursuer. Not only
does she repeatedly rebuke Dr. Flint's advances, but she attempts to
exert her own will by pursuing a relationship with a "young colored carpenter" in her neighborhood who was born a free man. Linda soon discovers that the "dream of her youth" is thwarted by the realities of her
own plight, for the civil laws to which she is subject as a slave give no
sanction to marriage or love. In her description of her first disappointment with love, Jacobs cleverly parodies the plot of the sentimental
romance novel, which often centers around the combatting tropes of
marriage based on love and mutual respect as opposed to the idea of

arranged marriages, which are tantamount to political or economic exchanges. Linda describes her relationship with her "lover" as one founded on "mutual attachment" and love; however, she undercuts this vision by pointing out that in order for them to realize their dream of happiness, her lover must offer to buy her (37). Denying her the right to choose her own partner, Dr. Flint, like an autocratic father, punctures Linda's "love dream" by denying the young carpenter's offer and suggesting instead that he arrange for her a union—though not sanctioned by law—with one of his own slaves, whom he would choose for her. In this episode Linda must come to terms with the fact that she is an object, a possession, much like a "piece of [parlor] furniture" which can be moved from place to place—a description which echoes the very language employed in Brontë's *Villette* (141).

As Beth Maclay Doriani points out in "Black Womanhood in Nineteenth Century America," Linda, being a black female slave, is faced with "a more complex standard of morality" than a white woman (210). For her, the ideals of silence, pious submissiveness and sexual passivity—all of which her free grandmother embodies—are tantamount to consenting to sexual exploitation and rape. Moreover, as Maclay Doriani has observed "bearing children does not define the slave as a true woman, since children are mere commodities" to the slave master (211). In self-defense, Linda thus breaks her vow of silence and rebukes her master.[30] After refusing his "proposal" with a verbal barrage which leaves the doctor almost speechless with anger, Flint offers her an opportunity to "redeem her character" by giving in to his advances (40). Defying the notion that a black woman's destiny lies not in legitimate marriage and motherhood but in rape and in her potential as a breeder of a new generation of slaves, Linda thus chooses her own sexual partner—Mr. Sands —and bears him a son and a daughter. In her own words,

I wanted to keep myself pure; and under the most adverse circumstances, I tried hard to preserve my self-respect . . . . but to be an object of interest to a man who is not married, and is not her master, is agreeable to the pride and feelings of a slave, if her miserable situation has left her any pride or sentiment. It seems less degrading to give one's self, than to submit to compulsion. There is something akin to freedom in having a lover who has no control over you, except that which he gains by kindness and attachment. (54-55)

Despite her defiance and her extraordinary assertion of will, Dr. Flint continues to persecute Linda. He repeatedly offers to "make her into a lady" by setting her up with her children in a cottage on his property, where he promises to leave her in "peace," though he would have constant access to her. In effect, he offers her a kind of perverse inversion of the Ruskinian, or perhaps it would be more correct to say Cowperian, ideal of domesticity (35).[31] Conscious that she cannot hold out much longer against this "fiend who bears the shape of [a man]," nor can she protect her own children, Linda conceals herself in the attic of her grandmother's garret—a claustrophobic space that recalls the nun's cell in the demi-convent which protected Lucy—and awaits an opportunity to flee to the North (27). As Nudelman observes, for Linda "visibility is a form of vulnerability and invisibility a means of freedom," much in the same way that cultural anonymity functioned for Lucy Snowe (959).

Upon discovering that Mr. Sands had failed to make good on his promise to free their children, Linda determines that she cannot remain in her hiding place any longer. Despite the fact that her grandmother's attic provides her with sanctuary and "freedom" from Dr. Flint's persecution and surveillance, she imagines that her only chance at true freedom both for herself and her children lies in the North, a territory as "foreign" to Linda as Villette was to Lucy. Just as Lucy Snowe abandons her native England, Linda flees her birthplace at the first opportunity; but upon her arrival in the North she too becomes disillusioned. Not only is she a stranger without references—a prerequisite for employment in polite society—but Linda quickly discovers that she is still pursued by, and subject to, the feared slave "hunters," a reality which was intensified by the passage of the Fugitive Slave Law, and that the "spectres" of slavery are everywhere evident (158, 186). Recalling Lucy's experience in Villette, Linda realizes, with great disappointment, that even though she is north of the Mason-Dixon line she must continue to be on her guard, for in her own words, "slaves, being surrounded by mysteries, deceptions, and dangers, early learn to be suspicious and watchful, and prematurely cautious and cunning" (155). However, Linda also encounters friends among strangers who are willing to protect and assist her.

Like *Villette,* Linda's narrative fails to resolve in the "usual way" with marriage. Rather, it concludes with Linda's having attained her primary goal—freedom—with the assistance of her benefactress, the second Mrs. Bruce. Like Lucy Snowe, Linda Brent "refuses to be destroyed by guilt" and forgives herself; by relying on her audience's empathetic identification and reaction, she both asks their forgiveness and calls them to political action.[32] In the closing paragraphs Linda expresses her desire to become financially independent in order to attain "the dream of [her] life": a home of her own, where she can educate her own children. Although her narrative steps beyond the "confines of genre," and Jacobs's narrator redefines not only true womanhood but motherhood as well, Jacobs, despite her independence, will always be "excluded" from white "domestic culture," as Nudelman points out.[33] Nevertheless critics continue to claim that Jacobs has created an "original" definition of motherhood and has "define[d] a womanhood different from the definitions advanced by the white world." Jacobs's narrative clearly demonstrates that black women could not be "judged by the same standards" as white women; however, scholars categorically fail to acknowledge that although she critiques patriarchal institutions and ideologies which support slavery and "articulate[s] the limitations of those standards," as Nudelman suggests, at no time does Jacobs reject the ideals of womanhood advocated by white bourgeois society (56). What she does do is point out the fact that her race, and consequently her position in society, precludes her from fulfilling these ideals. Again and again Jacobs's narrator "indulge[s] the hope" of attaining her "love dream"—to marry the man of her choice—and fulfilling her destiny as a "useful woman and a good mother"—traditional female destinies which Charlotte Brontë seems to reject (37-38, 133). By embracing and advocating the ideals of wifeliness and motherhood, Jacobs avoided a complete denunciation of patriarchal ideology just as Brontë did by establishing Lucy in a teaching career. In other words, in attempting to gain her audience's empathy by establishing not only her womanhood but her humanity as well, Jacobs posits a kind of counter-myth which, ironically, embraced the very ideals which white female writers such as Charlotte Brontë dismissed. In some sense, therefore, Jacobs simply reconstituted the terms and the conditions of her own slavery, for the sexist patriarchal system to which she— as a woman—was subject, regardless of her race, predetermined both her role, her behavior, and her prospects. Eventually, black female authors, such as Zora Neale Hurston, revised the traditional view of female destiny and women's social position and function that Jacobs seemed to advocate and disavowed the prescribed codes and mores that ultimately defined and limited women's role. However, one cannot lose sight of the fact that writers like Harriet Jacobs paved the way for later generations of female authors to protest the manner in which females in general were "enslaved" by patriarchy. Through her autobiography she advocated the black slave's fundamental human rights by establishing the fact that black women were capable of all of the functions and emotions that white society not only associated with being a woman, but with being a human being as well, rights and assumptions which Charlotte Brontë never dreamed of having to defend.

Notes

1. For more on the cult of the home and women's deportment during the Victorian period see Eric Trudgill, *Madonnas and Magdalens* (New York: Homes & Meier, 1976); Barbara Welter, "The Cult of True Womanhood," *Dimity Convictions: The American Woman in the Nineteenth Century.* Ed. Barbara Welter (Athens: Ohio UP, 1977) 21-41; Nancy Cott, "Passionlessness: An Interpretation of Victorian Sexual Ideology, 1790-1850," *Signs* 4.2 (1979): 219-36.

2. *Suffer and Be Still: Women in the Victorian Age* (Bloomington: Indiana UP, 1972) xi.

3. New York: Wiley, 1889.

4. See Martha Vicinus for more on this subject, *Independent Women: Work and Community for Single Women, 1850-1920* (Chicago: U of Chicago P, 1985).

5. See Vol. 1, chapter 14 of Elizabeth Gaskell's *The Life of Charlotte Brontë* (New York: Penquin, 1975) 289-90.

6. There are several stretches of time that go unaccounted for in Lucy Snowe's narrative, gaps that she often directly acknowledges and suggests that the reader imaginatively fill in.

7. That Charlotte Brontë was conscious of the artificial and contrived nature of gender roles seems to be indicated by the fact that Lucy literally takes on the role of a man in a play staged at the demi-convent. Although she appears on stage dressed as a man, Lucy insists upon wearing her own clothes beneath her costume, indicating, as some critics have suggested, the type of charading women like the Brontë sisters had to engage in (by assuming male pseudonyms) in order to compete in a public arena largely dominated by men. Brontë also seems to imply that the social roles allotted to women are pure artifice through the paintings that are mentioned, each of which depicts women in various stereotypical roles: the Cleopatra, the series *La vie d'une femme,* and the portrait of the "sainted" Justine Marie. Finally, note the reference to "play" on page 677 when Lucy struggles with the pillow-nun.

8. All quotations are taken from the Oxford edition of *Villette* (London: Clarendon, 1984).

9. *The Madwoman in the Attic: The Woman Writer and the Nineteenth-Century Literary Imagination* (New Haven: Yale UP, 1979) 209.

10. With the exception of M. Paul, the girls are not allowed to receive male visitors, and their daily schedules are divided up into three distinct periods—work or study, prayer, and a short interlude for rest or relaxation—which recall the Augustinian rules Edward Pusey adapted and then sought to impose upon his female religious communities. Though Madame Beck tends to be quite nasty, Lucy frequently praises her for her charitable benevolence and her maternal qualities. Like the Superior of a convent, she functions as a kind of surrogate mother; and like a demanding spiritual mother, she makes certain that her

charges adhere to a strict disciplinary code. In the same vein, Brontë designates Paul Emanuel—whose surname translates as "God is with us" and Christian name recalls the biblical Saul, who was struck blind on the road to Damascus—as a kind of resident secular priest, whom Lucy refers to as a "lay Jesuit."

11. Reinforcing this notion, Lucy repeatedly links Madame Beck with the spectral nun who haunts the demi-convent. Upon their first meeting she comments, "No ghost stood beside me, nor anything of spectral aspect; merely a motherly, dumpy little woman, in a large shawl, a wrapping-gown, and a clean, trim night-cap" (88). Nevertheless, Madame Beck "glides ghost-like through the house," and she appears and disappears, "noisless as a shadow" in her "shoes of silence" (100, 95, 88).

12. Robert B. Heilman was the first to identify Brontë's works as "new Gothic." See Heilman's "Charlotte Brontë's 'New' Gothic," *From Jane Austen to Joseph Conrad.* Ed. Charles Rathburn (Minneapolis: U of Minneapolis P, 1958) 118-32.

13. See Nancy Cott's "Passionlessness: An Interpretation of Victorian Sexual Ideology," 219-36.

14. Lucy's façade of self-possession and internalized restraint may also be viewed as a product of her Protestant upbringing. See especially Rosemary Clark-Beattie's essay "Fables of Rebellion: Anti-Catholicism and the Structure of *Villette,*" *English Literary History* 53 (1986); and Ruth Bernard Yeazell's *Fictions of Modesty* (Chicago: U of Chicago P, 1984) 169-93. As Nina Auerbach observes in *Communities of Women* (Cambridge: Harvard UP, 1978), Charlotte Brontë depicts the Catholic Church in a pejorative way in *Jane Eyre* as well. She states, "Eliza Reed, whom Jane defines as an anti-human personification of 'judgment without feeling' . . . embrace[s] the tenets of Rome and takes the veil" (102).

15. In his essay "The Brontës: The Self Defined, Redefined, and Refined," which appears in *The Victorian Experience: The Novelists,* ed. Richard A. Levine (Athens: Ohio UP, 1976), Frederick R. Karl comments, "All Brontë heroines must be tested by their confrontation with a male. They must, in a sense, pass through male experience" (129).

16. For more on this subject see especially Christina Crosby's "Charlotte Brontë's Haunted Text," *Studies in English Literature, 1500-1900* 24 (1984): 705-15; Linda Hunt's "*Villette:* The Inward and Outward Life," *Victorians Institute Journal* 11 (1982-83): 23-31; John Kucich's "Passionate Reserve and Reserved Passion in the Works of Charlotte Brontë," *English Literary History* 52 (1985): 913-37; and Ruth Bernard Yeazell's *Fictions of Modesty* 169-93.

17. As many critics have observed, Lucy Snowe's name (*luz* and snow) suggests this conflict. For more on the significance of names in *Villette* see George S. Dunbar's "Proper Names in *Villette,*" *Nineteenth-Century Fiction* 15 (June 1960): 77-80.

18. The nun in *Villette* has traditionally been treated as a single figure. (In general, commentators who have acknowledged that there are, indeed, two nuns, have placed little to no importance on this fact.) In the past, critics such as W. A. Craik, have dismissed "her" as a silly "neo Gothic" device "too trite for serious consideration," *The Brontë Novels* (London: Methuen, 1968) 187. Others have stressed the idea that the phantom nun appears to Lucy at key moments in her emotional development, an argument with which I concur. However, according to most accounts, she is merely a projection of Lucy's psychic state. See especially E. D. H. Johnson's "'Daring the Dread Glance': Charlotte Brontë's Treat-ment of the Supernatural in *Villette*," *Nineteenth-Century Fiction* 20 (1965-66): 325-36.

19. Lucy's almost masochistic sense of her own guilt and sinfulness or imperfection is encapsulated in the "mad" scene in which she goes into the Catholic church; when she reaches the confessional she discovers that she has nothing to say. As Robert Keefe observes in *Charlotte Brontë's World of Death* (Austin: U of Texas P, 1979), "Lucy buries herself before she can sin"; the only sin she has committed is against her own natural instincts (165).

20. In "The Brontës: The Self Defined, Redefined, and Refined," Frederick R. Karl points out that Lucy's desire to attain (male) independence without forfeiting her "feminine role" is epitomized in the scene, previously mentioned, in which she acts out a male role in a "vest, a collar, and a cravat, and a paletot" while "retaining" her "woman's garb," which she wears beneath her costume (209).

21. For more on this subject see for example Jean Fagan Yellin's introduction to the 1987 edition of *Incidents in the Life of a Slave Girl, Written by Herself* (Cambridge: Harvard UP) xiii-xxxiv; Deborah M. Garfield's "Speech, Listening, and Female Sexuality in *Incidents in the Life of a Slave Girl*," *Arizona Quarterly* 50.2 (1994):19-49; Joanne M. Braxton's *Black Women Writing Autobiography: A Tradition within a Tradition* (Philadelphia: Temple UP, 1989) 18-38.

22. Although many critics have written on this subject, see especially Hazel Carby's *Reconstructing Womanhood: The Emergence of the Afro-Amercian Woman Novelist* (New York: Oxford UP, 1987).

23. See Fagan Yellin's introduction to the 1987 edition of Jacobs's *Incidents in the Life of a Slave Girl, Written by Herself* (Cambridge: Harvard UP) xiii.

24. "Harriet Jacobs and the Sentimental Politics of Female Suffering," *English Literary History* 59.4 (1992): 959.

25. See note 39 of Jean Fagan Yellin's introduction to the 1987 edition of *Incidents* 257.

26. For more on this subject see especially Joanne Braxton's *Black Women Writing Autobiography* and Beth Maclay Doriani's "Black Womanhood in

Nineteenth-Century America: Subversion and Self-Construction in Two Women's Autobiographies," *American Quarterly* 43.2 (1991): 199-222.

27. For more on this subject see Beth Maclay Doriani's "Black Womanhood in Nineteenth-Century America," *American Quarterly* 43.2 (1991): 218-19.

28. All quotations are taken from the 1987 edition of *Incidents in the Life of a Slave Girl, Written by Herself* (Cambridge: Harvard UP).

29. *Reconstructing Womanhood: The Emergence of the Black Woman Novelist* (New York: Oxford UP, 1987) 47.

30. Granted, as critic Valerie Smith, among others, has observed, Harriet Jacobs had to observe these injunctions to some measure, as manifest in the gaps or silences in her work, in order to make her text palatable to her genteel white audience. As Smith notes in her 1988 introduction to *Incidents in the Life of a Slave Girl*, Jacobs's account is curbed by "cultural injunctions against woman's assertiveness and directnesss and speech" (New York: Oxford UP) xxxiii.

31. As Franny Nudelman points out, Linda dubs her hiding space "The Loophole Retreat," an ironic reference to William Cowper's "The Task," a poem that paints an idealized image of domesticity akin to Ruskin's, p. 958. In it, the domestic sphere is depicted as a safe haven from the chaotic outside world for women and children. According to Jean Fagan Yellin, Jacobs was not the first American to employ Cowper's phrase. See note 1, chapter 21, p. 277 in her edition of Jacobs's autobiography.

32. See Elizabeth C. Becker's "Harriet Jacobs's Search for Home," *College Language Association Journal* 35.5 (1992) 416 for more on Jacobs's guilt regarding her relationship with Mr. Sands. On the subject of the ability of "maternal sorrow" to override social and racial barriers, see especially Franny Nudelman's "Harriet Jacobs and the Sentimental Politics of Female Suffering."

33. See Becker's "Harriet Jacobs's Search for Home," 413; and Nudelman's "Harriet Jacobs and the Sentimental Politics of Female Suffering," 960.

Works Cited

Brontë, Charlotte. *Villette.* London: Oxford UP, 1984.

Carby, Hazel. *Reconstructing Womanhood: The Emergence of the Afro-American Woman Novelist.* New York: Oxford UP, 1987.

Doriani, Beth Maclay. "Black Womanhood in Nineteenth-Century America: Subversion and Self-Construction in Two Women's Autobiographies." *American Quarterly* 43.2 (1991): 199-222.

Gaskell, Elizabeth. *The Life of Charlotte Brontë.* New York: Penguin, 1975.

Gilbert, Sandra, and Susan Gubar. *The Madwoman in the Attic: The Woman Writer and the Nineteenth-Century Literary Imagination.* New Haven: Yale UP, 1979.

Jacobs, Harriet. *Incidents in the Life of a Slave Girl, Written by Herself.* Cambridge: Harvard UP, 1987.

Nudelman, Franny. "Harriet Jacobs and the Sentimental Politics of Female Suffering." *English Literary History* 59.4 (1992): 939-64.

Vicinus, Martha. *Suffer and Be Still: Women in the Victorian Age.* Bloomington: Indiana UP, 1972.

Yellin, Jean Fagan. Introduction. *Incidents in the Life of a Slave Girl, Written by Herself.* Cambridge: Harvard UP, 1987.

4

Breaking Loose from "Chin-Bands of the Soul": Barrett Browning's Re-Visioning of the Patriarchal Family in *Aurora Leigh*

Maureen Thum

Previous critics dealing with Elizabeth Barrett Browning's novel poem, *Aurora Leigh* (1857), have argued that Barrett Browning, despite an ostensibly feminist agenda, did not—and could not—effectively contest the hegemonic ideologies of the nineteenth-century bourgeois and patriarchal status quo. Although she offers sporadic critiques of patriarchy and bourgeois ideology, she maintains an essentially traditionalist, even an antifeminist stance.[1] She does not mount a sustained critique of bourgeois ideology. "What is really missing," contends Cora Kaplan, "is any adequate attempt at analysis of the intersecting oppressions of capitalism and patriarchy" (12). In *The Madwoman in the Attic,* Sandra Gilbert and Susan Gubar argue that the author subscribes fully to a traditionalist view of women and the family. Thus, at the conclusion of the novel, Aurora Leigh compromises her feminist ideals and acts out the "role of dutiful handmaiden" to Romney Leigh, "a blind but powerful master" (Gilbert and Gubar 578). Critics point, invariably, to the conclusion of the novel poem—Aurora Leigh's marriage to Romney—as representing Barrett Browning's return to the fold: her final, unambiguous reaffirmation of the traditionalist view both of marriage and of the nuclear family.

I wish to argue for a very different reading of *Aurora Leigh.* Contrary to critical consensus, Barrett Browning does not reaffirm the status quo. In exploring the relationship of her protagonist, Aurora Leigh, to a series of families depicted throughout the novel poem, Barrett Browning contests key tenets of bourgeois ideology, including the doctrine of separate spheres and the doctrine of the nuclear family. The doctrine of the nuclear family was, as numerous literary and cultural historians have demonstrated, an essential aspect of bourgeois ideology. According to this doctrine, the nuclear family is a static, typological monad or self-enclosed module (Robertson 159). Opponents such as Leploy argued that it was based on raw egotism and greed for gain. Proponents—by far in the majority—argued that it was the essential building block of a progressive, yet stable bourgeois society (Peterson 194). A corollary of this doctrine was the rigid separation of spheres associated with an equally rigid segregation of male and female roles. Women's roles, constrained by the domestic ideal of the Angel in the House, were limited to those of wife, mother, and subordinate helpmate to her husband (Matus 5). Men, by contrast, were granted a wider area of action in the public sphere (Fraisse and Perrot 321).

In arguing that she subscribes to an essentially traditionalist stance, critics have failed to note that Barrett Browning presents a sustained—if implicit—critique of bourgeois and patriarchal norms, and that her views diverge markedly from the doctrine of the nuclear family. Instead of presenting the bourgeois family as a static, self-enclosed unit, she argues for a wider, more inclusive view of family as a flexible, dynamic network of relationships capable of multiple transformations and even of drastic changes. From the outset, Barrett Browning presents the bourgeois family—namely Aurora Leigh's family—as a constantly changing, dynamic structure in a continuous state of metamorphosis. The changes, brought about by marriage, death, and adoption, radically alter what would otherwise be the protagonist's conventional bourgeois upbringing. Aurora's nontraditional education produces a critic of patriarchy who views conventional women's roles with estranged and distancing eyes.

Not only does Barrett Browning depict the nuclear family as unstable, and hence capable of change, but she also provides alternatives to the nuclear family. In part because of her unconventional upbringing, and her orphaned, relatively independent state, Aurora Leigh is shown as capable of envisioning and facilitating alternative family patterns and structures that fall outside the purview of the bourgeois family. These alternative arrangements carry out functions that the nuclear family, with its prescriptive roles and static relationships, cannot fulfill. The first alternative to the nuclear family is the living arrangement made by an independent, unmarried woman, Aurora Leigh. Aurora refuses an excellent and financially advantageous offer of marriage, and, contrary to expectations associated with spinsterhood, she assumes the unconventional role of writer, who is able to lead a self-supporting and autonomous existence in London, living, quite literally, in a room of her own without the guidance or protection of a father, a husband, or a brother.

The second alternative to the nuclear family is even more radically conceived. This unconventional "family" is formed by a choice that transgresses normative codes, since it includes an unmarried mother and her child. Both were, by definition, excluded from the respectable confines of the bourgeois family. A final family is envisioned but not yet realized by Aurora and Romney at the conclusion of the novel poem. It has the appearance of a conventional bourgeois family, since it involves marriage. Nevertheless, contrary to critical consensus, Aurora's marriage is not a reaffirmation but a contradiction of the twin doctrines of the separate spheres and the nuclear family. Indeed, by its very nature, her marriage flouts conventions, and removes the concept of family from the confines of bourgeois and patriarchal ideology. Thus, Barrett Browning represents the nuclear family and the doctrine of separate spheres only to deconstruct them and to offer a far more flexible set of alternatives.

Unlike some of her utopian and socialist contemporaries, the author does not directly attack marriage as an institution (Kaeppeli 485). Nor does she embrace the dualistic views espoused by such theorists as Ernest Legouve (Kaeppeli 484). Instead, she undermines, transforms, and supplants the bourgeois nuclear family by a very differently conceived marital relationship from that envisioned by proponents of the nuclear family as a static, fixed pattern of prescribed relationships and roles. In order to demonstrate Barrett Browning's nontraditional—indeed antitraditionalist—stance, I will examine the author's depiction of each of the above family structures in turn.

From the outset, Barrett Browning contests the nineteenth-century doctrine of the fixed, unchanging nuclear family. In Aurora Leigh's retrospective narrative of her childhood, depicted in Book One, Barrett Browning presents the bourgeois family not as a stable typological pattern, but as a dynamic, constantly changing series of structures characterized more by flux than by stasis. This portrait of the family in process implicitly puts into question the static image of the nuclear family as what A. F. Robertson calls a "fixed social module" (159). In her depiction of the family in flux, Barrett Browning is—as recent sociological studies have suggested—probably closer to many of the lived realities of family life than were the nineteenth-century proponents of the nuclear family doctrine. Robertson argues that the static view of the nuclear family promulgated by nineteenth-century cultural historians and guardians of the social order is inherently limited because it is based on theories of "fixed family types" which fail to account for the actual processes of family formation and change (159). "Reproduction," argues Roberston, "is unquestionably dynamic, but if we interpret it through fixed family types its active role in the making and remaking of human society will be lost to us" (159). In order to develop a historically more accurate view of family life, explains Robertson, it is necessary to view the traditional "nuclear" family from alternative perspectives, and to see it not as defined by fixed "snapshots," but as involving a continuous process of change.

In her depiction of Aurora Leigh's childhood, the author describes precisely such a changing family, and thus implicitly questions the static view of the bourgeois family. Looking back on her parents' marriage, Aurora Leigh at first presents what appears to be the idealized nuclear family fixed by custom and convention. But this portrait of family life transgresses the norm by presenting one of its key elements—the domesticated mother figure—in unconventional terms. Aurora's mother is not a proper, docile image of British womanhood. Instead, she is a foreigner and "intruder," an Italian woman who by her very nature disrupts the nuclear family and violates bourgeois values. As an outsider, Aurora Leigh's Italian mother is shown to have changed Aurora's father so profoundly that he abandons the role of the sovereign, distant family patriarch, of the "austere Englishman" who is comfortable in his "island scorn" for anything that falls outside the norm (1: 65-67).[2]

Her father, as Aurora recalls, "after a dry lifetime spent at home / In college-learning, law and parish talk" was suddenly and irrevocably altered by his encounter with his future wife (1: 65-67). His passion for Aurora Leigh's mother sets aside his "complacent past" and transforms him utterly. Aurora sees the marriage as a flouting of British convention: her father "had suddenly / Thrown off the old conventions, broken loose / From chin-bands of the soul" (1: 176-78).

His marriage to an Italian woman violates bourgeois expectations at least in part because it means the loss of the family fortune for any children resulting from this marriage. An ancestor, in a fit of xenophobic ire, had excluded all children of a foreign marriage from the line of inheritance. By marrying a foreign woman and forfeiting the family fortune, Aurora Leigh's father abdicates his bourgeois "duty," and disobeys the unwritten rules that shore up the bourgeois family and ensure the continuance not only of the individual family wealth, but of upper middle-class economic and political power all told.

The death of Aurora Leigh's mother, when the child is four years old, brings an additional marked change in an already disrupted bourgeois family pattern, demonstrating further the author's recognition that the traditional monad was at least potentially far more unstable than contemporary ideologues would allow. Instead of following the accepted route, and replacing his dead wife with a new "Angel in the House" to care for the child—that is, instead of reconstituting the normal and normative familial structure—Aurora's father makes a second unconventional move. Stricken by grief, he retreats to the mountains, where he lives, hermit-like with his four-year-old daughter, and the old Italian nurse, Assunta. Her father is, as Aurora Leigh tells the reader, no "common" man.

An unconventional husband, he is also an unconventional father, who provides his little daughter with an uncommon education, the education normally reserved for male children: "He wrapt his little daughter in his large / Man's doublet, careless did it fit or no" (1: 727-28). He does not teach her to respect and accept traditionalist views and ideological systems; instead, he teaches her to dismantle and distrust systems. Thus, she recalls, "He taught me all the ignorance of men" and "He sent the schools to school" to demonstrate the errors of building ideological structures that ignore the anomalies of lived existence. Fixed ideological systems are, as he demonstrates to his daughter, little more than "mistakes being ventured in the gross / And heaped up to a system" (1: 190-98). Her father thus equips his daughter with the tools she will later need to dismantle patriarchy and its underlying assumptions. His unusual approach to education also helps to shape Aurora into a woman who does not fit traditionalist molds and who will later choose to lead an unconventional life as a writer.

Having undergone two drastic changes, Aurora's already far-from-conventional bourgeois family now undergoes yet another radical alteration. When Aurora is thirteen years old, her father dies, casting her adrift as an orphan. As Florence Nightingale had already noted in *Cassandra* (1852-59), female orphans in literature were freed to lead a relatively independent life: "the secret charm of every romance . . . is that the heroine has generally no family ties (almost invariably no mother), or, if she has, these do not interfere with her entire independence" (qtd. in Reynolds and Humble 26).

This observation is certainly an accurate assessment of Aurora Leigh's condition as an orphan. She is suddenly thrust into an English context, into the house of a maiden aunt, who now attempts—without success—to eradicate effects of Aurora's previous, unconventional education, and to inculcate the "foreign" child with conventional notions of British womanhood. Aurora Leigh presents a scathing critique of women's education and women's roles, a critique epitomized by a single, biting analogy which the narrator uses to describe the aunt's unwittingly cruel attempt to reshape the unconventional child according to the domestic ideal:

> She had lived
> A sort of cage-bird life, born in a cage,
> Accounting that to leap from perch to perch
> Was act and joy enough for any bird . . .
> I, alas,
> A wild bird scarcely fledged, was brought to her cage,
> And she was there to meet me.
>
> (1: 304-11)

Aurora Leigh is twenty years old when her aunt dies, leaving her destitute. According to the restrictive clause in the documents governing the
inheritance, Aurora's claim to the family fortune is blocked because her
mother was not an Englishwoman. The inheritance, which had first
passed to her aunt, as the father's nearest relative, is now settled on her
cousin, Romney Leigh.

This conjunction of circumstances leads to a significant confrontation at the opening of Book Two. During a verbal sparring match,
Aurora Leigh, defender of unconventional views of women's roles, confronts Romney Leigh, symbolic male guardian of the social order. The
segregation of the sexes and the doctrine of the nuclear family, already
implicitly contested throughout Book One, are now explicitly debated.

The confrontation scene is fraught with irony and laced with telling
discrepancies that indicate the difficulties and the hostility—not to speak
of the deeply engrained prejudices—a nineteenth-century woman faced
if she wished to follow an unconventional path. Romney is a progressive
thinker, a utopian socialist who wishes to carry out his vision by his
own, personal intervention. Ironically, although Romney cherishes
unconventional political ideas and ideals, when it comes to the woman
question, he is the epitome of conventionality.

Given his progressive views in other areas, the certainty and conviction with which he defends traditionalist views of women's roles is
cast in an acerbically, if implicitly, ironic light. A further irony lies in
Romney's blindness. He insults Aurora, casts aspersion on her goals and
ideals, all the while seeing himself in the role of generous benefactor,
and munificent self-appointed guardian, who offers Aurora Leigh not
only the financial comfort of his wealth, and the stability of a traditional
marriage, but also a much needed "reality check." The constant discrep-
ancy between Romney's impenetrable and obtuse sense of superiority,
and Aurora Leigh's sprightly retorts lends this scene a somewhat dark
but consistent irony and humor that has not lost its edge even now, over
a hundred years after the initial publication of the novel poem.

The progressive thinker, now unmasked as a defender of the
status quo, urges Aurora to abandon aspirations unbecoming to a
woman, to acquiesce to her destiny, and to take his generous, financially advantageous offer. In the course of the debate, Romney deals
what he deems his most devastating blow: the argument that women,
by nature are restricted to the personal, individual, domestic and nonpublic sphere, and that their limited nature—rather than any action by
men or by society at large—prevents them from becoming poets and
influencing society:

> Women as you are,
> Mere women, personal and passionate,
> You give us doting mothers, and perfect wives,
> Sublime Madonnas, and enduring saints!
> We get no Christ from you,—and verily
> We shall not get a poet...
>
> (2: 220-25)

In an ingenious twist, Romney appeals to Aurora's better nature, arguing it is *below* Aurora to attempt such frivolous undertakings; she should not stoop to waste her talents in such vain endeavors as the unattainable career of writer and poet.

Aurora Leigh, who has countered his argument point by point with sharp and energetic retorts, concludes—to Romney's astonishment—by turning down not only his marriage proposal but also his generous but patronizing offer of financial assistance. Aurora refuses Romney Leigh in part because of her aspirations, but also in part because she buys into (or is forced by circumstances to buy into) what Barrett Browning demonstrates to be yet another patriarchal prejudice: the view that a woman's career and a woman's genius are entirely incompatible with her role as a member of a family who has a fulfilling relationship with a member of the opposite sex. Romney clearly demonstrates his incapability of envisioning anything but a traditionalist view of marriage; however, Aurora Leigh represents a view that proves to be just as ideologically anchored in the patriarchal mindset: that a public career is invariably to be pitted against and seen in opposition to her role in marriage.

By the conclusion of the novel poem, both alter their perspectives—Romney far more radically than Aurora—to re-vision a marriage that would depart from the bourgeois convention so markedly that it would no longer represent a compromising of Aurora Leigh's feminist principles. Indeed, this optimistic re-visioning of the patriarchal family would represent an implicit questioning of all the tenets of the bourgeois doctrines associated with women's roles and the nature of the nuclear family as a static, unchanging monad.

Barrett Browning not only destabilizes the concept of the nuclear family itself; she also presents alternative perspectives of living conditions that were not considered to be viable forms of existence as long as the nuclear family monad remained ideologically intact. Thus, she depicts Aurora Leigh as abdicating a traditional marriage, but, contrary to traditional portraits, exemplified by the maiden aunt, Aurora Leigh does not lead the frustrated and sterile life of a spinster. Unlike her maiden aunt whose sterility and frustration arise from her accepting and becoming the accomplice in enforcing patriarchal models of woman-hood, Aurora Leigh flouts these models, and demonstrates that a woman can, indeed, live an independent existence, even if she is deprived of financial means. In opposition to the negative concept of the spinster as an iconic figure symbolizing the lonely, rejected, frustrated life of a woman who does not marry, the author offers the view of a successful, financially independent and self-supporting writer who counters all con-ventional wisdom regarding the ability of women to live independently, without the support and guidance of a male mentor—whether husband, father, or brother.

The depiction of Aurora Leigh as an independent woman, living without patriarchal protection, is the first of three alternative arrange-ments Barrett Browning offers to the traditional bourgeois ideal of domestic womanhood with its stark limitations in the choice of viable living circumstances for women.

Probably the least conventional of all the alternative living arrange-ments explored by Barrett Browning is the supportive structure depicted in Book Six of the novel poem. This unconventional grouping takes the place of the nuclear family, and carries out functions that the nuclear family is not equipped to fulfill. This unconventional "family" is not based on the accepted biological and social ties which link members of the bourgeois family. It is neither legally authorized, nor theologically sanctified. Instead, it is formed by an act of will that transgresses norma-tive codes, since it includes an unmarried mother—Marian Erle—and her illegitimate child.

Aurora Leigh had already made the acquaintance of Marian Erle, an impoverished seamstress living on piecework among the urban, nonre-spectable poor—those Marx refers to by the collective, derogatory term *Lumpenproletariat*. A successful, published author, Aurora Leigh later travels to Paris, to continue her chosen life of writing and independent solitude. There, in the streets of Paris, she encounters Marian Erle once again. Unbeknownst to Aurora, Marian had been betrayed, sold into white slavery, and shipped to Paris, where she was, as Aurora Leigh dis-covers only later, drugged and raped while she lay unconscious. Alone, she gave birth to a child, and remained in Paris, where she has cared for her little boy with love and maternal solicitude.

In depicting Marian Erle, Barrett Browning is presenting a sym-bolic figure, a test case, and an intentional anomaly. Marian is an unusual figure who fits none of the clichés of fallen womanhood. Although branded with the label of fallen woman, she has not "sinned"; she has not been weak or complicit in her "fall." And, she has shown none of the treachery and perfidy which, as Higginbotham notes, was so frequently associated with the fallen woman (Higginbotham 2). Barrett Browning uses this anomalous figure in order to present a probing interrogation of traditionalist views of the fallen woman, to question her exclusion from the respectable bourgeois family, and to scrutinize her role as a "threat" to the patriarchal order.

Marian's name is significant. It is no accident that she is named after Marianne, the revolutionary female figure who symbolized freedom, liberty, and fraternity during the French Revolution. Marian is in some respects truly a revolutionary figure. Nor is it accidental that she is named after a popular carnival figure, Maid Marian, who ruled with Robin Hood over the May games of popular festivals. Maid Marian epitomized the flouting of normative codes, and even unruly licentiousness (Davis 138). In *Aurora Leigh,* Marian Erle plays the role of unruly outsider who is not decried but celebrated. Her name also suggests a third figure, Mary, who was, according to Christian tradition, *both* virgin *and* mother, and who has been celebrated throughout the history of Western culture as the icon of purity and maternity. Marian is not physically a virgin, and yet the complete absence of the knowledge of her rape puts her in an anomalous position, that of a nonvirgin who has not "known" any man. The conflation of seemingly contradictory figures suggested by Marian's name and role—the Virgin Mary, and, the fallen woman, the unruly outsider, and the harbinger of freedom and egalitarian principles—puts into question the polarized view of women as either pure or fallen, angel or whore by uniting them in a single figure.

As the resonant name suggests, in her portrait of Marian Erle, Barrett Browning dismantles and contests both the stereotype of the fallen woman and conventional narratives of fallen womanhood. Barrett Browning's polemical intent becomes evident if one compares her portrait of Marian to traditionalist depictions, current throughout the nineteenth century. According to tradition, the fallen woman was frequently seen negatively as the sexual predator who victimizes hapless, wealthy middle- and upper-class males. Throughout the nineteenth century, unmarried women with children were viewed both in literature, and according to law, from two contrasting but linked perspectives. On the one hand, they were seen negatively as "manipulative, immoral women in control of their sexuality which they used to overpower men" (Higginbotham 5). On the other hand, if portrayed sympathetically, the fallen woman was perceived almost invariably as a sinner whose bastard child "bore witness to a fall from purity" and was "evidence of sin" for which she must expiate, generally through death by illness or suicide (Higginbotham 2). The only alternative to death was rehabilitation and reincorporation into normative patriarchal models. Rehabilitation was a far less frequent occurrence since the fall itself was seen as producing an indelible stain which branded her, and marked her exclusion from the paternalistic Victorian family, and from the respectability accorded to married motherhood.

As Yvonne Kniebiehler has commented, the unmarried mother faced universal condemnation:

Ill-protected by the law, defenseless young women remained vulnerable in the countryside as well as in the cities. In fact, public opinion made no exception for rape. Any girl who gave in, even if forced to do so, was "ruined," "fallen," unworthy of respect or help. When pregnant, she was forced back on her own resources except in unusual circumstances. (351)

Contrary to expectations attached to images of fallen womanhood, Marian Erle is not a symbol of womanly shame and exclusion, who must expiate and die. Nor is she "rehabilitated" and thus prepared to become, in turn, an enforcer of patriarchal codes who works for the reform of fallen woman.

Instead, she is depicted through the eyes of the upper middle-class protagonist, Aurora Leigh, as a positive image of idealized motherhood. This is an unusual portrait since it flies in the face of an almost universally held nineteenth century consensus that, in Yvonne Kniebielher's words, "the unwed mother was not fit to be called a mother at all" (351). Indeed, she was denied the ability to feel motherly love for her child, just as the child was denied the ability to love such a mother. As Kniebiehler states, according to the officially sanctioned view "no woman could love the living proof of her sin, and no child could help feeling contempt for the woman who had inflicted such a life on him or her" (351).

Barrett Browning recognizes that, in order to depict a positive image of the unwed mother, she must attempt to deal with the contemporary reader's automatic negative responses. She does so by portraying her bourgeois protagonist as responding negatively and conventionally to Marian Erle as a fallen woman. Aurora, despite her own unconventionality in other areas concerning women's roles in patriarchy, has remained conventional in her view of the fallen woman. She looks at Marian initially, through her middle-class eyes, with the customary, condescending admixture of pity and distaste. Thus, when she first sees mother and child together, an almost idyllic picture of motherly love and affection, Aurora is alienated by her own warm response: "Must sin have compensations, was my thought" (613). She compares Marian's possession of a beautiful child to a theft and upbraids Marian for her unseemly joy in motherhood. A fallen woman, she argues, "is no mother, but a kid-napper" and her child is "a dismal orphan not a son" who will reject her because she has failed to provide him with a "pure home," "a pure heart" and "a pure good mother's name and memory" (6: 630-40).

The confrontation that follows represents both a parallel to and an ironic reversal of the earlier encounter between the unconventional Aurora and the conventional Romney. The latter, despite his progressive socialist views, acted as a stern guardian of the social order when it came to the woman question. Aurora Leigh, despite her progressive views about women and social class, also functions as a guardian of the social order when it comes to the question of the *fallen* woman. During her encounter with Marian in Paris, she calls upon all the stereotypical images of fallen womanhood shared by members of her class, castigating Marian for her impurity, her perfidy, her treachery, her disobedience to God's law, and for the affrontery and hypocrisy of her "pretense" that she is a good, loving mother to her illegitimate child.

In the confrontation that follows, Marian's stance vis-à-vis Aurora Leigh parallels Aurora's earlier stance when confronted by Romney at the end of Book One, with his seemingly impenetrable armor of complaisance, prejudice, and false superiority. Marian responds energetically and articulately to Aurora's charges that Marian is a fallen woman who deserves punishment. Significantly, although Aurora as narrator spoke for Marian and (re)told Marian's tale earlier in the novel poem, at this crucial juncture, she allows Marian to speak for herself and in her own voice. Marian—who, as the narrator has stressed, is self-educated—responds to Aurora's charges, and to the stereotypical images Aurora uses to label her, by calling upon her natural right as a mother:

> I have as sure a right
> As any glad proud mother in the world,
> Who sets her darling down to cut his teeth
> Upon her church-ring. If she talks of law,
> I talk of law! I claim my mother-dues
> By law,—the law which is now paramount,—
> The common law, by which the poor and weak
> Are trodden underfoot by vicious men,
> And loathed for ever after by the good.
>
> (6: 661-69)

Marian now turns the tables on her accuser, upbraiding Aurora for her hypocritical and patronizing stance: "What have you, any of you, to say . . . /Who are happy and sit safe and high" (6: 673-74). She refers to

Aurora as a collective "you," emphasizing the fact that these received opinions are communally held: Aurora Leigh is the guardian of a hypocritical social order that condemns without regard to the reality of the situation: "What have you in your souls against me then, / All of you? Am I wicked do you think?" (6: 739-40). And when Aurora responds—circumspectly—in the affirmative, Marian tells her story, demonstrating her innocence of all the charges normally leveled at the fallen woman. She concludes, "man's violence, / Not man's seduction, made me what I am" (6: 1226-27).

During this pivotal scene, Aurora Leigh, who had shared all the automatic responses and prejudices of her class about the "fallen woman" of the underclasses, discovers in an ironic reversal of perspectives and roles, the ludicrousness, the erroneousness, indeed, the patronizing hubris of her view of Marian as a "fallen" woman in need of philanthropic redemption.

Marian's story demonstrates the inadequacy and injuriousness of received images of fallen womanhood. The epithet "fallen woman" is shown to be a distorting, dehumanizing label. Marian's articulate voice and outlook are authorized by the narrator and by the narrative, undercutting official discourse that excludes the fallen woman from respectable society. Not only is the otherwise silent and silenced "fallen" Other allowed to plead her case, but the author provides an empathetic and informed perspective of the fallen woman via the mediation of her fictive narrator. Aurora Leigh's response serves as a model and invitation for a more sympathetic and enlightened reader response, presenting a view of the fallen woman that would otherwise be closed to the contemporary bourgeois reader, who would, conditioned by prescribed codes, automatically condemn Marian and regard her as less than human.

In depicting Marian, Barrett Browning thus presents a test case that will allow the sympathetic reader to see the fallen woman with different, unprejudiced eyes. Marian's absence of sin does not denote the author's prudish and fearful Victorian "delicacy" or her inability to deal with sexual matters as critics have contended. On the contrary, Marian's sinlessness as a fallen woman expresses the plight of women who are held, unjustly, as the hostages of the double standard. By removing the taint of complicity and the charge of evil-doing from Marian, the author demonstrates the perniciousness and the injustice of a label that is applied to women regardless of their circumstances, and completely without consideration of their "guilt" or "innocence." Indeed, Marian herself shifts the focus of the question from morality, and woman's complicity in her fall to the injustice perpetrated upon women by men—and women—who subscribe to the double standard, and who automatically ostracize nonrespectable women while countenancing as slight flaws and pecadillos the nonrespectable deeds of "respectable" men.

Her re-visioning of the fallen woman permits the author to justify an alternative view of familial networks. Since the proponents of the domestic ideal and the self-enclosed nuclear family have excluded the victims of society, and have erroneously branded them as "unworthy," it follows, logically, that those excluded are justified in finding an alternative nexus of support. As Marian clearly states, her child is "not much worse off in being fatherless" than she, herself, was with an abusive and cruel father (6: 646). This view, that a child could be nurtured not just adequately, but perhaps more successfully without a father, completely contradicts the ideology of the nuclear family, as does the mutually supportive surrogate family unit which Aurora Leigh, with her new-found empathy and acceptance, now helps to facilitate. Barrett Browning's positive depiction of two "deviant" women—Marian Erle, the fallen woman, and Aurora Leigh, intellectual, writer, and aspiring poet—as forming a nexus of mutual support represents a radical questioning of the nuclear family with its restricted views of womanhood, and its exclusivity of membership. Significantly, the surrogate family is not formed in England, but in foreign countries—namely France and Italy—where a foreigner's unconventionality was less likely to draw the disapproval of a society for whom foreigners were, by definition, representatives of an alien point of view.

The vision of the family presented at the conclusion of the narrative has been the continuing subject of critical debate. With few exceptions, previous critics have seen Aurora's marriage to Romney as the evidence that she, like the author, has compromised her principles, and has disclosed the traditionalist stance critics knew all along to be hiding behind Aurora Leigh's *and* Barrett Browning's feminist mask. The marriage, critics argue, reinserts Aurora unambiguously into patriarchy. In social, psychological and feminist terms, it represents the prodigal daughter's return "home" to the patriarchal and bourgeois fold (Gilbert and Gubar 578).

However, in castigating the author and her fictive narrator for their acceptance of patriarchy, previous critics have failed to note that although Aurora Leigh enters into a marriage with Romney, she by no means espouses the bourgeois view of marriage. This is no conventional marriage. As already indicated, the bourgeois marriage was based on the domestic ideal of womanhood. Gender roles were clearly defined. The segregation of (female) domestic and private role from the (male) public and active role in the wider social, economic, political, and cultural world was a sine qua non of the nuclear family doctrine.

Aurora's marriage, a radical departure from convention, does not even remotely conform to restrictive, officially promulgated views of marriage and family. By redefining men's and women's roles, it redefines the nature of the marriage itself. Aurora Leigh is no obedient and "dutiful handmaiden" who serves a "blind but powerful master," as Gilbert and Gubar have argued (578). On the contrary, she takes a leading role, and is recognized by her partner, Romney, as a creative genius. Toward the conclusion of the narrative, when Romney once again encounters Aurora, one of his first comments bears telling witness to his change of mind and heart, particularly considering his former rejection of her role as a serious writer. "I have read your book" (261), he states. And he adds that the book has changed him: "It stands above my knowledge, draws me up" (8: 285). This recognition alone counters the nineteenth-century conviction that—as Romney himself had argued earlier—poetic genius was essentially a "masculine" prerogative. It also contradicts the view that women whose literary and artistic endeavor demonstrated genius—i.e., a creative, imaginative impulse rather than mere imitation of models, or technical proficiency—were "abnormal or at best asexual" (Higonnet 249), and that women of genius could therefore not enter into "successful" relationships with men because "the attributes of femininity were diametrically opposed to those of genius" (Higonnet 249). According to conventional wisdom, a woman who "aspired to artistic greatness" was seen to have betrayed her "domestic destiny" (249) to such an extent that marriage was an unthinkable option.

In light of these nineteenth-century prejudices about female genius, the conclusion of *Aurora Leigh* is to be read as a radical questioning of the ideological restrictions placed on the bourgeois marriage. The marriage Romney and Aurora envision is clearly not restricted to women who live the "domestic ideal" or to men who act according to the accepted patriarchal role. On the contrary, for the female partner this revised view of marriage includes the unconventional role of artist and intellectual as an option, rather than as a state of deviancy.

Such an unconventional female role was by no means provided for within the context of the doctrine of separate spheres. As Higonnet points out, this doctrine clearly excludes the role of creative genius as a viable option for women:

Against the conflated values of activity, imagination, production, and masculine sexuality are pitted the similarly indivisible values of passivity, imitation, reproduction, and feminine sexuality. Men create original works of art; women recreate themselves in their children. (249)

In depicting Aurora's and Romney's marriage, then, Barrett Browning questions the very foundations of the bourgeois marriage, with its segregation of gender roles, its sovereignty of the patriarchal male "head of household," and its domestic ideal of womanhood.

By presenting this unconventional union, Barrett Browning makes a clear case that the static bourgeois view of the nuclear family represents a misconception of the dynamic potential of male-female relationships. Marriage, she argues, can be literally restructured along very different lines; the static nuclear family is a myth. Family relationships are, as her narrative discloses, both flexible and capable of the very changes that official discourses of the period proscribed.

Significantly, Romney has come to accept such an equal, cooperative relationship only with great difficulty. Indeed, he is portrayed as unable to abandon his conditioned responses as a patriarchal male until he is forced to do so by a physical impairment, and by the destruction of his utopian society. His blinding during a fire set by the *Lumpenproletariat* whom he—a self-styled Savior—had attempted to form into an ideal community, is not the expression of Barrett Browning's cruelty, and it is not to be seen as a "punishment" of her character. Instead, the author demonstrates that cultural conditioning is such a strong force that the patriarchal male, however benevolent his intentions, is unable to abandon his prescribed—here, Messianic—role unless forced—in this case by a physical disability—to do so. His impenetrable armor of patriarchal superiority must be damaged before he is capable of questioning his own prescribed role as husband and sovereign head of household. Only a traumatic alteration that renders him helpless allows Romney to reassess his former stance, and to view his—and Aurora's—roles in very different, nonpatriarchal terms.

Tellingly, Romney only begins to see when he is physically blinded. Only then can he recognize an alternative vision that contradicts his former convictions and stance. This is not to say that Romney finally comes to this recognition grudgingly, as one forced into submission. He states, "Thank God, who made me blind, to make me see!" (8: 830). The marriage *both* Aurora and Romney now envision is a full, interactive partnership in work, in love, and in mutual support: "Our work shall be the better for our love,/And still our love be sweeter for our work" (8: 925-26). In contradiction to Romney's and Aurora's earlier views, this work is neither Romney's alone, nor is it Aurora's alone. Instead, it is their work together. This is certainly an unusual, even an unlikely vision of marriage in the context of patriarchy. But, that it is not impossible is demonstrated by Barrett Browning's own marriage to Robert Browning. During their lifetimes *she* was the more widely recognized and acclaimed!

Significantly, this marriage, like the alternative family grouping depicted in earlier books of the novel poem, is established outside England, in a kind of limbo, a privileged space where Aurora Leigh, as a foreigner, is no longer inserted into the specific upper-middle-class context and structures that would be hostile to such radical departures from officially sanctioned marriage patterns. Barrett Browning recognizes implicitly that her re-visioned marriage must belong to a world which, as the vision at the conclusion of the novel poem suggests, has yet to be created.

Contrary to critical consensus, then, Barrett Browning as a member of the upper-middle-class was not trapped helplessly within the confines of bourgeois ideology, unable to envision models of womanhood "fundamentally different in style or content from men's images of women" (Higgonet 248). On the contrary, the author contests masculinist views both of the nuclear family and of women's roles within the family. She demonstrates that the bourgeois ideal of domestic womanhood, like the officially promulgated view of the nuclear family, is both restrictive and insufficient to account for the far more diverse and flexible realities of lived experience. Barrett Browning not only recognizes the flexible and fluid nature of the bourgeois family as a series of patterns in what A. F. Robertson refers to as a state of "dynamic process" (162) as opposed to the static image of families as "fixed social modules" or as "family portraits secure in their frames" (159). But she also uses her insight into the dynamic nature of family as the point of departure for offering alternative perspectives and future possibilities for radical change.

Notes

1. See, for instance studies by Angela Leighton, Barbara Gelpi, and Virginia Steinmetz. Gelpi and Leighton see Barrett Browning's Aurora Leigh as sharing an unconscious antifeminist stance. Both author and protagonist suffer, critics contend, from a "divided attitude toward being a woman" (Gelpi 41), and a "profound anxiety of womanliness" (Leighton 121) which cause them to reject their feminine and maternal nature, and to see women in antagonistic terms. Steinmetz argues that the protagonist—like the author—suffers from a form of neurosis. Both protagonist and author are unable to overcome mentally debilitating conflicts or to unite a painfully divided self into an integrated whole (353). Sandra Gilbert argues that the novel poem depicts the protagonist's at best partially successful attempt to undertake a "journey from disease toward what Sylvia Plath once called 'a country as far away as health'" (200). In short, Barrett Browning is seen to have produced a highly personal, confessional state-

ment fraught with contradictions demonstrating her narrowness of vision, and her failure to insert her voice into a wider social, cultural and philosophic dialogue.

2. All citations are taken from Cora Kaplan's 1978 edition of *Aurora Leigh.* All references to the novel poem will provide the book number followed by the line number(s).

Works Cited

Barrett Browning, Elizabeth. *Elizabeth Barrett Browning: "Aurora Leigh" and Other Poems.* Ed. Cora Kaplan. London: Women's Press, 1978.

Caine, Barbara. "Feminism and Political Economy in Victorian England—or John Stuart Mill, Henry Fawcett and Henry Sidgwick Ponder the 'Woman Question.'" *Feminism and Political Economy in Victorian England.* Ed. Peter Groenewegen. Brookfield, Vermont: Elgar, 1994: 25-45.

Davis, Natalie Zemon. *Society and Culture in Early Modern France.* Stanford: Stanford UP, 1965.

Fraisse, Genevieve, and Michelle Perrot, eds. *Emerging Feminism from Revolution to World War.* Vol. 4 of *A History of Women in the West.* 4 vols. Cambridge: Belknap P of Harvard UP, 1993.

——. "Family Is Women's Work." Fraisse and Perrot 321-24.

Gelpi, Barbara C. "*Aurora Leigh:* Vocation of the Woman Poet." *Victorian Poetry* 19.1 (1981): 35-48.

Gilbert, Sandra M. "From Patria to Matria: Elizabeth Barrett Browning's Risorgimento." *PMLA* 99.2 (1984): 194-211.

——, and Susan Gubar. *The Madwoman in the Attic: The Woman Writer and the Nineteenth-Century Literary Imagination.* New Haven: Yale UP, 1979.

Higginbotham, Ann R. "Madonnas and Magdalens: Changing Ideas of Illegitimate Motherhood." Unpublished paper delivered at the Midwest Victorian Studies Association Conference, Chicago, 20 Apr. 1991.

Higonnet, Anne. "Images—Appearances, Leisure, and Subsistence." Fraisse and Perrot 246-305.

Kaeppeli, Anne-Marie. "Feminist Scenes." Fraisse and Perrot 482-514.

Kaplan, Cora. Introduction. *Elizabeth Barrett Browning: "Aurora Leigh" and Other Poems.* London: Women's Press, 1978.

Kniebiehler, Yvonne. "Bodies and Hearts." Fraisse and Perrot 325-68.

Leighton, Angela. *Elizabeth Barrett Browning.* Brighton: Harvester, 1986.

Matus, Jill. *Unstable Bodies: Victorian Representations of Sexuality and Maternity.* Manchester: Manchester UP, 1995.

Peterson, M. Jeanne. *Family, Love and Work in the Lives of Victorian Gentlewomen.* Bloomington: Indiana UP, 1989.

Robertson, A. F. *Beyond the Family: The Social Organization of Reproduction.* Berkeley: U of California P, 1991.

Steinmetz, Virginia V. "Images of 'Mother-Want' in Elizabeth Barrett Browning's *Aurora Leigh.*" *Victorian Poetry* 21.4 (1983): 351-67.

5

(De)constructing the Patriarchal Family: Mary Louisa Molesworth and the Late Nineteenth-Century Children's Novel

Frank P. Riga

In discussing the use of fantasy and fairy tale in children's novels at the end of the nineteenth century, Jack Zipes argues that many of the important writers such as Julia Horatia Ewing, Mary Louisa Molesworth, and Edith Nesbit, adopted an essentially traditionalist approach. In Zipes's words:

[They] conceived plots conventionally to reconcile themselves and their readers to the status quo of Victorian society. Their imaginative world could be called exercises in complicity with the traditional opponents of fairy tales, for there is rarely a hint of social criticism and subversion in their works. After a brief period of disturbance, the fairies, brownies, elves or other extraordinary creatures generally enable the protagonists to integrate themselves into a prescribed social order. (xxii)

In an article on Edith Nesbit, U. C. Knoepflmacher seconds Zipes's argument, stating that for Victorian women writers such as Ewing, Molesworth and Nesbit, "fantasy serves an ideology that remains essentially anti-fantastic" (301). Although Zipes and Knoepflmacher agree that the above women writers appropriated what appear to be subversive fairy tale and fantasy motifs, nevertheless, in Knoepflmacher's words, their work "neither radically challenges a patriarchal order nor sharply departs from pronounced moralism" (302).[1] In this view, the above women writers tend, with a few after-thought exceptions, to reaffirm the validity of the bourgeois nuclear family as a sound, unquestioned social structure, and thus to validate an essentially patriarchal status quo.

Neither Zipes nor Knoepflmacher depart from a widely held critical consensus about nineteenth-century writers, and especially women writers for children. With few exceptions, critics have argued that nineteenth-century women writers did not seriously question the bourgeois ideology of the fixed and static nuclear family. As Jane Rendall states, central to this ideology is the "concept of the desirability of the private and domesticated family world, apart from the public world of the economic and political marketplace" (44). Nor did nineteenth-century writers, argue the critics, cast doubt upon the "doctrine" of separate spheres which underpinned the nuclear family, with its restrictive views of men's and women's roles. According to the doctrine of separate spheres, women were to play a passive, subordinate and domestic role. Men, by contrast, were to play a more public, active, superior and controlling role.

As some critics argue, this familial ideology was difficult, almost impossible, to challenge. In *Women and Fiction*, Patricia Stubbs observes that it was dangerous for a writer to question the stable image of the inviolate, idealized nuclear family with its inflexible roles for men and women. A writer who did so would be censored and silenced by "publishers, editors or librarians." Stubbs explains:

If a novel violated social and sexual conventions it was not just frowned upon or ignored. Society operated an extensive apparatus for banning and it did not hesitate to use it. This meant that if they wanted to be published at all, writers had to accept severe restrictions on the scope and treatment of their material. (19)

Critics have agreed that writers of children's books could seldom if ever be exceptions to this general rule. If women writers for children appeared to deconstruct the rigorously conventional image of the nuclear family, they invariably reaffirmed or reinstated it by the conclusion of the novel. The status quo thus remained essentially intact.

I wish to argue that, in contrast to this critical consensus, at least one late nineteenth-century children's writer, Mary Louisa Molesworth, does not merely reinstate traditional paradigms of social order. Instead, she questions the status quo by destablizing and subverting the rigorously paternalistic image of the nuclear family. Molesworth, well known at her death in 1921 as the writer of over 100 volumes for children, often depicts a traditional family structure that has been altered by various social, economic, and other factors. Parents are often in foreign countries, the army, or dead. In *The Carved Lions* (1895), for example, the Le Marchants leave Geraldine in a boarding school as they seek economic opportunity in South America. In *The Cuckoo Clock* (1877), Griselda is sent to live with her great aunts after her mother's death, and in *The Tapestry Room* (1879), the protagonist's family takes in an orphaned relative. Although the family at first "breaks down" in some of her plots, it appears by the novel's end to be reconstituted according to the "old" order. This reconstitution might lead the reader to see her as merely reaffirming this social order. But this is not the case. The nuclear family with its prescriptive roles only appears to be reconstructed along conventional lines. Molesworth's *The Palace in the Garden* (1887) is a case in point. The story seems to revolve around what might, under other circumstances, be a cliché: the finding of the lost mother figure, the full reconstitution of the nuclear family, and the reaffirmation of patriarchal order. By the conclusion of the novel, the family is restored; but the customary patterns and roles have been so altered and modified as to constitute an almost new reality. The newly structured family is analogous, but certainly not identical, to the conventional nuclear family.

Molesworth does not openly defy convention in *The Palace in the Garden*. Instead, she subverts it by indirection. The expected members of the nuclear family are present: a father figure, a mother figure, and children. But they either no longer play the expected roles, or their conventional roles have been modified in significant ways. The aging grandfather—an upper middle-class, stereotypical family patriarch and member of parliament—is transformed from a distant, benevolent authority figure into a man who learns to express the genuine affection he feels for his grandchildren. The children's great aunt, who takes the place of the dead mother, is not at all conventional. She is the former family outcast, who has been rejected because she had disobeyed her parents. All of the family members have ostracized her, including her brother, the children's grandfather. At best she is an unusual choice to assume the role of the absent mother. Since she has not played the restricted role mandated for women, her presence destabilizes the fixed view of the nuclear family. She has made decisions independent of fatherly and brotherly authority. The children are also exceptional. As orphans, they have far more scope for independence. Throughout the novel, they take the initiative rather than being passive, nurtured objects of cultural conditioning. In one sense, rather than be "educated" by their elders, they become the "educators" of their elders. They ultimately play a significant role in facilitating the transformation of the family along unconventional lines. Not only is the family reconstituted along more flexible and dynamic lines, but it is transformed emotionally so that the sterility resulting from unexpressed, even repressed, affection is replaced by a vitality that grows from mutual expressions of love.

This salutary change can be described as a magical transformation, mediated through fantasy and fairy tale. Gussie, the narrator and one of the children, repeatedly insists on the commonsense reality of her account, presenting the impression that she is striving to provide a realistic narrative. But the reality or authenticity of the narrative that reflects her experience does not deny the ethos of fairy tale. Instead, fairy tale elements are metamorphosed and incorporated into the narrative so that the novel itself appears as a contemporary fairy tale complete with a series of traditional motifs, including the magical transformation of the family, and two fairy tale intercessors, who are the equivalent of the fairy godmother or magic mediator and who facilitate the transformation. In Molesworth's novel, fairy tale is not seen as an infantile realm of fantasy which is displaced, as the child matures, by a world of experience based on the reality principle. Fairy tale does not give way to the dull quotidian of empirical reality. On the contrary, the realism of *The Palace in the Garden* in some ways serves as a mask for a literary fairy tale.

Quite aware of the restrictions placed on late nineteenth century novelists, particularly woman novelists, Molesworth has dressed her "fairy tale" in what appears to be the conventional garb of realism. In her study *Feminist Lives in Victorian England: Private Roles and Public Commitment*, Philippa Levine notes that women who wished to make the case for unconventional views often tempered their position to avoid overt hostility and censorship. "Feminists," she explains, "were sometimes cautious in their approach, favouring conservatism in dress as a means of deflecting the cruder criticisms of a bewildered public" (vii). Molesworth takes a similar approach, subverting rather than openly defying convention. I do not wish to make the case that she is a feminist; however, I do wish to argue that she brings—in the guise of a children's story—an approach to the nuclear family that is hardly conventional.

The events of the narrative are deceptively commonplace, and when order is disrupted, its restoration gives the impression of a traditional reaffirmation. The locus of family structure and authority never appears to be ambiguous. From this perspective, Molesworth's novel seems to resolve itself on the reconstruction of the patriarchal family. The story turns on a mystery concerning a family member whose identity has literally been erased (the grandfather has crossed out her name in one of the books they read as children) and hints at the disruption of the family's unity and nurturing function. But its ideology never appears to be put in question. When the three children protagonists—Gussie, the narrator; Tibs, her sister; and Gerald, their seven-year-old brother—are orphaned, the grandfather does not hesitate to assume what he sees as his responsibility as the head of the family. He says to the children, "what I do is no more than you have a right to" (104). Mrs. Munt, the old housekeeper at Rosebuds, the family's country cottage, tells the children that their grandfather could have done his duty differently; he could have sent them to a boarding school or entrusted them to the care of strangers, and thus have further disrupted the family. Instead, he chose to re-open his

London house in order to have them near him. Yet he remains emotionally distant from the children.

At the opening of the novel, the grandfather is a typical, remote yet benevolent patriarchal head of family. He seldom visits the three children, and when he does, he treats them ironically and demonstrates no affection. The children, in turn, are not encouraged to show affection. When the housekeeper, Mrs. Munt, explains that their grandfather does love them, but that his own troubles have caused him to withdraw into himself, Tib responds, "I wish he'd let us feel that he loves us, and then we would, indeed we would, love him" (91). This lack of overt affection gives the children a sense of emotional abandonment. Part of this breakdown in the expression of affection and love, as Mrs. Munt explains and the children sense, arises from the absence of a woman in the family: "A lady—a woman in the family makes all so different" (90). As we see from the developments of the novel, this statement does not finally suggest that love and affection are somehow rooted in woman's "nature," but rather that these qualities, encouraged by woman, are at the source of healthy family life.

The nuclear family is thus depicted as incomplete. It lacks the nuturing care of a mother figure. The paternal values of duty, responsibility, authority, and even a kind of love are present, but the informing affection and felt love, cultivated by a mother figure, are absent. And thus, the children feel unloved, resentful, and emotionally abandoned. While the formal order and structure of the patriarchal family remains intact, its emotional and spiritual substance is, if not vitiated, at least in abeyance. The narrative concludes with what appears to be a conventional restoration of the lost order: a mother figure is found and the nuclear family is thus reconstituted. The reader is presented, upon closure, with a family made whole again. The entire narrative appears to have been designed specifically for the reaffirmation of the bourgeois nuclear family, and of its domestic ideal.

The conventional surface of the narrative appears to be further corroborated by a series of intertextual references in the form of books which the narrator mentions during the course of the novel. Many of these are moral tales and behavior books which would seem to confirm not only the conventionality of the author's narratorial intent but also the mode of moral realism that apparently triumphs over fantasy and fairy tale. The works are significant: they include Maria Edgeworth's *Parent's Assistant* (1796), Mary Hughes's *Ornaments Discovered* (1815), and Catherine Sinclare's *Holiday House* (1839). Each of these texts reinforces what appears to be the didactic message of Molesworth's overt narrative. Edgeworth's *Parent's Assistant* is a collection of tales that demonstrate the unhappy repercussions of lying, thieving, bad company, and idleness. Edgeworth also challenges the notion that fairy tale and fantasy play a positive role in children's education. In the introduction, she explicitly challenges Samuel Johnson's views on children's proclivity for fairy tales, asking, "Why should the mind be filled with fantastic visions, instead of useful knowledge?" Hughes's *Ornaments Discovered* appears to be an intentional parallel to *The Palace in the Garden*. Like Molesworth's novel, it features a family disrupted by the death of the parents. The orphan, Fanny, learns her lesson on how to play the conventional domestic role; she discovers that "amiable manners and a well-regulated mind, are the only true valuable ornaments." In *Holiday House*, Sinclare seems to counter Edgeworth's message about the negative role of fantasy and fairy tale, declaring "All play of imagination is now carefully discouraged, and books written for young persons are generally a mere record of dry facts, unenlivened by any appeal to the heart, or any excitement to the fancy." Yet in the later chapters of *Holiday House*, she appears to modify her initial judgment. The children's better-behaved elder brother, who had become a sailor, is wounded in action and comes home to die a holy death, piously exhorting the younger children to reform and become sober and truthful. That is, it becomes a moral tale.

As the above intertextual allusions seem to imply, the moral tale with its didacticism and exhortations to conventional patterns of behavior appears to inform Molesworth's novel. At times, the influence is explicit, as the narrator, Gussie, occasionally expatiates on the wickedness of lying, cruelty, and prying into the private matters of adults. She also stresses the fact that while she is considered to be a "naughty" girl, her naughtiness is never cruel or harmful. And while the children undertake adventures without the knowledge either of the housekeepr or of the grandfather himself, they are well-behaved children, careful not to disobey the grandfather even indirectly. Thus, they obtain "permission" from the grandfather for exploring in the secret place behind the locked door in the high wall surrounding the cottage grounds. But they do so, as the reader recognizes, while the grandfather is in a state of absent-mindedness. On the surface, however, their lives are carefully regulated. For instance, they are forbidden to associate with the neighbors and are required to live in isolation from other families, an injunction which they do not understand but which they obey.

But this is on the surface of the narrative. In addition to the didactic books by Edgeworth, Hughes, and Sinclare, the narrator also refers to a different series of texts whose messages contrast sharply to the exhortations of the moral tales. While the moral tales appeared to corroborate conventional expectations, these other intertextual allusions point toward the subversive elements underlying the ostensibly unchallenged values of the narrative with its apparent return to patriarchal order. Among these texts, Gussie emphasizes a series of books which feature the essentially subversive world of fantasy, wonder and fairy tale: Lamb's *Tales from Shakespeare*, Nathaniel Hawthorne's *Wonder Book*, "and best of all perhaps, the dearest little shabby, dumpy, dark-brown book of real old-fashioned fairy tales" (18), which the "realistic" narrator intends to keep for her own children. The fact that the treasured book is worn from reading stresses the key function of such tales in the narrative. As these intertextual references suggest, the didactic and conventional surface of the narrative hides a different series of values which counter rather than reaffirm the ideology of the bourgeois nuclear family. The intertextual references are the cues or signals provided by Molesworth to suggest her apparent conventional narrative is not all that it seems on the surface.

From the outset, Molesworth provides a series of hints that indicate an unconventional view of the family. Gussie as narrator plays a significant role in the indirect subversion of patriarchal norms. From the beginning of the novel, Molesworth problematizes the narrative by providing a naive child narrator, who presents an unusual and by nineteenth century standards unconventional view of the bourgeois nuclear family. This unconventionality is corroborated by recent studies of how the nuclear family was viewed during the nineteenth century. In *Beyond the Family*, sociologist and cultural historian A. F. Robertson argues that previous views of the nineteenth century nuclear family were rigid and incomplete. Although the ideal of the nuclear family was promulgated as a doctrine and although nineteenth century sociologists and historians alike argued that it was fixed and stable, the nuclear family was far more flexible and dynamic than critics and theorists have assumed. According to Robertson, "static definitions" have prevented historians from seeing that reproduction, the central concern of the nuclear family, "concerns a continually changing ensemble of people" (162). In other words, people, then as now, found ways to vary the family structure in order to accommodate the needs of the different persons who wanted to be part of it.

Previous studies of the family were skewed by the fact that researchers relied on "a single informant," who was invariably the male "household head" (Robertson 162). This observation plays a key role in assessing the significance of Molesworth's child narrator. In providing an alternative perspective of the nuclear family—that of the naive and unformed female child—Molesworth is able to present a far more dynamic and flexible view of the family than was conventionally possible. As Robertson notes, previous studies, even during the twentieth century, have frequently relied entirely on the male head of household, and thus on the male perspective, for information. The result is an incomplete, unnecessarily static and even distorted view of the family. "Construing the life of the household as a function of a single person's career," explains Robertson, "produces patterns which diverge significantly from the more complicated and temporally more extensive growth, decline, and replacement of the entire group" (162). By presenting the narrative through the eyes of a female child, Molesworth provides what may be seen as corrective lenses, which allow a different view of the bourgeois family to come into focus. Throughout the novel the unconventional female view is sustained. This is so even when the first person narrative is suddenly destabilized and fragmented toward the conclusion of the novel, as different narrators are interposed to provide information for the same event. It is noteworthy that none of these narratives is given from the perspective of the male head of household, namely the grandfather, even though he participates directly or indirectly in each of them.

The child narrator as an unconventional informant presents an unusual, and potentially subversive perspective. The ability of the narrator to deconstruct—wittingly or unwittingly—conventionally held views of the family is further enhanced by the fact that she has been isolated from English society and from its conventions in a number of ways. Born in Spain and orphaned at an early age, she has no memory of what a "real" family is supposed to be like. Living with her grandfather has kept her in artificial isolation from other families, as she repeatedly acknowledges in her narrative. Although she states that her ignorance is a gap in her knowledge, this ignorance actually plays a positive role. It is the point of departure for conceiving the nuclear family in different and more dynamic terms. From the outset, for example, she does not perceive the grandfather's benevolent yet ironic and cold distance as normal. On the contrary, she perceives it as a lack, as a problem. She also connects it with the family mystery of the crossed out name that she and the children wish to resolve. She suspects that the answer to the family mystery will help to provide an answer to her grandfather's character, to his cold reserve and his distance. And finally, in a rough parallel to Huck Finn, she comes to believe that good has come out of what would be seen, conventionally, as "naughty" or reprehensible behavior. As she comments in her childlike way:

And even the great thing I have to write about, the thing that put it into my head to write it at all, would never have come but for our being in a way naughty— that is very queer, isn't it? To think that good and nice things should sometimes come out of being naughty! (23)

Her entire narrative may thus be seen as a process of undermining the values of the patriarchal family.

The mystery itself concerns a lost family member, a woman named Regina, whose outcast state is symbolized by the erasure of her name in one of the books the children have found in their grandfather's house. The mystery begins to take shape when the children, still in the London house, find out that they are to holiday at Rosebuds, the family's country cottage previously unknown to them. Gussie remembers that the name Rosebuds is written in one of grandfather's children's books, *Ornaments Discovered*, but she also remembers that, on the same page, another name has been scored out. On examining the book, the children discover that the scored out name is Regina, Tib's middle name. This clue to the mystery, however, puts them perilously close to what they consider their grandfather's "secrets," which they, as respectful and well-behaved children, cannot pry into. Yet they cannot stop themselves from wondering what the mystery is or what it means. Only later does the reader recognize the hidden irony of the crossed out name in the context of *Ornaments Discovered*. The name is that of a rebellious woman, the grandfather's sister and the children's great aunt. He had erased his sister's name from a conduct book that had clearly "failed" in its mission to shape her into an obedient embodiment of the domestic ideal. Gussie herself is "naughty" and the resolution of the novel turns on what she considers "naughty."

The mystery of Regina's identity remains concealed from the children. The retrospective narrator, Gussie, knows who she is at the time of writing, but conceals her great aunt's identity from the reader, who is only informed of her real status as rebellious woman and family outcast at the conclusion of the novel. And although great aunt Regina does not actually appear until the close of the narrative, she is indirectly present throughout much of the novel, represented by an ancestral portrait of a young woman named Regina, and by her daughter, who is also named Regina. Regina, the grandfather's sister, Regina the daughter, and Regina in the family portrait are linked not only because they bear the same name, but also because they have an uncanny physical resemblance to one another. Gussie's sister, Tib, whose middle name is Regina, also resembles the three women. The suggestive richness of this pattern of character quadruplets suggests the novel's attempt to demonstrate how varied individuals are accommodated to a single family. In particular, the multiplication of characters who appear to be identical implies that the family's identity and coherence seem to depend on the female line. As we also discover, however, these women are all different, each independent and active in her own way: the woman of the portrait is the enchanted princess of the children's imagining, the great aunt is the outcast rebel, her daughter Regina is the reconciling mediator, and Tib is the budding romantic who wants the different and unusual.

Through great aunt Regina's "representatives," the narrator is able to depict her in a positive light throughout much of the narrative, before the reader knows the truth about her being ostracized from the family. The children, not knowing who this mysterious figure is, cast her in the role of the princess in a fairy tale they have invented in order to account for circumstances they as yet do not understand. The fairy tale fantasy, far from being inconsequential, actually helps them to reshape reality. Ultimately, the fairy tale projection of the positive figure of the princess, or the good fairy, succeeds in transforming adult reality itself. The outcast woman, whose representatives have been benevolent figures for the children, is in turn revealed to the grandfather as the figure the children have imagined. The fairy tale becomes reality. The children can imagine her as a nurturing figure because they do not know her status as an outcast, a status that does not interfere with their acceptance of her as a magical intercessor and as a replacement for their lost mother. For the children, there is no social or emotional barrier to her reintegration into the family, or with her assumption of the maternal role. Indeed, through the eyes of the children, and especially through the eyes of the child narrator, the grandfather's erasure of her name and his banning her, and her daughter, from the respectable territory of the family, appears unwarranted and over-reactive.

The children's initiative to transform the family begins—outside of their awareness or intention—when they are moved to the family cottage, Rosebuds. Rosebuds had already been associated with the mystery of the erased name. Gussie's response to this new place signals her recognition that, despite her prosaic tendencies, she has somehow entered into a fairy tale and fantasy realm. On the first morning, she lies in an uncustomarily meditative state between sleeping and waking—the romantic area of the mixed states of consciousness—which she sees in terms of fairy tale:

Oh, it is too delicious—and when you hear all those sounds, as you are lying there still dreamy and sleepy, there is a sort of strangeness and *fairy-ness*—I must make up that word—that makes you think of Red Ridinghood setting off in the early morning to her grandmother's cottage, or of the little princess who went to live with the dwarfs to keep house for them. (53-54)

While still in the London house, Gerald and Tibs, her brother and sister, had already indicated a similar recognition when they first heard of the country cottage. Resisting the idea of a fantasy world, Gerald complains: "I don't like cottages with roses growing over them . . . There are always witches living in cottages like that, in the fairy tales." And to specify his insight, he adds, "There is in *Snow-white and Rose-red*" (16-17). Picking up the reference to witches, Tib then adds: "Well . . . it would be rather fun to have a witch at Rosebuds. I do hope there'll be something interesting and out of the common there—something *romantic*" (17).

After their arrival at Rosebuds, as their initial responses have already suggested, the children continue their attempt to make sense of the family mystery by incorporating what they know into a fairy tale or fantasy narrative. While playing in the cottage garden, in order to assuage their curiosity about the family mystery, into which they, as good, obedient children, cannot pry, Tib suggests that they fantasize about it, that they "turn it into a play."

We can't leave off wondering, as you say, but we can mix our wondering with fancy, and make up a plan of how it all was. It will be very interesting, for we shall know there is something real, and yet we can make it more wonderful than anything real could be now that everything's grown so plain—and—I don't know the word—the opposite of poetry and fairy stories, I mean—in the world. (42)

In her narrative or "plan" to represent "how it all was," the romantic Tib recognizes that the fairies have been exiled from the world, that the world has become "prosaic," and so in her narrative, she, like Wordsworth, wants to surround the events of every day with an aura of imagination, thus giving it a sense of the wonderful and the extraordinary. Gussie, though she thinks this a good idea, tells us, "I am not so fond of fancying or pretending as Tib—I like real things. And the idea of a real secret or mystery had taken hold of my mind, and I wanted to find out about it" (43). Tib wants a story of ancient times or ogres, that is, a romance or fairy tale; Gussie wants a prosaic, realistic story of detection. And yet, in the final count, what Gussie tells is a story laced and underpinned by fairy tale elements and motifs. The conflict between the two children and the two modes of perception dominates the attempt at narration and becomes a dialectic by which the children make sense of their growing but incomplete knowledge of the family mystery.

Once the children decide to act out their narrative, they must first construct a plot that will accommodate their knowledge and perceptions of the mystery. Tib, who "was all for a regular romance," proposes the initial plot in which "there was to be a beautiful lady shut up by a cruel baron, who wanted to get all her money by forcing her to marry his hump-backed son" (79). A prince, of course, will rescue the lady. Since they are to act out the story, however, they run into several problems immediately. While there is a garden wall at Rosebuds, for example, it is too high for the children to climb, and so the lady's escape from the dungeon by going over the wall must be revised: "And we fixed that, instead of 'scaling the wall,' the lady should escape by hiding in the wood till the prince who was to be her rescuer passed that way" (86). Similar problems of production, casting and setting, cause the children to revise their initial concepts to suit the actual conditions they have found, much as the fairy tale mode itself is being revised to have a contemporary significance. But they never lose sight of the essential motifs of the fairy tale.

A new discovery appears to corroborate Gussie's insight that real mysteries are as exciting and interesting as invented ones, and just as surprising. Discovering a locked door in the garden wall and the key to open it, they believe that they will enter a toolhouse which they could use as a "dungeon" in their invented tale. What they find outstrips their imaginings. When they pass through the door, they are greeted by a "perfect flood of light." It was "like the entrance to some fairy palace of brightness and brilliance. . . . *Was* it magic? Had we chanced upon some such wonder of old world times as our little heads were stuffed with" (129). Uncertain whether they are "awake or dreaming," they enter "the enchanted palace," and Tib exclaims, "*what* a bower for a princess!" (133). Gussie makes one of her expected disclaimers at this point in an aside to the reader: "this is not a fairy story; and in the end I think you will allow, when you have come to know the whole, that is is very interesting, perhaps more interesting than a fairy story after all" (131). It is not a fairy story for her, since it is not distant from the children or separated from reality by a clear barrier; instead, it is reality. But despite Gussie's objections, the alert reader notes that her account is suffused with the language, images, and motifs of a fairy tale, albeit transposed into contemporary terms.

The children find themselves in a house that appears to be unlived in, since it looks deserted and dust covers hide the furniture. And yet the place is obviously cared for. They enter what appears to be a conservatory. A second door leads to a hallway "which ends in a very large and handsome drawing room" (135). The doorway leading out of the drawing room is locked, but on one wall they discover a life-sized portrait. Although painted in a different, much earlier age, the portrait—as already mentioned—bears an uncanny resemblance to Tib. A further detail seems to connect the portrait to the family mystery: it is labeled "Regina," which is both the name crossed out in the grandfather's copy of *Ornaments Discovered*, and Tib's middle name. This unusual discovery prompts the children to believe that they have entered an enchanted palace. Gerald declares, "Perhaps that lady is *really* alive, and the fairies have fastened her up into that picture till—till" (139). The others find Gerald's inarticulateness amusing; yet in a sense his assessment proves to be accurate. Great aunt Regina, who resembles the picture, has indeed been banished by the grandfather—an act that has the equivalent effect of enchantment, since it prevents her from being part of the family and erects a "magical," i.e., an insurmountable, barrier between her and her family.

Tib immediately sees the portrait as the new basis for their fantasies, since the woman portrayed can become an enchanted princess. Gussie, by contrast, wishes to solve the mystery it presents. She indicates that this room is not part of an enchanted palace by making a practical move. Finding the key to the door leading into the drawing room, she hides it in a drawer, so that no one can return and lock the children out: "I took the key out of the lock and slipped it inside a drawer of one of the big cabinets where it may be lying still" (144). Gussie proceeds like a detective, who wishes to find the real explanation for what only appears to be enchantment. She recognizes that "the palace in the garden" is linked with the mystery surrounding the crossed out name; but she also understands that the grandfather must explain this to them voluntarily: "What I want is to find out about it from him" (151). Since the discovery of the portrait has given them a new tack, the children abandon their original plot: "For after a while we got tired of our play story about the baron and the hump back and all the rest of it, and then we pretended that we came to visit the princess in her beautiful palace, and that she was very kind to us indeed" (148). That is, by casting the princess in a maternal role, they have substituted an image closer to their true desire for that of the hackneyed romance.

At this point, the equivalent of the magical intercessor of fairy tale arrives in the person of Charles Truro. Charles, a cousin who is acting as a secretary to their grandfather, is kind and affectionate, an attentive listener who immediately wins their trust and confidence. They tell him the secret of their discovery in the garden, seeing him as "a sort of good fairy who was to put everything right" (176). Without their knowledge, Charles intervenes. As the reader discovers later, he is not only the grandfather's secretary, but also the good friend of great aunt Regina and her daughter. Thus, he knows the story of how the old man banished his sister for her disobeying their parents in her choice of a husband. Charles Truro and Regina devise a plan: since she has access to the "old house" which contains the "enchanted palace," she decides to enter the house and the children's fantasy tale, without explaining to them who she is.

Cousin Regina's entrance into the "old house" seems magical. The children recognize her arrival, almost instinctively, even before they see her. Gussie feels the difference in the room: "it seemed warmer, more alive, there was more feeling in it" (181). The family resemblance between Regina and the life-sized portrait in the abandoned house is so striking that when Regina steps into the drawing room for the first time, the children almost believe she has stepped out of the portrait. They accept her presence—her friendship, her kindness, her gifts, her enter-tainment—as if she were, indeed, a magical figure. When she leaves at the sound of a bell, Gussie comments, "Surely she must be a fairy of some kind, after all!" (197). When the children discuss the meeting later, the only way they can make sense of it is through fairy tale motifs. Gerald is convinced that "she is a fairy, and that she lives in Fairyland," and commenting on the summons by the bell, Tib responds, "That part of it was really like a fairy story" (200-01). The practical, reality-loving Gussie adds, "If only she had left a slipper behind her, it would have been a little like Cinderella . . . though the deserted, quiet room and that part of it, is more like the Sleeping Beauty" (201). And then, remember-ing their first entrance through the garden wall, she adds, "And the first day, when we were trying to get in at the door in the wall, was like one of the stories of dwarfs and gnomes in the woods. . ." (201).

The conclusion of the tale is not an abandonment of fairy tale, but instead an incorporation of fairy tale into everyday reality. The fairy tale which helped the children make sense of reality, now succeeds in reshap-ing reality. The transformation occurs through a series of improbable coincidences—the contemporary version of "magic"—to bring about the "happy ending." Precisely at this point, the hitherto unified view of the first person narrator is interrupted by Gussie's need to be in three places at the same time in order to make coherent sense of the complex ending. She solves this narrative problem by first stating her quandry and then by reporting a series of alternate perspectives that had been told to her later. The break-up of the narrative into multiple perspectives allows the reader to see that the transformation of the family is finally the work of many mediators, not just the children themselves.

In the first of many coincidences, which serve to bring about the denouement, the children break off the key to the garden and are locked in "the palace." The grandfather, who has arrived for a visit, is overcome by fear when they do not return. He believes that they have drowned in the deep pools in an area outside the cottage. Suddenly, his emotions and his imagination are activated; he imagines that they are dead, and is so convinced that he orders the dragging of the pools to find their bodies. This traumatic experience, living through what he believes to be the children's deaths, causes him to acknowledge and express his own emotions for the first time. And it causes him to recognize how much they mean to him. Thus he becomes vulnerable and open to what now occurs. By a further coincidence, his servants, in order to borrow dragging hooks, go to the house where great aunt Regina and her daughter are living. Regina's daughter immediately realizes that the children have not been drowned, but instead have been locked in the old house. She sends her mother, the family outcast, to the grandfather with the good news, while she goes to free the children from the locked up house. The grandfather is reconciled to his sister, whom he had adamantly refused to see for many years. A new family unit is now formed. Order appears to be restored, and the conclusion seems to reaffirm the normal status quo.

However, it is a much altered status quo, and a much more flexible and dynamic grouping than the "nuclear family" with its doctrine of separate spheres and its static, rigidly defined roles. Gerald, whose point of view is ostensibly dismissed by his two older sisters, is nonetheless accurate in his assessment: a fairy tale intercession has brought about a transformation in his life which surpasses the mere factual.

I do understand all I need . . . I understand that we've got an auntie, and that she's very kind, and that Regina is a cousin, and she's very nice too—so nice that I'm still going to think she's a fairy. That's what I've settled, and I think it's quite enough when only seven. (288)

As Gussie tells us in the last sentences of the novel, the new family grouping has transformed their lives and has transformed the family itself from a sterile grouping of human beings connected by duty and blood ties, to a far more vital unit of people, interconnected by strong and active emotional bonds: "We are almost always together, grandpapa and auntie and Regina and we children, and very often Mr. Truro too. Grandpapa says he is getting very old but he really doesn't look so, and even when he does get 'very old,' we shall all only love him the better" (298). The simplicity of the final statement, like the surface of the narrative itself, is deceptive. Hidden in the ostensibly naive account written by a child, Molesworth has put into question the view of family which was officially promulgated throughout the nineteenth century.

Instead of the domestic ideal of the obedient, passive Angel in the House, we have not one, but two mother figures: Regina, the rebellious woman, and her daughter, both of whom now act in place of the children's missing mother. Not only are these figures unconventional in themselves; they encourage nontraditional behavior on the part of Gussie. Cousin Regina helps the child, Gussie, to play what was, in the late nineteenth century, still an unconventional role: to write a narrative of her experience. Gussie consciously speaks throughout the narrative about the act of writing, reminding the reader again and again that she is struggling with a difficult narrative, trying to find adequate words to express her point of view. The difficulty lies not in the failure of the child narrator, but in the unusual nature of her task: to articulate an unconventional perspective and to authorize that perspective by the act of writing, an act faciliated by cousin Regina whom the narrator refers to as her writing mentor at several points in the novel. As Gussie's act of writing underlines, the literary heritage plays an important role throughout the novel. The children are always reading and referring to texts. When they first see great aunt Regina through the garden wall, she is reading rather than fulfilling the expected feminine activities of sewing and doing domestic work.

While both of the mother figures and the children themselves play unconventional roles in this family of articulate women, the family structure is also modified by the revised roles of the other characters. The grandfather is no longer the distant family patriarch, but a loving man who is close to his grandchildren, a metamorphosis that is remarkable given the requirements of the patriarchal role. The family is not limited to the mothers, father and children, but is extended to include Charles Truro. It is thus depicted as an open-ended, dynamic and inclusive structure, in which none of the members play a fully conventional role. As Robertson suggests, the nuclear family was, in reality, probably far more flexible and changing than the officially sanctioned paradigm would lead us to believe. Molesworth has thus provided not only a subversive, but perhaps a more accurate, picture of the realities of the bourgeois family than the various regulatory discourses of the nineteenth century would seem to permit.

Molesworth's subtle critique of mainstream values is of particular significance in the context of children's literature as a marginal or inconsequential literary genre. In her discussion of nineteenth century women artists, Anne Higonnet speaks of the difficulties women faced in charting their careers in territories traditionally reserved for men. Women, Higonnet argues, frequently negotiated positions not in mainstream endeavors, but in areas that were considered to be on the margins of the public artistic and literary domain. According to Higonnet, "Liminal careers provided women with uncharted terrain to claim as their own" (260), and as an example, Higonnet points to the illustration of children's books as one of these "unclaimed" territories. Women who specialized in "unusual or marginal" genres, she argues, "could go far without seeming to break any rules" (260). Molesworth, who specialized in what appears to be an inconsequential genre, that of children's books, charts precisely such a terrain. And in making this genre her own, she gently questions traditional roles in which women are relegated to the nonpublic, domestic sphere.

In terms of the Victorian nuclear family, *The Palace in the Garden* does not merely effect a simple reconciliation with the status quo to "enable the protagonists to integrate themselves into a prescribed social order," a reconciliation that "neither challenges a patriarchal order nor sharply departs from a pronounced moralism." On the contrary, this depiction of the family allows the older forms and images to contain new ideas, thereby preserving a sense of familiarity and security while negotiating new terms for family vitality. The fairy tale intertext thus becomes an especially appropriate medium for this kind of subversion, since the fairy tale's primary concern has frequently been to find a mode of transformation that can accommodate and reconcile new realities. And so, though the family seems to look like it always did, it has retained its integrity and stability by being transformed. A careful reading of Molesworth's book reveals that our current assumptions about the Victorian family are probably too narrow and formulaic to describe the vitality with which individuals adjusted the family structure to meet the changing needs of everyday life. It is scarcely surprising, then, to find that her novels—ostensibly straightforward, charming stories, with everyday plots and characters, written by and for children—should actually contain a different, subversive message beneath the tranquil surface of conventionality.

Note

1. See, however, *Forbidden Journeys: Fairy Tales and Fantasies by Victorian Women Writers* (Chicago: U of Chicago P, 1992), in which Knoepflmacher and Nina Auerbach make the case that Molesworth's writing may be more subversive than Knoepflmacher allows here. In "The Brown Bull of Norrowa," a Scottish tale rewritten by Molesworth and inserted into her novel, *The Tapestry Room*, they argue that the heroine challenges "the conservative ideologies of gender that often seem embedded in the very form of fairy tales" (17).

Works Cited

Auerbach, Nina, and U. C. Knoepflmacher, eds. *Forbidden Journies: Fairytales and Fantasies by Victorian Women Writers*. Chicago: U of Chicago P, 1992.

Higonnet, Anne. "Images—Appearances, Leisure, and Subsistence." *A History of Women in the West*. Vol. 4. *Emerging Feminism from Revolution to World War*. Ed. Genevieve Fraisse and Michelle Perrot. Cambridge, MA: Belknap P of Harvard U, 1993: 246-305.

Knoepflmacher, U. C. "Of Babylands and Babylons: E. Nesbit and the Reclamation of the Fairy Tale." *Tulsa Studies in Women's Literature* 6.2 (Fall 1987): 299-325.

Levine, Philippa. *Feminist Lives in Victorian England: Private Roles and Public Commitment*. Cambridge, MA: Basil Rockwell, 1990.

Molesworth, Mary Louisa. *The Palace in the Garden*. Illus. Harriet M. Bennett. London: Hatchards, Picadilly, 1887.

Rendall, Jane. *Women in an Industrializing Society: England 1750-1880*. Cambridge, MA: Basil Blackwell, 1991.

Reynolds, Kimberly, and Nicola Humble. *Victorian Heroines: Representations of Femininity in Nineteenth-Century Literature and Art*. New York: New York UP, 1993.

Robertson, A. F. *Beyond the Family: The Social Organization of Reproduction*. Berkeley: U of California P, 1991.

Stubbs, Patricia. *Women and Fiction: Feminism and the Novel, 1880-1920*. New York: Harper and Row, 1979.

Zipes, Jack, ed. *Victorian Fairy Tales: The Revolt of the Fairies and Elves*. New York: Methuen, 1987.

6

The "Muddle" of Step-Parenting: Reconstructing Domestic Harmony in James and Forster

Scott F. Stoddart

P. N. Furbank's biography of E. M. Forster recounts a single meeting between Forster and his idea of "a first-rate literary celebrity," Henry James. Forster was "thrilled" at the prospect of meeting the "Master"— but the afternoon tea was nothing short of a disaster. James mistook the young author for another acquaintance, and their subsequent conversation proceeded "stammeringly" (163-64). Forster, in a letter to his friend Edward Dent, claimed to enjoy the "funny sensation, going to see a really first class person. I felt all that the ordinary healthy man feels in the presence of a lord" (165). However, he later concluded that the esteem he felt for James related more toward his work. Thereafter, Forster felt James's notions of class "stuffy and precious," leading him not only to "distrust" James's fictive politics, but to question his own. It is at this time, according to the biographer, "during the summer the scheme for a new novel, the future *Howards End*, began to shape itself" (165).

While this amusing anecdote emphasizes one relationship between the figures of Henry James and E. M. Forster, their works reveal another, for many of the major works both authors wrote respond to the popularist domestic tradition of the nineteenth-century novel. James's *The Portrait of a Lady* (1881/1909)[2] and Forster's *Howards End* (1910) expand the formulaic genre to include the problems of alternate family situations—namely those connected with step-parenting—a highly charged, equally ignored subject by authors of domestic fiction. Both protagonists, Isabel Archer Osmond and Margaret Schlegel Wilcox, marry into "ready-made" family situations which not only complicate the domestic atmosphere of their immediate lives, but threaten the patriarchal construct of these familial structures. These male-authored texts deconstruct Edwardian "family values" to create a re-styled notion of a modern family—centered in an ethic of maternal power and familial community.

115

Victorian Domesticity vs. Edwardian Domesticity

Written largely by women throughout the nineteenth-century, the paradigmatic domestic novel illustrates a fundamentally Victorian ideology (Douglas 72). The female protagonist, usually parentless, desires to fulfill goals relating to her personal social situation, ensuring a basis for economic interdependence through marriage (Baym 36-37). As the "child" emerges into an adult, the reader follows her development to self-awareness, usually connected to a period of self-employment—her understanding of the "world" at large—and ending with her marriage. But, her episodic journey introduces the heroine to characters who help guide her in shaping healthy attitudes toward marriage, family, and motherhood, so this "final domesticity" institutionalizes a sense of family and solidifies the inherent needs of the protagonist (39). She, therefore, chooses marriage, establishing herself as an appropriate maternal model. This pedagogical use of the novel introduced its largely female audience to the limitations of Victorian culture, and showed how women could use patriarchal boundaries to mediate their personal desires.

James revised his *Portrait* and Forster composed *Howards End* during what literary historians now call "The Edwardian Age," which largely influenced their use of the domestic novel.[3] Both writers rely on omniscient narrators to detail their heroines, building stories which do not "end" in marriage, but continue through marriage, taking the domestic fiction to a new height. What makes these novels predominantly "Edwardian" is their on-going argument about the stasis of matrimony within a world of progress; questioning established codes, the protagonist faces shifts in social organization and rifts in personal morality, all the while speculating as to how one copes with societal change (Hunter 3-10). James and Forster use the domestic novel to articulate the condition of woman within the unsettling moral and social climate of this new century.[4]

With this in mind, there are a number of uncanny parallels between these novels which goes far to prove Furbank's (and my own) hypothesis that one text perhaps worked as a response to the other. Their narrators label both Isabel and Margaret "heroines," and as heroines, they share commonalities with those of nineteenth-century domestic fiction. But, in contrast to the Victorian domestic novel, both American and British, the novels do not end with the heroine's marriage (as a matter of fact, both marriages take place roughly at the halfway point) and a re-established equilibrium; instead, these marriages, which create new familial situations, further complicate the actions of each novel. With this departure, both James and Forster explore a new era of domestic fiction—one which turns on the position of married woman within the "muddle" of the phallocentric order.

Isabel and Margaret: Feminine "Single"-Mindedness

Isabel Archer's introduction to Gardencourt (and to us) comes in the form of a cryptic telegram sent by Mrs. Touchett to her son, Ralph. Beth Sharon Ash's close reading of this communique connects Isabel succinctly to the Touchett clan—emphasizing her "mother's absence" rather than her father's, with whom Mrs. Touchett fought (*PL* 128)—privileging a notion that Isabel's motherless condition predisposes her toward maternity.[5] However, what Ash ignores is the novel's lengthy discussion of Isabel's relationship with her father, and her paternal grandmother; it is this paternal connection, a form of hero-worship, that actively engages Isabel's "imagination," and shapes her self-awareness. The narrator takes us back to Albany, New York to "a large, square, double house, with a notice of sale in the windows . . . painted all over exactly alike, in a yellowish white which had grown sallow with time" (31-32)—after her initial introduction, we find Isabel "seated alone with a book" "fertilizing" her imagination (31). While Mrs. Touchett insists on removing her from this "very bad house" (35), Isabel recognizes the fertile capabilities of her paternal homestead. This brief reading of her paternal grandmother's homelife depicts it as a characteristic domestic space, where Isabel plots "the foundation of her knowledge" (33), a conception of her own individual design.

In a similar light, Forster introduces Margaret Schlegel, motherless, and newly fatherless, the "keeper" of her own homestead. The novel begins in crisis with another misunderstood communique, this time a series of letters written by the younger sister, Helen, vacationing in the country with the Wilcox family. While the dilemma of Helen's admission to having fallen "in love" with the profligate Paul Wilcox tests the abilities of Margaret's home management, the narrator subtly introduces us to the importance of the paternal home for the Schlegel women, described in a language reminscent of a battle-plan (*HE* 7-8). Wickham Place remains the final legacy from the Schlegel's newly deceased father, and the phrases used by the narrator not only characterize the transient heartlessness of the city in ultimately replacing the structure (I might add, a suggestion made by Mrs. Touchett to Isabel concerning *her* familial dwelling), but employ a rhetoric emphasizing military strategy.[6] Ernst Schlegel, "the countryman of Hegel and Kant, as the idealist, inclined to be dreamy, whose Imperialism was the Imperialism of the air" (29), bequeaths to his eldest daughter his militaristic ideals which enabled him to fight "like the blazes against Denmark, Austria, France . . . without visualizing the results of victory" (29), and provides her with the domestic ideal to maintain the Schlegel "empire" in London, despite the attitudes of other family members who see them as "half-breeds."

Margaret's social education, much like Isabel's, is labeled "unique," certainly not common to women of her social background, as Ernst wants his daughter to "use the intellect" rather than the "imagination" to survive in the modern world (30). Nurturing his daughter's curiosity causes their distant relations to think her "a most offensive child . . . a hateful little girl" (31), but we soon learn that this pedagogy creates a unique heroine of Margaret—a woman of many facets, with a unique perception of woman's place within the modern world: "she had grasped a dilemma that most people travel through life without perceiving. Her brain darted up and down; it grew pliant and strong. Her conclusion was that any human being lies nearer to the unseen than any organization, and from this she never varied" (31). Margaret represents the antithesis of the Victorian maternal figure—and the burgeoning Edwardian one.

As Margaret's reading of literature shapes her insights into the human condition, Isabel's reading also shapes her early consciousness. Even though Mrs. Touchett discovers her in "the office" "trudging over the sandy plains of a history of German Thought" (*PL* 34) we certainly conjecture as to what other readings shaped Isabel's early years. The narrator continues to employ the word "romance" to describe Isabel's demeanor throughout her interview with her aunt and immediately thereafter, while Mrs. Touchett arranges with the Ludlows (Isabel's in-laws) to bring Isabel to Europe. During a moment of reflection that evening, Isabel outlines her goals, which include her musings concerning her own self-awareness: "She had a desire to leave the past behind her and, as she said to herself, to begin afresh. This desire indeed was not a birth of the present occasion; it was as familiar as the sound of the rain upon the window and it had led to her beginning afresh a great many times" (39). Isabel's early life, including her reading, conditions her to perceive her goals: "She had a great desire for knowledge, but she really preferred almost any source information to the printed page; she had an immense curiosity about life and was constantly staring and wondering" (41). We can conclude that the "uncontrolled use of a library full of books with frontispieces" included books of a romantic variety—undoubtedly novels—which shaped her fanciful ideals (33). Isabel quickly articulates this singular attitude when Mrs. Touchett suggests they leave the house to the wrecking ball. This "experience" is our first inkling of Isabel's desire to remain a member of an established family unit, as her use of the phrase "full of experience" points to a house filled with "life," in other words "love"—all that has made the structure "a home" in the eyes of the young woman.

Margaret already operates as the maternal center of Wickham Place; but, as time passes, her siblings treat her more as an elder confidante.

Yet, this natural treatment does not prevent Margaret from envisioning a more fulfilling occupation for herself. For instance, as she reflects on her meeting of the suspicious Leonard Bast, during a concert of "The Four Serious Songs," she "sees" a broader purpose to her life, even though Bast hastily retreats from the overbearing philanthropist: "Most ladies would have laughed, but Margaret really minded, for it gave her a glimpse into squalor. To trust people is a luxury in which only the wealthy can indulge; the poor cannot afford it" (*HE* 36). This particular observation provides us with an insight into Margaret's own destiny; Margaret's precarious role in the household, as Helen grows "wilder," and Tibby begins to look toward attending Oxford, begins to affect the way she looks at the lower classes, a possible outlet for her maternal instincts. Margaret's conversations take on the language of the maternal as she manages her household—for instance, in her comparison of the Schlegel home to the new Wilcox establishment which takes the form of a dinner party—not simply feminine but maternal, in the sense of a female's orchestration in respect to domestic responsibility. She privileges this "feminine" home to the masculine as she refers to the residents, again, in the rhetoric of her father, as "inmates." Therefore, she understands that a woman's primary domestic duty protects the home from both crippling "effeminacy" *and* overpowering masculinity. This becomes, in essence, Margaret's goal in maintaining her "homefront" (45).

Given our cynical introduction to Mrs. Touchett through Ralph's conversation with Lord Warburton, we certainly understand that Gardencourt will never be mistaken for "a home," mainly because Mrs. Touchett does not regard her station as wife or mother as particularly self-defining. Isabel recognizes this absence almost immediately, and constructs a position within the Touchett household where she operates as the "lady" of the house. It is unlikely that the "something better" Mrs. Touchett has in mind for Isabel could be the reassignment of her own domestic duties, but marriage enters the conversation quickly when Mrs. Touchett speaks with Ralph about Isabel's goals. Of primary interest here is how Mrs. Touchett does not envision marriage as anything more than "a trick" played upon a woman, yet Ralph understands that his mother already has plans of her own for his ingenue cousin. Her accusation that Ralph, already, sees Isabel "as if she were a yard of calico" (*PL* 49), establishes the battlelines of this gendered warfare; obviously, James wishes us to see that men and women understand social responsibility through different methods that achieve similar ends.

Prior to Daniel Touchett's death, and her subsequent inheritance, Isabel declines invitations of marriage from two highly eligible bachelors, Lord Warburton, Ralph's friend and confidante, and Casper Goodwood, an enterprising American suitor from Isabel's past. She tells Warburton his offer represents a "great honor" to her immediate way of thinking, but, during a moment of solitary reflection, Isabel acknowledges that his offer will only limit her spirit: Marriage to the lord only represents further barriers toward her goal of "do[ing] something greater"—"something" nebulous at this point and time, but "something" which represents self-definition to her. Casper Goodwood catches Isabel off guard with his arrival from America, and her more assured refusal clearly substantiates her ideas that something more than marriage awaits her (*PL* 101-02, 139). These refusals validate Isabel's concern that marriage will limit her own aspirations toward another form of greatness.

Margaret has a similar attitude toward marriage, believing she will remain "an old maid" (*HE* 66) in her effort to combine her intellectual curiosity with her interest in social affairs. In her conversations with Helen, Margaret, in a fashion similar to Isabel, explains how marriage can empower women within the domestic sphere, while limiting the possibilities of women socially—outside the home. The narrator tells us that both women "cared deeply about politics, though not as politicians would have us care; they desired that public life should mirror whatever is good in the life within" (28)—a clear sign that women need control within the social sphere to replicate the "good" possible "within" the walls of one's home. She confirms this attitude, I believe, upon befriending Mrs. Wilcox, who embraces Margaret's attitudes about the female condition ideally, but ignores their impact on her own situation. In this initial conversation, Margaret's choice of the word "proportion" in respect to marital pleasure is important, as it relates not only to the relation of parts to a whole, but a desire to see those parts operate in a harmonious whole. Mrs. Wilcox does not reveal her wish to articulate the woman's purpose in such a well-reasoned manner, but Margaret assures her that she could pursue grander goals through maternal influence within the Wilcox establishment if she so desired (76). Both James and Forster delineate domestic goals for their heroines, with qualifications—this alteration in the domestic formula creates heroines who understand that domestic influence can reach beyond the hearth to larger social spheres.

Madame Merle and Mrs. Wilcox: Selective Surrogacy

Critical speculations abound as to why Isabel Archer agrees to marry Gilbert Osmond; almost as many question Margaret Schlegel's decision to wed Henry Wilcox.[7] My response suggests that the tradition of the domestic novel, in which the heroines *must marry* in order to fit the form, allows both James and Forster to concentrate on the marital conditions of ready-made families, and to bring the domestic novel into the realm of modern realism.

Isabel Archer's acceptance of Gilbert Osmond's proposal does not seem so large a mystery when contexualized in Isabel's attitude toward family, situated alongside her new acquaintance, Madame Merle, who actively selects Isabel—not only as a wife for Osmond—but as a surrogate mother to her own daughter, Pansy. Isabel's inheritance increases her value from an "interesting" person into an obtainable object. Madame Selena Merle arrives at Gardencourt, and openly represents to Isabel an ideal of modern femininity—a woman of the world who "does everything beautifully" (*PL* 155). Merle overtly selects Isabel to become the wife of Gilbert Osmond, her "partner" in the ultimate redefinition of Isabel's character. Upon meeting Merle, Isabel recognizes her not only as a "compatriot" (Merle's word, 152), but as a worldly role model, Merle, like Isabel, hailing from Brooklyn "born under the shadow of the national banner" (153). In their frequent talks, Merle shines in the eyes of the motherless Isabel; she actively takes part in the shaping of the recent heiress's assets. As Lyall Powers points out, the simple noting of Merle's hands throughout her scenes with Isabel reveal her as a consummate "manipulator" (39). As Merle continues befriending Isabel, the narrator shows how Merle functions as a maternal figure: "but she wandered, as by the wrong side of the wall of a private garden, round the enclosed talents, accomplishments, aptitudes of Madame Merle. She found herself desiring to emulate them" (165). No one, save Ralph, questions Isabel's emulation of her elder. It even seems that Mrs. Touchett, in a fit of wifely (and motherly) guilt, pushes the two toward each other. Ultimately, it is her elder's social polish and confidence Isabel desires to achieve, as Merle comes to represent a feminine ideal.

However, the narrator does not want us fooled by Merle's demeanor: "I may not count over all the links in the chain which led Isabel to think of Madame Merle's situation as aristocratic—a view of it never expressed in any reference made to it by that lady herself" (166). This rather lengthy narratorial aside calls attention to the paradoxical personality of the resident houseguest, revealing how Isabel might even suspect Merle's seamlessness (165). But, even with these dim reservations (note, Isabel does not see any problem with Merle's making domestic articles, even though she owns no permanent domestic establishment), Isabel "sees" Madame Merle as a complete woman—one who comfortably operates in all social situations—and one suited for emulation. Merle's many self-effacing comments as to her valueless position in society, and her lack of personal accomplishments, including "Neither husband, nor child, nor fortune, nor the traces of beauty that I never had" (173), help win Isabel's confidence. So much so that when Ralph tells his cousin, somewhat cynically, "Selena Merle hasn't a fault"—Isabel naturally replies, " If I didn't already like her very much that description might alarm me" (169).

Of course, Ruth Wilcox operates in a less covert, but fascinatingly similar way to Merle in her ensuring that Margaret becomes the surrogate mother of the Wilcox clan by leaving Howards End, her ancestral home, to her new acquaintance. Margaret appears to undergo two tests before Mrs. Wilcox's untimely death, which underscores Ruth's conscious acknowledgment of Margaret's suitability. In the first, Ruth tells Margaret about the "lore" of Howards End; she appears to consciously solicit an appropriate response from the genuinely interested Margaret (*HE* 74). The conversation here turns on Mrs. Wilcox asking Margaret not only if she would patronize such myth, but if she truly believes in its magic; Margaret's refreshing acknowledgment and sincere interest validate Ruth's first impression of Margaret—that she will act as a suitable surrogate mother. One receives the feeling here that Mrs. Wilcox has been loathe to find anyone interested in the familial legends of her people; Margaret's interest is a breath of fresh air.

After the fiasco of the Schlegel luncheon, Mrs. Wilcox invites Margaret to go Christmas shopping, a feminine bonding ritual which becomes the immediate precursor (in the text) to the bequeathal. As the scene opens, Margaret contemplates the blunder of the politically charged luncheon, fearing that she offended her new friend. So, when Ruth asks for assistance to beat the holiday traffic, Margaret quickly obliges. Margaret takes charge of the situation, attempting to organize the chaos of shopping randomly: " 'First of all,' began Margaret, 'we must make a list and tick off the people's names' " (83); the fact that Mrs. Wilcox admits to her lack of skill in shopping allows her to stand watch, so to speak, and observe Margaret in control. And, the fact that Margaret's name heads the list (according to Ruth's instructions) with "nothing written next to it" (84) highlights her giving nature—she would rather assist in the purchase of everyone else's presents, than help herself to something.[8] When Mrs. Wilcox points out their forgetfulness, Margaret makes the most of her naturally giving attitude—a selfless conversation that leads to another, concerning the impending destruction of Wickham Place, and the necessity for the Schlegels to find new lodgings; this imposed removal from their father's home worries Mrs. Wilcox: "To be parted from your house, your father's house—it oughtn't to be allowed. It is worse than dying" (86). Though Ruth's analogy strikes us, in hindsight, as an ideal instance of foreshadowing, it does not cause Margaret concern that Mrs. Wilcox likens moving to death because it affects Margaret in the same way—losing her father's home does preoccupy an inordinate amount of her time, and the fact that Helen and Tibby take no interest in relocating causes the burden to fall all the heavier upon the elder sister.

On the event of Isabel's "windfall" (*PL* 182), Madame Merle takes on the role of a catalyst, introducing the heiress to Gilbert Osmond, and sitting back to "witness" their nuptials; while orchestrating the match, Merle also consciously figures to place Isabel in a maternal light. For instance, the narrator crosses her consciousness prior to Mrs. Touchett's announcement of Isabel's wealth; we see here the calculating posture, suspecting Isabel played a hand in her "achievement" (181). This brief glimpse into the character of Merle underscores just how calculated her previous suggestion appears to be. For just before leaving Gardencourt (prior to Mr. Touchett's passing), she intrigues Isabel with an image of "Mr. Gilbert Osmond . . . who lives *tout betement* in Italy. No career, no name, no position, no fortune, no past, no future, no anything" (171-72). By now, Merle obviously understands that neither the rugged forceful-ness of Goodwood nor the patriarchal position of Warburton interests Isabel; she seems to play her "trump" casually by letting Isabel under-stand what Osmond can offer and what the others cannot (172). While this obviously intrigues Isabel, who quickly gives her consent to meeting this "excellent father," it begins to become apparent, even to the unen-lightened, that Madame Merle seeks someone to step in and "mother" her daughter, Pansy. In a further conversation with Isabel, she denigrates her position, which in turn, reveals just what might be missing from Pansy's upbringing: "What have my talents brought me? Nothing but the need of using them still, to get through the hours, the years, to cheat myself with some pretence of movement, of unconsciousness. As for my graces and memories the less said about them the better. You'll be my friend till you find a better use for your friendship" (173-74). Isabel brushes aside this pathetic (and prophetic) call for sympathy, and contin-ues to ignore the warning that Merle consciously selects her for the role of Pansy's mother—particularly when we later see that Merle is truly incapable of maintaining her own relationship with her daughter.

And it is Merle's inability to play the appropriate maternal role that springs the trap set by Osmond; however, it pleases Merle to maintain her delicate position on the sidelines, as she watches Isabel slowly bond with Gilbert and Pansy. After the introduction, Merle's conversations with Isabel, alone and in the presence of others, revolve around Osmond's parenting, and the place of Pansy in the order of the house-hold. For instance, Merle attempts to mother Pansy during their introduction: "'I hope they always see that you wear gloves,' she said in a moment. 'Little girls usually dislike them'" (203). But, later, after Osmond asks Isabel to check on Pansy as she passes through Florence, Madame Merle takes a form of jealous exception. This scene falls well after we understand Merle and Osmond's plans for Isabel, but when we look at it in hindsight, Merle's attitude seems curious, for once she establishes Isabel as surrogate, she begins to understand her own, now precarious, situation (266).

Gilbert Osmond and Henry Wilcox: Paramours of Patriarchy
One interesting point of comparison between these texts is the overall effect of marriage on the ideals of the heroines. Osmond is clearly James's idea of an antagonistic force in Isabel's life, a point readily recognized; however, Forster labels Henry Wilcox as his "hero" throughout the second half of *Howards End* (262)—indicating a positive position in Margaret's story—a point often ignored in critical judgments.[9] One significant similarity between this hero and antagonist lies in the fact that each spouse comes to represent the patriarchal society of Edwardian England; both Osmond and Wilcox create obstacles which seek to limit the heroines' idealistic effect as step-mothers within their new familial situations and, in essence, within their larger social spheres.

I have already speculated that Isabel Archer decides to wed the Florentine dilettante, Gilbert Osmond, because of what he possesses—the ready-made family in his daughter, Pansy. She is, after all, the one thing he contributes to their union, other than his status as an "original—original, as one might say by courtesy" (*PL* 224). The narrator records Isabel's initial reading of Osmond's character throughout these early meetings in a language which replicates her impressions, while it clues us into Osmond's "real" demeanor in pursuing the marriage (255). Here, the narrator qualifies Isabel's reaction in the past tense, as if Isabel herself were in the act of justifying what will come later; placing the last thought in the conditional specifies what Isabel does not appear to infer from her impressions. This is further understood in the narrator's initial description of Osmond's villa, "a long, rather blank-looking structure . . . the mask, not the face of a house [with] no eyes" (195), and in his initial detail of Osmond's appearance, qualified, again, so as to show Isabel's inability to recognize his prescriptive nature (197). Harkening a look of a sixteenth-century portrait, the narrator directly connects Osmond to the vestiges of traditional patriarchy. In a similar vein, the narrator's direct address to the reader reveals what Isabel cannot (or does not) decipher for herself. Therefore, we never judge Isabel in her decision to marry Osmond, as do her family and friends, because we understand precisely what she sees, even though the narrator proves Isabel's confidantes correct.

In a similar way, Forster presents Henry Wilcox through the speculation of Helen Schlegel, before employing his narrator, causing him gradually to become representative of his class-at-large. Our first glimpse comes from one of Helen's letters recounting a typical Wilcox evening at Howards End: "He says the most horrid things about women's suffrage so nicely, and when I said I believed in equality he just folded his arms and gave me such a setting down as I've never had" (*HE* 5). At another early point, Helen's insights position Henry at the center of his children's lives (24). These two early glimpses into Henry Wilcox's character reveal how he represents patriarchal order; his attitudes toward suffrage, and women in general, specify a purely middle-class trust in the status quo. Also, we can witness through Helen's impression that Henry actually galvinizes the familial bond—rather than the more maternal Ruth; in this light, we understand the middle-class ethic in respect to family responsibility—women operate in a pro-creative manner, leaving the grooming of the child, mentally and socially, to the father. This image solidifies the idea that the Wilcoxes not only represent but embody the middle-class Edwardian ethic.

Forster's narrator does not pause long over Henry Wilcox, as he does over other characters, forcing us to infer Henry's nature through his main concerns: his occupation, which coincides with his political and social attitudes, and through his conversation. Take, for instance, the scene where Margaret, Helen and Wilcox discuss the "fate" of the Schlegel protege, Leonard Bast. After attending an evening paper on the subject, "How ought I to dispose of my money?"—the reader professing to be a millionaire on the point of death, inclined to bequeath her fortune for the foundation of local art galleries, but open to conviction from other sources" (131)—the women pose the hypothetical to Mr. Wilcox. However, Henry's attitudes and actions compose his overall philosophy. Labeling Wilcox as a "man of business" at the outset of the conversation, the narrator reveals his singular priority; life having "no mysteries" shows how consciously and confidently Henry orchestrates his new existence. As the conversation continues, and Wilcox offers his off-hand advice that the Porphyrion Fire Insurance Company will be in "the receiver's hands before Christmas," he, again, reveals his confident worldliness to the Schlegel women—he claims to "advise nothing" but certainly urges the women to "let [their] young friend clear out . . . with all possible speed" (140). Henry's attitude toward both the poorer classes and the philanthropic nature of the middle-class remains superior and confidently fixed.

And, above reproach when his "hypotheticals" become the Schlegel's "responsibilities." During Leonard Bast's next visit to Margaret and Helen, as they urge him to leave his post, Leonard causes a scene, accusing them of meddling in his affairs; Wilcox's response to this is characteristic of his capitalist concern for maintaining the class structure: "I know the world and that type of man, and as soon as I entered the room I saw you had not been treating him properly. You must keep that type at a distance. Otherwise they forget themselves. Sad, but true. They aren't our sort, and one must face the fact" (151). Trading on Margaret and Helen's self-defined reputations as "emancipated" women (153), Henry sees their genuine concern as a parlor game; he positions himself to remain above their self-imposed stature.

So, again, we find ourselves wondering what it is the heroine sees in her prospective husband; Forster's narrator directly responds to this concern through Margaret's psyche. For instance, after Bast's outburst, and Henry's shirking of his involvement, Margaret pauses to contemplate the more worldly Wilcox: "A woman and two men—they had formed the magic triangle of sex, and the male was thrilled to jealousy, in case the female was attracted by another male. . . . It is jealousy, not love, that connects us with the farmyard intolerably, and calls up visions of two angry cocks and a complacent hen" (154). This reading of Henry Wilcox through Margaret lies at the heart of her reasons for, ultimately, accepting his proposal of marriage. Looking "back to the real man," Margaret sees what the former Mrs. Wilcox once saw—Henry has a distinct vulnerability in his position as extreme traditionalist; therefore, there *is* a reason for her prolonged interest, once invited. The extended analogy to "the farmyard" not only calls to mind the baser nature of males, but the rural upbringing of Mrs. Wilcox, and the rustic romanticism of Margaret—who both prove to be "earth-mothers" in contrast to the "civilized" exteriors of the class-based city.

This fascination intrigues Margaret as she contemplates Henry Wilcox's proposal of marriage. Margaret, immersed in the painful process of relocating the family home from Wickham Place, solicits Henry's assistance in finding a suitable home during a luncheon with him, Evie and her fiance. This scene reveals how Wilcox's traditionalism and Schlegel's humanism translate into marriage. While Margaret distresses over the lack of suitable housing, Henry pontificates on proper fare and the importance of adhering to standard rules of etiquette (158-59). Here, the prospective battlelines are drawn between the patriarchal foundations of Henry, preoccupied with not only preserving certain rules of thumb, but with appearing in complete control—right down to changing Margaret's order to one more suitable. This delicate balancing act initially attracts Margaret, as she appreciates the lure of Simpson's "old English" ambiance and the traditional posturing exhibited by the gallant Henry Wilcox. While the tipping of the carver seems a meaningless gesture of class, in one respect, it remains a subtle clue to Henry's attitude toward capitalism specifically, and gender roles, generally, as the male figure, here, maintains order.

So, after writing of his decision to let his Ducie Street "apartment," Margaret recognizes the invitation as the foundation for a prospective proposal. In traveling to town, Margaret realizes her "solitary and old-maidish" demeanor as she begins to face change—not only as her family experiences displacement from their family home, but from Tibby's attendance to Oxford, and Helen's desire to travel. Margaret, in acknowledging her inability to find comfort in familial change, sees that the "Wilcox" name represents a mediation of sorts—an excuse to set aside her philanthropic ideals to lend a feminine touch to the masculinized tradition. In reading Henry at the time of his proposal, she sees only possibility: "Some twenty years her senior, he preserved a gift that she supposed herself to have already lost—not youth's creative power, but its self-confidence and optimism" (169); her response suggests her momentary lapse in her own desires, as she again looks to see what she might offer the Wilcox name: "She had too much intuition to look at him as he struggled for possessions that money cannot buy. He desired comradeship and affection, but he feared them, and she, who had taught herself only to desire, and could have clothed the struggle with beauty, held back, and hesitated with him" (172). The fact that Margaret senses the spirit of Ruth Wilcox as "a welcome ghost" at this time (174), confirms for her the appropriateness of his request. Margaret ultimately agrees to marry Henry because she acknowledges her ability to mediate her desires, in a way similar to Isabel Archer—these women set aside their individualized goals to become the feminine, namely matriarchal, presence in the patriarchal conditions of their intended spouses; these marriages *will* offer challenges that each interpret as both necessary and exciting.

Osmonds and Wilcoxes: Maintaining Familial Control

The announcement of Isabel's engagement to Osmond meets with a backlash of criticism, similar in scope to that which follows the reading of Mrs. Wilcox's penciled message leaving Margaret Schlegel the mistress of Howards End. Both marriages create new family situations for the parties involved, introducing each to the concept of step-parenting. However, both Isabel and Margaret do not, at first, comprehend their role as step-mothers, allowing their husbands to continue their patriarchal rule over the hearth. It is only after each "family" reaches its crisis, which coincides with each heroine's personal self-awareness, that these women, rather than leaving their marriages, redefine their roles, transferring the real seat of power from the paternal to the maternal. Each novel illustrates how this transference not only reorganizes the familial community, but re-enforces its value within the capitalist super-structure.

Isabel's response to the wave of skepticism only solidifies her intention to wed Osmond. For instance, in her tête-à-tête with her cousin Ralph Touchett, Isabel clarifies her desires for this particular marriage, despite Ralph's warnings against the "sterile dilettante" (*PL* 292-93). We can see here Isabel's determination to marry Osmond on her own terms—central to her earlier idealized sense of self: "One has human feelings and needs, one has a heart in one's bosom, and one must marry a particular individual . . . Mr. Osmond's simply a very lonely, very cultivated and a very honest man—he's not a prodigious proprietor" (293). Isabel believes she will enter a partnership—a state of equal individualization she developed earlier from her reading.

In a walk through the Cascine prior to their nuptials, Osmond seemingly concurs with Isabel's reading of the marital state. The narrator shows us Osmond's desire to marry honestly and maturely—without the trappings of naive sensitivity: "Contentment, on his part, took no vulgar form; excitement, in the most self-conscious of men, was a kind of ecstacy of self-control. This disposition, however, made him an admirable lover; it gave him a constant view of the smitten and dedicated state" (295). Osmond even appears honest in his assessment of Isabel's fortune, and she recognizes this honesty as a positive regarding their new life together: "I won't pretend I'm sorry you're rich; I'm delighted. I delight in everything that's your's—whether it be money or virtue. . . . It has made me better, loving you; it has made me wiser and easier and—I won't pretend to deny—brighter and nicer and even stronger" (296-97). Stating his response to all the familial criticism in such a manner, Osmond gives Isabel the assurance she needs that their marriage establishes itself in a communal bond. With his clever analogy of reading against the light, Osmond allows Isabel to see herself as this lamp, creating a space where her creative desires will flourish in the very "light" she will bring to Osmond's household.

Of course, what Osmond really offers Isabel is the chance to become an "immediate" mother to his daughter, Pansy, who takes an instant liking to her new parent. At their first meeting, Pansy "had on a scant white dress, and her fair hair was neatly arranged in a net; she wore her small shoes tied sandal fashion about her ankles. . . . Even the little girl from the convent, who, in her prim white dress, with her small submissive face and her hands locked before her, stood as if she were about to partake of her first communion, even Mr. Osmond's diminutive daughter had a kind of finish that was not entirely artless" (218-19). Isabel's impressions, taking on a religious tone, quickly record Pansy as the true victim of patriarchal society, recognizing her objectified state will only serve to make a successful marriage. Pansy's own "sweetly provincial" attitude quickly idolizes Isabel (221), who in turn, begins to actively create a bond between them (238). Isabel's reading of Pansy reveals her desire to become the girl's mother, especially in hoping to influence the "edifying text" which might compose her "blank page"; she shows here, in the early stages of their relationship, more attention and care than toward any other relation, with the possible exception of Ralph Touchett, another in need of a mother-figure.

This bond not only becomes stronger after the marriage but it also becomes more intense as Pansy enters society. We witness the marital alteration of Isabel, while we sense a slight change in Pansy since reaching the age of 19—namely, her attraction to Ned Rosier, a young collector of Spanish lace and Dresden teacups, rather than to Lord Warburton, whom Osmond wishes to join with his daughter. To Isabel's way of thinking, "she was at present very thankful for Pansy. Pansy was dear to her, and there was nothing else in her life that had the rightness of the young creature's attachment or sweetness of her own clearness about it" (341). Here, the narrator calls attention to how primary this bond remains on behalf of both women; he also implies this bond capable of overthrowing the duplicity of Osmond. And, with this innuendo, the narrator peaks the interest of the reader, as we, perhaps cynically, begin to look for clues to witness how Isabel will triumph over her marital malaise.

A similar situation arises for Margaret, who finds she must also justify her decision to marry Henry Wilcox to her immediate family who fear that this particular marriage will compromise the individuality of the elder Schlegel. However, in conversing with Helen, Margaret almost appears to be convincing herself that she will not lose sight of that which composes her character (*HE* 181-83). This conversation reveals much in the way Margaret will conceive of her role within the marriage—and within the ready-made, established family. Being older, Margaret does not see this as a "romantic" marriage—but one of "prose"—she will not fool herself into thinking she can alter the elder Wilcox, or redesign the workings of their family; however, she does show she can effect the methods of the Wilcoxes through her quality of consciousness—walking into the situation with her eyes and ears open—the same method she employs to "peer into her past." In this way, Margaret's confidence rests in her ability to work within the boundaries Henry draws.

Margaret joins into a much more precarious relationship with her "family-to-be," mainly because of the Wilcoxes' suspicions stemming from their mother's death-bed bequeathal. The narrator carefully records the responses of Charles and Evie at the news: "Brother and sister were not callous . . . partly because they avoided the personal note in life. All Wilcoxes did" (96)—Charles is "vexed" initially; to his wife Dolly's request to read the note, "Little lumps appeared in front of either ear—a symptom that she had not yet learnt to respect"; Evie on the other hand, "was scowling like an angry boy" (101-02). This spoiled demeanor continues through the Wilcox/Schlegel engagement, and into their marriage. For instance, turning back to the scene at Simpson's, we can see that Evie seems far from comfortable with Margaret, having "scarcely addressed her" throughout the meal (163). And, much later, we become privy to Charles's thoughts after Margaret leaps from his moving motor-car to see about a wounded dog he hit, all on the way to his sister's wedding at Oniton: "Charles had never been in such a position before. It was woman in revolt who was hobbling away from him, and the sight was too strange to leave any room for anger. . . . That woman had a tongue. She would bring worse disgrace on his father before she had done with him" (222-26). Though Henry's children, Charles and Evie, are older than Pansy Osmond, Forster's narrator seems to delight in drawing them as petulant brats used to obtaining their way in moments of familial crisis. Neither child seeks to draw Margaret into the family, as neither finds the need of a mother figure. Therefore, it becomes much more central to Margaret's interaction with the Wilcox progeny to behave as a reasoned equal, rather than try to reforge a maternal bond. In this way, Margaret reserves her maternal attributes for Henry, and, ultimately, to the heir of Howards End, the son of her sister Helen.

In witnessing the significant alteration marriage makes in Isabel Osmond, the narrative underscores the simple maintenance in the spirit of Gilbert Osmond. In addition to the infamous depiction of Isabel "dressed in black velvet . . . framed in the gilded doorway . . . the picture of a gracious lady" (*PL* 309-10), we understand some rather serious events which contributed to this change, foremost among these the fact that Isabel "had a poor little boy, who died two years ago, six months after his birth" (305)—a point merely tossed off in conversation.[10] These singular changes in Isabel, who grows, gradually, more introspective as we approach her internal monologue of Chapter 42, highlight the more overt sterility of Osmond, as he begins to orchestrate his greatest score—to make his daughter Pansy "Lady Warburton." In soliciting the assistance of his wife to "woo" Warburton toward Pansy's availability, building upon Isabel's previous relationship with the Lord, Gilbert draws specific boundaries in which he expects his wife to operate. But, the sight of Osmond in conference with Madame Merle "in her bonnet" causes Isabel to rethink her role in his expectations (342-43). Actually, we see in this "flicker of light" that Osmond himself never really alters in his three-year marriage to Isabel—he still represents sheer duplicity—but Isabel's real alteration begins with her midnight vigil, where she "becomes," in essence, an advocate for her step-daughter, Pansy.

Both Margaret Wilcox and Isabel Osmond undergo a period of reflection which allows them to observe, in a more objective fashion, their place within this social order, and to speculate how they can rechannel their individual spirits in the face of the prescriptive roles designated them by their husbands. A close reading of Isabel's midnight vigil, which takes the form of an internal monologue, reveals much concerning this change that pervades her character. She begins by replaying Osmond's jealous ideal concerning the place of Warburton in her life; Osmond suggests that the unmarried Lord, who once pined for Isabel's affections, will marry Pansy with her assistance. In other words, Osmond wants Isabel to take a more traditional interest in her step-daughter by playing matchmaker, using her wiles to entice Warburton to such a proposition. She decides the request is "not an agreeable task; it was a repulsive one" (355). In this respect, she begins to fully realize Osmond's duplicitous nature, and how he actively seeks to manipulate her to behave in an equally shady manner. Isabel adopts an offensive language, now understanding the "rules" that Osmond outlines for her position in the matter of Pansy's prospects for marriage. Phrases such as "blight," "gulf," "either side a declaration" and "opposition" mark a significant change in Isabel's character, as she formalizes her own strategy for asserting domestic control.

This contemplation shifts as Isabel begins to understand her position within the marriage, and how Osmond used her innocence against her, limiting, in essence, the freedom she once felt so important. This gradual change engulfs her as she measures her options: "It was her deep distrust of her husband—this was what darkened the world. . . . Suffering, with Isabel, was an active condition; it was not a chill, a stupor, a dispair; it was a passion of thought, of speculation, of response to every pressure" (356). Isabel sees how Osmond restricted her involvement in creating a nurturing sense of family. The fact that she suffers through these reflective moments as she sits into the night provides her with the insight to see how Osmond controls the home environment—even to the point of "deliberately, almost malignantly" controlling the lights. This vision of his position of power, in essence, the man of the house, degenerates Isabel's ideas about the marital bond; destroying her ideals is his first step toward assimilating her into his idea of domesticity. Later, in an extended analogy, where she sees Gilbert as "a skeptical voyager strolling on the beach" (357-58), Isabel understands how commodification limits women of means within the patriarchal code: What proves interesting in this turn of logic is first, Isabel's drawing of the maritime analogy—seeing herself as some modern-day Queen Isabella, seduced, in a fashion, to bankroll the ultimate goal of Osmond's journey—to establish a more lucrative image of Pansy Osmond. Second, the fact that she initially undertook this "voyage" in a "maternal" frame of mind reminds us of Isabel's precarious maternal role—with her own son dead, Isabel remains only an "adopted" form of mother to Pansy—now, she is capable of behaving in a manner similar to her uncle, who provided the money which "put wind" in her sails.

This turn in Isabel's thinking permits her to assess her responsibility toward Pansy, and the recognition of how masterfully Osmond (and, in fact, Madame Merle) manipulated the situation. Isabel entered into the marriage with the understanding "that he had no superstitions, no dull limitations, no prejudices" concerning a more modern state of marriage "caring only for truth and knowledge and believing that two intelligent people ought to look for them together" (359); in hindsight, she now realizes she lives with Osmond's limitations, which built "the house of darkness, the house of dumbness, the house of suffocation" (360)—which now restricts her liberty. Because of this, Osmond's machinations seem all the more sinister. Isabel's recognition of Osmond's patriarchal motivations assists her in seeing that her only offense "as she ultimately perceived, was her having a mind of her own" (362)—an ability to "march" to the beat of her own drummer, in an effort to redefine her role as maternal power. She soon sees that her step-daughter Pansy will be the site of their ultimate battle.

Of course, the point of reflection Margaret undergoes comes prior to her marriage to Henry, during her orchestration of Evie's wedding at Oniton. At this point, Margaret sees herself as a bridge between the two worlds that compose her life, and a visit to Howards End on the way to Oniton causes her to reflect on her future position as the second Mrs. Wilcox: "She forgot the luggage and the motor-cars, and the hurrying men who know so much and connect so little. She recaptured the sense of space, which is the basis of all earthly beauty, and starting from Howards End, she attempted to realize England" (*HE* 213-14). This brief detour to Howards End serves as Margaret's first realization of her "connection" between these two familial factions, and, more symbolically, between the differing philosophical camps which constitute the British commonwealth. This only confirms Margaret's belief that she will, in marrying Henry Wilcox, serve a more profound purpose in the lives of her families and within society. She continues contemplating the wych-elm and its connection to the house itself: "It was neither warrior, nor lover, nor god; in none of these roles do the English excel. It was a comrade, bending over the house. . . . House and tree transcended any similes of sex. Margaret thought of them now, . . . but to compare either to man, or woman, always dwarfed the vision. Yet they kept within the limits of the human. Their message was not of eternity, but of hope on this side of the grave" (215). Margaret confirms the ideals she believes possible with her marriage into the Wilcox clan through her vision of pure connection. Margaret comes back to this vision of Howards End as a stabilizing agent: "Her only ally was the power of Home. The loss of Wickham Place had taught her more than its possession. Howards End had repeated the lesson" (232).[11]

And, the circumstances further test Margaret's fortitude shortly thereafter. During the reception, Helen arrives with Leonard and Jacky Bast in tow, there to confront Henry Wilcox with the fruits of his cavalier advice (which, inadvertently, led to Leonard's losing his job). It is at this time that Margaret realizes Henry proved unfaithful to his first wife with a mistress—Mrs. Bast. During the initial confrontation, Margaret reprimands her sister, calling her arrival "theatrical nonsense" (235), all the while trying to maintain order in the social proceedings, by getting Helen to remove the Basts to the local hotel, and by promising to approach Henry about the prospects of hiring Leonard in her own time. Margaret instantly sees the precarious nature of her diplomatic role: "She was ashamed of her own diplomacy. In dealing with a Wilcox, how tempting it was to lapse from comradeship, and to give him the kind of woman that he desired!. . . How wide the gulf between Henry as he was and Henry as Helen thought he ought to be! And she herself—hovering as usual between the two, now accepting men as they are, now yearning with her sister for Truth, Love and Truth—their warfare seems eternal" (239-41). Margaret's attitude here mirrors that of any step-parent caught between the two spheres of familial continuity; the use of the "diplomatic" imagery and words like "hovering" reflect the tenuous nature of her position, forced into taking a position, while fighting for the sake of the whole.

Of course, Henry's subsequent accusation concerning Margaret's role in bringing the Basts to Oniton fuels her moment of crisis and reflection, causing her consciously to examine her future. When Henry recognizes Jacky Bast, he imparts the secret of his infidelity and he, believing Margaret a part of the coup d'état, offers to "release" her from the engagement (243). Immediately, she decides, "it was not her tragedy: it was Mrs. Wilcox's" (244), but Chapter 28 leaves Margaret alone to fully contemplate her options—to plot her own "battle-plan" so to speak. The chapter opens with her foremost thoughts: "She was too bruised to speak to Henry; she could pity him, and even determine to marry him, but as yet all lay too deep in her heart for speech. On the surface the sense of his degradation was too strong. She could not command voice or look, and the gentle words that she forced out through her pen seemed to proceed from some other person" (251). While her words to Henry ring maternal, opening her note to him using "My dearest boy" as a salutation, her subsequent thoughts turn to the social situation which allows the double-standards to pervade the culture (251-52). Again, we can take note of the narrator's word choice in recording the thoughts of Margaret—words which further the notion that Margaret consciously measures her actions and weighs the ramifications for all sides prior to taking action. Her movement from her personal circumstances to the larger social questions is very similar to the course Isabel Archer's thoughts take during her vigil—not only are men accorded a privileged condition within the patriarchy, but woman's response, in order to be effective, needs to take more than just her immediate situation into consideration because the patriarchy draws the boundaries. She concedes that her actions against the Basts are "practical" in denying responsibility for their situation, but her response toward Henry, upon encountering him later in the kitchen, appears reserved, cautious in its hesitancy. She does not respond impulsively, but only after careful reflection (254). Some might argue that this cautiousness reveals Margaret's inability to realize fully the implications of Henry's infidelity; however, Margaret is not really a pseudo-philosopher—she is truly maternal. Margaret's reflection here acknowledges the real limitations of woman within Edwardian culture—her only two choices are to break off the engagement to Henry, or to accept the proposal, forgive the indiscretion, not simply forget it. Instead, she can consciously use her feminine sensibilities to effect a "make-over" for Wilcox, changing him from the imperialist entrepreneur to a man of deeper social conviction, "made better by love" in honor of "that unquiet and kindly ghost" which joins with Margaret's own conscience to forge a stronger maternal network.

Reconstructing Domestic Harmony in The Portrait of a Lady

These moments of introspection permit each heroine to further understand her precarious situation; and this clarity focuses the decisions both make in respect to their marriages and, most importantly, toward their familial obligations. Even before Amy Osmond Gemini confirms Isabel's suspicions concerning Osmond and Merle's relationship, Isabel positions herself for reconstructing order. Ultimately, we see Isabel assaulted on three different fronts in this battle royal, causing the plot to seem more Dickensian than realistic. Yet, it is in the face of this onslaught that Isabel truly triumphs as she seizes control in the midst of chaos.

James's decision to end *The Portrait of a Lady* with Isabel's return to Osmond continues to be a source of critical disagreement; however, those who question Isabel's course of action have not considered the novel's source—the formulaic domestic fiction.[12] To end the plot with a divorce, or, worse yet, with Isabel's becoming another Mrs. Touchett— an absent maternal force—denies the strength of her character, and her willingness to remain true to her original conviction. Her first course of action assures us that she is in control of her own situation. After Warburton's retreat from the disinterested Pansy Osmond, the child turns to Isabel for assistance in securing Osmond's blessing for Ned Rosier's proposal: " 'It's difficult for me to advise you,' Isabel returned . . . 'you must get his advice and, above all, you must act on it.' At this, Pansy dropped her eyes . . . 'I think I should like your advice better than papa's,' she presently remarked. 'That's not as it should be,' said Isabel coldly. 'I love you very much, but your father loves you better' " (PL 391). While some question this advice, Isabel, in order to maintain control, must remain above any suspicion Osmond will level. As Pansy continues to beg for her intervention "as if she were praying to a Madonna" (392), Isabel does sense some insincerity in denying her step-daughter— but Isabel recognizes that Pansy will only suffer more if she attempts to fight Osmond. Taking this avenue not only maintains Isabel's "self respect" (393), but strengthens her resolve ultimately to stand up to Osmond—and win control of the situation. Shortly thereafter, when Warburton takes his final leave of the Osmonds, Gilbert makes his final accusation against his wife; with her conscience free, Isabel can leave the room, with us, knowing she has not betrayed her husband, nor contributed to his prescriptive vision for his daughter.

It is after this episode that Isabel finds herself surrounded by her friends, all of whom wish her to walk away from her marriage. Yet, while this seems an easy solution to a rather complex problem, it is no option for Isabel. In a conversation with her confidante, Henrietta Stackpole, Isabel details her personal reasons for not leaving Osmond (407). This affirmation of the self is central to understanding Isabel's position within the context of the culture, and within the construct of her marital and familial responsibility. This is not a simple resignation to patriarchal power, but a calculated understanding of her cultural limitations. If Isabel wants to retain control of her domestic situation, she must remain constant to herself. This becomes, in fact, a tribute to her feminine nature, as it underscores the passion of her convictions.

Her first assault takes the form of restraining Madame Merle's influence within the home. When Isabel encounters Merle, who hopes to change Pansy's mind toward Lord Warburton, Isabel's confidence overpowers the visitor, who now believes she resorted to trickery in ending the child's interest. Merle questions how Isabel affects Pansy's mind and the images of battle reflect the urgency of Isabel's situation, and help underscore the confident nature of her plan of action (427-28). Isabel seems tuned into Merle's duplicity, and uses her newly empowered state to chip away the foundation of Merle's fragile position. It is this assuredness that later assists Isabel in graciously accepting the news her sister-in-law the Countess Gemini imparts: that Osmond's first wife died childless, and that Pansy is the daughter of Merle's indelicate affair with Osmond.

Yet, this confirmation of Merle's real stake in her masterful manipulation of Isabel's prospects does not completely unsettle Isabel because she comes to expect the worst; therefore, she establishes a carefully chosen course of action which assaults Merle instead. During their final meeting, which takes place at Pansy's convent school, Isabel feels "she had had absolutely nothing to say to Madame Merle" (457); and, as Merle pushes for recognition, it is Isabel's silence which unnerves her: "That Madame Merle had lost her pluck and saw before her the phantom of exposure—this in itself was a revenge, this in itself was almost the promise of a brighter day. . . . She left her there for a period that must have seemed long to this lady, who at last seated herself with a movement which was in itself a confession of helplessness" (458-59). Isabel controls the moment with quiet dignity as she later informs Merle of her intention to leave Italy to attend her dying cousin Ralph at Gardencourt, placing her in the light of victor. After seeing Pansy, Isabel returns to the parlor, finding that Merle remained to attend to her one last time. Isabel's conviction of her appropriate place within her household permits a confidence to translate authority. Taking control of the situation with a quiet dignity reveals the subtle form her maternal power takes as it seeks to reconstruct the equilibrium of the Osmond household.

The second assault comes in the form of Osmond himself; as the plot draws to a close, we witness only one significant scene between husband and wife, and it allows Isabel to display the real force of her newly realized empowerment. Isabel goes to his room to inform him of her decision to leave to attend to her ailing cousin: She finds Osmond "seated at the table near the window with a folio volume before him . . . open at a page of small coloured plates, and Isabel presently saw that he had been copying from it the drawing of an antique coin" (444). While this occupation may appear trivial at first, it reveals much about Osmond's inferiority concerning his position within the household. By copying the coin, Osmond concentrates on controlling transference; usually, he conducts this practice through people—first, Madame Merle, second, his daughter—Isabel continues to resist this objectification. Throughout their conversation, Isabel remains calm and resolute; in response to Gilbert's protest concerning her decision to leave, Isabel simply replies: "Why should I mind that? You won't like it if I don't. You like nothing I do or don't do" (445). The narrator's commentary focuses the reader on Isabel's mounting fortitude, and her resolve to succeed:

They were as perfectly apart in feeling as two disillusioned lovers had been; but they had never yet separated in act. Isabel had not changed; her old passion for justice still abode within her; and now, in the very thick of her sense of her husband's blasphemous sophistry, it began to throb to a tune which for a moment promised him the victory . . . "I know you're a master at the art of mockery," she said. "How can you speak of indissoluble union—how can you speak of being contented? Where's our union when you accuse me of falsity? Where's your contentment when you have nothing but hideous suspicion in your heart?"

"It is in our living decently together, in spite of such drawbacks."

"We don't live decently together!" cried Isabel. (446-47)

But, it is not enough to have the narrator assure us that Isabel remains conscious to Osmond's "blasphemous sophistry," but Isabel articulates the idea to Osmond that she is a "victim," not a "dupe" of his clumsy manipulation. Presenting the matter in this way gives Isabel the vantage point from which to fully confront her husband. As she threatens to defy him, the narrator qualifies his utterances with phrases which reflect his lack of assurance in matters of the house, highlighting Isabel's recognition that Osmond's attitude, remaining "deliberately indifferent yet most expressive," is key to understanding that Isabel maintains power within the context of the confrontation. With her subtle control, she not only lets Osmond know that she fully understands the degree of his falsity, but, with her abrupt exit from the room, she asserts a quiet authority. Isabel's leaving the home throws the order of the household into chaos, and we see here that Osmond has "lost" composure—control. The fact that Isabel leaves *and* returns on her own condition places not only the construction of the domestic in her hands, but places the future of it in her control as well.

I do not believe Isabel's final assault comes in the form of Casper Goodwood and his kiss "like white lightning" (489)—an act which might suggest a maddening ambiguity on James's part. Instead, my reading suggests that Isabel's final assault remains between herself and Pansy Osmond, and that Pansy is the real reason Isabel returns to Osmond at the novel's end.[13] Just prior to their final conversation, Osmond announces to Isabel that he sent Pansy back to Mother Catherine's convent. Again, Isabel's mental response shows her comprehension of Osmond's calculations: "She could only dimly perceive that he had more traditions than she supposed" (441). Osmond's justification of his actions underscores his patriarchal ideals concerning the place of a daughter—and, through innuendo, the place of a wife: Osmond reads the importance of his daughter's education in respect to "families"; he obviously recognizes that the traditional role of the convent is to re-enforce the prescriptive condition of woman within society as a whole. And, it is this aspect that causes Isabel to see "poor little Pansy" as "the heroine of a tragedy" (443). Isabel's momentary, silent reflection not only reveals her complete comprehension of Osmond's motives but also allows us to understand the fear she feels for Pansy, who cannot conceive of such objectification. Isabel also recognizes that the limitations of the convent will prohibit Pansy from ever seeing her father for what he is, and from realizing any individual potential.

I believe it is this recognition which ultimately pulls Isabel back to Rome after Ralph's death, as she realizes her own real potential as an assertive maternal force. Before leaving for England, Isabel visits Pansy at the convent; their private conversation provides evidence of Pansy's place in Isabel's most important decision. Though the scene is brief in comparison to others in the novel, it is, undoubtedly, one of James's most poignant interchanges between an adult and child. A narratorial aside helps render the emotions: "She [Pansy] made her reflexions, Isabel was sure; and she must have had a conviction that there were husbands and wives who were more intimate than that. But Pansy was not indiscreet even in thought; she would have little ventured to judge her gentle stepmother as to criticize her magnificent father" (461). This provides the only insight into Pansy's perspective, and it shows how her consciousness simply maintains the mold prescribed by Osmond's machinations. Isabel recognizes that Pansy is cognizant of their marital malaise, but it is Isabel—not Osmond—who figures highly in the child's developing mind. As Pansy reiterates the previous advice of her stepmother, recognizing the importance of obeying Osmond, Isabel responds with a bit of embarrassment: "Then as she heard her own words, a deep, pure blush came into her face. Isabel read the meaning of it; she saw the poor girl had been vanquished" (462). Isabel now realizes the central position within this familial situation—even though she is not Pansy's mother, she sees in the scene just how Pansy incorporates *her* advice—not Osmond's. As their conversation continues, Pansy looks "pleadingly" toward her step-mother, as she solicits the ultimate promise from her step-mother not to leave her (462-63). This last qualifier, "a voice that Isabel remembered afterwards," stays with us as we follow Isabel to Ralph's death-bed. Isabel concludes that her serving as a positive conduit is the very thing she has looked for throughout. While she marries Osmond to help someone without means realize their potential, she sees, for the first time, that the money is insignificant—the real effect lies in the change she witnesses in Pansy, and how the girl incorporates her own style, conviction—even rhetoric—into her maturation. This allows Isabel to leave Merle quietly after learning that Ralph was her real benefactor; and, it is this quality which allows her to forgive Ralph on his death-bed. In this simple exchange, Isabel understands the importance of maternal influence within the patriarchal household, and she returns to Rome to solidify this maternal empowerment within her familial community.

Reconstructing Domestic Harmony in Howards End

Similar to the mis-readings of Isabel's decision to return to Rome, discussions of Margaret's course of action focus not only on her "connection" to Howards End but also on her compromise in respect to her position at the novel's end. Again, these critics do not take the domestic tradition into consideration and it is with this ideal in mind that one can acknowledge Margaret's triumph over marriage, her newly reconstituted family, and herself.[14] Forster does not want us to see Margaret's situation as a tragic negotiation of her talents; he wants us to acknowledge Margaret's fortitude in her reconstruction of the Wilcox/Shlegel clan—to see this as her singular triumph.

Margaret and Henry marry shortly after her decision to forgive Henry's indiscretion, and their rather business-like wedding ceremony mirrors the conflict inherent in woman's changing role in society. For instance, while explaining Henry's attitude toward his nuptials, the narrator draws a parallel with Edwardian society, as women began to take a more active role in the world-at-large (*HE* 271). It is remarkable how Forster's narrator builds the extended image of the Wilcox marriage in a masculine language so characteristic of Henry's being. Here, the male appears to humor the woman for frolicking in the pleasure of books, and for playing at argument and social debate—but only if she remains willing to "clap the book up" when he calls. The image becomes metaphor, as man takes on the active role of "warrior," and woman assumes a passive role because she "cannot win the real battle." Herein lies Henry's central mistake, as *he* believes he controls the new familial situation in much the way he controlled his former life with Ruth; his willingness to allow his new wife "triumph" on occasion assures us of Henry's confidence in this world order.

However, the following spring, Dolly informs Margaret of a grave mistake: Mrs. Avery, the caretaker of Howards End, has unpacked the Schlegel furniture (sent there for storage), believing the newly married couple will soon reside there. This mistake causes a series of increasingly ominous events to occur, forcing Margaret into a more advantageous domestic role. As Margaret heads toward Howards End, she senses another force present—the narrator's voice blends with her own as her thoughts drift toward loftier concerns: "Why has not England a great mythology? Our folklore has never advanced beyond daintiness, . . . it has stopped with the witches and the fairies. England still waits for the supreme moment of her literature—for the great poet who shall voice her, or, better still, for the thousand little poets whose voices shall pass into our common talk" (279). It is significant that this curious inter-mingling occurs as Margaret approaches the house, as it recalls her earlier conversation with Ruth Wilcox concerning the "lore" of the country. As she wanders through the mistakenly unpacked house, furnished with her belongings, Margaret seems struck with how right everything feels, knowing full well Mrs. Avery's confusion involves more than the furniture: "In the house Margaret had wondered whether she quite distinguished the first wife from the second" (286). Ruth's ghost seems to guide Margaret through these crises indicative to step-parenting.

Margaret soon finds herself in the midst of the warring factions of her two family commitments; she soon realizes that she alone needs to work with both sides to bring them together. Helen abruptly decides to leave for Germany, which not only hurts Margaret, but causes Henry to voice an opinion of the wayward sister: "when it comes to a case like this, when there is a question of madness—" (297). Perhaps Henry only uses this to justify Helen's outburst at Evie's wedding, but his opinion hurts Margaret—assuring her that she must take action (298). Margaret's attitude dispels the notion that she passively resigns herself to a fate for her sister, prescribed not only by her patriarchal husband, but by Charles and a local doctor. Again, the language here takes on the metaphor of battle, Helen becoming the fox in a twisted hunt master-minded by the strategically placed patriarchal re-inforcements.

As they leave to attend Helen, Margaret becomes more and more irritated by the doctor's questions. She begins to formulate her own plan as she comes to understand the divisive nature of Henry's control—this, ultimately, gives her the upper hand in reconstructing familial security. Of course, the sight of the pregnant Helen, now the third maternal figure of the novel, only underscores Margaret's decision to support her. With her sister's interests at heart, Margaret finds the courage to implement her spontaneous battle-plan: "A new feeling came over her; she was fighting for women against men. She did not care about rights, but if men came into Howards End, it should be over her body" (303). Howards End, in this single sentence, truly becomes a maternal fortress defended by the Schlegel women, empowered by the spirit of Mrs. Wilcox, and even supported by Mrs. Avery and her niece.

Once Margaret sends Henry on his way back to Dolly's, she formulates another plan—one which will unite these families once and for all. As she and Helen stroll through the house, they are struck by how suited the dwelling is for their furniture; their talk becomes more "natural" (311), and Margaret continues to recognize the importance of not simply remaining a link between the two families, but bridging them somehow. It is in this respect that the epigram which opens the novel becomes Margaret's mantra: "Only connect . . ." not only refers to the practice of bridging the erudite classes to the land and lore of England—but refers to Margaret's ability to bring her family together under one roof—truly, she is not only mother to her own siblings, but to Henry and his tenacious clan. The act of connection becomes her method for re-establishing the harmony.

It is, however, another "connection" which, momentarily, brings tragedy to Howards End. Helen's arrival causes Henry to speak curtly to his wife as Margaret requests leave for the sisters to stay the night at the abandoned home: "Ducie Street is his house. This is ours. Our furniture, our sort of people coming to the door" (315). During their subsequent conversation, Henry's refusal not only insults Helen, but becomes the impetus for Margaret to wage her initial assault, not simply on Henry, but on the Edwardian code which permits the double standard against women (319-20). Margaret's request illustrates her natural ability to negotiate between two such diverse familial factions. Using her sister's emotional state as a basis, not as false justification, she appeals to the human quality she knows to be an implicit component of Henry's nature—an aspect she understands through his loving treatment of her during their marriage. Margaret does not expect this request to become a problem, but the narrator's qualifications of Henry's responses show us that his singular priority will separate the families, rather than bring them to some accord. It is Henry who involves Charles in the request, as "the future owner of Howards End," and Margaret appropriates his

entrepreneurial language to counter their masculine concern: "Will
Helen's condition depreciate the property?" (321). It is important to note
here that Margaret sees the request as the one way Henry can assist her
in bridging the needs of the Schlegel and Wilcox families; Henry's
denial and criticism shows her that he is not ready to redefine his patriarchal boundaries to create a *new* idea of familial order. He fights to maintain his hold on the order of *his* house—characteristic of the old order.
As the conversation rises to a climax, Margaret asserts her position by
employing a collective feminine power:

She was transfigured. "Not any more of this!" she cried. You shall see the connection if it kills you, Henry! You have had a mistress—I forgave you. My sister
has a lover—you drive her from the house. Do you see the connection? Stupid,
hypocritical, cruel—oh, contemptible!—a man who insults his wife when she's
alive and cants with her memory when she's dead. A man who ruins a woman
for his pleasure, and casts her off to ruin other men. And gives bad financial
advice, and then says he is not responsible. These, man, are you. You can't recognize them, because you cannot connect. (322-23)

Margaret's "transfiguration" underscores the feminine quality of her own
connection. Here, she defends not only her sister but also Mrs. Wilcox
and Mrs. Bast—defining both by their patriarchal tags—qualifying her
position as mediator. In addition, Margaret's use of the word "connection" shows her ability to see the entire picture—the patriarchal code's
double-standard—as opposed to simply those portions which validate
the masculine ideal. Obviously, Margaret does not understand the divisive nature of the request—only that the denial divides the families further.

The tragedy of the novel's catastrophic "muddle" primes Margaret
to solidify the connection which reconstitutes family order. Of course,
Margaret defends her sister by remaining with her through the night; and
Leonard Bast's arrival the next morning, and Charles's subsequent
manslaughter charge brought down once he beats Leonard with the
Schlegel family sword reminds us that patriarchal "order" easily
becomes patriarchal "disorder." Margaret appears shattered as Chapter
43 opens, but her reflection on the "causes and effects" which led
Charles to destroy one man for his own selfish gain causes her to recognize "hope" "on this side of the grave" as the inquest begins (345). Margaret's initial decision, to leave Henry, becomes moot as she contemplates not only the future of her family—but the future of her England:
"To what ultimate harmony we tend she did not know, but there seemed
a great chance that a child would be born into the world, to take the great

chances of beauty and adventure that the world offers" (345-46). What changes Margaret's mind is her connection—not simply to Henry—but to her new maternal presence. While she cynically sees that Henry "would grow into a rich, jolly old man, at times a little sentimental about women, but emptying his glass with anyone" (348), Margaret obviously still feels for him as she ponders his fate further: "But in time he must get too tired to move, and settle down. What next? The inevitable word. The release of the soul to its appropriate Heaven. Would they meet in it?" (348). When they later meet, sitting on the grass at Howards End, Margaret still resolves to accompany Helen to Germany; it is the witnessing of Henry's shattered being—the giving way of his "fortress"—which affirms Margaret's station, forcing her to take action: "She did not see that to break him was her only hope . . . he shambled up to Margaret afterwards and asked her to do what she could with him. She did what seemed easiest—she took him to Howards End (350). This removal represents a triumph of the maternal spirit, Mrs. Wilcox's ancestral home finally the home of the pater Wilcox, the present Mrs. Wilcox forging the connection between her new family and her own siblings. The last chapter, taking place fourteen months later, shows the outcome of Margaret's work—Helen's child now romping in the fields with the neighborly Tom, Margaret consoling Helen while taking care of the shell that once was her powerful husband. Even Margaret's philosophy, once simple rhetoric, becomes more honest as she reflects on the newly constituted order she polices. This singular reflection shows the selfless quality of Margaret in respect to the order she maintains. Again, place is the essential quantity in the familial equation, and Helen recognizes her sister's humility in her passing of the credit to God: "You did it all, sweetest, though you're too stupid to see. Living here was your plan—I wanted you; he wanted you; and everyone said it was impossible, but you knew" (354), but Margaret does not see this as extraordinary—only natural: "I did the obvious things. I had two invalids to nurse. Here was a house, ready furnished and empty. . . . No doubt I have done a little towards straightening the tangle, but things I can't phrase have helped me" (355). Forster closes the novel with Henry signing his will, leaving Howards End to his wife; the house becomes the site of a maternal empowerment which re-connects the two worlds of privileged England under the roof of a harmonious domesticity.

Margaret's maternal victory is not an emasculating one; her commitment to familial order mirrors Isabel's decision to return to her family responsibilities. In each case, the female protagonist wages war against the patriarchy to remain true to her single-minded roots, testing the false boundaries that prescribe female behavior within a masculine code of ethics. These women do not simply desire an individual quality—they desire familial community, a partnership where their actions account for the development and well-being of their families. Each woman triumphs in spite of the formulaic organization of the domestic novel as they become the center of a newly defined step-parenting tradition; however, as James and Forster detail the complexities of marriage, they reveal how women can assert a maternal power to reconstruct familial harmony where it did not previously exist.

Notes

1. According to Furbank, Forster re-examined his recent *A Room With a View* after this meeting with James, and realized that it "would gratify the home circle, but not those whose opinion I value most" (165). At this time, he felt it important to begin examining broader subjects of more universal importance.

2. James's *The Portrait of a Lady* was originally published in 1881; in 1909, in constructing his *New York Edition*, James heavily revised the text, creating, in the words of Nina Baym, "a new work": "The changes of 1908, transforming the story into a drama of consciousness, overlaid and in places obliterated the coherence of the 1881 version . . . the version of 1881 is a different work" (119-20). For purposes of my comparison, I have consciously selected the *1909 New York Edition* because of its proximity to the 1910 publication of *Howards End*; if Baym is correct in seeing the two "versions" as "different," we can further witness how the new *Portrait* embodies James's attitude toward the emerging social changes in the Edwardian world. All my subsequent references to James's *The Portrait of a Lady* are from this *1909 New York Edition* (labeled *PL* in my text); all my page references to Forster's *Howards End* are from the original 1910 edition (labeled *HE* in my text).

3. In making my argument, I refute Stuart Hutchinson's earlier claim that James's novel is best understood through a Victorian sensibility; reading Isabel as a proper Victorian lady leads to the many ambiguities that critics like Hutchinson use to construct artificial readings of Isabel's intent and character.

4. I purposely rely on Jefferson Hunter's revisionist reading of Edwardian society in his *Edwardian Fiction* (1982), rather than on more "established overviews," such as John Batchelor's *The Edwardian Novelists* (1982), which limits the Edwardian novelist to being British, and to writing solely about British concerns, namely in respect to imperialist capitalism. Hunter's new historic approach expands the parameters of Edwardian fiction to include American expatriots, such as Henry James.

5. Ash's most significant point in this respect concerns Mrs. Touchett's lack of maternal connection to Ralph Touchett, her son, and, consequently,

toward her husband. She suggests, as she goes on, however, that Mrs. Touchett is capable of "unconsciously" replacing Isabel's mother, and builds her argument, a bit unconvincingly, around Mrs. Touchett's desire to act in this capacity (128-29).

6. Douglas H. Thomson's deconstructionist reading of Margaret's rhetorical patterns successfully argues that Margaret must appropriate this discourse in order to maintain control within the context of the changing social system of Edwardian England.

7. In respect to Isabel's decision, see William Veeder's "The Portrait of a Lack," Annette Niemtzov's "Marriage and the New Woman in *The Portrait of a Lady*," and Alfred Habegger's "The Fatherless Heroine and the Filial Son: Deep Background for *The Portrait of a Lady*." Each of these articles uses a psychoanalysis to a degree in order to justify Isabel's decision to marry Osmond. In respect to Margaret's decision, Michael Levenson's "Liberalism and Symbolism in *Howards End*," Daniel Born's "Liberalism and Guilt," and Jeane N. Olson's "E. M. Forster's Prophetic Vision of the Modern Family in *Howards End*" employ new historist techniques in order to simply justify Forster's creation of plot. Each of these essays looks toward Forster's personal politics in order to establish a realistic basis for such a marriage.

8. Again, see Douglass H. Thomson's "From Words to Things: Margaret's Progress in *Howards End*" for a detailed reading of Margaret's rhetorical strategies.

9. As a matter of fact, Henry Wilcox himself figures very little in the collective criticism of *Howards End*. While there is much discussion of "The Wilcox Family" as such, Henry as a particular character takes a backseat to discussions of Mrs. Wilcox and Charles. Even a prescriptive reading of the novel, such as Alistair M. Duckworth's *Howards End: E. M. Forster's House of Fiction* relegates him to the background, a symbolic figure that serves to represent class and the mercantile ethics of society.

10. Not even "classic" readings of the novel touch upon the subject, including those of Leon Edel, Tony Tanner, or William H. Gass.

11. Alistair M. Duckworth provides a nice reading of the novel's epigram "Only connect . . ." as a method for reading the entire novel; his argument focuses on the idea that connection is the only way Forster could conceive of maintaining England's authority as a major world power.

12. For instance, Annette Niemtzov suggests that divorce was not an option for Isabel simply because it had no bearing in Henry James's upbringing. Her argument, "New Woman in *The Portrait of a Lady*" makes the case that James's heroine's morality is his morality; therefore, divorce cannot enter in the musings of Isabel. This sort of psychoanalysis seems rather reductive in comparison to one which focuses on cultural or gender role differences.

13. For an interesting reading of Isabel and Pansy's relationship, see Elizabeth Allen's "Objects of Value: Isabel and Her Influence."

14. Two such readings are Peter Hughes's "Mothers and Mystics: An Aspect of *Howards End* and *A Passage to India*" and Jeane N. Olson's "E. M. Forster's Prophetic Vision of the Modern Family in *Howards End.*"

Works Cited

Allen, Elizabeth. "Objects of Value: Isabel and Her Inheritance." *Henry James's The Portrait of a Lady.* Ed. Harold Bloom. New York: Chelsea House, 1987.

Ash, Beth Sharon. "Frail Vessels and Vast Designs: A Psychoanalytic Portrait of Isabel Archer." *New Essays on The Portrait of a Lady.* Ed. Joel Porte. New York: Cambridge UP, 1990.

Batchelor, John. *The Edwardian Novelists.* New York: St. Martin's, 1982.

Baym, Nina. "Revision and Thematic Change in *The Portrait of a Lady.*" *Major Literary Characters: Isabel Archer.* Ed. Harold Bloom. New York: Chelsea House, 1992.

——. *Woman's Fiction.* Ithaca: Cornell, 1978.

Beauman, Nicola. *E. M. Forster: A Biography.* New York: Alfred Knopf, 1993.

Born, Daniel, "Private Gardens, Public Swamps: Howards End and the Revaluation of Liberal Guilt." *Novel: A Forum on Fiction* 25.2 (Winter 1992): 141-59.

Douglas, Ann. *The Feminization of American Culture.* New York: Alfred Knopf, 1977.

Duckworth, Alistair M. *Howards End: E. M. Forster's House of Fiction.* New York: Twayne, 1992.

Edel, Leon. *Henry James: The Conquest of London, 1870-1881.* New York, Avon, 1962.

Forster, E. M. *Howards End.* New York: Random House, 1989.

Furbank, P. N. *E. M. Forster: A Life.* San Diego: Harcourt Brace, 1977.

Gass, William H. "The High Brutality of Good Intentions." *The Portrait of a Lady.* Ed. Robert D. Bramberg. New York: Norton, 1975.

Habegger, Alfred. *Henry James and the "Woman Business."* Cambridge: Cambridge UP, 1989.

Hughes, Peter. "Mothers and Mystics: An Aspect of *Howards End* and *A Passage to India.*" *Modes of Interpretation: Essays Presented to Ernst Leisi.* Ed. Richard J. Watts and Urs Weidmann. Tubingen, Germany: Narr, 1984.

Hunter, Jefferson. *Edwardian Fiction.* Cambridge, MA: Harvard, 1982.

Hutchinson, Stuart. *Henry James: An American as Modernist.* Totowa, NJ: Barnes and Noble, 1982.

James, Henry. *The Portrait of a Lady*. New York. Norton, 1975.

Levenson, Michael. "Liberalism and Symbolism in *Howards End.*" *Papers on Language and Literature* 21.3 (Summer 1985): 295-316.

Niemtzow, Annette. "Marriage and the New Woman in *The Portrait of a Lady.*" *On Henry James: The Best from American Literature*. Ed. Louis J. Budd and Edwin H. Cady. Durham: Duke UP, 1990.

Olson, Jeane N. "E. M. Forster's Prophetic Vision of the Modern Family in *Howards End.*" *Texas Studies in Literature and Language* 35.3 (Fall 1993): 347-62.

Powers, Lyall H. *The Portrait of a Lady: Maiden, Woman, and Heroine*. Boston: G. K. Hall, 1991.

Tanner, Tony. "The Fearful Self in *Major Literary Characters: Isabel Archer*. Ed. Harold Bloom. New York: Chelsea House, 1992.

Thomson, Douglass H. "From Words to Things: Margaret's Progress in *Howards End.*" *Studies in the Novel* 15.2 (Summer 1983): 122-34.

Veeder, William. "The Portrait of a Lack." *New Essays on The Portrait of a Lady*. Ed. Joel Porte. Cambridge: Cambridge UP, 1990.

7

Virginia Woolf's Dialogues with the "New Woman"

Wendy Perkins

During the first few decades of the twentieth century, feminist thinkers engaged in a rigorous investigation of female identity as it related to all aspects of a woman's life. A dialogue resulted among these women that incorporated radical as well as conservative points of view. For example, at the fin-de-siècle, novelist Mona Caird declared the institution of marriage to be a form of slavery and thus recommended its abolition. This period's other radical feminists, notes Gail Cunningham in *The New Woman and the Victorian Novel* (1978), "jeered openly at the ideal of the maternal instinct," rejecting the notion that motherhood should be the ultimate goal of all women. They also deemed the family, "long regarded as a microcosm of the state, if not of the divine order . . . , [to be] a nest of seething frustrations, discontent, and deception" (2-3).

The Saturday Review offered a less caustic view of maternity in an 1895 article entitled "The Maternal Instinct":

The only woman at the present time who is willing to be regarded as a mere breeding machine is she who lacks the wit to adopt any other role. . . . The only good mother is one prepared to limit her breeding capacity, one who has more to offer her child than an endless succession of siblings and a vapid ideal of maternal devotion. (qtd. in Cunningham 13)

The more conservative feminists of this age considered marriage and motherhood acceptable roles only if guidelines were set in order to prevent a woman from assuming an inferior position to her husband in any area of their life together. A woman granted equality in marriage would serve as an exemplary role model for her children by encouraging the development of an independent spirit.

Of course, dialogues also developed between the New Woman[1] and those opposed to her, and these tended to be much more vitriolic. Lynn Linton, a vocal opponent of the feminist thinkers—especially Mona Caird—supported the intention-of-nature argument, insisting that "the

149

raison d'etre of a woman is maternity. For this and this alone, nature has differentiated her from man, and built her up cell by cell and organ by organ" (79). Caird responded by wondering how, if a woman's sole function is maternity, she can be differentiated from a cow or a sheep (Fernando 3).

Virginia Woolf's works enter into this dialogue, as they illuminate contradictory visions of women—visions that were at the heart of debates between many of Woolf's contemporaries. *Mrs. Dalloway* (1925) expands traditional subject matter to accommodate the study not only of the marital union but also of the bonds that can arise between women. *Orlando* (1928) playfully deconstructs accepted notions of gender identification and roles as it traces the hero's development through four centuries, including his transformation into a woman.

Anti-feminist attitudes arise in the characterizations of Evelyn Murgatroyd in *The Voyage Out* (1915), Mrs. Seal in *Night and Day* (1919), Julia Hedge in *Jacob's Room* (1922), and Miss Kilman in *Mrs. Dalloway*—all suggesting how blind devotion to a cause can produce callousness and narrow minds. In *Three Guineas* (1938), Woolf rejects "Feminism" because it causes men to reassert their dominance and thus interferes with "men and women working together for the same cause" (102). In *A Room of One's Own* she explains that cause to be "the union of man and woman"[2] which "makes for the greatest satisfaction, the most complete happiness" (98).

The multiple voices and attitudes toward female identity that emerge in Woolf's work result from her own ambiguous attitude toward male and female relationships. While she remained committed to the struggle for women's rights, she was reluctant to sever her ties completely with the Victorian age and its promotion of marriage and family.[3] Woolf considered herself to be one of the "explorers, revolutionists, reformers" of her generation, yet admitted "the cruel thing was that while we could see the future, we were completely in the power of the past" (*Moments* 126-27).

Woolf's rejection of accepted roles for men and women clashed with her reverence for family life which sprung from her own childhood memories. In *Feminism and Art* (1968), Herbert Marder concludes that she viewed marriage "from two essentially different points of view, describing it, in an intensely critical spirit, as a patriarchal institution, but also expressing a visionary ideal of marriage as the ultimate relation." Thus marriage became for her a state of oppression as well as "a profound symbol of community" (53).

This epistemological ambivalence becomes the complex subject matter of *To the Lighthouse* as the intricate narrative illuminates fragmentary and contradictory images of female identity. Throughout the novel, Lily Briscoe strives to define Mrs. Ramsay and her relation to her world and thus to define herself. Lily's internal explorations give rise to dialogues on several levels: between Lily and Mrs. Ramsay, between the text and Woolf's contemporaries, and between the text and its readers— all of us engaged in the process of discovery. Woolf's chaptering in *To the Lighthouse* frames aspects of these oppositional discourses on marriage and motherhood, suggesting the difficulties inherent in a woman's quest for an authentic self.

Lily struggles to achieve a concrete vision, to find the essential nature of Mrs. Ramsay and to represent on canvas her roles as wife and mother. Lily's task is complicated, though, by the shifting personal and cultural lenses through which her gaze is filtered—lenses that delineate Lily's own varied roles as artist, spinster, friend, and surrogate daughter. The tension among these multiple perspectives leads Lily to admit, in frustration, that "one wanted fifty pair of eyes to see with. . . . Fifty pair of eyes were not enough to get round that one woman with" (198). These diverse points of view create a fragmented narrative that becomes Woolf's critique of representation and of any absolute vision of female identity.

Book 1 centers on particular moments during one day in the life of the Ramsays, their children, and their guests as they gather together at the Ramsays' summer home. Woolf focuses here on the enigmatic Mrs. Ramsay, of whom we catch glimpses through the other characters' points of view. In Book 2 these fragmentary but powerful impressions of Mrs. Ramsay are deconstructed as we view the slow decay over time of the Ramsay summer home. In Book 3 Lily tries to recreate in her memory the moments sketched in Book 1 as she struggles to complete her painting.

Woolf structures the nineteen chapters in Book 1, "The Window," around two central moments: the Ramsays' discussion of the trip to the Lighthouse and the dinner party that evening. In the first five chapters, which center on the discussion, she discards traditional linear structure in favor of a unique spatial design that propels the narrative not by means of developing action but through rhythmic currents of reflection centered around a single brief moment of dialogue.

Double frames focus added attention on Mrs. Ramsay in these chapters: the window frames her as she sits in front of it with her son James playing beside her, and Lily's canvas frames the scene in the window as she attempts to capture Mrs. Ramsay's essence. Moreover, each of the first five chapters, with the exception of Chapter 4, begins with a line of dialogue about whether they will be able to take a trip to the

Lighthouse the next day. Woolf employs these techniques to explore the implications of this seemingly unimportant conversation. The significance of this moment becomes clear as Lily observes the interactions among Mrs. Ramsay, Mr. Ramsay, Charles Tansley, and her son James—interactions that define her various roles as a woman. The exploration of a moment in these first five chapters initiates the question "how do we know others?"—one that is inextricably linked to questions asking how we know ourselves. Woolf makes it Lily's task in *To the Lighthouse* to try to provide us with answers.

Throughout the five chapters, Woolf scatters fragments refracting the moment of dialogue, each heralding shifting and sometimes contradictory visions of Mrs. Ramsay's conduct with her family, house guests, and community. Thus the dialogue becomes a trope for the complex nature of Mrs. Ramsay.

Chapter 1 presents fragments of all of the various visions of Mrs. Ramsay that will be repeated throughout the novel. In this chapter we see her as a nurturer, a protector, a creator, a manipulator, a rebel, and a conformist. The various reflections on the nature of Mrs. Ramsay, marked by lines of dialogue, create an ambiguous portrait that establishes the narrative pattern of the first five chapters as well as the thematic thrust of the entire novel.

Chapter 1 contains the following portions of the dialogue that will trigger each new vision:

"Yes, of course, if it's fine to-morrow," said Mrs. Ramsay. (7)

"But," said his father, stopping in front of the drawing-room window, "it won't be fine." (8)

"But it may be fine—I expect it will be fine," said Mrs. Ramsay. (8)

"It's due west," said the atheist Tansley. . . . "There'll be no landing at the Lighthouse tomorrow." (9, 10)

Woolf exploits the natural stress points at the beginning and end of a chapter, framing Chapter 1 with a traditionally "feminine" image—Mrs. Ramsay's nurture of her family and her community. The first line of dialogue opens the chapter as Mrs. Ramsay sits in front of the window, framed in the domestic scene. "Yes, of course, if it's fine tomorrow" is her response to her son's fervent desire that they will be able to make the trip to the Lighthouse. James's reaction, which creates for us a strong opening impression of his mother, immediately follows her statement:

To her son these words conveyed an extraordinary joy, as if it were settled, the expedition were bound to take place, and the wonder to which he had looked forward, for years and years it seemed, was, after a night's darkness and a day's sail, within touch. (7)

Mr. Ramsay's insistence that the bad weather will cause them to cancel their plans produces another response from James, who considers his mother to be "ten thousand times better in every way" than his father (8). Woolf makes rapid shifts in point of view in this scene and throughout the novel between the characters and an omniscient narrator who often appears to echo their sympathies. Thus her narrator succeeds in dramatizing the inner processes of her characters' responses to family tensions.

Here, at the beginning of chapter 1, the narrator champions James's critical view of his father, who grins "sarcastically" after "disillusioning his son and casting ridicule upon his wife." The narrator also points out in a narrative digression Mr. Ramsay's obsessive devotion to the truth and his "secret conceit at his own accuracy of judgement" (8). This obvious contrast between Mr. and Mrs. Ramsay helps to reinforce James's more positive view of his mother.

Mrs. Ramsay's counter-declaration that the weather might very well be suitable sustains the impression of her nurturing role, but introduces a note of independence as she offers a slight challenge to her husband. Her reply also suggests her desire to maintain control of this hopeful moment with her son. All of these perceptions of Mrs. Ramsay are reinforced by the reflections that follow this scene. Her continuing knitting of the stocking for the Lighthouse keeper's tubercular son presents another challenge to her husband's prediction, as well as an example of her care for the welfare of her community. A hint of her desire to control appears at the end of this passage as an admonition to her daughters, made at some indeterminate moment in the past, to remember their duties to those less fortunate. Mrs. Ramsay's attempts at the manipulation of the lives of her family and guests will be sketched more fully in succeeding chapters.

The dialogue itself illustrates the difficulties in arriving at any definitive statement about her nature. Her words present her as a nurturer who exhibits the independence and confidence necessary to stand up to her husband's negativity and devotion to the facts in order to support and encourage her child's hopes. Yet her language also suggests her ultimate deference to her husband.

In Chapter 1, as well as in succeeding chapters, Mrs. Ramsay speaks less assertively than does her husband, especially when she hedges her statements with vague qualifiers so as not to challenge him directly. For example, she qualifies her statement about going to the Lighthouse when she says, "*if* it's fine tomorrow." Then her husband's negative assertion prompts her to disclaim certainty about the weather: "But it *may* be fine—I *expect* it will be fine."

The dialogue in Chapter 1 presents readers with an epistemological conundrum, thus charting the thematic direction of the novel. On the one hand, we could interpret Mrs. Ramsay's choice of words here as a reflection of her strength: even though Mr. Ramsay becomes enraged at what he considers to be her irrationality, she appears to know exactly what effect her words will have on her son. Thus, we could conclude, she hedges to prevent James's disappointment, not because she is unsure about predicting weather conditions. If, however, we consider further examples in this chapter of Mrs. Ramsay's promotion of conventional roles for women, we could consider her language to be inspired by a desire to assuage her husband and to nurse his formidable self-regard.

The reflections that follow Mrs. Ramsay's response in Chapter 1 ("But it *may* be fine—I *expect* it will be fine") support this contradictory image of independence and deference. Here she shows her altruism toward her community when she stresses the importance of offering comfort to the poor. Yet by encouraging this quality in her daughters and not in her sons, she will help create another generation of women whose main function becomes attendance to the needs of others.

The next lines of dialogue in this chapter are offered by Charles Tansley in support of his colleague, Mr. Ramsay: "It's due west. . . . There'll be no landing at the Lighthouse tomorrow." Tansley's statement reinforces but slightly alters the expression of deference. Woolf does not have Mrs. Ramsay contradict this second challenge to her position at this point, suggesting instead that a period of silence follows Tansley's presumptuous remarks. Moreover, she breaks up Tansley's portion of the dialogue with Mrs. Ramsay's and her family's contradictory responses to him, offered either internally or beyond earshot.

After Tansley insists that the wind's direction would prevent their landing at the Lighthouse, Mrs. Ramsay thinks him odious for contributing to James's dashed hopes. Yet as she muses about his character, she reveals past incidents in which she forbade her children to criticize him. She envisions herself as a protector of the male sex, ultimately because of their benign attitude toward her, "which no woman could fail to feel or to find agreeable, something trustful, childlike, reverential" (9). Here, as her urge to defer becomes entwined with a desire for power, she becomes a Magna Mater figure.

This complex image of Mrs. Ramsay infuses the next digression in Chapter 1, as her attention suddenly shifts to her daughters' hopes for a different life than hers—"not always taking care of some man or other."

When she characterizes their "mute questioning of the deference and chivalry . . . of ringed fingers and lace" as "infidel ideas," we are reminded of her previous insistence that only her daughters should continue her devotion to the needs of others (10).

Chapter 1 ends, however, as it begins—with an image of Mrs. Ramsay as selfless nurturer. Tansley's insistence that "[t]here'll be no landing at the Lighthouse" the next day and Mrs. Ramsay's continued silence signal the last section of this chapter with its focus on Mrs. Ramsay's memory of a trip she made one afternoon with Tansley to town. Her attention to this awkward and insecure man's needs had prompted an invitation to accompany her on a charitable visit to an ill woman. During the trip, her charity clearly extends to Tansley as well. As the point of view in this flashback shifts between the two, one vision of Mrs. Ramsay emerges—her unselfish attention to others. Even though she often considers Tansley to be "an insufferable bore," she "flatter[s]" his intellectual abilities during their walk to town and thus "sooth[es]" and "revives" him (13). After she encourages him to speak about his impoverished childhood, she pities him, deciding to redouble her efforts to "see to it that [her children] didn't laugh at him any more" (14).

The chapter's final paragraphs are given over to Tansley, as he watches Mrs. Ramsay administer to the poor. We gain our last impression of her in this chapter through Tansley, who is overcome with "an extraordinary pride" while gazing at her standing framed by a portrait of Queen Victoria—the symbol of traditional Victorian womanhood (16).

Chapter 2 deconstructs the closure achieved in the previous chapter in its few short lines—Tansley's declaration, "No going to the Lighthouse, James" followed by Mrs. Ramsay's interior reply, "Odious little man." When Woolf shaped Chapter 2 around this portion of the dialogue, she reinforced the ambiguous nature of Mrs. Ramsay and underscored the social pressures on her behavior. The unique construction of this chapter serves as an example of Bakhtin's theory that no single voice exists in narrative. In "Toward a Feminist Narratology," Susan Lanser applies this theory to women's writing which, she argues, often contains a public, "socially acceptable" voice and a private, "rebellious and individual" voice. She explains that "the condition of being a woman in a male-dominant society may well necessitate the double voice, whether as conscious subterfuge or as tragic dispossession of the self" (349).

Mrs. Ramsay's "double voice" in this chapter provides a complex example of both motives. Her public voice—her silence—reveals a dispossession of her self when she refuses to respond directly to Tansley's contradiction of her position and his dashing of James's hopes. Her private voice—her internal declaration of Tansley's odiousness—presents a conscious subterfuge of his domination. This double voice produces a dialectic between an external view of reality, where conventional assumptions of appearance remain intact, and an internal view, where those conventions are deconstructed. The lack of closure at the end of this chapter, which results from the ironic and dramatic juxtaposition of contrasting points of view, prevents us from attaining any absolute vision of Mrs. Ramsay.[4]

In Chapter 3, Woolf finally allows Mrs. Ramsay a response, but it is directed toward James rather than Tansley. As she smoothes her son's hair, she tells him, "Perhaps you will wake up and find the sun shining and the birds singing." A few lines later she reiterates, "Perhaps it will be fine to-morrow," as she continues to pat his head affectionately (17). By opening this chapter with Mrs. Ramsay's attempt to repair the damage done by her husband and his colleague, Woolf reinforces her protagonist's traditional role as nurturer/protector.

Woolf soon overturns this image of Mrs. Ramsay, however, when she suggests that Mrs. Ramsay's support will not last. As she sits in the window with James at her side, she hears "the monotonous fall of the waves on the beach," which "beat a measured and soothing tattoo to her thoughts and seemed consolingly to repeat over and over again as she sat with the children the words of some old cradle song, murmured by nature, 'I am guarding you—I am your support.'" At other times, however, "suddenly and unexpectedly" the waves "had no such kindly meaning, but like a ghostly roll of drums remorselessly beat the measure of life, made one think of the destruction of the island and its engulfment in the sea, and warned her whose day had slipped past in one quick doing after another that it was all ephemeral as a rainbow" (17). Here Woolf alludes to Mrs. Ramsay's death and the ephemeral nature of her moments of nurture, which will become the focal point of the novel's last two Books.

Often the chapters in *To the Lighthouse* are shaped around moments which reveal Mrs. Ramsay's attempts to control and imbue the events in the lives of her family and friends with her integrating vision. This vision usually involves the protection of others from her husband's uncompromising empiricism. She creates consoling fictions, as when she suggests the weather will be fine the next day, or drapes her shawl over the skull in the children's room to allay their fears, or envisions the happiness of a young couple she has helped propel towards marriage. In these instances we gain a clear image of her as nurturer/protector; but the moments, like the image, prove transitory. She will not be able to protect her children or herself from life's harsh realities—a fact that becomes the poetic subject of "Time Passes." Moreover, a close examination of Mrs. Ramsay's creation of perfect moments reveals her often destructive manipulation of others—a point Woolf illustrates through her careful shaping of the dinner-party scene at the end of "The Window."

Chapter 3 ends with the introduction of Lily, whom Woolf presents at this point in the narrative to help readers with the difficult task of reconciling the contradictory visions of Mrs. Ramsay presented in the first three chapters. Yet Lily's own struggles to capture Mrs. Ramsay's elusive nature ultimately deconstruct any expectations we may have of epistemological certainty.

Mrs. Ramsay's description of Lily, which reveals more about herself than her friend, closes Chapter 3: "With her little Chinese eyes and her puckered-up face, she would never marry; one could not take her painting very seriously; she was an independent little creature, and Mrs. Ramsay liked her for it" (18). Mrs. Ramsay's thoughts here act as a summary of the various images we have previously glimpsed of her: her support and promotion of traditional roles for women as well as her appreciation of rebelliousness. The chapter's last line—"so remembering her promise [to keep her head in the same position as Lily paints her], she bent her head"—reframes Mrs. Ramsay in the window and on Lily's canvas, thus refocusing our attention back onto her.[5]

Woolf gives Chapter 4 to Lily, as the artist attempts to recreate her friend on canvas. Here Lily begins her task of interpreting Mrs. Ramsay. Yet as she struggles to explain Mrs. Ramsay's devotion to traditional roles, she also examines her own departures from them.

Chapter 4 opens with Mr. Ramsay almost knocking over Lily's easel as he strides around the yard, reciting lines of poetry. This action symbolizes his and his wife's rejection of nontraditional roles for women and Lily's struggle against these forces in her quest to discover her own identity. Lily's insecurity about her artistic abilities surfaces as she tries to keep all eyes except William Bankes's away from her painting. As long as Mr. Ramsay "kept like that, waving, shouting, she was safe; he would not stand still and look at her picture. And that was what Lily Briscoe could not have endured." Even while she concentrates on her painting, "she kept a feeler on her surroundings lest some one should creep up, and suddenly she should find her picture looked at" (18-19). The unobtrusive Bankes, another of the Ramsays' guests, represents a second way Lily may choose to define herself—through marriage and family.

Like Edith Wharton's *The Age of Innocence*, *To the Lighthouse* expresses the dual forces of nostalgia for a Victorian past and the rebellious, revolutionary spirit of the modern age. The first three chapters have revealed the complex reality of a woman's role as wife and mother, especially during the transitional fin-de-siècle, a time when marriage not only defines a woman but often confines her as well. Elsewhere, Woolf acknowledged the limited role of motherhood and suggested how difficult it is for mothers to establish a sense of self:

Often nothing tangible remains of a woman's day. The food that has been cooked is eaten; the children that have been nursed have gone out into the world. Where does the accent fall? What is the salient point for the novelist to seize upon? It is difficult to say. [A woman's] life has an anonymous character which is baffling and puzzling in the extreme. ("Women and Fiction" 146)

Here she shows how Lily's quest for self-discovery is complicated by her shifting images of Mrs. Ramsay—images that sometimes attract and sometimes repel her. She notes the fatigue that results from the duties of wife and mother: the constant attention to meals, errands, repairs, and all the trivial and wearing tasks involved in running a household. She has observed Mrs. Ramsay's selfless devotion to the needs of others, the sublimation of her desires, and her deference to her husband. Indeed, she thinks to herself, "there was scarcely a shell of [Mrs. Ramsay] left for her to know herself by; all was so lavished and spent" (35). Yet Lily has also observed Mrs. Ramsay's loving connection to her family and the transcendent force of her female energy, creating moments of unity that express the beauty and value of life.

Woolf reinforces her vision of the problematic nature of knowing as presented in the first three chapters by extending Lily's gaze in Chapter 4 to other objects in her field of vision. Acquiescing to Bankes's suggestion, she leaves her work to join him in a walk. As Lily gazes at the surrounding scene, she observes objects through her own unique point of view. Yet, since her visions are only transitory, she has difficulty recreating the object of her gaze on canvas: "Such she often felt herself—struggling against terrific odds to maintain her courage; to say: 'But this is what I see; this is what I see,' and so to clasp some miserable remnant of her vision to her breast, which a thousand forces did their best to pluck from her" (20).

Lily then shifts her attention to Mr. Ramsay and Bankes—two figures that represent the world of marriage and family to her. Lily's perceptions of Mr. Ramsay vacillate between visions of his disruptive eccentricities and his tiresome demand for sympathy, and his "fiery unworldliness," his seriousness, and his "sincere love of dogs and children." Her views of Bankes shift in a similar fashion until "[a]ll of this danced up and down, like a company of gnats, each separate—danced up and down in Lily's mind" (24). Woolf concludes this chapter as she opened it, by focusing on Lily's confusion: "How then did it work out, all this? How did one judge people, think of them? How did one add up this and that and conclude that it was liking one felt, or disliking?" (24).

In Chapter 5, Woolf refuses to end Lily's or the readers' perplexity. While she frames the chapter with an image of Mrs. Ramsay as nurturer, she integrates within it, as she did in Chapters 1 through 3, conflicting images: Here we note her decision that Lily and Bankes should marry, her impatience with her son, her worry over the household finances, her inability ever to find the time to read, and her inspirational beauty. The chapter begins and ends with a line of the continued Lighthouse dialogue, both spoken by Mrs. Ramsay and revealing her continued attentiveness to her son's needs: "And even if it isn't fine to-morrow . . . it will be another day. Let us find another picture to cut out. . . ." Woolf employs another double frame at the end of this chapter as readers perceive Mrs. Ramsay not only framed by the window but also "outlined absurdly by the gilt [picture] frame" behind her. The narrator describes the latter framing as "absurd," perhaps, because the conflicting images contained within the chapter cannot possibly add up to a single, fixed portrait of her.

The remaining chapters in "The Window" build on the images of Mrs. Ramsay gained from Chapters 1 through 5 and culminate in the dinner-party scene (Chapters 12 through 19) that ends Book 1. While the dinner party, orchestrated by Mrs. Ramsay, constitutes a perfect moment of feminine domestic creativity, these chapters also frame instances of manipulation, exhaustion, and deference, announcing once again the theme of ultimate impermanence. At the end of the dinner party, Woolf underscores this theme when the narrator describes Mrs. Ramsay framed in the doorway of the dining room, gazing at the results of her efforts:

With her foot on the threshold she waited a moment longer in a scene which was vanishing even as she looked, and then, as she moved and took Minta's arm and left the room, it changed, it shaped itself differently; it had become, she knew, giving one last look at it over her shoulder, already the past. (94)

Book 2, "Time Passes," serves as a transitional section in *To the Lighthouse*, separating the object (Mrs. Ramsay) from the subject (Lily), thus complicating the artist's epistemological quest. The ten brief chapters in this book chart the decay and restoration of the Ramsays' house, a process that becomes the poetic representation of Lily's struggles to render permanent her fleeting moments of perception.

Chapters 1 through 3 map out the destruction of the Ramsay home and end by announcing Mrs. Ramsay's death. Woolf fuses these two events, suggesting a cause-and-effect relationship between them, at the end of Chapter 3. Speaking in general time, the omniscient narrator, who controls most of "Time Passes," paints a scene of dissolution in the chapter's penultimate paragraph:

The nights now are full of wind and destruction; the trees plunge and bend and their leaves fly helter skelter until the lawn is plastered with them and they lie packed in gutters and choke rain pipes and scatter damp paths. Also the sea tosses itself and breaks itself, and should any sleeper fancying that he might find on the beach an answer to his doubts, a sharer of his solitude, throw off his bedclothes and go down by himself to walk on the sand, no image with semblance of serving and divine promptitude comes readily to hand bringing the night to order and making the world reflect the compass of the soul. . . . Almost it would appear that it is useless in such confusion to ask the night those questions as to what, and why, and wherefore, which tempt the sleeper from his bed to seek an answer. (110)

The following sentence closes the chapter: "[Mr. Ramsay stumbling along a passage one dark morning stretched his arms out, but Mrs. Ramsay having died rather suddenly the night before, his arms, though stretched out, remained empty.]"

By juxtaposing these two passages at the end of the chapter, Woolf creates a metaphoric relationship between man and nature. We assume Mr. Ramsay to be the lonely sleeper of the penultimate paragraph and that the omniscient narrator is relating his vivid sensory impressions of a dissolute world that provides no comfort—a dissolution created by the death of Mrs. Ramsay.

Chapter 4 serves as a transition chapter that begins the process of reconstruction as the questions posed by the sea airs that wind through the Ramsay house ("Will you fade? Will you perish?") are answered, "we remain" (111). Yet this rebirth proves difficult. The succeeding chapters in "Time Passes" present a battle between the forces of destruction and regeneration as Mrs. McNab, the housekeeper, works to restore the house. The time markers placed in Chapter 4 reinforce the theme of transience. After her son Andrew dies in the war, her daughter Prue dies in childbirth (providing another ambiguous example of motherhood), and Mrs. Ramsay herself dies—probably as a result of her endless sacrifices to the needs of her family—we question whether her moments of transcendence can be restored, moments that might lend us an absolute vision of her. In Book 2's final chapter, the remaining family and guests return ten years later to the partially restored Ramsay home to begin the process of answering this question.

Book 3, "The Lighthouse," opens as Lily wonders "What does it mean then, what can it all mean?" It closes with her answer, revealed in her painting, and her declaration, "Yes . . . I have had my vision." The intervening chapters form a contrapuntal yet progressive pattern that oscillates between Lily's point of view as she completes her painting and the viewpoints of three members of the Ramsay family as they complete their journey to the Lighthouse. Book 3 charts a gradual movement from fragmentation and chaos to reconstruction and unity. This unity, however, is achieved through the artist's integrating vision, not through any objective representation of reality. Woolf suggests that Lily assumes control in each of these chapters as her artistic imagination creates a successful completion of the journey to the Lighthouse.

The first three chapters in "The Lighthouse" describe Lily's and the family's preparations and provide the foundation for the contrapuntal chapter design that follows. Chapter 1 details the "world of strife, ruin, [and] chaos" which Lily finds upon her return to the Ramsay home (129). Her epistemological confusion after Mrs. Ramsay's death results in a "blankness of . . . mind" (125). Without Mrs. Ramsay's guidance and support, the children are ill-prepared for their trip, which causes Mr. Ramsay to rage against them. The entire chapter centers on this chaotic state and the detrimental effects it has on Lily's creative energies.

Family members and guests all feel "as if the link that usually bound things together had been cut, and they floated up here, down there, off, anyhow" (126). As a result, Mr. Ramsay looks to Lily for sympathy that she feels incapable of providing. His constant pleas for attention, coupled with her own insecurities concerning her artistic abilities, prevent her from achieving her vision of Mrs. Ramsay. Ten years earlier Lily had been unable to complete her work, for she could not find the "relations" between the masses or shapes she had painted on her canvas. Now she acknowledges that she has some of the parts, but wonders still "how [to] bring them together," especially now that her model is gone (126).

Lily, like Woolf, refuses to follow the realist tradition, painting instead according to her own personal vision. As she explains to William Bankes in Book 1, her work makes "no attempt at likeness . . . the picture was not of [mother and child] . . . not in his sense." It is, she continues, "a matter of relations" between the objects and between the fragments of her individual perceptions (46-47).

At this point, Lily, unable to find these relationships, feels she is only "playing at painting" (128). Mrs. Ramsay's death has left unanswered questions about the value of traditional roles for women—questions Lily needs to have answered before she can find her own place and worth. Her recreation of Mrs. Ramsay's image as nurturer helps her to begin the process of self-definition. At the end of the chapter, Lily determines to "imitate from recollection the glow, the rhapsody, the self-surrender she had seen on so many women's faces (on Mrs. Ramsay's, for instance) when on some occasion like this they blazed up . . . into a rapture of sympathy. . . ." Thus, when Mr. Ramsay returns to her side and demands her attention, she decides "she would give him what she could" (129).

Chapter 2 centers on Lily's successful attempt to sympathize with Mr. Ramsay, which provides the first step toward her unifying vision. As she watches him on the lawn she sees "how his gaze seemed to fall dolefully over the sunny grass and discolour it. . . . Look at him, he seemed to be saying, look at me." Lily thinks that, as a woman, "she had provoked this horror; a woman, she should have known how to deal with it. It was immensely to her discredit, sexually, to stand there dumb" (131). When she finally responds by praising his boots, his joy at her attention inspires her vision of "a sunny island where peace dwelt, sanity reigned and the sun for ever shone" (132). The family now is ready to complete the trip to the Lighthouse.

Chapter 3 documents how this new sympathy Lily feels for Mr. Ramsay sparks her creative energies. During the chaos and confusion outlined in Chapter 1, Lily had taken up the wrong brush and rammed her easel into the ground at the wrong angle. Now she puts it right; yet when she begins to paint, old insecurities resurface. She remembers Tansley's insisting, "Women can't paint, can't write" at the dinner party, and her canvas becomes a "hideously difficult white space" (136). When Lily again recalls the image of Mrs. Ramsay, however, her confidence returns.

Woolf draws on a Proustian sense of time as Lily recreates her visions of Mrs. Ramsay. In Chapter 3, Lily's memory recaptures the past, recalling a morning on the beach near the Ramsay home. In this scene, Mrs. Ramsay sits and writes letters as guests and family frolic on the beach. Lily recalls playing a game with Tansley that morning and the camaraderie she felt with him:

[It] seemed to depend somehow upon Mrs. Ramsay sitting under the rock, with a pad on her knee, writing letters. . . . [She] resolved everything into simplicity; made these angers, irritations fall off like old rags; she brought together this and that and then this, and so made out of that miserable silliness and spite (she and Charles squabbling, sparring . . .) something—this scene on the beach for example, this moment of friendship and liking, which survived, after all these years complete, so that she dipped into it to re-fashion her memory of him, and there it stayed in the mind affecting one almost like a work of art. (137)

As she remembers Mrs. Ramsay, Lily chooses to focus only on an angle of vision that defines her as nurturer and unifier. Lily's memory of Mrs. Ramsay's creation of this moment of unity, "almost like a work of art," inspires her own creativity—for she has now found an image she can employ in the discovery of herself. In this particular memory, Mrs. Ramsay embodies both the traditional and the nontraditional image of woman: her nurture of others in her role of wife and mother creates a moment of artistic unity. When Lily expresses sympathy toward Mr. Ramsay, she models herself after this narrowed image of his wife and creates her own moment of unity (the trip to the Lighthouse)—a moment that *becomes* "a work of art" when it is expressed in her painting. Thus Lily is able to embrace and reconcile conflicting definitions of "woman" as nurturer and artist.

At the end of Chapter 3, Woolf suggests that Lily not only helps set the trip to the Lighthouse in motion, but also creates the narrative that describes the successful completion of the trip. The chapter's final scene centers on Lily walking down the beach, trying to spot the boat. When she sees one boat apart from the others, "she *decided* that there in that very distant and entirely silent little boat Mr. Ramsay was sitting with Cam and James" (138).

The contrapuntal design of the remaining chapters reinforces the suggestion that Lily envisions what happens on the boat. Woolf continually shifts the focus from the narrative of the trip (Chapters 4, 6, 8, 10, and 12) to Lily on shore (Chapters 5, 7, 9, 11, and 13), completing her painting while she speculates on the progress of the boat. This section begins as Woolf hints that Lily, not an omniscient narrator, relates details about the trip, while repeating the conditional "would": "Now they *would* sail on for hours like this"; "James *would* be forced to keep his eye all the time on the sail"; "Mr. Ramsay *would* say sharply, 'Look out! Look out!'" (140).

The end-points of the novel's two final chapters also highlight Lily's gaze. At the end of Chapter 12, the novel's penultimate chapter, Woolf describes the family's landing at the Lighthouse. She then begins Chapter 13 with Lily's declaration: "He must have reached it. . . . He has landed. . . . It is finished." When, at the end of this final chapter, Woolf accords Lily the last lines, "it was finished. . . . I have had my vision," she effectively fuses the image of the landing with Lily's completed painting. Woolf's diary records her careful attention to the shape of this final chapter:

At this moment I'm casting about for an end. The problem is how to bring Lily and Mr. R. together and make a combination of interest at the end. I am feathering about with various ideas. The last chapter which I begin tomorrow is In the

Boat: I had meant to end with R. climbing on to the rock. If so, what becomes of Lily and her picture? Should there be a final page about her and Carmichael looking at the picture and summing up R.'s character? In that case I lose the intensity of the moment. If this intervenes between R. and the Lighthouse, there's too much chop and change I think. Could I do it in a parenthesis? So that one had the sense of reading the two things at the same time? (98)

Woolf's shaping of the final two chapters creates a sense of spatiality that solves this problem.

To the Lighthouse closes as Lily achieves a vision of Mrs. Ramsay that is also a moment of transcendent unity for Lily, as she struggles to define herself, and for the Ramsay family, who find comfort and support in each other as they complete their journey. We know that this vision is ephemeral, however, because it is based on a single, transitory point of view. Lily shows that she understands this as well when she admits that the "great revelation" about the meaning of life would never come. Instead she can only glimpse transitory moments—"daily miracles, illuminations, matches struck unexpectedly in the dark"—when one could make "Life stand still here" (137-38).

Woolf provides Lily with her own perfect moment in the final chapter, as she achieves a clear confidence in her knowledge of herself as a woman and an artist. Here she discovers a nexus for the dialogues of identity that have been framed in the novel. Yet Lily acknowledges the fragility of this brief moment of unity when she admits that her painting will probably "be hung in the attics" or "rolled up and flung under a sofa" (152). The glimpses we have been given of Mr. Ramsay's difficult nature suggest that any harmony he has achieved with his family during the trip to the Lighthouse will soon be overturned. Lily's new-found confidence also appears tenuous in a world where men *and* women often claim that "women can not paint or write" and are, therefore, better suited for domestic life. Thus we suspect that the unity achieved by the strong sense of closure at the end of the final chapter would be undercut if more chapters were to follow. David Lodge concurs, arguing that the novel's "cut-off point is essentially arbitrary, and it is clear that if the text were to continue, another down-beat must inevitably follow" (181).

Woolf's artful shaping of the novel has made the inevitability of a "down-beat" clear. As the chapters in *To the Lighthouse* frame fragmentary and contradictory images of Mrs. Ramsay, our imposed gestalt of the text disintegrates and we cannot consider any one perception of her or of Lily to be absolute. Lily has viewed Mrs. Ramsay through cultural lenses, producing a vision of her as a traditional wife and mother who subjugates herself to the needs of her husband and children. She has also gazed at Mrs. Ramsay through more personal lenses that produce conflicting images: an independent woman whose creativity encourages harmony and life, and a manipulative woman who imposes her will on others, including Lily, whom she has tried to pressure into marriage.

Woolf focuses our attention ultimately on the epistemological *process*—not on the permanence of individual vision but "on what it attempted" (152); for the vision must be continually reconstructed, as the relationship between its fragments must forever be reestablished.

Notes

1. The phrase "new woman" has been attributed to novelist Sarah Grand, whose 1894 article in the *North American Review* identified an emergent group of women, influenced by J. S. Mill and other champions of individualism, who supported and campaigned for women's rights.

2. By "union" Woolf refers not only to the marital union, but also to a union between the masculine and feminine principles contained within each of us. Borrowing the concept of the androgynous mind from Coleridge, Woolf insists that both principles operate in the human brain and that "the normal and comfortable state of being is . . . when the two live in harmony together, spiritually co-operating" (*Room* 948).

3. Scholars agree that this dichotomy springs from Woolf's ambiguous attitude toward her parents and her family life. Woolf admits, in "A Sketch of the Past," that in *To the Lighthouse*, the most autobiographical of her works, she "did for herself what psycho-analysts do for their patients. I expressed some very long felt and deeply felt emotion. And in expressing it I explained it and then laid it to rest" (*Moments* 81).

4. Jane Lilienfeld observes that Mrs. Ramsay is frequently silent with her husband. These silences "always retain their ambiguous character. . . . [Each] serves to insulate her against her husband, while it equally grants a medium in which to give herself to him in a manner both can accept" (159).

5. Woolf perhaps has another motive for scripting Mrs. Ramsay's death. In "Professions for Women," she stresses the need to kill the "Angel in the House," a term taken from a popular Victorian poem by Coventry Patmore, in order for a woman to write: "I turned upon her and caught her by the throat. I did my best to kill her. My excuse, if I were to be had up in a court of law, would be that I acted in self-defence. Had I not killed her she would have killed me." Woolf refers here to a woman, much like Mrs. Ramsay, who "sacrificed herself daily. If there was a chicken, she took the leg; if there was a draught, she sat in it" (285).

Works Cited

Cunningham, Gail. *The New Woman and the Victorian Novel.* New York: Harper, 1978.

Fernando, Lloyd. *"New Women" in the Late Victorian Novel.* University Park, PA: Penn State UP, 1977.

Lanser, Susan. "Toward a Feminist Narratology." *Style* 20 (1986): 341-63.

Lilienfeld, Jane. "Where the Spear Plants Grew: the Ramsays' Marriage in *To the Lighthouse.*" *New Feminist Essays on Virginia Woolf.* Ed. Jane Marcus. Lincoln: U of Nebraska P, 148-69.

Linton, Lynn. "The Wild Women as Politicians." *Nineteenth Century* 30 (1891): 79-88.

Lodge, David. *The Modes of Modern Writing: Metaphor, Metonymy, and the Typology of Modern Literature.* Ithaca, NY: Cornell UP, 1977.

Marder, Herbert. *Feminism and Art: A Study of Virginia Woolf.* Chicago: U of Chicago P, 1968.

Woolf, Virginia. *Moments of Being.* London: Sussex UP, 1976.

——. "Professions for Women." *Collected Essays.* Vol. II. London: Harcourt, 1966. 284-89.

——. *A Room of One's Own.* New York: Harcourt, 1981.

——. *Three Guineas.* 1938. New York: Harcourt, 1966.

——. *To the Lighthouse.* Ed. Susan Dick. Cambridge: Blackwell, 1992.

——. "Women and Fiction." *Collected Essays.* Vol. II. London: Harcourt, 1966. 141-48.

8

Competing Mothers:
Edith Wharton's Late Vision of Family Life

Hildegard Hoeller

During the first two decades of this century, America experienced a "revolution in morals and manners" (Yellis 368) and within it a dramatic change in feminine ideals from the Gibson girl to the flapper. Most important in this changing image of femininity was the way in which female sexuality was conceived of and constructed. The flapper began to signal that female sexuality was not a passive response to male advances, but an independent, active force. It is this presence of an active female sexuality that most decidedly marks Wharton's late vision of motherhood and family life and differentiates it from that in her earlier fiction.

Wharton had always been a cynical critic of marriage as an institution, as she had always seen in motherhood a potential space of fulfillment for women: one need only look at *The House of Mirth* (1905) and its furious critique of the marriage market, as well as its surprising and sentimental celebration of the organic powers of motherhood in the working class kitchen of Nettie Struther, which serves as a redeeming alternative to the cold calculations of Lily Bart's managing, upper-class mother.

In Wharton's later fiction, motherhood gains a more and more central role: Elizabeth Ammons talks about the author's "near obsession with the subject of motherhood" (168); R. W. B. Lewis observes "almost a new compulsion: what might be called the maternal imagination" (446). Most critics see this concern as a reflection of the aging author's preoccupation with her own childlessness and a need to recompense for a childhood lack of her own.[1] Yet, such needs can hardly account for the strikingly complex and unconventional ways in which Wharton chooses to reflect on motherhood. Her novellas "The Old Maid" (1924) and "Her Son" (1933) as well as other late fictions center around illegitimate, even semi-incestuous motherly love that is troublingly connected to female desire.[2] Unlike her earlier fiction, Wharton's late fiction negotiates moth-

167

erhood and marriage within the context of illegitimacy and female desire. The result is a vision of motherhood that is both anarchic and tragic.

Wharton presents two forms of motherhood: the passionate mother love for an illegitimate child and the moderate feelings of motherly love within marriage. The former is intricately and dangerously linked to female sexual desire, the latter independent of it and thus sterile and meaningless. For this reason, Wharton's women characters compete for the former and disregard the latter; in the process, they exploit, injure, or even destroy each other. Wharton's late vision of family life suggests that while traditional, "legitimate" families render motherhood meaningless, excessive motherly love for an illegitimate child is fulfilling but leads to a monstrous struggle between women.

* * *

In "The Old Maid," a novella that, as Wharton puts it in a letter to William Berenson in 1921, "apparently every self-respecting American magazine has refused [. . .] on the ground of immorality" (*Letters* 441),[3] Wharton tells the story of two cousins, Delia Lovell Ralston and the "old maid" Charlotte Lovell. At its center is the conflict between Charlotte's passionate mother love and Delia's powers as the established, married Ralston woman who tries to use money, society, the law, and medicine to obtain "motherhood" of Charlotte's illegitimate daughter Tina. Wharton's fiction opens with the impending marriage between Charlotte Lovell and Joe Ralston, a cousin of Delia's husband Jim. Shortly before her wedding, Charlotte confesses to Delia that one of the "orphans" she, as an "old maid," has cared for is her own child. Tina is hers and Clem Spender's—Delia's own former love—and was conceived in one passionate night. As a young woman, Delia had rejected the artistic and impecunious Spender in favor of the more wealthy, established, and altogether reasonable Jim Ralston. Although Delia has children in her suitable marriage to Ralston, she shows truly passionate motherly feelings only for Tina. Envious of Charlotte's child by Spender and Joe Ralston's love for Charlotte—which she suspects to be stronger than her husband's love for her—Delia manages to prevent her cousin's marriage by telling Joe about Charlotte's lung disease. Consequently, she makes Tina and her mother dependent on herself. When Delia's husband Jim dies, the two women and their children establish a household together. Tina grows up calling Delia "mother" and considering Charlotte as her "old maid" aunt. Their lifelong competition for Tina's love and the role of the girl's "real" mother reaches its climax when the two women face the issue of Tina's marriageability; Charlotte accuses Delia of stealing her child in order to relive her own repressed love for Spender. Yet, in the end, Delia adopts Tina and enables her to make a suitable marriage by providing her with a dowry. Tina never knows the truth about her birth.

In "The Old Maid," Wharton's men merely orchestrate the central conflict between the two competing "mothers." There is Clem Spender, whose name suggests his quality as an uneconomical, sexual young man. Even though both women had only a fleeting moment with him, their lives are dominated by his memory. Both cherish his "gifts": Charlotte has his child Tina while Delia has only a French ormolu clock that Spender delivered to her as Mrs. Mingott's wedding gift. The clock "represented a shepherdess sitting on a fallen trunk, a basket of flowers at her feet. A shepherd stealing up, surprised her with a kiss" (83). "Odd and foreign" (83), Clem Spender has become the symbol of all of Delia's dreams. As a man who "steals" kisses rather than owning real estate or running a business, Spender signifies romantic dreams about Europe and pastoral fantasies about free love. Importantly, Spender is never present in the text. He is a mere fantasy of both women; later, Wharton makes sure we learn that Spender also married and that his sense of freedom is only an illusion.

In the memories of the two women, Spender's independence functions as a foil to the Ralstons, whom Wharton describes with a mock-anthropological voice: The "primitive" (80) Ralston "tribe" (78) represents the "conservative element" (78), in which one "regarded heroism as a form of gambling" (77). They "had not come to the colonies to die for a creed but to live for a bank account" (77). Unsentimental, stiflingly economical and rational, the Ralston world forbids individual thought and action and only allows the replication of precise social conventions. "Charlotte was making a match exactly like Delia's own: marrying a Ralston, of the Waverly branch, than which nothing could be safer, sounder, or more—well, usual" (81f). Later, "Delia [. . .] noticed how much her husband and her cousin Joe were alike; it made her feel how justified she was in always thinking of the Ralstons collectively" (105). That the Ralstons can only be looked at "collectively"—as Wharton's repeated use of "them" underlines—makes them particularly unsentimental; they almost have a "corporate" character. They are types who embody a male corporate social order, which—importantly—depends on marriage as an economic institution.

In contrast, a typical sentimental heroine, Charlotte is a character of heightened sensibility in conflict with the rational social conventions of the world she inhabits. She is not a "product of particular material and social conditions"—as Wharton postulates for characters of realist fiction in *The Writing of Fiction* (7)—but is driven by her private emotions and passions. Charlotte's fierce motherly sentiments as well as her sexual knowledge outside of marriage, both results of her illegitimate affair, set her apart from the stiff and conventional world of the Ralstons. She is—literally and metaphorically—"consumed" by her feelings. Employing nineteenth-century sentimental iconography, Wharton individualizes Charlotte through her lung disease; her illness poses a threat to the "healthy" Ralston world. Charlotte, indeed, suffers from a mild case of lung weakness—she does cough blood; however, her lung disease was also used to hide her pregnancy since she was officially sent away to a sanatorium for her lungs when in fact she had Tina during that time. Both Wharton and her characters use and understand Charlotte's lung disease as a metaphor for her sexual passion.[4] Unlike the Ralstons, who economize, Charlotte spends both literally—her blood and tears—and figuratively—in form of passionate "illegitimate" motherhood; and this sentimental expenditure is a form of anarchy, an excess, in the economy of the Ralston world.

Wharton dramatizes the conflict between the rational, calculating world of the Ralstons and the passionate nature of Charlotte's motherhood in Delia's character. More than once she juxtaposes Delia's feelings toward her own children—born into the Ralston marriage—and her feelings of motherhood for Clem Spender's child Tina. For example, after hearing Charlotte's confession, Delia realizes that "the child came first—she felt it in every fibre of her body" (97); "feverishly" (97), Delia leaves to see Tina. But, on the way, she "saw her rosy children playing, under their nurse's eyes, with the pampered progeny of other square-dwellers" (98). And while the nurse tries to get her attention, Delia "shook her head, waved at the group and hurried on" (98). Delia's own children make no impression on her and leave her uninterested and empty; in her own eyes, they prevent her from living a meaningful life. "Delia Ralston sometimes felt that the real events of her life did not begin until both her children had contracted—so safely and suitably—their irreproachable New York alliances" (125). Almost like a lover, Tina, on the other hand, reaches "every fibre" of Delia's body; to be Tina's mother appears to Delia exciting and fulfilling, almost like a "fever." Whereas "[Delia] always knew beforehand exactly what her own girl would say [. . .] Tina's views and opinions were a perpetual delicious shock to her" (127). It is in the passion of her love for Tina, which is fueled by her repressed desire for Clem Spender, that Delia finds the fulfillment that the conventional, asexual motherhood within marriage cannot give her. Indeed, the very illegitimacy of Tina and perhaps of Delia's love for her provides the "delicious shock" Delia seeks.

Tina's marriageability in general and the appearance of suitor Lanning Halsey specifically bring into the open the competition and conflict between the two women. It becomes the hour of truth not only about who the "real" mother is but also about the true nature of the relationship between the two "mothers." In Tina's suitor, history seems to repeat itself for both cousins. Just like Charlotte, Delia sees in Halsey her former lover: "Clement Spender stood before her, irresolute, impecunious, persuasive. Ah, if only she had let herself be persuaded!" (135). Both Delia and Charlotte judge the relationship between Tina and Halsey from the angle of their own experience. Charlotte knows that Halsey will not marry Tina because of her social position and is worried that Tina will repeat her own fate—that she will have sex with Halsey without being married and become an "old maid": " 'Tina an old maid? Never!' Charlotte Lovell rose abruptly, her closed hand crashing down on the slender work-table. 'My child shall have her life . . . her own life . . . whatever it costs me' " (136). She decides that she and her daughter should move away. Delia, on the other hand, wants to adopt Tina and make her a Ralston, thus marriageable to Halsey; she hopes to combine passion and respectability. Both women realize that "only Tina's mother had a right to decide what Tina's future should be" (139) and that they need to clarify who Tina's "real mother" is as quickly as possible.

And while Charlotte believes in her decision "whatever it costs her," Delia is incapable of "independent action" (148) and consults with the old physician Dr. Lanskell about the advisability and the legalities of adopting Tina. Compared to a "king," "pope," and "elder," the "fatherly" (150) Lanskell seems to incorporate patriarchy; his "soundness" makes him the voice of reason. He advises Delia to adopt Tina and even lets her know that her late husband would (even had implicitly) approve. With both Lanskell's patriarchal backing and the implicit consent of the Ralston men, Delia confronts Charlotte with her plan to adopt Tina. Charlotte initially resists this last renunciation of her own motherhood, but, just as in King Solomon's story, so also in Wharton's story the real mother eventually renounces her rights for the best interest of her child. Wharton writes without irony: "The same fierce maternal passion that had once flung her down upon those same cushions was now bowing her still lower, in the throes of a bitterer renunciation" (155). Charlotte is capable of renunciation, of sentimental love for her child. She is living up to the most ancient sentimental myth of the true mother; in Wharton's world that means that she is willing to pay any price for her child's well-being.

Delia, on the other hand, is neither able to form her own convictions nor able to renounce. In her adopted motherhood she quite openly relives her past and "the road not taken" with Spender. In contrast to Charlotte's passionate mother love, Delia's motherly love, driven by sexual desires and backed by the means of money and the law, is not capable of renunciation; "sometimes, when she watched Tina's changing face, she felt as though her own blood were beating in it, as though she could read every thought and emotion feeding those tumultuous currents. [. . .] Delia saw displayed before her, with an artless frankness, all the visions, cravings and imaginings of her own stifled youth" (160). In Tina's stormy sentiments, Delia sees the silences of her own life; her "motherhood" to this illegitimate child allows her to become the spectator of a sentimental version of her life that she never dared to live or even speak. And yet, Delia's dreams are once more illusions. By choosing "the law" to fulfill her sentimental fantasies, ironically, she has acted once again like a Ralston, and with the support of the Ralston men. By legalizing her illicit passionate desire, by making it "legitimate," she has changed its very nature. When Tina hears about her adoption, she whispers to Delia: " 'I've always thought of you as my Mamma; and now, you dearest, you really are' " (160). And yet, Delia replies: "Well, if the lawyers can make me so!" (160).

"WHICH OF US IS HER MOTHER?" (166), is the central question both women face as they finally confront each other on the night before Tina's wedding. Since "A girl ought to have a mother's counsel, a mother's . . . ," before entering marriage, the two competing "mothers" need to decide who will go up to Tina's room to give her final, motherly advice on marriage.[5] In this final passionate confrontation Charlotte reveals to Delia that "hate" is the word that has "been between us since the beginning" (166). And, like Charlotte's words, Wharton's language becomes more violent and unrestrained: "Charlotte's words flamed up as if from the depth of the infernal fires" (166). She tells Delia that "everything you've done has been done for Clement Spender" (167), and while Delia denies her cousin's allegation, the story supports its truthfulness. Charlotte bursts out, "You've always thought of him in thinking of Tina—of him and nobody else! A woman never stops thinking of the man she loves. She thinks of him years afterward, in all sorts of unconscious ways, in thinking of all sorts of things—books, pictures, sunsets, a flower or a ribbon—or a clock on the mantelpiece" (167). Charlotte reveals that Wharton's sentimental, maternal tale is, in fact, about the exclusive power of love and sexual passion.

In the crescendo of this final clash, Charlotte accuses Delia of "robbing [her] of [her] child" (168) and tells Delia that "tonight [Tina] belongs to me. Tonight I can't bear that she should call you 'mother'" (168). And again Delia is awed by Charlotte's passion. She responds, "How much you must love her—to say such things to me" (168). Delia wonders: "With what divination her maternal passion had endowed her"

(169). Like Delia, we see that Charlotte's fierce sentimental nature, 'the divination that maternal passion brings,' is the most reliable, truthful voice in "The Old Maid"—more truthful than Delia's repressed passion for Spender. Charlotte is shouting out the truth of the story—the sentimental truth about Delia's one love for Spender. Delia realizes that Charlotte is right and that "here in this bridal joy, so mysteriously her own, was the compensation for all she had missed and never renounced" (169).

Characteristic of Wharton's fiction, after this momentous and momentary narrative outburst, the narrative takes a turn. When Charlotte tries to give Tina a mother's advice for her wedding, she realizes that she is not able to tell her the truth about her motherhood and thus about love, sex, and motherhood outside of marriage. Charlotte's final renunciation lies in silence. She decides to protect her daughter from the painful truth of her own "illegitimate" life experience. Instead she asks Delia to see Tina. The narrator tells us that "they did not say much, after all; or else their communion had no need of words" (171). Tina will enter marriage as ignorantly as Delia herself did once, and as the young Edith Jones did. Tina's life, like that of the young Wharton, will be "falsified and misdirected" ("Life and I," 1088). Protected from the "illegitimate" truth of female sexual desire, Tina will enter the meaningless, legitimate world of marriage.[6]

Wharton ends the narrative on a tragically ambivalent note. Delia makes Tina promise "that [she'll] give [her] last kiss to Aunt Charlotte. Don't forget—the very last" (172). And this last kiss may signify both that Delia is acknowledging Charlotte's rights as a mother and that she is saying good-bye to her real, "illegitimate" mother in order to enter her other mother's "legitimate" world of marriage. And the ambivalence of this kiss carries Wharton's anarchic critique of family life. It is a kiss of allegiance to a meaningless life within marriage and a kiss of betrayal to everything that makes a woman's life meaningful: illegitimate, female desire.

In "The Old Maid" Wharton engages in a complicated renegotiation of the concept of motherhood. On the one hand, the narrative sentimentally celebrates Charlotte's fiercely passionate motherly love, which gives her the "divination of a mother" and makes her capable of renunciation; it makes her a character who is willing to protect her child "whatever it costs her." The narrative also never wavers in its conviction that Charlotte's motherly love is stronger and better than that of Delia, who deliberates, legitimizes, even legalizes where she desires, and whose love for Tina is more overtly driven by her repressed desire for Spender. Wharton deviates from nineteenth century sentimental celebrations of motherhood in her fervent belief that it is *only* in illegitimacy that women can find emotionally fulfilling motherhood and that this motherhood is dangerously closely related to illicit female desire. And Wharton's realist eye perceives that a mother who is willing to 'pay any price' for her child will have to do so in a world where everything has a price; potentially a form of anarchy, such excessive feelings are utterly exploitable in a world of economy. She envisions no sentimental community of sympathy between women and mothers, but instead she shows in the two competing mothers that the public, societal forces of the law, medicine, money, and reputation and the private forces of passionate, infinite love of the mother remain incompatible and irreconcilable. In the struggle between these two forces, her competing "mothers" spend themselves and erase the possibility of a meaningful, fulfilling existence for themselves, each other, and the daughter. In Wharton's world there is no space between meaningless legitimacy and realistically unlivable illegitimacy.

* * *

"Her Son" also centers around the desperate competition between two "mothers" over one illegitimate child. Like "The Old Maid," it offers a sentimental celebration of motherhood, a linking of motherhood to female desire, and the frightful vision of motherhood as a means of oppression among women. Wharton presents in "Her Son," as she did in "The Old Maid," the tragic struggles and exploitations that take place when sentimental visions and realistic calculations come in close contact. And, devoid of a biological mother and embellished with an almost incestuous twist to its plot, "Her Son" offers perhaps an even more radical, anarchic negotiation of motherhood than "The Old Maid."

While both fictions show great similarities in plot and theme, they differ in narrative perspective. Whereas in "The Old Maid" men are relegated to the background, "Her Son" is told through the eyes of Mr. Norcutt, an aging bachelor who has only very traditional notions of parenthood and no conception of illicit female desire. He provides Wharton with the ironic lens of a rather inept sentimental reader, who cannot understand the story about two competing mothers seemingly unfolding in front of his eyes. Norcutt's prudishly limited notions of womanhood, which link female identity closely to motherhood and marriage, blind him to the central issue of Wharton's tale: illegitimate motherhood and female, sexual desire. In that sense, the narrative is as much about Norcutt's awakening as it is about motherhood and the struggle between two disparate women.

After the death of her husband and her son, Mrs. Glenn is in search of her first, illegitimate son Stephen. Although her late husband is also Stephen's father, their first son was born before Mr. Glenn was divorced and able to marry Mrs. Glenn, then Catherine Reamer. Stephen was given up for adoption to a couple named Brown, and even after their marriage the Glenns did not try to reclaim their first son. When Norcutt meets Mrs. Glenn many years later, she asks him to help her find her now thirty-year-old son Stephen with only the help of a baby photograph. Working for the consulate in Paris, Norcutt gets involved in Mrs. Glenn's search and soon hears that she has found her son and the Browns. Norcutt then witnesses in intervals of years the relationship between the Browns, the "son" Stephen, and Mrs. Glenn until the consumptive "son," now on his death bed, finally confesses to Norcutt that he is neither "mother's" son; instead, in order to save his life, he and the Browns deceived Mrs. Glenn and exploited her motherly need for her first illegitimate son through a well-staged charade. He does not, however, reveal to Norcutt that he is Mrs. Brown's lover.

When Norcutt first receives Mrs. Glenn in his office, he is astonished by her looks and demeanor. Knowing that the men in her life—her husband, her son, and her uncle—had died, Norcutt is surprised to see Mrs. Glenn more beautiful and vibrant than he had imagined. His amazement grows when he meets Mrs. Glenn next, and she has found her lost son Stephen. What Norcutt considers "incredible," Mrs. Glenn regards as "'not incredible—inevitable. When one has lived for more than half a life with one object in view it's bound to become a reality. I *had* to find Stevie; and I found him.' She smiled with the inward brooding smile of a Madonna—an image of the eternal mother who, when she speaks of her children in old age, still feels them at the breast" (21). To Norcutt, Mrs. Glenn is as unreal as the image of a Madonna, an icon of eternal motherhood. For Mrs. Glenn, on the other hand, her feelings are quite real; her universe is one in which love and desire seemingly triumph over likelihood. In her tale, as in most sentimental tales, the construction or re-construction of a family is the purpose and inevitable goal. Wharton lets those two sensibilities stand in contrast; she apparently identifies neither with Norcutt's limited and conventional lack of imagination nor with Mrs. Glenn's driven and "unreasonable," sentimental imagination.

Mrs. Glenn then tells Norcutt about her highly sentimental encounter with Mrs. Brown and her reunion with her lost son: "the lady, snatching the miniature from her, and bursting into tears, had identified the portrait as her adopted child's, and herself as the long-sought Mrs. Brown" (21). The staple elements of sentimental reunion scenes, the miniature, the tears, the overwhelming emotion, are framed by Wharton, not only through Mrs. Glenn's account and Norcutt's lens, but furthermore through the irony of a second reading, which reveals that Mrs. Brown stages this stock sentimental scene as the beginning of her exploitative plot. Mrs. Glenn's sense of inevitability has been rightly diagnosed by Mrs. Brown as sentimental and then has been played out skillfully according to the genre conventions. Like Delia in "The Old Maid," Mrs. Glenn can only focus on her passion for one particular illegitimate child: "She seemed to have forgotten that there had ever been a war, and that a son of her own, with thousands of young Americans, had lost his life in it" (23). It is this ahistorical, focused, overpowering vision—in its nature typical of the sentimental—that makes Mrs. Glenn a perfect victim of Mrs. Brown's scheme.

It is thus that Mrs. Brown exploits Mrs. Glenn's overpowering motherly feelings by claiming her "recompense" for her years of parenting. And it is unclear what the price tag of 30 years of parenting versus nine months of pregnancy is. Repeatedly, Mrs. Glenn explains to Norcutt the debt she owes the Browns: "They love Stephen so much they won't give him up; and how can I blame them? What are my rights, compared with theirs" (37). And about Mrs. Brown: "She was there—all the years when I'd failed him" (40); "she's his *real* mother . . . I'm nothing . . . " (65); and "Why should I deny what's so evident—and so natural? When Stevie's ill and unhappy it's not to me he turns. During so many years he knew nothing of me, never even suspected my existence; and all the while *they* were there, watching over him, loving him, slaving for him" (67). But while Mrs. Glenn brings forward these arguments for the Browns's rights, she, like Norcutt, also has a deep sense of her own biological motherhood as "naturally" deeper and more essential.

Throughout the tale, one crucial element distinguishes Mrs. Brown from Mrs. Glenn: taste—a concept exceedingly important for Wharton. Like Norcutt, Stephen also instinctively understands Mrs. Glenn's mother love to be superior. His illness, a "mode of clairvoyance" (74), is a metaphor for a sensibility that forces him to recognize, respect, and ultimately reciprocate Mrs. Glenn's pure maternal feelings for him. Although Mrs. Brown's lover, he is genuinely moved by Mrs. Glenn's "pure" emotions—so much so that he at first cannot endure to keep up the lie and then, for the same reason, will follow Norcutt's urgent advice and endure the lie to please her. Stephen's silence is a form of expiation; he gives Mrs. Glenn what Norcutt believes a mother needs and does, indeed, grow very close to her. In the end, like Norcutt, he apparently prefers Mrs. Glenn's intense feelings of motherhood to Mrs. Brown's aggressively sexual desire and possessive love for him. A sentimental "family" reunion of sorts is achieved when the loving mother cares for the dying son. The tastefulness of Mrs. Glenn's motherly love is an externalization of its inherent goodness and it makes her, in the eyes of Wharton, her characters, and the readers, ultimately Stephen's "true" mother.

After Stephen's death, Norcutt's belief that Mrs. Glenn is the "true" mother is once again challenged since it cannot account for Mrs. Brown's grief:

It seemed like profaning Catherine Glenn's grief to compare Mrs. Brown's to it; yet, in the first weeks after Stephen's death, I had to admit that Mrs. Brown mourned him as genuinely, as inconsolably, as his supposed mother. Indeed, it would be nearer to the truth to say that Mrs. Brown's grief was more hopeless and rebellious than the other's. (80 f.)

In his traditional imagination, Norcutt can only see Mrs. Glenn as the saintly mother. His worldview has no words or concepts to account for Mrs. Brown and her "genuine" feelings, only a vague sense of "profanation." Indeed, both Norcutt and Mrs. Glenn are blinded by their belief in the power of natural (that is, biological) motherhood. Mrs. Glenn, who doubted her own rights as long as her son was alive, is now ready to value her own motherhood (reduced to nine months of childbearing and the few years at the end of Stephen's life) as infinitely higher than Mrs. Brown's claims as the adoptive parent who seemingly raised and lived with the child for thirty years.

When Norcutt sees Mrs. Glenn for the last time, his self-righteousness about his decision to let Mrs. Glenn live a lie is shaken. Now in a hotel room in Nice, both women are almost "spent." Mrs. Glenn is ill and bedridden while Mrs. Brown is drunk and clearly out of control. Mrs. Glenn's countenance reflects the ways in which Mrs. Brown has exploited her for years: "The face that looked out from [a lace cap] had still the same carven beauty; but its texture had dwindled from marble to worn ivory. Her body too had shrunk, so that, low in her chair, under her loose garments, she seemed to have turned into a little broken doll" (91). Norcutt learns that Mrs. Glenn's checking account has been plundered and is now, like its owner, reduced to a skeleton. Typical of a sentimental character, Mrs. Glenn "dwindles" away once her loved one has died. But Wharton's sentimental logic functions only outside of marriage—in the realm of the "illegitimate." While the death of her second son and her husband left Mrs. Glenn beautiful and vibrant, the death of her illegitimate son destroys her.

Mrs. Brown—now under the heavy influence of alcohol—demands more and more funds from the suffering Mrs. Glenn. Norcutt witnesses how she now loudly proclaims the old formula for extraction: "The fact that for years I looked after the child she deserted weighs nothing with her. She doesn't seem to think she owes us anything" (93). Years of consistent struggle and exploitation between the two women finally end in a violent revelation. Norcutt threatens Mrs. Brown with exposing her and Stephen's scheme to Mrs. Glenn, but again the tables turn on the innocent bachelor. Mrs. Brown uses the same threat on him. And there is, of course, one element, the sexual element, the most offensive of all, that Norcutt is ignorant of, and which Mrs. Brown now reveals to both of them. Mrs. Brown's crescendo solves the mystery of Wharton's plot: "What he doesn't know is why we fixed the thing up. Steve wasn't my adopted son any more than he was your real one. Adopted son, indeed! How old do you suppose I am? He was my lover. There—do you understand? My lover! That's why we faked up this ridiculous adoption story, and all the rest of it— . . . There—I'd rather have told you that than have your money. I'd rather you should know what Steve was to me than think longer that you owned him . . . " (103). As in "The Old Maid," in "Her Son" the issue of "property" between the two women finally shifts from monetary to sentimental and sexual issues. The sentimental claim to the son, be it as mother or lover, ultimately counts more than the money negotiations the two mothers have engaged in before. Mrs. Brown rather voices her true relationship with her "son" than continues to extract money from the other "mother."

In a dramatic final scene, Norcutt relates that this speech apparently kills Mrs. Glenn:

A tremor convulsed her face; then, to my amazement, it was smoothed into an expression of childish serenity, and a faint smile, half playful, half-ironic, stole over it.

She raised her hand and pointed tremulously to the other's disordered headgear. "My dear—your hat's crooked," she said.

For a moment I was bewildered; then I saw that, very gently, she was at last returning the taunt that Mrs. Brown had so often addressed to her. The shot fired, she leaned back against me with the satisfied sigh of a child; and immediately I understood that Mrs. Brown's blow had gone wide. A pitying fate had darkened Catherine Glenn's intelligence at the exact moment when to see clearly would have been the final anguish. (104)

In this final death bed scene, Mrs. Glenn's innocence once again triumphs over Mrs. Brown's vulgarity. But Norcutt's role is crucial in this last scene. Protecting her through a lie, Mr. Norcutt believes that Mrs. Glenn—a woman who had extramarital sex and bore a child out of wedlock—dies in a childlike purity shielded from the fact that, in an ironic, almost incestuous twist, her rival "mother" slept with the man she considered her son. Wharton's ironic treatment of Norcutt suggests that, while Mrs. Glenn is perhaps protected from this last blow, it is Norcutt's innocence more than Mrs. Glenn's that is preserved through his reading of this last scene. He, more so than Mrs. Glenn, is protected from the meaning of Mrs. Brown's "vile" remarks.

In "Her Son" Wharton tells a sentimental tale about "motherly" love as well as a tragic tale of the exploitations of a sentimental character. On the one hand, Mrs. Glenn's passionate mother love for Stephen overcomes even the boundaries of lacking biological ties and becomes in its purity, tastefulness, and passionate goodness a self-fulfilling prophecy. As in many sentimental novels, a family of affinity rather than biology is established through the narrative. Importantly, though, this family of affinity is used by Wharton to critique the meaninglessness of Mrs. Glenn's previous "legitimate family." Only when she is freed of her marriage and legitimate son can Mrs. Glenn follow her true passion and constitute an illegitimate family that fulfills her. Yet, on the other hand, her pursuit of such an illegitimate family becomes the source of her exploitation and oppression. Misguided in her passionate need for her illegitimate son, she falls easy prey to Mrs. Brown's scheme. Like Charlotte, she pays any price and is consumed by her illegitimate drive. Indeed, both sensitive and sentimental characters die, are consumed by their virtuous feelings for each other. Stephen dies out of guilt, informed by his true feelings for Mrs. Glenn. Mrs. Glenn dies because she is, as so many sentimental heroines, too sensitive for the harsh realities of "real" life.

Even more explicitly so than Delia's love for Tina, Mrs. Brown's motherly feelings for "her son" are a disguise for her sexual desire for the "child." Her almost incestuous feelings for Stephen are the hidden core, the "heart of darkness," of Wharton's tale from which Norcutt tries to protect Mrs. Glenn until the end. Through the limitations of Norcutt's inept lens, so utterly blind to illicit female desire, Wharton exposes the limitation of nineteenth-century sentimental celebration of motherhood: its repression of female sexual desire and its unreflected use of semi-incestuous plots. In Mrs. Brown's "vulgar" admittance to her own sexual desire for her "son" Wharton lets the central theme of female desire surface and violate Norcutt's tasteful but misguided notions of motherhood.

* * *

Edmund Wilson relates that "Professor Charles Eliot Norton [. . .] had once warned [Edith Wharton] that 'no great work of imagination' had ever been based on illicit passion" (30). In view of these stories, we have to be particularly grateful that Wharton did not take Norton's warning to heart. Wharton's stories, overtly dealing with motherhood, are driven by the secret force of female "illegitimate"—that is extramarital—desire. Wharton's anarchic celebration of a particular, "illegitimate," passionate motherhood allows her to launch a devastating critique of "legitimate" family life within marriage and to reveal the centrality of female, sexual desire to her tales and the lives of her characters. Wharton's heroines—the "real" mothers—in these tales are willing "to pay any price"; they are driven by a sentimental passion for their children that is unrestrained and unconditional. Like the heroines of sentimental fiction, Wharton's protagonists stand in sharp contrast to the world around them—a world that calculates and schemes. In that legitimate world of calculation, most forcefully symbolized by marriage for Wharton, none of her women characters can find fulfillment. All of her characters seek meaning in the space of illegitimacy, a space that dangerously mingles female sexual desire and motherhood. Yet, such a world is embedded in a world of calculation, money, and patriarchal power; in a desperate search to fulfill their desires and driven by envy for other women's illegitimate passions, Wharton's competing mothers exploit and destroy each other.

Both "Her Son" and "The Old Maid" are centrally concerned with "legitimacy." Wharton's mothers can only find meaningful passion in their love to illegitimate children, even as they, as in Mrs. Glenn's case, are by the same man as her legitimate children. "Illegitimacy," in its connection to female desire and excessive motherhood, represents a form of anarchic truth, as do the loud, expressive, passionate voices of Wharton's heroines that tell their stories. In that sense, the question of legitimate motherhood is linked to the question of legitimate authorship. As her characters try to find truth in illegitimate passion, Wharton tries to find a true voice in the "illegitimate"—that is critically not approved — realm of the tradition of sentimental writing. Wharton locates the meaningful story in her heroines' sentimental voices and against a background of "male," economic restraint, which she shows to be an evasion of the "real." In that sense, Wharton's "real," "illegitimate" mothers can be compared to Wharton herself, as she becomes the author of the "real," "illegitimate" sentimental story. And it is in this voice that she asserts that illicit female passion is the only "reality" her women characters and her stories consider meaningful. In it lies the fulfillment, anarchy, and tragedy of her heroines.

Notes

1. See Cynthia Griffin Wolff (342). Also, in her discussion of "The Old Maid" and "Roman Fever," Elizabeth Ammons notes the "fierce, maternal passion" that Wharton's women characters feel "toward an extraordinary daughter . . . [who] is the offspring of an illicit affair her mother had as a young woman." And she comments: "How much Edith Wharton as an older woman may have longed, at least at times, for such a daughter is only barely concealed in the two fictions" (169). Like Wolff, Ammons accounts for Wharton's interest in the subject of motherhood in biographical ways. However, I believe that such a biographical reading cannot explain the complicated pattern Ammons herself reveals.

2. Wharton uses the same pattern in her famous short story "Roman Fever" (1934). However, the scope of this essay makes it impossible to include a discussion of it. Also, in her novel *The Mother's Recompense* (1925) Wharton examines motherhood and female desire through a plot that plays with incest.

3. Lewis adds in a footnote that "the editor of the *Ladies Home Journal* said of 'The Old Maid,' 'It's a bit too vigorous for us.' The spokesmen for the *Metropolitan Magazine* declared it to be 'powerful but too unpleasant' " (Letters 443).

4. In *Illness as Metaphor*, Susan Sontag describes how tuberculosis was mythologized and used as a literary convention in nineteenth-century fiction. It became a metaphorical expression of "a secret love" (37). "[It] was understood as a disease that isolates one from the community" (37-38); the "tb-prone character . . . was an amalgam of two different fantasies: someone both passionate and repressed" (39). "TB is the disease that makes manifest intense desire" (45).

5. I agree with Catherine M. Rae that "this [scene] is so unrestrained, so noisy, that one is tempted to wonder if the mature Edith Wharton is sighing to herself and saying, 'How much better things might have been had there been a few rousing scenes. They might have cleared the air' " (124).

6. Susan Goodman argues, "In this story Charlotte receives her recompense when Tina escapes repeating her own folly and is safely married" (116). But isn't Wharton showing that such a "safe" marriage is a worse folly, that it is like death, like entering a "grave"?

Works Cited

Ammons, Elizabeth. *Edith Wharton's Argument with America*. Athens: U of Georgia P, 1980.

Goodman, Susan. *Edith Wharton's Women*. Hanover: UP of New England, 1990.

Lewis, R. W. B. *Edith Wharton: A Biography.* New York: Harper, 1975.

Rae, Catherine M. "Edith Wharton's Avenging Angel in the House." *Denver Quarterly* 18.4 (1984): 119-25.

Sontag, Susan. *Illness as Metaphor.* New York: Farrar, 1977.

Wharton, Edith."Her Son." *Human Nature.* New York: Appleton, 1933.

——. *The Letters of Edith Wharton.* Ed. R. W. B. Lewis and Nancy Lewis. New York: Scribner, 1988.

——. "Life and I." *Edith Wharton Novellas and Other Writings.* New York: Library of America, 1990. 1069-98.

——. "The Old Maid." *Old New York.* New York: Scribner, 1924.

——. *Writing of Fiction.* New York: Scribner, 1925.

Wilson, Edmund. "Justice to Edith Wharton." *Edith Wharton: A Collection of Critical Essays.* Ed. Irving Howe. Englewood Cliffs: Prentice, 1962. 19-31.

Wolff, Cynthia Griffin. *A Feast of Words.* Oxford: Oxford UP, 1977.

Yellis, Kenneth A. "Prosperity's Child: Some Thoughts on the Flapper." *Women's Experience in America.* Ed. Esther Katz and Anita Rapone. New Brunswick: Transaction Books, 1980. 367-88.

9

Demythifying Motherhood
in Three Novels by Fay Weldon

Aleta F. Cane

Kristeva is right, we know very little about the inner discourse of a mother; and as long as our own emphasis, encouraged by psychoanalytic theory and by the looming presence of the (mostly male) mother fixated writers, continues to be on the mother-as-she-is-written rather than on the mother-as-she writes, we shall continue in ignorance.

—Susan Rubin Suleiman, "Writing and Motherhood"

The twentieth century's preoccupation with the Freudians' explanation that all human behavior is centered around the phallus, or the lack thereof, has controlled the discourse about motherhood until fairly recently. Myths of feminine passivity, penis envy, and female masochism have been shown by Juliet Mitchell, Elizabeth Janeway and Nancy Chodorow to be more culturally created than inborn. Chodorow's important book *The Reproduction of Mothering* states, as its thesis, that women mother as they do because they are brought up by mothers who have culturally accustomed them to do so. Coppelia Kahn, citing Chodorow, argues that "motherhood . . . is the cause of the oppression of women in the sense that it is necessary for that oppression, and the oppression of women is inevitable given the institution of motherhood" (73). In *Puffball, The Lives and Loves of a She-Devil,* and *Life Force,* three novels of Fay Weldon, the women are all oppressed by their culture in many ways. Interestingly, the mothers represented in the novels cut across all class levels. The hallmark trait that they each share is the lack of healthy roles upon which to model their own mothering. Every dysfunctional mother in these three novels, is herself the daughter of a dysfunctional mother. Chodorow's emphasis on mothering, as a product of acculturation, would suggest that mothering, in the modern era, must continue to be dysfunctional until the cycle of women's marginalization is broken. Weldon's mothers comprise a convincing case for this hypothesis. In these three novels, Weldon parodies the Freudian myths of motherhood and rejects patriarchal society's marginalization of women and of women's role as mothers. Although various postmodern critics argue that feminism and postmodernism are incompatible projects, in her parodic explosion of the accepted mother myths, Weldon shows herself to be both a feminist and a postmodern novelist.

Weldon takes aim at several misappropriated myths of motherhood. Here are but a few of the more significant issues with which these three novels deal. First, Weldon focuses on the notion that mothers are figures of self-abnegation and altruism, or as the psychoanalyst, Helene Deutsch, prefers "feminine masochism." The second myth is that good mothers have no interests outside those of their families. Thirdly, Weldon debunks the belief that because all mothers are creatures created by nature, they are therefore the best source of nurturing for their own children. The belief that western mothers accept the Madonna as the supreme role model is the fourth myth which Weldon takes to task. Lastly, she explodes the cliche which states that mothers do not write, they are written.

Fay Weldon's novels present a wide variety of dramas which are distinctly those of the mother-who-writes herself. In her novels *Puffball, The Lives and Loves of a She-Devil,* and *Life Force*, all the protagonists are mothers. Interestingly, about half the chapters in *Puffball* deal solely with the activity in the protagonist's uterus, as she prepares to conceive, conceives and develops a fetus. This focus on the physical rather than the social function of mothering makes an important statement. Activity in the womb occurs because evolution has decreed that it will. All outside forces, whether social or cultural, including indecision about the pregnancy, evil medicinal machinations by a neighbor and abandonment by a husband cannot stop the process. As Mabs, the novel's antagonist, proclaims, "The only winners are Auntie Evolution and Mother Nature. Bitches both" (101). Evolution and Mother Nature are the ever present dialectic, and the narrative style which plays them off against one another presents the inescapable nature of the supreme conflict within human life.

Mother Nature herself is the über-myth, and all the psychoanalytically accepted parts of the Mother Nature myth are opened to observation and speculation in these three novels. According to the Freudian analyst, Helene Deutsch, the *sine qua non* of normal motherhood is the masochistic feminine willingness to sacrifice—a sacrifice made easy by the impulse of maternal love whose chief characteristic is tenderness (Suleiman 354). To subvert this notion, Weldon introduces us to women who are anything but sacrificing. In *Puffball*, Weldon introduces us to Mabs and Madge. Mabs is Liffey's (the protagonist) neighbor and Madge is Liffey's mother. Mabs is a farm woman, who at first glance leads a perfectly natural life. But she is unnatural in fundamentally dangerous ways. She is a witch with powerful knowledge of herbal remedies and poisons. Dosing everyone around, in order to have them do her bidding, Mabs seems to have power over nature in that when she is jealous or angry she can cause storm clouds to gather on the local mountaintop. She loves being pregnant and likes small babies: it is children she cannot and does not abide. She is jealous of her teenage daughter Audrey's adolescent allure, and angry at her for being intelligent. Audrey was "a young woman with rounded hips and bosom and Mabs' raised fist fell as she felt for the first time the power of the growing daughter" (*Puffball* 90). Mabs forces Audrey to take on most of the mothering and household chores. Audrey is usually not fed and Mabs takes her books from her. Eddie, Mabs's eight-year-old son, takes the worst share of Mabs's moods. He is beaten and cuffed constantly. She dislikes her daughter Debbie because she moves slowly. The children cannot win. If one is too quick, the mother dislikes him or her, if the other is slow, the mother cannot abide that characteristic either. Mabs's maternal, nurturing instinct only extends as far as the infant state, a state where the child has not yet differentiated or separated itself from its parent. Thus, Mabs's mothering instinct is more self focused than other directed. When her daughter, Debbie, complains of violent stomach pains, Mabs doses her with some poisonous herb and locks her in her room. She is being a bother, her mother thinks. The child nearly dies of appendicitis. It is only through Audrey's quick thinking that Debbie is saved. The characteristic in Audrey, which her mother most dislikes, is what saves Debbie from the machinations or simply the indifference of the mother.

The Freudian psychoanalyst, Melanie Klein, speaks rather sympathetically of the murderous impulses children often harbor against their mothers. Suleiman remarks that very few people show sympathy for mothers who harbor murderous thoughts against their children (363). Infanticide can be accomplished consciously by malignant action or unconsciously through neglect. Mabs is Weldon's example of a woman who really does not like her children and harms them alternately through both her violence and her indifference. When Mabs puts her arm around Liffey, the narrator remarks that "that's more than she did for her children" (44). Mabs refuses to allow any of her children to wear protective florescent arm bands so they might be seen at dusk getting off their school bus. She says, "If they're daft enough to get run over they're better off dead" (47). Mabs was raised by a witch and is raising her children exactly as she was raised: indifferently.

Liffey's mother, Madge, gave birth to Liffey as a slap in the face of convention. She had wanted to have a "warrior son" but instead got Liffey who only wanted to please and be loved. Her mother says, "You'll never be a born mother if you take after me" and "I was never one for nature" (135). Madge tells Liffey not to become pregnant and to be wary of Mabs when she visits. Liffey realizes that her mother did not love her and that she would fly right out of her mother's thoughts as soon as her mother left her house. "She realized that children do not forget mothers, mothers forget children" (165). And Liffey knew that she was intensely forgettable to her mother. As if to underscore that point, her mother immediately loses her daughter's new address.

Mabs and Madge (whose very names are so euphoniously alike) are opposite sides of a single coin. They both have children for idiosyncratic reasons and primarily selfish reasons. Each woman is either incapable of or indifferent to mothering the children that she has. Yet their children cling to them, because children want and need more than clothing and food to grow up whole: they want to be loved. Even the adult children in this novel make that very clear. Liffey comments that one day she will outgrow desiring her mother's approval. Neither Mabs nor Madge has a shred of what the Freudians refer to as maternal altruism. That is the significant point that Weldon is making here about motherhood. She creates a world where there is no maternal instinct, no instant mother love or sacrifice. The children who survive live to repeat the same parenting patterns.

The main character, Liffey, becomes pregnant as a bargain with her husband. Her reasoning is every bit as self focused as was her mother's. She wants to move to a country cottage and out of London. The bargain is, "if we move to the country, I'll have a baby." She does not want a child, at this point, but she does want the cottage. As the child of her mother, she has learned her mother's methods in spite of herself, and she exhibits not Deutsch's concept of the innate good mother but Chodorow's belief that mothering is culturally inculcated. She becomes a mother not to nurture but for a reason outside familial considerations.

In *The Life and Loves of a She-Devil*, Ruth gives away her children to their miserable father and his lover, Mary Fisher. In her adventures on the way to remaking herself in the image of Mary Fisher, Ruth encounters other mothers and other children. When she lives with a young unmarried and pregnant mother of two, who is on the dole, Ruth encourages her to sell her children to people who will care for them more than she does. She suggests that the young woman, Vickie, use the money to have a holiday somewhere warm. Ruth says:

If I were you I would sell the unborn baby, in advance for a large sum to adoptive parents. . . . There are many rich people in the world only too anxious to adopt pretty, healthy, white children. By doing so you will be . . . ensuring them longer life, more interesting friends, more beautiful sexual partners, and a much more rewarding life in general than if you condemn them to scrape away down here with you, at the bottom of the world's barrel. Sell them! (207)

When Vickie protests, using the age-old argument about maternal and child connection—"but what about the bond?"—Ruth's (alter ego and) sympathetic omniscient narrator writes:

There was much talk of "the bond" down at the clinic and a good deal to foster it. It was less taxing on welfare funds to have mothers looking after their own progeny than leaving the state to do it. (207)

Weldon takes a dim view of the idea that natural mothers are the most fit people to bring up their own children. As in the case of Vickie's neglect of her children, so again in *Puffball*, Mabs is surely an unfit mother. The doctor and the visiting nurse both question the inordinate number of times they have seen Eddie beaten up and bruised but choose not to do anything about it because of the government's belief that children are better off with their parents.

But if Ruth's remarks about children being better off with rich parents than with poor ones seem to be a manifesto in *Puffball*, we see a similar situation in *Life Force*, which raises doubts about the notion of selling children so that life will be better for them. In this novel, Marion agrees to become pregnant by the "Life Force," Leslie Beck, in order to sell a baby to an infertile South African couple. The deal will make Leslie's business solvent again and will afford Marion sufficient funds to open up her own art gallery. Just as she is about to give birth, Marion muses:

A baby brought up in some squalid inner city room, which was the best a single mother on an ordinary wage could provide. What is natural, careless maternal love, we both agreed, fetus and myself, compared with the love of nonnatural parents who care profoundly, even unto a million pounds worth of love? (165)

At this point in *Life Force*, Weldon is restating views similar to those in *Puffball* and *She-Devil*. However, true to the postmodern precept that there are no hard and fast answers or truths to be found in art (or anywhere), Weldon has Marion's teenage son return to her from South Africa, to announce that his adoptive father is dead and that he does not get along with his adoptive mother who is an alcoholic.

"I paint pictures," he said. "That's what drove my adoptive mother to drink." I thought being called an adoptive mother by the child you rear might be the more likely cause, but children twist the world to suit themselves. (210)

Here Weldon not only subverts the idea that adoptive parents will bring up happier or better adjusted children, but she also calls into question the child's creation of his own drama, apart from that of his mother. Deliciously, Weldon has the son of the gallery owner turn out to be a painter. Marion sells the creations of others professionally and has sold her own creation to subsidize that work. Now the creation (the child) turns up a painter himself whom she believes is creating the drama of his own life by telling his perception of his adoptive mother to the woman who gave birth to him. He has seen fit to put a reason to her drinking based upon his own actions or desires. The adoptive mother's own story is of little consequence to him because the Freudian psychoanalysts only seem to valorize the story of the child, never that of the mother. For Weldon, the only good mother is the one who has had a good mother. In these novels, such mothers do not exist.

As Susan Suleiman notes, writing about mothers is problematic on two fronts. It is not only that male writers focus on the dichotomy within the female population when they write about mothers and others, but that Anglo-American feminist critics tend to write polemically about motherhood from the perspective of the daughter almost exclusively. As Suleiman writes, "it is as if, for psychoanalysis, the only self worth worrying about in the mother-child relationship were that of the child" (355). Why is it, she asks, that the drama in art always belongs to the child? Weldon's mothers answer that question by existing as a paraphrase of Wordsworth: the child is mother to the woman. Weldon shows how mothering is passed down from generation to generation. As Chodorow observes, "women are prepared psychologically for mothering through the developmental situation in which they grow up, and in which women have mothered them" (39). The abused or ignored child becomes the abusive or ignoring parent. Feminist polemicists emphasize the drama of the child's development, and Weldon shows us children (and the adults that they will become) as eternally linked to the ways they were mothered.

In *Puffball*, we encounter many sets of parents who were brought up in dysfunctional households and are repeating the sad pattern in their own children's lives. Liffey and Richard both come from dysfunctional families. We have already met Madge, Liffey's mother. Richard's mother never loved Richard because he was not his father's child. One can only interpolate the family life that Richard and Liffey will subsequently experience together. Two of the children in the novel, Tina and Tony, are the children of Bella and Ray, self-proclaimed Marxists and renowned food writers. They have conveniently set up child care arrangements with Helga, as an au pair. Helga is the only truly maternal figure in the novel, although she is no one's mother. When she leaves Bella and Ray's employ, the children are devastated. "Both children were weeping over Helga's leaving but neither parent showed much concern. 'For God's sake,' snapped Bella, 'stop whining. She was only the maid. It's not as if she was your mother'" (204). But that is the point exactly; she was a mother to them. Bella has so little interest in the children that she leaves them, without feeding them, in the country with Liffey and goes off to a publisher's party without a second thought. Helga was indeed their mother, if not biologically, at least through caring. Here then is another alternative view of mothering—that of the paid caretaker. But, lest a reader believe that this is a solution being offered to the question of who should mother children, it is not. Helga leaves and the children are once again in need. The open-endedness of possible solutions is a hallmark of Weldon's, and indeed most, postmodernist novels.

Just as she questions the psychoanalytic myths of maternal altruism and feminine masochism, so too Weldon reworks the Madonna myth. As Linda Hutcheon writes in *A Poetics of Postmodernism*, "What is important in all these internalized challenges to humanism is the interrogating of the notion of consensus. . . . In its most extreme formulation, the result is that consensus becomes the illusion of consensus . . ." (7). Weldon employs the Madonna myth to remind us that cultures have shaped us, but also to call into question the validity of the power we still afford this myth in modern life. In her essay, "Heretique de l'amour," Kristeva explores the ways in which this myth functions in the Western imagination.

Her tentative conclusion is that in the image of the Virgin Mother, Christianity provided what was for a long time a satisfactory compromise solution to female paranoia: a denial of the male's role in procreation (virgin birth), and a fulfillment of the female desire for power (Mary as Queen of Heaven). (Suleiman 368)

For Kristeva and for Weldon, as well, the myth has lost its power. "It leaves too many things unsaid, censors too many aspects of female experience" (Suleiman 369). Weldon presents the myth in all its glory in *Puffball* and does so parodically. Not only is Liffey's pregnancy planned and worked at, but her intimacy with Tucker makes most of the characters question whose baby it is. Richard wants to think of Liffey as pure, once she is pregnant. He takes his sexual pleasures with every other woman he meets. Isolated in the country, with no car, no phone, Liffey is living an existence which suggests a throwback to the simpler, natural life that Richard now associates with a Madonna. He wants Liffey separated from the sordid world—for she is to be the mother of his children.

He wanted her to be above the sexual morass in which he as a male could find his proper place but she as a wife and mother could not. He wanted her to be pure, to submit to his sexual advances but not to enjoy them, and thus as a sacred vessel, sanctified by his love, adoration and respect, to deliver his children unsullied into the world . . . he had offered her all his worldly goods, laying them down on the altar of her purity, her sweet smile. (89)

This is Richard's perpetuation of the Madonna/whore dichotomy— a great favorite of most patriarchal cultures. Levi-Strauss observed that a major function of a myth is to be "the template of mental operations that have already taken place and are taking place within the speaker and the listener. The themes are expressed and experienced anew for each generation in the group" (Van Buren 56). Richard is reliving the cultural myth, expressing, and perpetuating it. According to Suleiman:

Rich and Dinnerstein are convincing on the ways in which woman's body becomes the carnal scapegoat for the fears of the flesh and mortality or the idol in which we recreate our lost union with mother as flesh . . . Women are encouraged to behave narcissistically as mothers, either position being a defense against the female body's resonance with primitive fears and needs. (369)

Liffey wishes that Richard would treat her more like a woman than a holy vessel, because her sexual needs have changed during her pregnancy. She no longer wishes merely to cuddle, but rather to experiment with some of the ideas she had learned from dabbling in pornography.

It is wonderfully ironic then that when Liffey first senses quickening, she views it as an annunciation. "The Holy Ghost or something descended and inhabited me" (128) she imagines telling her mother. Liffey has been as exposed to the Madonna myth just as Richard has. Even though she clearly understands the irony in being both a sexual being and an immaculate mother, Liffey sees the Madonna myth as a powerful affirmation of herself within nature and as a continuum of culture. Indeed, it may well represent her only source of power within her marriage. But it is just this myth which Adrienne Rich has shown isolates women "creating internal conflicts which are the results of institutional forces which result in women's isolation, women's victimization by the motherhood myth in patriarchal society" (Suleiman 363). Liffey's isolation at Honeycomb Cottage underscores not only the singularity of her current life but foreshadows the emotional isolation that new mothers without a network of friends and extended family must feel. In her isolation she is threatened by natural (placenta praevia) and unnatural (Mabs) dangers with which she is not able to cope alone. Weldon opens to speculation the question of how safe it is to be a Madonna on a pedestal with a rotten societal base.

In *Life Force*, Marion looks at a painting of the Madonna and child and has an epiphany of her own. She "picked up the notion that a visitation by the Holy Ghost would be okay and you'd know it was Him from the dozen red roses He'd offer you first" (95). Marion feels herself to be superior because she is childless and unfettered. Is she better off than her friends? Does she have the politically correct feminist attitude toward the Madonna myth? Since postmodernism "reveals rather than conceals the tracks of the signifying systems that constitute our world—that is systems constituted by us to answer to our needs" (Hutcheon, *Poetics* 13). Weldon is showing us the power of the Madonna myth and how two different women use that signifying system (myth) to explain their own lives to themselves.

In *Life Force,* there is one more use of the Madonna myth which is worth examining. Susan, an aloof social scientist, goes off with Leslie Beck while they are both visiting France. They stop in "Les Ice Caves des Madones." It is almost impossible to see the shapes of the Madonna and Christ child in the cave, yet someone is making money from people's desires to connect with the myth. The story shows the impregnating of the ice maiden (Susan), lying in a brackish green puddle, in a hokey tourist trap which exists to enrich itself by association with the immaculate conception and people's universal desire to connect in some way with that myth. In her use and explosion of it, Weldon is enjoying an ironic comment on the Madonna myth, completely created and transcribed by generations of men writing about women.

The final myth that I would like to explore, in reference to these novels, is Helene Deutsch's perception that "Mothers don't write, they are written." Nancy Chodorow, discussing the work of the psychoanalyst Alice Balint, quotes her as saying, "the ideal mother has no interests of her own" (77). Deutsch writes that "The urge to intellectual and artistic creation and the productivity of motherhood spring from common sources, and it seems very natural that one should be capable of replacing the other" (Suleiman 359). A woman is either mother or writer, not both at the same time. Suleiman quotes the Freudian psychoanalyst, Winnicot, "The good . . . mother is characterized . . . not only by tenderness and the masochistic-feminine willingness to sacrifice but above all by her exclusive and total involvement with her child" (355). Over the years it has been taken as a truth that women do not write; they have children. Kristeva rejects the mother or writer dichotomy saying that motherhood and creativity go hand in hand.

Motherhood which establishes a natural link (the child) between woman and the social world, provides a privileged means of entry into the order of culture and language. . . . If to love her child is for a woman, the same thing as to write, we have that conjunction of the modern, secular equivalent of the word made flesh. (Suleiman 367)

Weldon parodies the myth that mothers don't write, but are themselves written, in all three of the novels under discussion. In *She-Devil*, Ruth gives her children to Bobbo and Mary Fisher, a writer of pulp romances. Mary has been highly successful writing novels comprised of false dreams of love and life. When Bobbo's children come to stay, her editors notice that a "gritty realism" is creeping into her work. Yet she continues to write. Her forced motherhood does not stop her from creating—rather it changes the nature of her work. The only thing which makes her work unsalable is the artistic intrusion of Bobbo, not the children.

Life Force is narrated by Nora. She writes about herself and her friends and the havoc on friendship (and sometimes on marriages) that their pleasure in Leslie Beck's "magnificent dong" has given all of them at one time or another. If Melanie Klein's belief that "art represents a stand in for the mother's body," then Nora's journal would meet that criteria, but again in a parodic way. For Nora is the only one of Leslie's women who actually has a long-term affair with him and would have liked to have had more from him than sex (which is all that he is willing to give). She would have liked to have been the mother of one of his children, but of all the women, she is the only one who never conceived his child (she was on the Pill). So the retelling of the stories of all his women allows her not only to assuage her feelings of guilt about Leslie's wife Anita, but also to create for herself a child substitute. She has actually done the inverse of what Kristeva says about the mother as writer dichotomy. She has created Leslie's book instead of his child. And it is a book much like its pseudo-parents, self-serving and self-centered. By creating the narrator, Nora, Weldon has again opened up a myth to speculation. In so doing, Weldon exhibits her political agenda which is to show women in several relations to the cultural, religious and psychoanalytical myths which dominate western culture. Merely by setting up her characters in such a way as to make us see that they are acting idiosyncratically in relation to these widely-held beliefs makes us question not only the characters' reactions but the very nature of the myth itself.

Since a hallmark of postmodern thought is the absence of received "truth," and since Weldon explores the myths which are currently a focus of feminist polemic, it is not difficult to disagree with Linda

Hutcheon when she writes that "Feminist artists and theorists have resisted the incorporation of their work into postmodernism for fear of diffusing their own political agendas" (*Politics* 2). I believe that Weldon examines motherhood in order to show the range of women's responses to it, and to call into question the patriarchal society's view of motherhood. If the responses of some of her characters are ambivalent, this would certainly dovetail nicely with the open-ended nature of postmodern fiction. If Weldon's characters demythify currently held visions of motherhood, by parodically reliving some elements of the myths, while blithely disposing of others, then clearly a feminist agenda is displayed. Weldon's novels show a strong relation to Umberto Eco's remark that identifies postmodernism as "the orientation of anyone who has learned the lesson of Foucault . . . that power is not something unitary that exists outside us" (Hutcheon *Politics* 3). For Weldon, the desire to be a mother, or not to be and the ability to be both a mother and a sexually active woman, represent personal and political power which must come from within. I believe these ideas to be both feminist and postmodern, as well.

The film critic E. Anne Kaplan suggests that "patriarchy is not monolithic, not cleanly sealed" (201). Judith Wilt, commenting on Kaplan writes, "Gaps appear through which women can begin to ask questions and introduce change" (2). By presenting a variety of women who act and react to the long held myths of the patriarchy, Weldon pushes these "gaps" open a little further. Literarily, she presents her characters in a postmodern framework. Politically, she is unquestionably feminist. She blasts open the commonly held beliefs of the Freudians, which so dominate modern western thought. Thus she opens the way for speculation about other ways of seeing and other ways of being a mother.

Works Cited

Chodorow, Nancy. *The Reproduction of Mothering: Psychoanalysis and the Sociology of Gender*. Berkeley: U California P, 1978.

Hutcheon, Linda. *A Poetics of Postmodernism: History, Theory, Fiction*. New York: Routledge, 1988.

——. *The Politics of Postmodernism*. New York: Routledge, 1989.

Kahn, Coppelia. "The Hand That Rocks the Cradle: Recent Gender Theories and Their Implications." *The (M)Other Tongue: Essays in Feminist Psychoanalysis*. Eds. Shirley Nelson Gardner, Claire Kahane, and Madelon Sprengnether. Ithaca: Cornell UP, 1985. 72-83.

Kaplan, E. Ann. "Motherhood and Patriarchal Discourse." *Women and Film*. New York: Methuen, 1983. 201-13.

Rich, Adrienne. *Of Woman Born: Motherhood as Experience and Institution.* New York: Harper, 1976.

Suleiman, Susan Rubin. "Writing and Motherhood." *The (M)Other Tongue: Essays in Feminism Psychoanalysis.* Ed. Shirley Nelson Gardner, Claire Kahane, and Madeline Sprengnether. Ithaca: Cornell UP, 1985. 352-79.

Van Buren, Jane Silverman. *The Modernist Madonna; Semiotics of the Maternal Metaphor.* Bloomington: U Indiana P, 1989.

Weldon, Fay. *The Life and Loves of a She-Devil.* New York: Ballantine, 1983.

——. *Life Force.* New York: Viking, 1992.

——. *Puffball.* New York: Summit, 1980.

Wilt, Judith. *Abortion, Choice and Contemporary Fiction: The Armageddon of Maternal Instinct.* Chicago: U of Chicago P, 1990.

10

Updike's Rabbit Novels
and the Tragedy of Parenthood

D. Quentin Miller

Post-World War II America is frequently described as fragmented, entropic, and fearful of the impending doom of nuclear apocalypse. In this world the foundations of once-reliable structures have been shaken; religion, economy, political ideology, and community all suffer a fundamental breakdown as a result of the devastation and potential for complete annihilation posited by the existence of the Bomb. Parenthood suffers a similar fate in the years between the detonation of the first Soviet atomic bomb in 1949 and the destruction of the Berlin Wall in 1990; whereas raising a family was once seen as a stabilizing and strengthening force in a chaotic world, children in the Cold War era had the potential to become a burden to the individual who strove to maintain sanity amidst the chaos of the nuclear age. American novels of this period are often characterized by young Americans who wander away from domestic responsibilities such as parenthood, but toward nothing in particular; take, for example, Saul Bellow's *The Adventures of Augie March*, or Jack Kerouac's *On the Road*. Of course, a similar movement away from parental duty can be observed in American novels from the first half of the twentieth century—Kate Chopin's *The Awakening* and Ernest Hemingway's *A Farewell to Arms* come immediately to mind. But in the post-World War II novel, the fragmentation of the family is so prevalent—and its implications are so great for the fragile, post-atomic world—that some novelists of social realism turn their attention toward the more tragic implications of parenthood.

The relationship between Harry "Rabbit" Angstrom and his son Nelson in John Updike's Rabbit tetralogy is a striking example of the antagonism and resentment that can arise between parents and children in a world obsessed with the potential for its own destruction. Jealousy and resentment develop between this father and son, largely as a result of their sense that the American dream—the ideal of individual liberty and the promise of prosperity—is inhibited not only by the threat of the

195

Soviet "other," but by the failure of parenthood to provide any comfort against this threat. The conflict between Harry and Nelson seems an obvious inroad into the Rabbit novels, especially given its ubiquity in the final two novels in the tetralogy; yet critics often overlook the importance of this relationship in favor of investigating Harry's character alone. In *John Updike's Novels*, Donald J. Greiner mentions Nelson only once (54) in his analysis of *Rabbit, Run* (1960), and only three times (73, 78, 80) in his essay on *Rabbit Redux* (1971); all four citations regard Nelson as an unproblematic, passive recipient of his parents' actions. But Nelson holds a prominent place throughout the tetralogy; Harry does everything he can do to destroy Nelson's life, from neglecting his paternal responsibilities in *Rabbit, Run* to sleeping with Nelson's wife in *Rabbit at Rest* (1990). Nelson for his part tries to kill Harry by degrees; he wrecks his father's car in *Rabbit Is Rich* (1981) and completes the gesture by ruining Harry's car dealership and squandering his fortune in *Rabbit at Rest*. At crucial moments, a father-son bond is evident between these two men, but it is generally a bond that arises out of the shared pain of their condition. Updike's Rabbit novels are largely about this pain; they chronicle the life of a man unfit to accept fatherhood and the lives of those he destroys in the slow process of realizing this fact.[1] The four novels cover the entire turbulent era that was Cold War America and they reveal how parenthood, like so many other institutions, is not necessarily the most effective way to cope with the ängst of the contemporary world.

The first paragraph of the Rabbit tetralogy concludes with Harry Angstrom's thought, "The kids keep coming, they keep crowding you up" (*Rabbit, Run* 9). Although Harry is thinking specifically about a group of young basketball players as opposed to his own children, the words serve as a paradigm for a motif that spans the long curve of Updike's Rabbit novels: all of the kids in Harry's life keep crowding him up and threatening his precious sense of individualism. The tetralogy begins with Harry's fear of "the kids" and ends with his sense of inadequacy as a father; on his deathbed in *Rabbit at Rest*, he tries in vain to communicate with Nelson: "Rabbit thinks he should maybe say more, the kid looks wildly expectant, but enough. Maybe. Enough" (425). Placed as they are at the beginning and at the end of one of the most expansive novel sequences to come out of post-World War II America, these quotations indicate that Updike's project in the Rabbit novels is partially to explore how parenthood—the perceived source of comfort and stability for so many postwar Americans—is a source of tremendous anxiety and antagonism to others. Of the many disastrous aspects of Harry's life, his sense of inadequacy as a parent is the most devastating;

there is a nagging feeling throughout the tetralogy that, though sabotaging your own life may be a shame, sabotaging your children's lives is a catastrophe. Viewed this way, the tetralogy as a whole can be recognized as a tragedy, with Nelson's rehabilitation and renewed commitment to his wife and his family as the only catharsis.

Buried somewhere in Harry's unconscious is the idea that parenthood is a rude awakening from the American dream. For him, this dream is characterized by the uninhibited freedom of the individual, including freedom from responsibility. He values his "Goddam precious American rights" (*Redux* 47) to the point that he thinks the American ideals of life, liberty, and the pursuit of happiness exist for him and him alone. For Harry, being a good American involves exercising one's individual rights even (or especially) at the expense of others. There is the sense in these novels that our nation's global competition has its downside in internal competition, manifested in the actual Cold War as the divisiveness of McCarthy-era red-baiting or Vietnam-era upheaval, and manifested in Updike's novels as domestic strife.[2] In the name of being a good American, he stands apart from most of his countrymen on countless issues, including the issue of the importance of good parenting. During Harry's formative years, parenthood was accepted as a national duty as much as a biological obligation; in her book *Homeward Bound*, social historian Elaine Tyler May writes,

Procreation in the cold war era took on almost mythic proportions . . . children were a "defense—an impregnable bulwark" against the terrors of the age. For the nation, the next generation symbolized hope for the future. But for individuals, parenthood was much more than a duty to posterity; the joys of raising children would compensate for the thwarted expectations in other areas of their lives. For men who were frustrated at work, for women who were bored at home, and for both who were dissatisfied with the unfulfilled promise of sexual excitement, children might fill the void. (135-36)

Against this consensus, Harry and Janice Angstroms' lives illustrate that children decidedly might *not* fill that void. For the Angstroms, parenthood is just another of the thwarted expectations of their lives. Consequently, they fail at parenthood, to put it mildly; they find that the burdens and anxieties of the Cold War world prove too great to be remedied by childrearing.

These burdens and anxieties include their suspicion that the American dream—which includes the promise that one will live more comfortably than one's parents did—will not be realized. The Cold War world, realigned and polarized after a globally devastating world war, and plagued by mounting concern over the growing stockpiles of nuclear weapons, does not offer a stable future. Working-class guys like Harry are certain only of the fact that they have been cheated out of their birthright—to enjoy the prosperity of a powerful nation, and to exercise the freedom that comes with it. Thus Harry's resentment over his dead-end job as a MagiPeel salesman in *Rabbit, Run* manifests itself immediately in a critique of Janice and their life together. Early in the novel, he takes time to criticize her at length and to watch some television[3] before asking, "Where's the kid?" (15). Clearly, Nelson's well-being is not foremost in his mind. This lack of concern is soon compounded by overt hostility toward his status as a father: "[Janice] stands up and her pregnancy infuriates him with its look of stubborn lumpiness" (15). We soon learn that Janice was pregnant with Nelson when Harry married her, a circumstance which caused him "fright" (16), or more likely one which added to his anxiety over his very existence in this volatile world. He eventually gives in to a tug of compassion for Nelson, who is at Harry's mother's house; he tells Janice, "I'll run over and get the car and bring the kid back. The poor kid must think he has no home" (17). This compassion is false, though; Harry is really lamenting his own loss of a proper home. He sneaks around his parents' home like a burglar, and spies on the scene inside:

He sees himself sitting in a high chair, and a quick odd jealousy comes and passes. It is his son . . . His mother's glasses glitter as she leans in from her place at the table with a spoon of smoking beans at the end of her fat curved arm. Her face shows none of the worry she must be feeling about why nobody comes for the boy and is instead narrowed, her nose a faceted beak, into one wish: that the boy eat. (25)

Harry is jealous of his own son because he wants to relinquish the responsibilities of parenthood, and he also wants to be spoon-fed an easy existence like the one Nelson currently has. Part of his jealousy might also stem from the fact that he lacks the instinct for parental care exhibited here by his own bird-like mother.[4] Since he has never grown up, in many senses, Harry is barely prepared to accept responsibility for himself, much less for others. His reaction upon seeing this peaceful domestic scene, this happy child who is his but who is not him, is to flee; he slips into his own car as if he were a thief and drives, as all restless young Americans seemed to do in the Fifties, with no particular place to go.

Of course, Harry Angstrom is different from his fictional contemporaries such as Bellow's Augie March and Kerouac's Sal Paradiso in that he has a family to take care of. Updike has spoken of this difference; in a 1990 interview he says,

I read [*On the Road*] with some antagonism because it seemed to me to be so very unreal, so very evasive—about these more or less privileged people zipping back and forth across the country with no visible means of support. And I was trying to make the good Protestant point that we're all involved with our fellow man, and we're all members of families, and so the basic image of [*Rabbit, Run*] is of a man running or leaving or going on the road and disrupting his own family. (Plath 224)

There is a sense that Harry, when fleeing from the scene between his son and his mother, is desperately attempting to undo everything he has done in fathering Nelson and marrying Janice. He yearns, like Kerouac's drifting characters, to lead a carefree, rambling existence, but he is trapped by the fact of his domestic situation, represented metaphorically by the tangled net of American highway on which he finds himself on that fateful night. He manages to untangle himself and to return to his home town; briefly, he "wonders where his son slept" (43), but he shrugs off this guilt and moves in with his former basketball coach before moving in with his new girlfriend Ruth. During his vacation from fatherhood, the various figures Harry encounters fulfill his fantasy to return to the lack of responsibility associated with childhood; a sage gas station attendant calls him "son" (30). Tothero, his former coach, repeatedly calls him "boy" (46) and is himself compared to "a proud mother" (51). When Harry and Ruth meet for the first time, Tothero muses, "Where shall my little ones go [to dinner]" (56), and when it is time for them to order drinks, he addresses them as "children" (58). Even when Harry reminisces about the night he lost his virginity to a Texas prostitute, he recalls that her seductive invitation to him is said in a "motherly" (48) manner. All of this amounts to Harry's profound need to be parented, which is the ultimate gesture of relinquishing his own duties as a parent, to remove himself not only from "Janice's crowding presence," as most critics contend, but especially from "the kid and his shrill needs" (50).

Harry's affair with Ruth is an attempt to recreate his marriage properly, without the pressure of pregnancy. Before their first sexual encounter, he insists that they pretend they are married. After she succumbs to this game, he insists that she forego the precaution of wearing a diaphragm. He has learned nothing about responsibility from his marriage to Janice; he is like a child playing at marriage with Ruth. Following their first sexual encounter, he tries to appease himself of his guilt in a dream in which his mother absolves him of blame, declaring, "My good boy wouldn't hurt anyone" (85). He is able to maintain a guilt-free existence with Ruth for a while because he has recreated a domestic situation without the responsibility of children, something he never had with Janice, who was two months pregnant at their wedding. Although critics such as Donald J. Greiner[5] blame Harry's actions on "sexual dissatisfaction and marital tension" (47), it is important to note that Harry does not fear marital love or domesticity, but rather fears the condition of parenthood, which directly threatens his sense of uninhibited freedom. One of the things he likes best about Ruth is "the soft way her belly looked" (89), which is due as much to her childlessness as to his sexual preference for her body type. When Ruth realizes that she is pregnant with Harry's child, her impulse is to shelter him from this fact. She asks him, "Don't you ever think you're going to have to pay a price?" (136) as if to warn him, but she stops short of saying what's really on her mind: "you dope, don't you know you're a *father*! But no. She mustn't tell him. Saying a word would make it final" (139). Ruth senses Harry's aversion to parenthood here; she uses the word "final," signifying the termination of their happiness. She protects Harry from the fact of his fatherhood just as he absolves himself of the very idea of blame: "If you have the guts to be yourself," he says, "other people'll pay your price" (140). In the name of personal freedom, Harry has set up himself and his family for the tragedy that follows.

Immediately after Harry's declaration of independence from blame, Reverend Eccles observes Nelson being treated unfairly by another boy. Janice's mother, who sees Nelson as an extension of his wayward father, shows no compassion for her grandson; she tells Eccles, "Well, he's like his dad: spoiled. He's been made too much of and thinks the world owes him what he wants" (143). Eccles, who has begun to sympathize with Harry in spite of himself, intervenes in the conflict and commands the other boy with his authoritative "male voice" (142) to give Nelson's toy back to him. Harry's philosophy that other people will pay his price has proven itself accurate, at least for now; Eccles fills in the role of Nelson's father while Harry shirks his parental duties. Yet we see how Nelson's life is already affected by his father's absence, which fosters in him the grief, anger, and confusion which will characterize his personality from this point onward. Eccles notices this moment and "pities Nelson, who will be stranded in innocent surprise many times before he locates in himself the source of this strange reverse tide" (146). He sees Nelson's anger even at the age of two, foreshadowing Nelson's disturbing adult personality, which can be traced to this crucial, fatherless time in his childhood. Eccles rescues Nelson from a dog the boy has provoked, but he is "troubled" by Nelson's reenactment of the dog's snarl, "the harmlessness yet the reality of the instinct: the kitten's instinct to kill the spool with its cotton paws" (147). Nelson's more destructive forces are already loose, and these impulses, far from being kept in check by his parents, are linked directly to his parents' neglect. His unsympathetic grandmother provides a poor substitute for parental love; rather than offering him comfort, she promises him a "whipping" (140) if he teases the dog again.

Paradoxically, despite Harry's and Janice's neglect of their son, the birth of their next child reunites them. Relieved that his wife and daughter are fine after the potentially dangerous event of childbirth, Harry feels pity for Janice and Nelson and remorse for his actions; he declares, "I don't know why I left" (189). He experiences a "warm gust of pride" (202) upon seeing his daughter, perhaps feeling that he is now prepared for parenthood since it will not force him into marriage. He takes care of Nelson for the first time in the novel, sharing an idyllic father-son experience while Janice is recovering at the hospital. Yet this nascent bond between them is tainted by Harry's renewed realization that his freedom is gone, his life essentially over, as he sees it. Playing with Nelson at a playground, "he feels the truth: the thing that has left his life irrevocably; no search would recover it. No flight would reach it. It was here beneath the town, in these smells and these voices, forever behind him. The fullness ends when we give Nature her ransom, when we make children for her. Then she is through with us, and we become, first inside, and then outside, junk" (208). In coming to terms with his responsibility, Harry has realized how much he resents his fatherhood. The fullness in his life is gone; trying to recapture his youth through flight or through adultery is futile. His vision of fatherhood as a trap casts a dark shadow over his fleeting joy at his daughter's birth. Seeing Janice interact with the baby causes him to think of his wife not as a sexually alluring woman but as "a machine, a white, pliant machine for fucking, hatching, feeding" (216). Harry believes that parenthood has made him and Janice less human, and this attitude heightens the tragedy that follows.

After his return, Harry's lust grows and becomes unbearable to him, and it is complicated by the baby's incessant crying, a "wild feeble warning" (225) that confuses Harry and causes him to flee again after a vain attempt to seduce his recently pregnant wife. Their two primary flaws as parents throughout the novel—Harry's absence and Janice's drunkenness—resurface to cause Rebecca's death by drowning, an occurrence Janice immediately recognizes as "the worst thing that has ever happened to any woman in the world" (244). The tragedy of Rebecca's death is intensified by Harry's continued inability to accept any part of the blame for it; he externalizes his actions immediately, convinced that "something held him back [from returning to his home] all day. He tries to think of what it was because whatever it was murdered his daughter" (249). The reader is fully aware that this "something" is Harry's ongoing refusal to accept the responsibility of parenthood. Harry eventually comes around to this realization: "What held him back all day was the feeling that somewhere there was something better for him than listening to babies cry" (250). He is still haunted by the threat that his American dream will not be fulfilled because he has fathered children. The comfort that parenthood is supposed to provide comes only after extreme tragedy; he holds Nelson close after returning home and realizes, "It is himself he is protecting by imprisoning the child" (251). Parenthood for Harry is always about himself throughout *Rabbit, Run*. Despite everything, he is not able to behave unselfishly, even at his daughter's funeral, when he tries to blame the baby's death entirely on Janice. He runs from the funeral and runs again from Ruth who, he discovers, is pregnant with his child.

There can be no way to view Ruth's pregnancy as positive. Parenthood in *Rabbit, Run* is a curse, and far from providing a bulwark against the instabilities of the age, parenthood drives the Angstroms apart, splitting the nuclear family just as the superpowers continued to stockpile atom-splitting weapons. It is noteworthy that the only time Harry, Janice, and Nelson are together in the same place in *Rabbit, Run* is during the tensest scene in the book, when Rebecca's crying causes Harry to resent the home he has returned to. This fragmentation of the family carries over to *Rabbit Redux* (1971), in which Harry, Janice, and Nelson are again hardly ever together. The world has obviously changed since *Rabbit, Run*, but the Angstrom family essentially remains the same. Despite monumental reconfigurations in the global duel between the superpowers—notably the space race and Vietnam—Harry's world has not changed much by the beginning of *Rabbit Redux*; he is still unwilling to accept his role as a typical middle-class dad. Yet through the course of the novel he is forced to come to terms with his status as a father. At the end of the book, when Janice asks Harry, "Who matters more to you, me or Nelson?" he responds quickly, "Nelson" (345). This bond evolves over the course of *Rabbit Redux*, and it is positive only in the sense that Harry has grown and matured ever so slightly in terms of parental duty. Still, his bond with Nelson comes at the expense of his bond with Janice, undermining the Cold War consensus that parenthood is supposed to strengthen a marriage. Furthermore, when Janice follows up her original question by asking Harry if Nelson or his own mother matters more to him, he answers just as quickly, "My mother" (345). Parenthood is a part of Harry's identity by this point, but he still longs to be taken care of more than he longs to take care of his son.

Harry's partial acceptance of the duties of parenthood in *Rabbit Redux* must be taken as a positive development; readers of the Rabbit novels must take what little they can get when it comes to Harry's growth. In this novel Harry's life is on the way to recovery, as the title indicates, and his acceptance of his role as a father has something to do with this development. His ability to change has much to do with the turbulence of his world. Americans in the late 1960s had lived with sweaty palms through the near-apocalypse of the Cuban Missile Crisis and observed with horror the assassinations of political and spiritual leaders such as the Kennedys, Martin Luther King, Jr., and Malcolm X. In 1969, the year that *Rabbit Redux* takes place, Americans were coming to terms with a national identity rendered fragile by divided opinion over Vietnam, racial tension, and conflict over the many ideological differences that separated the generations.

The U.S. Manned Space Program, a largely successful attempt to unify Americans, was a sort of nonaggressive victory over the Soviet Union. But Harry stands apart from his fellow citizens on this issue just as he refuses to take comfort in parenthood. Nelson declares jubilantly when Harry returns from work that the moon-bound astronauts have "left earth's orbit!" Harry responds curtly, "Good for them . . . your mother here?" (23). Harry goes on to criticize Nelson for watching television all day, as opposed to playing basketball as he did at Nelson's age. Harry also notices with disdain that Nelson seems weak and effeminate, more like Janice than himself: "[Nelson's] long eyelashes come from nowhere, and his shoulder-length hair is his own idea. Somehow, Rabbit feels, if he were taller it would be all right, to have hair so long. As is, the resemblance to a girl is frightening" (23). In order to make his son more manly, Harry shares a beer with him; yet he realizes on some level that the boy will never be the man he wants him to be. The mutual jealousy that arises between them at this point continues to plague their relationship throughout their adult lives; both father and son feel that they have been denied certain privileges which would have led to their individual fulfillment, and each of them blames the other for this circumstance. Harry feels some guilt for Nelson's disinterest in life in general and sports in particular, but in typical fashion he puts most of the blame on his own mother, who keeps a scrapbook from Harry's heyday that makes Nelson aware of his own physical inferiority to his father.

In terms of fidelity and responsibility, the tables are turned in *Rabbit Redux*, forcing Harry to face up to his parental duties. When Janice leaves him for Charlie Stavros, Harry cannot rely on other people to pay his price, as he did in *Rabbit, Run*. He does not see caretaking as a fulfilling activity, though: "His son and father seem alike fragile and sad to him. That's the trouble with caring about anybody, you begin to feel overprotective. Then you begin to feel crowded" (26). He experiences the same sensation of crowding that he had in the earlier novel, but since he cannot run, he expresses his restlessness in ways that do violence to his domestic world, eventually destroying his home in fire.

Nelson is, as usual, caught between one parent's destruction of his home and the other parent's absence from it. Just before Janice moves out, the Angstroms go out to dinner and are joined by Charlie Stavros, Janice's lover. Harry and Charlie engage in a heated debate over American involvement in Vietnam, so heated that Nelson is neglected and reduced to tears. Harry and Janice use Nelson as a pawn in their argument: "Harry," Janice asks, "do you want Nelson to die in Vietnam? Go ahead, tell him you do." Harry turns to their child and says, "Kid, I don't want you to die anyplace. Your mother's the girl that's good at death" (50). This exchange proves that both Janice and Harry have yet to discover that their son is fragile, or even that he is human, not some weapon to be used against one another. The debate over Vietnam indicates why Janice is now the one who leaves home and Harry is more inclined to stay and raise Nelson; discussing the issue with Charlie, Janice says

Something is very real to [Harry] about [Vietnam], I don't know what it is . . . Maybe he came back to me, to Nelson and me, for old-fashioned reasons, and wants to live an old-fashioned life, but nobody does that any more, and he feels it. He put his life into rules he feels melting away now. I mean, I know he thinks he's missing something, he's always reading the paper and watching the news. (54)

Harry senses that the world is going on without him since he has decided to make an honest project of the "old-fashioned" ideal of responsible parenthood. His commitment to the old-fashioned reasons that Janice refers to is not enough to make Harry a good father, though. He has already caused Nelson great pain, and his irresponsible and selfish actions in *Rabbit Redux* compound this pain exponentially.

The wounds inflicted upon Nelson as a child are apparent at the beginning of *Rabbit Redux*, and they serve as a basis for his developing personality over the course of the novel. His reaction to the news that his mother has left home signifies how troubled he is: "The boy's face . . . goes rapt, seems to listen, as when he was three and flight and death were rustling above him. Perhaps his experience then shapes what he says now. Firmly he tells his father, 'She'll be back'" (81). Nelson's life up until this point has been characterized by loss—the temporary loss of his father, the permanent loss of his baby sister, and the irrecoverable loss of his childhood. Harry's foundling lover Jill represents a chance for Nelson to retrieve something that has been lost; she fulfills the role of a sister for Nelson as well as a mother, teacher, and first love. Harry's sexual relationship with her is conflicted because he also thinks of her as a daughter of sorts. She is initially introduced to Harry as "a poor child [who] needs a daddy" (122); Harry is of course someone who needs a daughter, but also someone who needs a wife, since Janice has left him. Jill fulfills both roles for him, though his conception of her body as "a child's" (129) initially prohibits him from making love to her, and even after they have repeatedly made love, "he finds the unripe firmness of her young body repels him" (224). The fact of Jill's youth and vulnerability is a constant reminder of her role as his surrogate daughter, and the feelings of guilt generated by this situation explain Harry's increasing anger and increasingly irresponsible behavior.

Harry is also angry about the effect that Jill might have on Nelson. He tries to convince Janice that Jill "is like a sister" (140) to Nelson, but he is wary that she is something more than that, negatively influencing his child by teaching him the ways of the new generation; he yells at her in a fit of anger, "you're turning my kid into a beggar and a whore just like yourself" (151). He also worries that there may be some sexual connection between Jill and Nelson (which causes him no small amount of jealousy), and he is concerned that she may lead his son into drugs. Still, the bond that evolves between Nelson and Jill is strong and inevitable. When Jill dies in the fire that destroys Harry's home in the novel's tragic climax, Nelson's reaction demonstrates how the novel's turbulent events have transformed him from a fragile child to a bitter adolescent who will have to live with deep scars. He attempts to rush into the burning building to save Jill, but a fireman prevents him from doing so: "Seeing his father, Nelson clamps shut his eyes and draws his lips back in a snarl and struggles so hard to be free that the two men holding his arms seem to be wildly operating pump handles" (278). For the first time in his life (but certainly not the last), Nelson demonstrates outright hostility toward Harry: "Nelson screams up at Harry's face: 'You fucking asshole, you've let her die. I'll kill you. I'll kill *you*.' And though it is his son, Harry crouches and gets his hands up ready to fight" (278-79). Jill had represented to Nelson the only possible recovery of his life, which seemed hopelessly devoid of meaning before her arrival. He directs the resentment that he feels upon learning of her death at Harry, who dares ask him, "Blame me, huh?" (283). When Nelson responds affirmatively, Harry tries in vain to pass the blame off: "'You don't think it was just bad luck?' And though the boy hardly bothers to shrug, Harry understands his answer: luck and God are both up there and he has not been raised to believe in anything higher than his father's head" (283). This is Harry's first admission of blame for anything he has or hasn't done as a parent, but the realization comes far too late to do any good. Nelson's soul has essentially died along with Jill, which intensifies the effect of Rebecca's death earlier in Nelson's life to set up the tragic circumstances of his adulthood.

Harry's reunion with Janice at the end of *Rabbit Redux* seems positive and is, on some level, the catharsis that follows the tragedy of this novel. Yet Harry is aware that the effects of the tragedy will remain in Nelson:

The one disturbing element, new and defiant of assimilation, is Nelson. Sullen, grieving, strangely large and loutish sprawled on the caneback davenport, his face glazed by some television of remembrance: none of them quite know what to do about him. He is not Harry, he is sadder than Harry ever was, yet he demands the privileges and indulgence of Harry's place. (305)

The connection between father and son is the next item in the long list of things Nelson has lost: "His father can't reach him, and lives with him in his parents' house as an estranged, because too much older, brother" (306). All of the conflict and turbulence of the 1960s is captured in the middle section of this novel, and Nelson bears the brunt of it. Janice realizes and regrets their poor parenthood twenty years later, in *Rabbit at Rest*, and Harry tries to appease her by blaming the times, "The Sixties. The whole country was flipping out back then. We weren't so bad. We got back together" (267). Though Harry and Janice succeed in reuniting despite all that has happened, they fail, once again, as parents because of their own self-indulgence and the confusion of their times.

The conflict between Nelson and his parents is foregrounded in the last two books in the Rabbit tetralogy. Nelson's adulthood is characterized by violence, depression, drug addiction, and profound hostility toward his father which goes beyond typical Oedipal tensions.[6] Updike's aim in *Rabbit Is Rich* and *Rabbit at Rest* is partially to show how the legacy of a young couple not ready for parenthood in the late 1950s is a pathetic and angry son who is unable to cope with the difficulties of the 1980s. As the focus of the Rabbit novels shifts to Nelson, the tragedy of parenthood enters its next logical phase. Nelson's adult life is devoid of happiness, self-respect, and economic prosperity, all of which are finally enjoyed by his father, to some degree, in *Rabbit Is Rich*. Harry has found and caught a piece of his version of the American dream; Nelson, it seems, never will.

Much of the conflict in *Rabbit Is Rich* stems from Nelson's notion that Harry is trying to deny him his birthright, and from Harry's notion that Nelson is trying to move into his territory before Harry has had a chance to indulge himself in his newfound prosperity. Harry's ongoing sense of being crowded, as on the basketball court in the first scene of *Rabbit, Run*, applies now exclusively to Nelson, the kid whose sole purpose as an adult is to crowd Harry up. Upon receiving the post card that announces Nelson's impending return home, Harry reveals his fear of being crowded and his rejection of his son; he says angrily to Janice, "This house is awkward upstairs, you know that. There's too much hall space and you can't sneeze or fart or fuck without everybody else hearing; it's been bliss, frankly, with just us and Ma. Remember the kid's radio all through high school to two in the morning, how he'd fall asleep to it?" (37). More than just an invasion of his privacy, Harry's jealousy of his son is partly a threat to his sexual self,[7] one of the last remaining vestiges of his waning youth. Harry acknowledges that his resentment of Nelson began at the time of Nelson's sexual activity, made evident to Harry by the absence of some of his condoms when Nelson was a teenager: "From about that time on he began to feel crowded, living with the kid. As long as Nelson was socked into baseball statistics or that guitar or even the rock records that threaded their sound through all the fibers of the house, his occupation of the room down the hall was no more uncomfortable than the persistence of Rabbit's own childhood in an annex of his brain; but when the stuff with hormones and girls and cars and beers began, Harry wanted out of fatherhood" (197). He later confirms the fact that Nelson's manhood is what makes him so threatening, and he explains to Janice that he is so against his son "because Nelson has swallowed up the boy that was and substituted one more pushy man in the world, hairy wrists, big prick. Not enough room in the world" (209). Once Nelson moves home and makes it clear that he intends to stay indefinitely, Harry's reaction is predictable; he essentially runs from the problem, buying a new house in the wealthy section of town and leaving Nelson and his newlywed Pru to live in his old house. In the meantime, the conflict between father and son becomes so intense that it is a miracle they escape the novel alive.

Harry believes that Nelson is weak and inept, and he is once again jealous of him for having opportunities that he himself did not have as a young man. He communicates his resentment of Nelson to Janice: "I wasn't so fucking fortunate as to get to college and the guys that did didn't goof off in Colorado hang gliding and God knows what until their father's money ran out" (64). Harry is not about to hand out to his son the advantages he himself was denied when he was younger. When Nelson appeals to Harry to allow him to sell cars at the lot, Harry's anger rises again. Janice's mother reminds Harry that her husband gave him a leg up in the world when he was younger, but Harry resists the idea; he says,

"I was a forty-year-old man who'd lost his job through no fault of his own. I sat and did Linotype as long as there was Linotype."

"You worked at your father's trade," Janice tells him, "and that's what Nelson's asking to do."

"Sure, *sure*," Harry shouts, "when he gets out of college if that's what he wants. Though frankly I'd hoped he'd want more. But what is the *rush*? What'd he come home for anyway? . . . Take over, young America. Eat me up. But one thing at a time, Jesus. There's tons of time." (112-13)

Harry is unaware at this point that there is not all that much time; Nelson is to be married to the pregnant Pru within a couple of months, in the same way Harry had to marry his own pregnant girlfriend twenty years before. Prior to his knowledge of Pru's pregnancy, all Harry knows is that he is "scared" (83) of his own son, and that he does not want him selling cars at the lot, even if it means that he must act like a child to get his point across. He tells Charlie Stavros, "I *know* he wants in, and I don't *want* him in. He makes me uncomfortable" (119). Far from paternal affection, Harry's attitude toward his own son degenerates to the point of bitter enmity, and he renounces parenthood, likening it to murder: "[Harry] can't shake his depression, thinking of Nelson. Thanks for being such a bastard. He misses Janice [who is vacationing]. With her around, his paternity is diluted, something the two of them did together, conniving, half by accident, and can laugh together about. When he contemplates it by himself, bringing a person into the world seems as terrible as pushing somebody into a furnace" (165). Harry clearly realizes his own failure as a parent, and the failure of parenthood to provide stability or domestic happiness. After regarding fatherhood as a joke, he accepts it as a horrible mistake.

The reason that parenthood has been such a miserable endeavor for Harry has much to do with his own self-indulgence; but Webb Murkett—Harry's mentor for wisdom, financial advice, and good living in *Rabbit Is Rich*—indicates that Nelson's generation in general has been given short shrift. " 'They're disillusioned,' Webb Murkett asserts in that wise voice of tumbling gravel. 'They've seen the world go crazy since they were age two, from JFK's assassination right through Vietnam to the oil mess now' " (164). In short, young Americans witnessed the American dream turn into a nightmare in the 1960s and 1970s, and Nelson is no exception. Yet his situation is exacerbated by Harry's lack of sympathy for his child and his inability to communicate with him. Webb counsels Harry to keep Nelson away from the car lot, but Harry ultimately has no say in the matter, since Janice and her mother control the company. Harry tries to use the differences between his opinion and the opinion of the Springer women against Nelson, accusing him of being weak: "In my day kids *wanted* to get out in the world. We were scared but not so scared we kept running back to Mama. And Grand-mama. What're you going to do when you run out of women to tell you what to do?" (193). This aggressive assault on Nelson's character gives way to Harry's true reasons for being so upset with Nelson's behavior; he is frightened because Nelson is in the same predicament he was in just before he married Janice. "'I just don't like seeing you caught,' he blurts out to Nelson. 'You're too much me'" (194). Though Nelson resists this label, we can see clear parallels between Harry in *Rabbit, Run* and Nelson in *Rabbit Is Rich*; the main difference is that Nelson has to deal with all of the same problems, *plus* an aggressive and uncaring father.

We are allowed direct access to Nelson's point of view for the first time in *Rabbit Is Rich*. His actions—notably his temporary disappear-ance during and immediately after the birth of his daughter—are much like Harry's; yet we get a clear sense that he is not and will never be the same person as Harry. He is far more serious, for one thing, and he lacks his father's charisma, a trait which helps Harry through countless crises. Like Harry, Nelson is also given to running, but his characteristic gesture is destruction, most notably in the form of his wrecking Harry's own car, cars at the lot, and his grandmother's car, all within a three-month period. From Nelson's perspective, the effect of all of Harry's poor par-enting is that he has given his son nothing—no job, no love, and espe-cially no cause for self-esteem. In a soul-searching conversation with his erstwhile lover Melanie, Nelson vents his aggression toward his father: "'He *is* bad, really bad. He doesn't know what's up, and he doesn't *care*, and he thinks he's so great. That's what gets me, his *hap*piness. He is so fucking *hap*py.' Nelson almost sobs. 'You think of all the misery he's caused. My little sister dead because of him and then this Jill he let die.'" Melanie points out that Harry is not God and cautions Nelson that Pru's pregnancy isn't Harry's fault. "'It *is*,'" Nelson insists. 'Everything's his fault, it's his fault I'm so fucked up, and he en*joys* it, the way he looks at me sometimes, you can tell he's really eating it up, that I'm fucked up" (124). This assessment isn't quite accurate; though Harry is somewhat spiteful, his attitude toward Nelson is actually a mixture of pity and fear, evident by his reaction to Nelson's first car wreck in the novel: "He wants to put his hands on the boy, whether to give him a push or comfort his instinct is obscure" (97). He has the same reaction when Nelson totals the cars at the lot; he narrates to his friends, "'The only thing I could think of to do was go stand by the Olds with my arms out like *this*.' He spreads his arms wide, under the benign curve of the mountain. 'If the kid'd come out swinging my gut would've been wide open'" (158). These contrary impulses to hug or strike Nelson represent Harry's attitude toward his son, whom he ultimately loves, but outwardly resents. Nelson's interpretation of Harry's attitude as enjoyment arising from competitiveness stems from abysmally low self-esteem. He feels as though he has been completely dispossessed of anything worthwhile; he feels undeserving even of pity, telling his father, "Don't feel sorry for me. Don't waste your feelings on me" (192). This is a crucial difference between Harry and Nelson; Harry has indulged himself in everything except self-pity. He is self-involved to the point that he cannot respond to Janice's painful, sobbing admission that Nelson "*hates* himself" (399), directing attention instead to the fact that Nelson's running has deprived him of the partner-swapping opportunity of a lifetime. By contrast, Nelson pities himself to the point of self-destruction, manifested by his excessive drinking in this novel and his cocaine addiction in *Rabbit at Rest*.

The resentment of parenthood is passed down from one generation of Angstroms to the next. Nelson takes out his anger on Pru because she is pregnant; he allegedly pushes her down a flight of stairs after a drunken argument at a party, and once she has recovered he tells her, "the only thing you know is how to hang on to that damn thing inside you, *that* you're really good at" (336). Since he has been denied his piece of the American pie, and has had to accept a life without parental love, Nelson is no more equipped to deal with an unexpected pregnancy than Harry had been two decades earlier. The crisis is resolved quietly in *Rabbit Is Rich*; Nelson returns to college and exits the novel as he had entered it—with a post card to his parents. "The kid's a father and doesn't seem to know it," Harry complains to Janice, and declares his son "'a hopeless loser,' but his heart wasn't in it. The kid was no threat to him for now. Harry was king of the castle" (427). The legacy of bad parenting that Harry passes on to Nelson is not as important to him as preserving his own rights and privacy. He is more relieved that his son is out of his hair than he is concerned that his son is an unfit father, which indicates that his conflict with Nelson is largely about jealousy and the threat of being crowded.

Nelson continues to represent to Harry a threat to his enjoyment of an uncomplicated bourgeois life. Harry has written off his son as a hopeless loser, and rather than try to correct for his misguided parenthood, he spends time searching for his lost daughter—Ruth's daughter, Annabelle, who preserves for him the possibility of another chance at producing a "winner," and who can symbolically fill the void for Jill and Rebecca, his two daughter-figures who died. He visits Ruth in order to confirm his belief that Annabelle is indeed his child; he studies the girl's school picture approvingly, noticing his qualities in her. The fact of this resemblance is enough to begin to make up for Nelson's physical shortcomings, in Harry's mind, but his satisfaction is undercut by Ruth's insistence that he has again been neglectful as a father; she says, "you didn't give a simple shit what had happened to me, or my kid, or anything. . . . When I think of you thinking she's your daughter it's like rubbing her all over with shit" (419). Ruth's tough assessment of him as an utter failure jars him into admitting some blame: "I never was too good at thinking things through" (420).

This realization again comes too late to do any good, and the only hope left for Harry is to be an adequate grandfather. The final sentences of *Rabbit Is Rich* prove that he cannot reconcile his individual needs with the presence of grandchildren; upon seeing his granddaughter he reflects, "Fortune's hostage, heart's desire, a granddaughter. His. Another nail in his coffin. His" (437). Harry has concluded that parenthood leads to disappointment, which leads to grandparenthood, which signifies death. Death becomes Harry's enduring obsession in *Rabbit at Rest*, and it frightens him that death may be the only point to his life. His old age is characterized by his simultaneous fear of death and of the younger generation; he observes, "There is something hot and disastrous about Nelson and Pru that scares the rest of them. Young couples give off this heat; they're still at the heart of the world's business, making babies. Old couples like him and Janice give off the musty smell of dead flower stalks, rotting in the vase" (82). He tries to put off the depressing thought "that the whole point of his earthly existence has been to produce little Nellie Angstrom, so he in turn could produce Judy and Roy, and so on until the sun burns out" (38). The end product of Harry's fatherhood is this existential ängst; far from a comfort against the trauma of his world, his child is simply an intensification of this trauma. Nelson lives up to this assessment in *Rabbit at Rest* by becoming horribly self-indulgent and destructive, and a worse father than Harry himself ever was.

Part of Harry's ängst stems from the waning of the Cold War, the geopolitical structure that dictated his definition of America and the American dream all through his adult life. Harry senses the end of something fundamental with the collapse of the Soviet empire: " 'I miss it,' he says. 'The cold war. It gave you a reason to get up in the morning' "

(293). Collapsing is in fact the dominant image in *Rabbit at Rest*; Harry twice collapses from heart attacks, Nelson's life collapses utterly due to his cocaine addiction and subsequent theft from Springer Motors, and the Eastern bloc collapses, quietly and suddenly, in the distance. Harry muses, "Without the cold war, what's the point of being an American?" (367). Without the Cold War it is difficult for Harry to define what he wants from life, and he begins to realize his faults as a parent; Janice acknowledges that Harry "had a hard time when we were younger giving up his dreams and his freedom but he seems to be at peace now" (120). By the novel's conclusion he no longer has the stamina to pursue his dreams, and he finally makes some sort of peace with Nelson. But this reconciliation comes after some of the most momentous mistakes he has ever made, and after some of the most turbulent moments in his relationship with his son.

Rabbit at Rest opens with Harry's realization that "facing Nelson has made him feel uneasy for thirty years" (1). The early pages of the novel reveal variations on this theme; Harry describes his son as "a real sore spot" (6) and "shifty" (8), and frequently observes that Nelson frightens him. Resentments between the two exist as a result of the differences between their generations; when Harry reiterates to Nelson that he worked long and hard hours at Nelson's age, Nelson retorts, "That was *then*, Dad, this is *now*. You were still in the industrial era. You were a blue-collar slave. People don't make money an hour at a time any more; you just get yourself in the right position and it *comes*. . . . It's *easy* to be rich, that's what this country is all about" (31). Nelson is clearly misdefining the American dream for himself here in a desperate effort to achieve the prosperity Harry enjoyed in *Rabbit Is Rich*; his philosophy is mocked by the revelation that he has embezzled hundreds of thousands of dollars from his parents' car dealership to support a cocaine habit. Harry realizes that something has gone wrong to result in this type of attitude from his boy: "Nelson's the one who needs parenting; he always did and never got enough. When you don't get enough of something at the right biological moment, Rabbit has read somewhere, you keep after it until you die" (73). We see Nelson enacting his animosities toward his parents and toward his own wife and children in an attempt to make up for some of the tragic misfortunes of his childhood, notably Jill's and Rebecca's deaths. Once the dealership collapses and Janice takes a firm hand with Nelson, Harry and Janice begin to make retributions for their poor parenting. When Harry asks Janice how Nelson reacted to her tough talk about his problem and the company, she responds, "he liked it. He's just been begging for the rest of us to take over, he knew he was way out of control" (250). Nelson's cocaine addiction is much more than a chemical dependency, in this sense; it is a desperate attempt to be taken care of as he never had been as a child.

The situation is complicated for a number of reasons, though. In the first place, Nelson is an adult now, and by all accounts he must take some responsibility for his own actions. In the second place, Harry is still behaving territorially, continuing to compete with his son rather than to father him. Nelson at some point realizes that he must take control of his own life, and it appears that his initiative to rehabilitate himself is going to work. Harry, on the other hand, has not essentially changed, and cannot face up to his problems, a fault which continues to render him a tragic figure. He has learned nothing, even a month before his death when his sleeping with Pru was, as Janice accurately points out, "the worst thing [Harry has] ever done, ever, ever" (359), and she exhorts him to "help undo some of the damage [he has] done for once in [his] life" (361). But Harry's incapacity to change causes him to follow his lifelong instinct to run away from his problems, and he dies without ever resolving them. His failure as a parent is complete; his son has at least learned to take some responsibility for his own actions, but Harry has not.

Perhaps Nelson has learned something from Harry's mistakes through observation; as the Japanese representative from the Toyota corporation points out to Harry, "Good teacher not always good parent" (326). The fact that Nelson seems to have learned a lesson by the end of the novel sequence enables the catharsis that follows the tragedy. In their final phone conversation, Nelson tells Harry that he and Pru are trying to get pregnant as part of his commitment to a new life after his addiction; he says to his father, "All this has made us realize how much we've been neglecting our marriage and how much really we have invested in making it *work*. Not only for Judy and Roy, but for our*selves*. We love each other, Dad" (400). This sense of family and cooperation is something that Harry has never experienced; he thinks at first that Nelson is admitting it to him "to make him feel jealous" (400), but he soon retreats from this emotion and tells Nelson for the first time in his life, "I'm proud of you" (401). Harry has made some sort of peace with his son after so many years of turbulence, though his conflicts with Janice remain unresolved after his death. Harry, like Lear or any number of tragic fathers, realizes his mistakes too late; but since he does realize them, and since it does seem like a new order can arise from the ashes of his mistakes, there is hope for parenthood.

Harry is thirteen in 1946 when the Yalta treaty was signed ending World War II, and he dies at the age of fifty-seven in 1990 when the Soviet Union surprisingly dissolved. His adulthood, burdened by

unwanted parenthood, coincides exactly with the longest war in American history. The Cold War lurks in the background of Updike's tetralogy, and there is more than a suggestion that the fate of parenthood in
these novels is inextricably linked to the pressures of the Cold War as
it intersects with the popular notion of the American dream. The
threats posited by the existence of a global "other"—threats to our
democratic ideology, our military hegemony, and our economic prosperity—cause anxiety in middle-class Americans like Harry Angstrom,
forcing him to redefine his ideals of individual liberty. Looking at
Nelson's transition into the post-Cold War era, such threats still exist;
for instance, the terrorist bombing of Pan Am flight 103 is a recurrent
concern in *Rabbit at Rest*. But it seems as if some hope exists for
Nelson as a father and for his family as a functional unit, despite the
extent of the pain he has endured as a son. We can glean no optimism
from Harry's life, but his son's life—though it was raked over the hot
coals of the later decades of the Cold War—emerges with a glimmer of
hope. There is hope for parenthood in the post-Cold War era, just as
there is hope for a world free from the anxieties that hung over the
globe like a mushroom cloud throughout the Cold War, making all of
our endeavors—including the fundamental one of raising a stable
family—difficult, if not tragic.

Notes

1. Margaret Gullette writes briefly of "the Laius complex" in *Rabbit Is
Rich*, and acknowledges that "Updike's early novels and stories describe better
than anyone's how threatening children can feel to male parents" (76); yet she
sees Updike's version of the Laius myth as a parody "in the comic mode" (78),
whereas I view it as tragedy, in the context of the entire tetralogy.

2. For a discussion of history in the first three books of the Rabbit tetralogy, see Dilvo I. Ristoff, *Updike's America: The Presence of Contemporary
American History in John Updike's Rabbit Trilogy*. New York: Peter Lang, 1988.

3. The prevalence of television in the Angstroms' world adds another
dimension to their dissatisfaction with their lives; in a discussion of 1950s t.v.
shows such as *Leave It to Beaver, Father Knows Best*, and *The Adventures of
Ozzie and Harriet*, David Halberstam points out, "To millions of Americans,
coming from flawed homes, it often seemed hopelessly unfair to look in on
families like this" (512). The idyllic television family provides a sharp contrast
to the Angstroms' dysfunction, a contrast made ironic by the fact that Nelson's
first name is the surname of the most enduring of these perfect-family television
portraits: Ozzie and Harriet Nelson.

4. For an extended discussion of family metaphors and the redefinition of family roles in Updike's Rabbit novels, see Kerry Ahearn, "Family and Adultery: Images and Ideas in Updike's Rabbit Novels." *Twentieth Century Literature* 34 (1988): 62-83.

5. Greiner is not the only critic who fails to recognize parenthood as the motivation for Harry's running; Matthew Wilson, in an essay that covers the entire tetralogy, also overlooks the link between Harry's actions and Nelson's existence, focusing instead on Janice and Ruth; he writes, "women are, centrally, the representatives of society in the constraints of marriage" (8), ignoring the boy who is more constrained by the marriage than either of his parents are.

6. See also Jack DeBellis, "Oedipal Angstrom," *Wascana Review* 24 (1989): 45-59. Margaret Gullette argues that *Rabbit Is Rich* "leads us out into post-Oedipal light" (71), but she is focusing, as most critics do, on Harry rather than on Nelson.

7. Margaret Gullette recognizes this sexual rivalry as well, and she notes that "By the time this rivalry is fully apparent . . . the novel is wedded to comic outcomes" (69). It is noteworthy that *Rabbit Is Rich* is the only novel in the tetralogy that does not follow a tragic pattern, but the tensions that arise between Nelson and Harry fuel the eventual tragedy in *Rabbit at Rest*, which had not been written when Gullette published her study.

Works Cited

Ahearn, Kerry. "Family and Adultery: Images and Ideas in Updike's Rabbit Novels." *Twentieth Century Literature* 34 (1988): 62-83.

DeBellis, Jack. "Oedipal Angstrom." *Wascana Review* 24 (1989): 45-59.

Greiner, Donald J. *John Updike's Novels*. Athens: Ohio UP, 1984.

Gullette, Margaret. *Safe at Last in the Middle Years*. Berkeley: U of California P, 1988.

Halberstam, David. *The Fifties*. New York: Villard, 1993.

May, Elaine Tyler. *Homeward Bound: American Families in the Cold War Era*. New York: Basic, 1988.

Plath, James. *Conversations with John Updike*. Jackson: UP of Mississippi, 1994.

Ristoff, Dilvo I. *Updike's America: The Presence of Contemporary American History in John Updike's Rabbit Trilogy*. New York: Lang, 1988.

Updike, John. *Rabbit at Rest*. New York: Knopf, 1990.

——. *Rabbit Is Rich*. New York: Knopf, 1981.

——. *Rabbit Redux*. New York: Knopf, 1971.

——. *Rabbit, Run*. New York: Knopf, 1960.

Wilson, Matthew. "The Rabbit Tetralogy: From Solitude to Society to Solitude Again." *Modern Fiction Studies* 37.1 (1991): 5-24.

11

Fatherhood Lost and Regained
in the Novels of Anne Tyler

Elizabeth Mahn Nollen

Understandably, the most common critical approach to the works of Anne Tyler is to study her depiction of the American family. Doris Betts claims that "Family and its clutter remain her metaphor for life" (31). John Updike notes her "fascination with families" (qtd. in Salwak 115) while Ann Romines details Tyler's use of "the home plot" (qtd. in Salwak 163). Jay Parini praises her ability to "celebrate family life without erasing the pain and boredom that families almost necessarily inflict" (qtd. in Salwak 170). And finally, Jessica Sitton describes the "signature element" of Anne Tyler's work, which she says is evident in *The Accidental Tourist*, as "lovingly drawn, eccentric characters who come into conflict with themselves and each other as they either slip or jostle their way through life, simultaneously nurtured and stifled by their families and their past" (qtd. in "Anne Tyler" 320).

Paralleling recent sociological and psychological research, there is much emphasis in studies of Tyler on her portrayal of the many and varied forms of dysfunction—or "ultra-functionality"—represented in her thirteen novels (Humphrey qtd. in Salwak 148). While much attention is paid to her disquieting pictures of broken marriages, failed relationships, and child abuse, some critics complain that her novels do not represent the reality of the contemporary family, lack realistic portrayals of sex and violence, and provide parallels with low art, like soap operas, that appeals to the escapist, wish-fulfillment fantasies of its audience. These critics speak of Tyler's candy-coated, saccharine, even "Nutra-Sweet" quality (John Blades qtd. in "Anne Tyler" 321). Or, in a more positive light, her fiction is classified as belonging to the comedy of manners (Salwak 179, 189). In either case, the redemption/regeneration of certain characters has not been taken as seriously as it might be. One example of this, which becomes very important given the emphasis on family in the Tyler canon, is the insufficient attention paid to the striking representations of effective parenting, especially fathering, in her works.

217

While critics have praised her male characters, they have largely over-looked their sometimes impressive fathering skills. Nevertheless, a notable oversight in Tyler criticism to date, one that is apparent in liter-ary criticism generally, is a study of fathers who provide essentially posi-tive, if complicated, examples of parenthood.[1]

Three fathers come immediately to mind: Jeremy Pauling in *Celes-tial Navigation* (1974), Ian Bedloe in *Saint Maybe* (1991), and Macon Leary in *The Accidental Tourist* (1985). The stories of these three fathers, albeit not chronologically, lie along a continuum of parental effectiveness in the Tyler canon. Linda Wagner-Martin rightly pro-nounces that "fathering has come into its own in a very positive sense in Tyler's work" with the publication of *Saint Maybe* (qtd. in Salwak 171). I contend, however, that it is earlier, with the publication of *The Acciden-tal Tourist*, that fathering really comes into its own, and in a more posi-tive sense than in *Saint Maybe*.

Before moving to a more extended discussion of the three novels in question, a brief overview of this continuum of parental effectiveness and how Tyler's three father figures fit into it will be presented. Initially, *Celestial Navigation*'s artist figure, Jeremy Pauling, is humanized by his experience with step-fatherhood and then fatherhood as he becomes increasingly involved with Mary Tell almost despite himself. When there at last seems to be a chance for Jeremy to become a real full-time father to Darcy and his children by Mary, he finds he lacks the strength to rescue them from the squalid existence they share with their mother in the fishing shack. In the end, as Jeremy tearfully returns to his lonely life at the boarding house, art wins out over life. In *Saint Maybe*, Ian Bedloe reluctantly assumes the "burden" of caring for Danny's children as penance for his brother's suicide and then is given a "second chance" at effective parenting with his own child, which promises to be a more joyful, if still worrisome, undertaking. Whereas art won out over father-hood in Jeremy's life, fatherhood wins out over religion as Ian Bedloe turns down the leadership of the Church of the Second Chance, offered to him by "Father" Emmett, to himself become a father. *The Accidental Tourist*'s Macon Leary is also given a "second chance" at parenting after the tragic accidental death of his son Ethan as he accepts the role of step-parent to Muriel's sickly son, Alexander. Knowing that Muriel cannot give him his own child, Macon shows that his commitment to fatherhood is totally unselfish and complete.

Thus, in Tyler's continuum of effective fathering, we move from Jeremy, who is neither allowed to nor capable of developing his budding paternal instincts, to Ian who has the potential to become an effective father to his own biological child after forcing himself out of misplaced religious zeal to parent his brother's children as a penance. Finally, in Macon Leary, the author presents what is, in the Tyler canon, the apogee of good fathering. This is a man who only learns to be a positive parental role model after the loss of his only son and the subsequent step-parenting of his lover's son.

Of the three Tyler novels containing good or potentially good central father figures, it is only *The Accidental Tourist* that has an unqualified happy ending. Although this ending has been criticized for its "sugar coated sweetness"—Tyler herself considering an alternate ending—it is the only closure the author could choose to get her message across: that fatherhood matters—that it can be a redemptive and healing force. After an examination of Tyler's depiction of fatherhood in *Celestial Navigation* and *Saint Maybe*, I will turn to a full examination of parenting in *The Accidental Tourist* with emphasis on Macon Leary's impressive development of fathering skills.

Fatherhood is thrust upon the needy sculptor, Jeremy Pauling, in *Celestial Navigation* when he is forced to take in boarders after his beloved mother's death. Tyler presents Jeremy as the sickly favored child who lives at home with his mother. In an ironic recasting of Tennessee Williams' tragic drama *The Glass Menagerie*, Jeremy becomes a male version of Laura Wingfield, a "pasty and puffy-faced" (13) agoraphobe whose existence is just as colorless as his body (11).[2] The significantly named Mary and her young daughter Darcy intrude on Jeremy's "silent golden period" when "childless, wifeless, friendless" (153) he could devote all his time to his sculpture (153). Very much like the post-Sarah/pre-Muriel Macon Leary, Jeremy is described as a man marooned on an island (97) in need of mothering. Mary is indeed an earth mother who is never happier than when she is in her nearly perpetual state of pregnancy (61).[3] From the very beginning, she, like Muriel, seems to be a total mismatch for Jeremy. Whereas Mary is able to meet real life head-on, unlike the neurotic sculptor, she is out of her element in his world. Her limited artistic vision is represented by her domestic doodles of "steam irons and tricycles and Mixmasters" (128) while Jeremy's sculpture is worthy of one-man shows. However, much as Macon slips "accidentally" under Muriel and Alexander's spell, so too is Jeremy entranced by Mary and Darcy, and before either he or the reader can imagine it, he has fathered five children with Mary. Curiously, Jeremy, like the Biblical Joseph of the nativity story, seems to have little real importance in his family's life. The births of Jeremy's five biological children are described as virgin births; his children, like Jesus to Joseph,[4] seem to have no real links to him:

He could find no physical resemblance to himself. He thought that was natural, for Mary's pregnancies appeared to be entirely her own undertakings. . . . Where had *all* of them [the children] learned to march so fearlessly across the teeming streets, to brave their way through the city schools, and shout and cheer and throw oranges without a trace of self-consciousness? (141)

We are reminded here of the striking differences between the huddled figure of Macon Leary and his biological son, Ethan. We are also reminded that later on it will be Macon who is responsible for Alexander's transformation from a sickly, germy (significantly, Jeremy's childhood nickname) boy to a healthy, sunny child reminiscent of Ethan.

Mary herself nevertheless comments that Jeremy loves children, and this seems to be borne out by certain touchingly paternal gestures in the novel. The painfully agoraphobic Jeremy forces himself on one occasion to walk seven blocks to attend Darcy's school play and proceeds to embarrass her by loudly applauding all by himself the moment she delivers her line. Before what turns out to be his extremely painful final leave-taking of his children in the fishing shack, Jeremy shops for special surprises for each of them. Thus it is all the more disappointing for the reader when this sensitive artist figure, who has indeed shown what is for him a "stubborn, hidden strength" in dealing with his new domestic responsibilities, allows himself to be thrust out of his family's lives at the end of *Celestial Navigation* (195).

Ironically, as Jeremy Pauling returns to his lonely life at the boarding house, his final work of art reflects his situation. Voelker, in an interesting discussion of "Tyler's boardinghouse of fiction" notes the emptiness and lifelessness of Jeremy's final work in the novel, a miniature boarding house (76). Tyler describes it this way:

Only in Jeremy's piece there were no people. Only the *feeling* of people—of full lives suddenly interrupted, belongings still bearing the imprint of their vanished owners. Dark squares upstairs full of toys, paper scraps, a plastic doll bed lying on its side as if some burst of exuberance had flung it there and then passed on, leaving such a vacancy it could make you cry. (221)

Tyler sees the "imaginary family" Jeremy has suggested through this final work as clearly inferior to the one he has lost (223). As Barbara Bennett states, finally "Jeremy successfully communicates with society only through his art" (73). In the final sentence of the novel, as he and Miss Vinton lock themselves away behind their drawn window shades, the reader mourns the loss of a fragile yet promising father figure. In this portrait of the conflicted artist/parent figure, we see mirrored

Tyler's own ambivalent feelings about art versus family. Despite her comments about needing a "stern white cubicle" of her own much like Jeremy's attic room in order to practice her art, her enviable family situation is living proof, unlike the tragic reversal at the end of *Celestial Navigation* —a promising father shunned and a once enviable example of motherhood now allowing her children to live in squalor—that art and domestic responsibility can successfully coexist ("Because I Want" G7).[5]

In *Saint Maybe*, we see another reluctant father figure in the character of Ian Bedloe as he accepts the "burden" of caring for Danny's children to assuage his own terrible guilt feelings for the part he played in his brother's suicide. Like Jeremy, Ian proves to be a better father than either he himself or the reader might have expected. Ian, without the full weight of neurotic baggage that Jeremy carries, is in fact a very effective father, despite his complaints of "wasting" his youth and his self-aggrandizing talk of penance (234). The theme of penitence, however, becomes so heavy handed in *Saint Maybe* that the reader is not convinced by the end of the novel that Ian will be able to embrace fatherhood enthusiastically when his own wife Rita becomes pregnant. Thomas, Agatha, and Daphne have turned out well, and Ian claims that "You could never call it a penance to have to take care of these three. They were all that gave [my] life color, and energy, and . . . well, life" (229). Ian has paid a price, however. He resembles the agoraphobic Jeremy Pauling as he is described as an "eccentric, middle-aged . . . uncle" that the children "loved" and "winced for" at the same time (267).

Nevertheless, there is definite hope for Ian Bedloe at the end of *Saint Maybe* as he turns down Rev. Emmett's offer to be the next minister of the Church of the Second Chance. Unlike Jeremy Pauling, who ultimately chooses art over fatherhood, Ian promises to place fatherhood above the religion he had convinced himself he was serving by fathering Danny's children. As he turns down the offer to become the next "Father" of the Church of the Second Chance, he accepts the challenge of becoming a real father himself. He sets about the task of creating a home after he discovers that the "family" of the Church of the Second Chance is a poor substitute for a family of his own. As Ian Bedloe carves a cradle for his first biological child, much as the carpenter Joseph might have done for Jesus, he thinks to himself, "All his years here, he had worked with straight lines. . . . Now he was surprised at how these shallow U shapes satisfied his palm" (347-48). He, like Jeremy, has become more flexible as a result of his parenting experience.

However, as he ponders his own imminent fatherhood, "the notion brought forth . . . worry and excitement and also, underneath, a pervasive sense of tiredness" (346). He tells Rita that as he served as step-father for Danny's children, he alternately felt boredom and terror: "Some days I felt like a fireman or a lifeguard or something—all that tedium, broken up by little spurts of high drama" (344). These are certainly plausible responses for a "fortysomething" father-to-be, but what is missing is the sheer wonder and joy that parenthood brings.

At the end of *Saint Maybe*, the reader is left with a touching picture of Ian holding his new son, but also with lingering doubts about the parenting abilities of this middle-aged father. Will he come to perceive his son as a burden as he did Danny's children, who devoured his youth? As he picks up the baby from the cradle, the child is described as "a burden so light it seemed almost buoyant; or maybe he was misled by the softness of the flannel" (372). Perhaps here Tyler is simply registering the realities of parenthood as she does for the family as a whole in her works—that it comes with inherent burdens as well as blessings. Even earth mother Mary Tell describes her cherished children as tent poles holding her down at one point in *Celestial Navigation* (126). Nevertheless, the ending of *Saint Maybe*, with this final picture of father and son and Ian's flashbacks of Danny and the adulterous Lucy, is not an unqualifiedly happy one. Although Tyler leads the reader to believe that Ian, Rita, and Joshua will have the happy family life that so tragically eluded Danny and Lucy, the ending is purposely left open-ended.

The Accidental Tourist's Macon Leary, more than either Jeremy Pauling or Ian Bedloe, learns to enjoy, and indeed joyfully embraces, fatherhood by the end of the novel. Jeremy of course tearfully forsakes fatherhood at the end of *Celestial Navigation* (246) and is tragically presented as one half of "an elderly couple . . . arriving at the end of their dusty and unremarkable lives," locked away from the world (248). Tyler ends *Saint Maybe* with the possibility of a happy life for Ian, Rita, and their new son, Joshua. In *The Accidental Tourist*, however, Tyler presents the most complex and ultimately satisfying picture of the blessings and burdens of parenthood, especially in regard to fatherhood and step-fatherhood. Although Macon Leary has suffered what many people consider to be the ultimate loss, that of a child, he learns to be an even better parent to Muriel's son than he was to his own—and teaches her to be a better mother in the bargain. While Ian Bedloe takes the first tentative steps toward seemingly model fatherhood at the end of *Saint Maybe*, the reader actually sees the process unfold in the second half of *The Accidental Tourist*. Therefore, this novel affords a unique opportunity in the Tyler canon to view the reciprocal regenerative process in which Macon is both humanized and transformed into a truly effective and joyful parent at the same time Alexander is humanized and transformed into a healthy, happy little boy.

The Accidental Tourist has been criticized for what some perceive to be its candy-coated, sentimentalized ending. Alice Hall Petry provides a useful summary of these negative reviews:

> Lee Lescaze argues that Tyler's "plot is conventional and telegraphs its twists in advance," while occasionally it "totters toward sentimentality" (22). Adam Mars-Jones bemoans its "patches of cuteness or banality," while admitting that "they are always surrounded by passages that treat the same material with confident freshness" (1096). The anonymous commentator in *The Antioch Review* 44 (Spring 1986) called it "a standard soap-opera plot" (249). Even Updike admits that Muriel's regenerative impact on Macon is "predictable" (108). (*Understanding Anne Tyler* 232, note 15)

What these critics and reviewers have overlooked is the importance of the regenerative process and Alexander's key role in it. They seem to believe that such a process should be relegated to examples from children's literature such as Darcy Niland's *The Shiralee*,[6] Johanna Spyri's *Heidi*, Frances Hodgson Burnett's *Little Lord Fauntleroy*, and particularly the latter's *The Secret Garden*. They tend to overlook the fact that *The Accidental Tourist* shares this important theme with George Eliot's *Silas Marner*, which may stand as the premier example of effective fathering in the novel.[7] One must also remember that Tyler herself sees Alexander's character, and by inference Macon's special relationship with him, as crucial to her work. In a 1989 interview with Alice Hall Petry, Tyler said, "I wrote an entire final chapter in which Macon stayed with Sarah and then realized I couldn't do it—not only because it spoiled the dramatic line of the plot but also because it meant abandoning Alexander" (Salwak 160; Petry, *Understanding Anne Tyler* 231-32, note 14). Much has rightly been made of Muriel's role as "improbable therapist," but little critical attention has been paid to the crucial relationship between Macon and Muriel's son (Voelker 155). Alexander is much more than a plot convenience, and his presence in the novel becomes as important as Ethan's as Tyler sets up a crucial counterpoint between the remembered father-son encounters of Macon and Ethan and the current step-father/step-son encounters of Macon and Alexander.

In addition to this revealing counterpoint of fathering scenes, Tyler's tenth novel presents a unique opportunity to explore parent-child relationships as they affect both the major characters in the novel, especially Sarah, Muriel, and Macon, and certain minor ones. These parent-child relationships all have a crucial impact on the dynamic relationship of Macon and Alexander. What sets *The Accidental Tourist* apart in the Tyler canon is the wide variety of parent-child relationships, excluding of course the overt violence of *Dinner at the Homesick Restaurant*. There are, for example, many variations of parenting, ranging from the neglect of Macon by his mother, Alicia, to the well-intentioned, but ineffective, parenting of Ethan by Macon, and finally to Macon's regenerative and transformational relationship with Alexander. It is appropriate that an effort be made to recover "the good father" in the novel, and there is no better place to start than Anne Tyler's *The Accidental Tourist*.

When we are first introduced to Macon Leary, he is an unhappy middle-aged man left childless by the senseless murder of his only child a year earlier. Ethan's death has not brought him and Sarah closer together but, like his birth, has only served to bring out the differences between them. Sarah is "haphazard, mercurial" whereas Macon is "methodical and steady" (16). She has been suffering deeply, wrestling with the problem of senseless, random evil in the world while Macon has been unable to comfort her in her despair. She is angry and hurt by his apparent inability or lack of desire to confront his grief. Meanwhile he has been trying unsuccessfully to bury his sorrow by erasing all visible reminders of Ethan from the house as quickly as possible and by retreating into a series of increasingly bizarre systems for daily living. When Sarah can no longer cope with her husband's seemingly uncaring attitude, his "muffled" (135) reaction to this ultimate family tragedy, she leaves him. Macon then slips further and further into neurotic, self-destructive behavior in a futile attempt to escape the pain of memory.

This neurotic behavior, characterized by such bizarre inventions as the Macon Leary Body Bag, is simply a parodic extension of the obsessive behavior he exhibited as Ethan's father. Their entire strained twelve-year relationship is neatly and tragically summed up by Tyler in one telling sentence: "And Macon (oh, he knew it, he admitted it) had been so intent on preparing [Ethan] for every eventuality that he hadn't had time to enjoy him. . . . A chortling, sunny little boy, he'd been, with Macon a stooped shape above him wringing his hands" (16). Of course, no one could have prepared Ethan for the terrible day of his death, yet Macon guiltily tortures himself through much of the book for not doing exactly that. Only through his relationships with Muriel, and then Alexander, will Macon free himself from the haunting memories of Ethan's youth and the ineffective parent he then was. Only through interactions with his new family will Macon learn to embrace the "accidental" in life, both good and bad, and become not only a whole person but a wonderful father.

From the day his son is born, over Sarah's protestations, Macon has attempted to turn him into a child he cannot be, someone like himself. When Ethan is six, Macon is "fierce" in teaching him how to swing a bat fearing his son will be chosen last for the team (16). And during the entire fall of Ethan's third-grade year, even after his son has lost interest, Macon "doggedly" brings home Wacky Pack stickers in a vain attempt to get the one final sticker that has eluded them (16). Even when Ethan is old enough to make fun of his father and his systems, Macon still tries to systematize every aspect of his son's life, even their seating arrangements at the movies.

Macon's excuse for his obsessive, inept version of fathering is that it represents his attempt to avert the few possible evils we have some control over in this "accidental" life. Sarah, of course, whose mode of mothering is a hands-off, come-what-may attitude, is bemused and somewhat confused by Macon's intrusive parenting style. When Ethan is alive, she seems to pass off his worried fathering as relatively harmless and probably somewhat touching. After Ethan's death, however, she cannot fathom his apparently uncaring attitude as he immediately strips the Wacky Pack stickers off his son's walls and embarrasses the neighbors by virtually forcing the dead child's belongings on them.

A fascinating passage provides a clue to Macon's strange behavior after the murder. Once, when Ethan was no more than two or three, Macon had watched helplessly as his son ran out into the street to retrieve a ball and had been nearly killed by a pickup truck. After Ethan's death, nearly a decade later, Macon marvels at how easily he had "released his claim" on the boy at that moment and wonders if that experience had made it somehow easier for him to face his son's death when it actually happened: "In one split second he adjusted to a future that held no Ethan—an immeasurably bleaker place but also, by way of compensation, plainer and simpler, free of the problems a small child trails along with him" (136). It is this sense of paternal detachment that Sarah cannot accept and that leads directly to their divorce.

This sense of self-imposed insularity must be deeply rooted in Macon's own childhood experiences. His own father, like Jeremy Pauling's, is fundamentally absent from Macon's life. When his father is killed in the war, Macon and his sister and two brothers are left in the care of their mother, Alicia, an endlessly enthusiastic, "giddy young war widow" who always seemed "about to fall over the brink of something" (65). Her strained relationship with her four children is effectively represented by the image of her Macon conjures up as he gazes at the portrait of the four young Learys: he imagines Alicia standing "just outside the gilded frame in a pink kimono," lustfully eyed by the artist who clearly would much rather be painting her than these four glum children (63).

The portrait still hangs in Grandfather Leary's home where Macon's sister, Rose, cares for "the boys," Porter and Charles, who have retreated there after their own failed marriages and where Macon, after his accident, will also retreat. The old maid, Rose, has become the mother she and her brothers never had. In the unconventional mother-child relationship between Alicia and her daughter and sons, it is the children who are described as dependable and steady (64) and who are constantly being made uncomfortable by their mother's antics, such as the time she enrolled them in a combination school and nudist colony.

The Leary children have much in common with the Pauling children and Alexander Pritchett, as none of them seem to have anything in common with one of their two parents. The Leary children's childhood is marked by an ever-changing series of father figures and new addresses as Alicia regularly changes boyfriends. There is no comforting stability in their young lives. One year the family moves so much that every day after school Macon has to make a conscious effort to remember where he lives before setting off for home. And Rose is often pictured pathetically sucking her thumb and stroking her mother's old fur stole as the little girl awaits her return. Macon remembers his childhood with Alicia as "a glassed-in place with grown-ups rushing past, talking at [not with] him, making changes, while he himself stayed mute" (65). There was neither real communication nor comfort there.

To compensate for the lack of parental supervision in his own childhood, Macon goes to the other extreme with Ethan. Instead of Alicia's flighty and careless approach to parenthood, Macon will prove an obsessive, intrusive parent. Luckily he has such a carefree, normal child in Ethan, partly due to Sarah's normalizing mothering and partly due to "accident," that Macon apparently finds it impossible to warp him. Eventually, when Alicia finds that her serious children are cramping her style, she ships them off to their "severe, distinguished" Leary grandparents in Baltimore and "flits" off on her way to four husbands (65). From this time on, she is like a "foreigner" to her own children, "some naughty, gleeful fairy [who] . . . darted in and out of their lives leaving a trail of irresponsible remarks" (65). She and her "guarded and suspicious" children apparently have nothing in common either physically or spiritually (65). Of course, when Macon meets a younger version of Alicia in Muriel, he will discover that he is not completely a Leary after all.

Fortuitously, it is Ethan's dog, Edward, who brings together Macon and the wild-haired dog trainer, Muriel, who will prove to be not only Edward's, but Macon's, "improbable therapist" and savior (Voelker 155). Edward, like his master, has not responded well to Ethan's death. Macon has suppressed his anger and grief over his son's murder by cocooning himself off from all normal human interaction and burying himself in a job whose goal is to eliminate the foreign, the spontaneous, the "accidental" from life. Macon's buried anger at the uncontrollable in life that claimed his son breaks out in Edward's angry, uncontrolled attacks. When Macon ponders whether dogs can have nervous break-downs, he is effectively bringing into question his own precarious mental stability.

Tellingly, Muriel proves to be the only person capable of control-ling Edward, who falls in love with her at first sight, as she does with his master. As she sternly takes the incorrigible corgi in hand, she trans-forms him from a dog who "hates the whole world" to a happy, well-adjusted animal (117). Of course, as she trains her charge, so does she train his owner. Her unrelenting chatter and brashness turn Macon from the limping, "encased" neurotic, literally and figuratively crippled by his crazy systems, into a healthy, socially adept man, who can finally con-front Ethan's death and the frightening, yet thrilling, uncertainty of life (136). Although Muriel's version of tough mothering is critical to Macon's recovery, it is ultimately Alexander who, in filling the void left by Edward's master, will restore Macon to full health.

Fittingly, Macon gets his first glimpse of Alexander, "a small, white, sickly boy with a shaved-looking skull," in the doctor's office (185). Just before meeting the child, when Muriel tells Macon that her son is seven, the grieving father flashes back to a fond memory of his own son at the same age. Macon pictures Ethan pedaling away from him on his bicycle for the first time, in one of those critical preparatory leave-takings of childhood that prepare parents for the final leave-taking from home and family. The description of Ethan in this fondly remem-bered scene is in stark contrast to the description of Alexander, further underlining his painfully isolated, abnormal status. As Muriel's son sits alone like a miniature adult, "His eyes were light blue and lashless, bulging slightly, rimmed with pink, magnified behind large, watery spec-tacles whose clear frames had an unfortunate pinkish cast themselves. He wore a carefully coordinated shirt-and-slacks set such as only a mother would choose" (184-85). Ethan, on the other hand, "rode away from [Macon], strong and proud and straight-backed, his hair picking up the light" (184).[8] Muriel had earlier explained to Macon that Alexander's biological father, Norman, had only married her because of her preg-nancy and had quickly left because he was unable to cope with the responsibility of a sickly, non-human-looking child. This is yet another example of failed parenting in the novel.

Muriel seems to have done little to guide Alexander on the road to physical and mental health as Macon will. In an initial fatherly gesture, Macon questions whether such a young child should be left on his own. As Muriel assures a doubting Macon that Alexander's "used to it," we get a first hint of her strange mothering style—at once smotheringly intrusive and neglectful (185). We soon learn that Muriel, in her endless pursuit of gainful employment and/or a new meal ticket for herself and her son, passes Alexander off to an endless array of baby sitters. This worries Macon throughout the book but, strangely, never seems to concern Muriel, who enthusiastically enumerates Alexander's enormous list of medical woes on several occasions. It seems he is even "allergic to air" (185), an unfortunate trait that makes him "a living emblem of the dangers of the outside world," as Alice Petry suggests (*Understanding Anne Tyler* 226). We are reminded here too of the Leary children's favorite game, Vaccination, their unique card game whose strange rules make it impossible for any "outsiders" to play, setting these children even further apart from their "ordinary" peers. At the very time Muriel is ignoring her son by leaving him to his own care or to the care of others, she seems intent on feeding into the myth of Alexander's fragile physical state by maintaining strict control of his diet and lifestyle and convincing everyone she talks to that without her supervision, he would be dead the next day. She even seems intent on maintaining his "nerdish" outsider status as she buys him incredibly out-of-style clothing.

Even though Macon would have been more comfortable with a more serious child, as the Leary grandparents were, his efforts to counter Sarah's influence and turn Ethan into a quiet, careful child failed. Muriel, on the other hand, seems to have been wonderfully successful in creating a sickly social outcast who, because of his largely imaginary physical ills and poorly-chosen wardrobe, has trouble coping with all facets of life from homework to mechanical projects to the neighborhood bullies. Three important scenes showing Macon's and Alexander's mutual regeneration are directly related to Muriel's efforts to maintain her son's status as abnormal outsider and Macon's attempts to reverse this. These are the faucet-fixing lesson, the encounter with the school bullies, and the shopping trip.

Several scenes in the book serve to point out the steps in the mutual regeneration of Alexander and Macon. It is significant that they are all very low-key, ordinary encounters between human beings, either family members or soon-to-be family members. There is no high drama here, and that is surely no accident on Tyler's part. There is simply a series of apparently innocuous everyday happenings that show us the steps in the regenerative process between man and boy.

The first scene comes soon after the initial meeting in the doctor's office. Macon is pictured driving to Muriel's home on Singleton Street, humming to himself and getting the steering wheel messy as he steals toppings from the pizza he is delivering to his newfound family. This happy, impulsive man is a far cry from the guilt-ridden neurotic who would never have considered contributing to the ill health of a minor by encouraging him to eat something he was allergic to. Ironically, as Macon arrives, Muriel is berating her mother for neglecting Alexander and never inquiring about his health.

The next scene is an especially revealing one. Tyler uses a simple faucet-fixing lesson to underline the traditional teacher-student scenario that defines many parent-child relationships. Instead of Dommie Saddler, the baby sitter, giving lessons to Alexander about waxing a car, it is now Macon teaching his future step-son how to complete a simple household task, but one that will, in Macon's words, make him a *"real man"* (206). Over Muriel's protestations that Alexander is not up to the job, Macon patiently guides the nervously intent child through the steps until he proudly completes the task by himself. Macon reminds Alexander that he will be able to fix the faucets for his own wife one day, a comment that suggests that, with Macon's help, this dysfunctional child will grow up to be a dependable, loving husband as Macon will likely be with Muriel. At the close of this important scene, Macon happily resigns himself to the fact that he has "got himself involved" once again in an important family relationship (206).

Soon afterwards, Macon takes the big step of truly moving in with Muriel and her son as he moves in his dog, Edward, whom Anne Ricketson Zahlan calls "the id in canine form" (88). The budding relationship between Macon/Edward and Alexander parallels the earlier remembered ball incident between Macon and Ethan, but now with a much more positive tone. It is true that Macon, by giving up his house for Muriel's, is sacrificing part of his freedom. By extending himself as a father figure to Alexander, he is accepting the same countless responsibilities and risking the same awful hurt he suffered as Ethan's father. However, he and Alexander have much to gain. As Voelker rightly points out, this is just one of several scenes in the novel that "quietly and credibly [mark] the stages in Alexander's blossoming under the influence of Macon and his dog" (162). Of course the blossoming is mutual. As Ethan's dog, Edward, takes an immediate liking to his new young master and demonstrates his devotion by playing fetch with him, Macon can turn the painful memory of his own son's nearly being killed in another ball incident into a pleasant plan for the future with his step-son-to-be. As Edward joyfully bounds after the matchbox Alexander has thrown for him, "Macon made a mental note to buy a ball first thing in the morning and teach Alexander how to throw" (222).

In preparation for the next key encounter between Macon and Alexander is a short, but important, scene in which Macon helps the child with his homework. We learn that up until Macon's joining their house-hold, the seven-year-old Alexander had been the quintessential latchkey child coming home to an empty house. As Alexander now comes home to milk and cookies lovingly supplied by the new house-husband-in-residence, Macon, Tyler offers yet another critical description of this pathetic child:

Macon had the feeling that school never went very well for Alexander. He came out of it with his face more pinched than ever, his glasses thick with finger-prints. He reminded Macon of a homework paper that had been erased and rewritten too many times. His clothes, on the other hand, were as neat as when he'd left in the morning. Oh, those clothes! Spotless polo shirts with a restrained brown pinstripe, matching brown trousers gathered bulkily around his waist with a heavy leather belt. Shiny brown shoes. Blinding white socks. Didn't he ever play? Didn't kids have recess anymore? (226-27)[9]

It is obvious how far Macon has progressed when it is he who describes Alexander as "limited" and "constricted," two words that would have aptly described him when he first met Muriel (227). Although he is now very much involved in this little boy's daily life in "all sorts of complicated ways," Macon feels he can still withdraw from him, and he considers this option a luxury he did not have with own son (227). He catches himself thinking of Ethan and being thankful and relieved that this is "not his own child" (227). Of course, in the next crucial scene, when Macon decides he can never leave Alexander, he is still neither his biological child nor a replacement for Ethan: he is simply, and importantly, a beloved human being Macon has come to realize he cannot live happily without.

The second key episode involving Macon and Alexander comes when Leary defends the little boy from some jeering bullies. It should be noted that Macon uses his dead son's dog, Edward, to come to the rescue. The dog, who has become healthy and whole once again through Muriel's training and Alexander's love, momentarily turns into his old angry self, but this time, of course, for a very different reason, as he scatters his new master's tormentors. It is during this climactic scene that Macon steps over that threshold from which there is no return. As Alexander slips his hand into Macon's:

Those cool little fingers were so distinct, so particular, so full of character. Macon tightened his grip and felt a pleasant kind of sorrow sweeping through him. Oh, his life had regained all its old perils. He was forced to worry once again about nuclear war and the future of the planet. He often had the same secret, guilty thought that had come to him after Ethan was born: *From this time on I can never be completely happy.*

Not that he was before, of course. (246)

This is the point at which *Saint Maybe* ends. *The Accidental Tourist* allows us to read beyond the worries of a middle-aged father to see Macon, in the final portion of the work, finally coming to terms with his past, present, and future. Whereas the conclusion of *Saint Maybe* is open-ended, *The Accidental Tourist's* is not. By the end of this novel, the father has come to terms with his ex-wife, his family, his future wife and step-son, and most important, his son's death.

Soon after the encounter with the school bullies comes the last important scene involving Macon and Alexander. By this point in the novel, Macon seems to have taken over all the important roles of both mother and father, as he takes the child clothes shopping. In an apparent final gesture in his ongoing battle to erase Muriel's negative influence from Alexander's life, Macon transforms the hesitant, "nerdish" child with his navy polyester blazer into a happy, confident little boy who is proud of his oversized T-shirts and jeans. All this happens as a result of a simple shopping trip to a store where Macon used to take Ethan. While there, Macon encounters not only an old friend of Ethan's and his mother, but his fashionable ex-mother-in-law, Paula Sidey. His encounter with Ethan's now teenaged friend causes Macon to confront the fact that life does indeed keep flowing, a favorite theme of Tyler's, despite its sometimes tragic "accidents" along the way. This sets up the final scene in the book in which Macon, devoid of the "baggage" of his former life, encounters the French teenager who so reminds him of Ethan; at this moment, he decides once and for all to return to his life with Muriel and Alexander. Finally, Macon's encounter with Sarah's mother allows him to show her publicly that he has moved on with his life.

As Alexander exits the dressing room wearing his new clothes, he is a child transformed:

He wore an oversized T-shirt that slipped a bit off one shoulder, as if he'd just emerged from some rough-and-tumble game. His jeans were comfortably baggy. His face, Macon saw, had somehow filled out in the past few weeks without anybody's noticing; and his hair—which Macon had started cutting at home—had lost that shaved prickliness and grown thick and floppy. (253)

We are immediately reminded of Colin Craven in Hodgson Burnett's *The Secret Garden*. Just as Colin finally did not have a humped back and crippled legs and was not doomed to an early death, Alexander has gradually, yet seemingly suddenly, been transformed into a healthy, fun-loving child who can finally embrace life as can his father. Of course in Hodgson Burnett's work, the agent of change is not the father, as it is in Tyler's novel. At the end of the scene, Tyler has Alexander confidently exclaim, "I look *wonderful!*" (253). She uses the same language to describe the character of Alexander when she tells the interviewer, Alice Hall Petry, that she could not bear to eliminate the child from her work for both artistic and personal reasons. Tyler views her chosen ending as a positive one for Macon and Muriel, and especially for Alexander: "I see Macon and Muriel in an edgy, incongruous but ultimately workable marriage, Macon forever frustrated by Muriel's behavior and yet more flexible than his old self. Alexander turns out *wonderfully.* (By that I mean: happy)" (Petry, *Understanding Anne Tyler* 232, note 14).

It becomes clear that Macon has triumphed in his role as step-father extraordinaire shortly after the shopping scene. When Muriel insists that Alexander wear a suit to Rose's wedding, Macon says that a white shirt and jeans are sufficient. She ends up deferring to him as the narrator tells us she has been doing of late where Alexander's shoes and diet have been concerned. We learn that despite his mother's dire predictions, like the housekeeper's in *The Secret Garden*, the worst her son has suffered from lately is an occasional skin rash.

Thus, Macon has established a full, healthy relationship with the child he has come to look upon as his own. The trouble, however, is that Macon has still not totally exorcised the haunting guilt surrounding Ethan's death. Although he has been able to discuss Ethan with Muriel, as a troubled patient would with his therapist, he is still having trouble adjusting to the notion of committing himself totally to a new life with a new wife and child.[10] He slips temporarily into his old way of life with Sarah, but he finds that her now tragic outlook on life does not square with his new positive one. Zahlan suggests that this final attempt to flee Muriel results from the fear and resentment he felt toward his own mother during his childhood and that he is reacting to the fact that the free-spirited Muriel reminds him of Alicia (93).

The reason for his temporary return to Sarah is much more complicated than that, however. Macon Leary is no longer the repressed Lucas Loomis or Miss MacIntosh but the smiling savior of Mrs. Daniel Bunn. He does not want to return to the old life and even turns down Sarah's proposal to have another child in order to spend the rest of his life with a woman who he knows can have no more children. Only when he is finally able to face the painful memory of identifying Ethan's body in the morgue, can he bury the tormenting pain of the past and start living for the future. When he has confronted once and for all the fact that what remained of his son after the murder was no more than a "shell" of his former lovable self (306), can Macon embark on "the real adventure" of living (342). Sarah, embittered and paralyzed by her grief, is unable to do this.

In the hotel room in Paris, Macon chooses not to swallow Sarah's tranquilizer, thus making the conscious choice to confront life head-on, hazards and all. By consciously refusing to climb back into the shell that he once used to encase himself, Macon is symbolically reborn—this time from an emotionally dead father to a vital, effective step-parent. By becoming one half of a mismatched couple, life will not always be easy. It will, however, be full of fascinating challenges and delightful surprises. With Muriel—and especially Alexander—at his side, Macon will at last be able to appreciate fully its "good parts" (100). And through his newfound parenting skills and the second chance at fatherhood he has been granted, Macon will be able to guide a second son to a fulfilling, "wonderful" adulthood.

Therefore, in *The Accidental Tourist*'s Macon Leary, Anne Tyler clearly represents the apogee of effective fathering. Whereas Jeremy Pauling turned away from his family and society to once again concentrate on his art, Macon has broken out of his shell of self-destructive grief and memory to forge strong bonds of sympathy with his newfound family and with the world at large. Like *Saint Maybe*'s Ian Bedloe, Macon has been granted a second chance at parenting. Ian, however, has not proved he can live up to his full potential as a good father to Joshua. Macon Leary, through the transformational relationship he shares with Alexander, shows that fatherhood skills, once lost as a result of the tragic accidents of life, need not be lost forever. They can be regained and improved upon through confronting the pain of the past and moving on to face the thrilling challenges of the future.

Notes

1. The abandoning, murdering, or suicidal mother figures of such works as Kate Chopin's *The Awakening*, Charlotte Perkins Gilman's *The Yellow Wallpaper*, or Gail Godwin's short story "A Sorrowful Woman" have monopolized critical attention. Neither parallel negative father figures nor positive mother or father figures have received the critical attention they deserve.

2. There are many obvious allusions to *The Glass Menagerie* in *Celestial Navigation*. For example, Jeremy's sister is named Laura, and when the Paulings' father leaves the family, he bids them farewell by way of a simple postcard as the Wingfields' father did.

3. For interesting reading on Anne Tyler's special brand of "feminism," see Petry's "Tyler and Feminism" in Salwak 33-42.

4. My colleague Renate Muendel reminded me that Joseph is the patron saint of adoption, which gives this interpretation added relevance.

5. See Betts and Voelker 3, 67, and 82.

6. *The Shiralee* is a relatively obscure Australian novel that tells the story of a tough swagman named Macauley, who reluctantly cares for his young daughter, Buster, as he treks across the outback in search of work. *Shiralee* is an aboriginal word for the swag or blanket-roll carried by such itinerant tramps as Macauley. The title thus calls attention to the novel's main theme, one common in Tyler's work, of children as both burden and blessing. After the little girl is kidnapped by her mother and nearly killed in an automobile accident, Mac no longer considers her a burden and becomes an exemplary father. The same theme of children as mixed blessings is explored in Margaret Drabble's *The Millstone*, in which the female protagonist Rosamund's out-of-wedlock baby, Octavia, who is born to her as she is attempting to write her dissertation, is the "millstone" of the title. Like Buster, however, Octavia serves to be both burden and sustaining and humanizing agent for her initially reluctant parent.

7. If *Silas Marner* is the premier example of "good fathering" regained, perhaps Hester Prynne in *The Scarlet Letter* is the corollary example of "good mothering." Both Eppie and Pearl are viewed as burdens by the society that scorns their parents. Another striking example of a "good father" who warrants critical attention is the protagonist of E. Annie Proulx's *The Shipping News*.

8. This scene is reminiscent of the one at the center of the poem "To a Daughter Leaving Home" by Linda Pastan. In this poem, a mother has just taught her eight-year-old daughter to ride a two wheeler, and as the child rides away, the mother describes her as "screaming/with laughter,/the hair flapping/behind you like a/handkerchief waving/goodbye."

9. Critics have noted the special significance of clothing in Tyler's work. See, for example, Ruth O. Saxton's "Crepe Soles, Boots, and Fringed Shawls: Female Dress as Signals of Femininity" in Salwak 65-76.

10. Another key scene that shows Macon's growing parenting skills is that in which he invites his niece Susan to accompany him on a business trip to Philadelphia, probably not coincidentally the Quaker city of brotherly love, and sensitively listens to her reminiscences and worries about Ethan.

Works Cited

"Anne Tyler: *The Accidental Tourist.*" *Contemporary Literary Criticism* 44 (Yearbook 1986). 311-22.

Betts, Doris. "The Fiction of Anne Tyler." *Interviews with Seven Contemporary Writers*: 23-37. *Southern Quarterly* 21.4 (1983): 23-38.

Petry, Alice Hall. *Understanding Anne Tyler.* Columbia: U of South Carolina P, 1990.

Salwak, Dale, ed. *Anne Tyler as Novelist.* Iowa City: U of Iowa P, 1994.

Stephens, Ralph, ed. *The Fiction of Anne Tyler.* Jackson: UP of Mississippi, 1990.

Tyler, Anne. *The Accidental Tourist.* New York: Berkley, 1985.

——. "Because I Want More Than One Life." *Washington Post* 15 Aug. 1976: G1, G7.

——. *Celestial Navigation.* New York: Ivy, 1974.

——. *Saint Maybe.* New York: Ivy, 1991.

Voelker, Joseph C. *Art and the Accidental in Anne Tyler.* Columbia: U of Missouri P, 1989.

Zahlan, Anne Ricketson. "Traveling Towards the Self: The Psychic Drama of Anne Tyler's *The Accidental Tourist.*" *The Fiction of Anne Tyler.* Ed. Ralph Stephens. Jackson: UP of Mississippi, 1990: 84-97.

12

Moynihan's "Tangle of Pathology": Toni Morrison's Legacy of Motherhood

Michelle Pagni Stewart

Throughout the 1960s, African Americans[1] faced battles on many fronts as they strived for political, economic, and social equality. They were attempting to erase the dichotomy under which they had suffered for so long: they were tired of being treated as different, as nonwhites, as if "white" were whole and "black" were not. In the midst of these battles, the Johnson administration issued the Moynihan report, which brought both African Americans and their families to the forefront. Not surprising was the bias and blindness inherent in the report: the black family depicted was one fraught with stereotypes, blamed for the ills more likely attributable to white society. According to the Moynihan report, the typical African American family was characterized by matriarchal tendencies, the failure of youths and the alienation of men, characteristics which fed on themselves, producing a vicious circle.

Toni Morrison's novels are often characterized by what the Moynihan report considered "typical" African American families—that is, matriarchal families with absent fathers. In Morrison's *Song of Solomon* (1977), Pilate's matriarchal family is composed solely of women, and the third generation, Hagar, never able to sustain a normal relationship in part because she has never been exposed to one, dies of unrequited love; in *Beloved* (1987), Sethe's family is similarly matriarchal and contains only women since her sons have fled the haunted house for reasons that also cause her daughter Denver to seclude herself from the outside world. Yet Morrison is not depicting African American families that validate the myth of the Moynihan report since the more traditional families in both novels are also dysfunctional. Although Macon Dead's family in *Song of Solomon* is characterized by having a strong father figure with a good income and so would be considered by the Moynihan report as "normal," Macon's son Milkman is not much better off than his cousin Hagar. Likewise, while Halle's family in *Beloved* would also be viewed as more traditional since it has a father and mother who are "married," white society will never recognize it as a real family since it consists of slaves who were denied the rights of humans and aligned more closely with animals. Through Morrison's depictions of the various families in these two novels—both of which have troubled children—we can see what many of the Moynihan report's enthusiasts overlooked: the family structure is not what leads to failed youth; rather, the white society that constantly treats the African American as an object lacking in human wants, needs and rights is to blame for the cycles of dysfunctionality that are depicted in these novels. Furthermore, Morrison's novels suggest that this oppression has its roots in the system of slavery and the ideologies that continued to support its premises even long after it was supposedly prohibited.

Sociological research has been concerned with families since its inception as a field of study, but the term "family" has rarely been used in a generic sense and if so, only more recently. As African American scholars gained prominence in the sociology field in the 1930s, so did studies that dealt with the African American family, studies which were soon subordinated to issues of war, industrialization and bureaucratization. It was not until the early sixties, when there was a new push for studies on poverty, that the African American family again became an object of research (Billingsley 204-06). In the fifties and sixties, "the family" was a key issue—popular magazines continually did features or series on the "typical American family." Not surprisingly, all pictures were of Caucasian families, and no references were made to minority families. A 1960 anthology of sociological studies on the family included only one report on the African American family, written by E. Franklin Frazier (the Frazier Thesis became a standard for later studies) (Billingsley 198). As Andrew Billingsley noted in a discussion of the treatment of African American families in American scholarship: "Two tendencies, then, are current in studies of American families. The first, and most general, is to ignore Negro families altogether. The second is to consider them only insofar as they may be conceived as a social problem" (198). And this is just what happened when Lyndon B. Johnson's administration undertook a study of the African American family. With preconceived notions about the African American family and a set agenda in mind—not to mention a former leader whose Catholic views influenced his idea of social welfare and the role the family should play—the Moynihan report was produced.

Published "for official use only" in March 1965, the Moynihan report caused a furor among the media and civil rights leaders over its use and implications. The Moynihan report, *The Negro Family: The Case For National Action*, came to the conclusion that "at the heart of the deterioration of the fabric of Negro society is the deterioration of the Negro family" (Rainwater and Yancey 5), citing almost a quarter of urban Negro marriages dissolving, of Negro births being illegitimate, and of Negro families headed by females (5). Daniel P. Moynihan traced the problem to the roots of slavery, something Frazier had done as early as 1939, yet the report went much further in imputing the African American family as a "tangle of pathology" (Rainwater and Yancey 6). While Billingsley, among others, faulted Moynihan for making conclusions despite contrary evidence, at the time the Moynihan report was leaked to the media, the data was assumed conclusive, and the results were constantly distorted when presented to the public.

The media used the report for various purposes, one being to cite the failure of the family as a possible cause of the Watts riots (Rainwater and Yancey 139). The *Washington Star* even went so far as to say it was up to the middle class *Negroes* (my emphasis) to help the lower class, something that the report did not propose (in fact, the Moynihan report proposed no solutions, but only defined the problem): "Taken as a whole, the effect of the press coverage of the Moynihan report was to subtly exaggerate the already dramatic and sensational aspects of Moynihan's presentation and as a result to considerably deepen the impression that the report dealt almost exclusively with the family, its 'pathology' and 'instability,' as *the* cause of the problems Negroes have" (Rainwater and Yancey 152-53).

Thus, the Moynihan report perpetuated the stereotypes of the African American family. For the next few decades sociologists would continue to debate whether these characteristics were more typical of an African American family than of a white family. And while some studies show these characteristics as more typical in an African American family than in a white family, that does not necessarily make them *typical* of an African American family or make them abnormalities leading to dysfunction. The three most common stereotypes include female-headed households, absent men and thus broken homes, and children who were destined to fail because they were not brought up in "normal" homes (the failures of the youth ranged from lack of success in education and work; to lower intelligence; to tendencies to engage in pre-marital sex, which led to unwanted pregnancies). If these standards were to be applied to today's youth, many families of a variety of ethnicities and races—including Caucasian—would be included in Moynihan's tangle of pathology.

What the Moynihan report said, then, was that the African American family's dysfunctional qualities were snowballing to affect the African Americans' way of life. What the report hinted at was that the

African Americans themselves had to do something to rectify this problem, failing to recognize that because this was society's problem, all of the nation was at fault. In Toni Morrison's novels *Song of Solomon* and *Beloved*, we can see an application of Moynihan's "theory" of families;[2] however, both the "typical" dysfunctional family and the "nontypical" white-like family in her novels lead to failures (of a sort) of the youngest generations. Thus, unlike the Moynihan report, Morrison's novels are not pointing a finger at the family structure; instead, through her fiction, Morrison seems to be making underlying criticisms about the way society has treated African Americans as being different or as being objects, rather than treating them as citizens, a practice at the heart of as well as perpetuated by slavery. As a result, the white societies in *Song of Solomon* and *Beloved*—though rarely seen—are just as blind and biased as the Moynihan report.

Lorraine Liscio sees a connection between Morrison's *Song of Solomon* and *Beloved* in that they both "celebrate a lost love, [in the former] between adults, [in the latter] between a mother and child, here a child lost to slavery" (44). It seems to me, though, that Morrison is reaching deeper in these novels to explore what caused the love to be lost in the first place—the white beliefs and social structures that severed the bonds of love and family and planted the seeds of hate and guilt, often directed at oneself rather than at those at fault, the creators of these social institutions and beliefs. Just as Giulia Scarpa believes all of Morrison's novels are essentially about "the relationship between present and past" (91), so do I see Morrison discussing the present (the matriarchal tendencies) with respect to its roots (slavery and economic/social oppression), which the Moynihan report elided so as not to make white society to blame for what "ailed" some African American families.

Pilate's and Sethe's families could have been constructed on the basis of the stereotypes fostered by the Moynihan report, for both families have all the tendencies Moynihan cited as pathological. Pilate is a strong, independent woman who has had to fend for herself since she was a young girl. She acts as both supporter and protectorate of her family, her daughter Reba and granddaughter Hagar. She does what she must, including illegal bootlegging, in order to provide for her family. She threatens a man at knife point when he tries to take advantage of her daughter, and she vows to avenge Hagar's death. Despite Pilate's care and protection, however, both Reba and Hagar display aspects of what Moynihan called the cyclical matriarchal tendencies since both engage in pre-marital sex, and neither is able to keep a man. Childlike, Reba simply "live[s] from one orgasm to another" (*Song* 151), merely fulfilling her sexual appetites and winning things while Pilate supports her and Hagar. Hagar also shows the failure of youth that allegedly results from a matriarchal structure. She is never shown how to have or how to keep a relationship with a man—or how to handle one that does not work out. "There was something truly askew in this girl . . . Not the poverty or dirt or noise, not just extreme unregulated passion where even love found its way with an ice pick, but the absence of control" (138). Hagar dies of fever after she fails to win the man she loves; she follows her mother's footsteps of being easy with her sexual favors, yet this is ironically what drives Milkman away. Throughout the novel, Hagar is unstable, but her "dysfunctional" upbringing is not necessarily the cause.[3]

In contrast to Pilate's household which not only is dominated by a woman but consists solely of women, Macon Dead's family is more "normal," at least in the eyes of Moynihan's report. Macon had the same "beginnings" as his sister, but as a male, his becoming independent at an early age only made him more successful. Macon is not a typical African American male as the Moynihan report stereotyped him, for he had a prosperous business and was able to mix in somewhat with "real" society. Macon's attitudes suggest he had expectations similar to those in the Moynihan report with respect to what made a man successful: "These rides that the family took on Sunday afternoons had become rituals and much too important for Macon to enjoy. For him it was a way to satisfy himself that he was indeed a successful man . . . there were very few among them [the black people] who lived as well as Macon Dead" (*Song* 31-32). Equally important to the Moynihan report's idea of what made for a "successful," "traditional" family, Macon is a strong force in his household: he keeps an eagle-eye over his children, requiring Milkman to work for him, the girls to go to school, and Corinthians to leave her boyfriend who does not meet Macon's approval. The only control Macon lacks is occasional moments when his wife temporarily gains the upper hand, but this is not public knowledge.[4] Outwardly, Macon's family is what Moynihan thought all African Americans should strive for: a two-parent household with a strong-willed, present father who has a good income and is a success in the community—the African American one at least (although Macon buys and mortgages houses from the whites, he rents only to African Americans). As Valerie Smith points out, Macon Dead's family represents "the patriarchal, nuclear family that has been traditionally a stable and critical feature not only of American society, but of Western civilization in general." The Deads degenerate and Macon's individualism is destructive, both suggesting the invalidity of American and Western values to black American families (278-79). Thus, Morrison shows us that even this family is not perfect: its strengths are also its weaknesses, and its perfection is only superficial—and in the eyes of the white society.

Milkman pays the price for having a successful father. According to the Moynihan report and many other studies of the African American family, the failure of the youth, particularly the males, resulted in part from a lack of strong role models. Ironically, while Moynihan's report would see Macon as an appropriate role model, Milkman wants to be nothing like his dad:

Macon was clean-shaven; Milkman was desperate for a mustache. Macon wore bow ties; Milkman wore four-in-hands. Macon didn't part his hair; Milkman had a part shaved into his. Macon hated tobacco; Milkman tried to put a cigarette in his mouth every fifteen minutes. Macon hoarded his money; Milkman gave his away. (*Song* 62-63)

Nor does Milkman have strong feelings for his mother: "[H]e would not pretend that it was love for his mother. She was too insubstantial, too shadowy for love . . . Never had he thought of his mother as a person, a separate individual, with a life apart from allowing or interfering with his own" (75). Milkman throughout the novel wants to disassociate himself from everything that involves his family and the past: "He just wanted to beat a path away from his parents' past, which was also their present and which was threatening to become his present as well" (180-81).

Milkman, then, is also a failure in society's eyes, at least those of Moynihan's persuasion: he is not interested in making money—because "no one had ever denied him any, . . . it had no exotic attraction" (108); nor does he feel he has a future: "It was becoming a habit—this concentration on things behind him. Almost as though there were no future to be had" (35). Furthermore, he cannot maintain a relationship with a woman, Hagar, or his best friend, Guitar. Guitar, upset that the inheritance he is promised turns out to be bones instead of money, suspects Milkman of trying to double-cross him. Guitar decides to hunt Milkman down and kill him. So Macon's money ironically results not in Milkman's success but in distancing him from his family and friends and leading, depending on how one reads the ending, to his death.[5]

Even worse in society's eyes is Milkman's attraction to Pilate's house since he is attracted to and is emulating the "wrong people." Many critics, however, argue that Pilate's family is a better influence than the "normal" family that the Moynihan report viewed as necessary to raise stable younger generations: for example, Barbara E. Cooper finds Pilate's matriarchal family, founded on love, as being a positive force compared to Macon's patriarchal family which is founded on the negative forces of hatred and greed (146-47); Smith finds that Pilate is not destroyed by her values as Macon is by his, in part because she does not get her sense of self from following the American myth (280), a myth which does not function for African Americans in the way it does for whites. Thus, the prescription the Moynihan report seemed to see as the answer for the problems facing African American youths—that is, to have a traditional, patriarchal, nuclear family—was as detrimental to the youths, if not more so, as what the Moynihan report considered pathological.

A similar dichotomy between matriarchal and patriarchal families can be found in Morrison's *Beloved*. One hundred twenty-four is filled with women: first with Baby Suggs, her daughter-in-law Sethe and her granddaughter Denver, and later with Sethe and her two "daughters," Denver and Beloved. Sethe's two sons Howard and Buglar have run away, and the only other man to live at 124, Paul D, is eventually driven out by a mother's love that is "too thick." Sethe's actions—although founded on love like Pilate's—are harmful to her daughters: she begins to drive Denver away, making her feel unloved and, as Stephanie A. Demetrakopoulos argues, she protects Beloved, which keeps her from growing up (similar to the way Milkman and Hagar are unable to grow up because they are overprotected) (56-57). While Beloved has been murdered by her mother, Denver seems to suffer the most. She fears her own mother yet is outcast from the community because of her mother. Her mother overprotects her to the point that Denver cannot allow other people—especially a man like Paul D—into their family. Yet she is such a lonely child that she appropriates the new visitor with a possessiveness and a jealousy that soon leads to her plottings and manipulations to secure Beloved's favor. Her obsession becomes so great that her own needs are forgotten—except the need to be with Beloved:

This is worse than when Paul D came to 124 and she cried helplessly into the stove. This is worse. Then it was for herself. Now she is crying because she has no self. Death is a skipped meal compared to this. She can feel her thickness thinning, dissolving into nothing. She grabs the hair at her temples to get enough to uproot it and halt the melting for a while. (123)

Denver's situation, then, is not a healthy one, nor is that of Sethe's other daughter, Beloved, who is killed by her mother and then returns to haunt her mother in her unrest. While some blame Sethe for killing her own daughter—many of the people in town do, as do some critics[6]—Morrison's novel suggests the verdict is not that simple: the white society and its institution of slavery are complicit as well, if not more so.

The more traditional, seemingly more stable families in the novel are not any more propitious to the younger generations. Sethe's relationship to Paul D, particularly at the end of the novel when he tells her she's her own "best thing" (*Beloved* 273), helps her to find her way past the guilt she feels for her past actions so she can focus on the present. In fact, contrary to Moynihan's man who runs away, Paul D runs *to* Sethe and leaves only when Beloved moves him away (and, even then, he does return). Yet while Paul D's actions seem beneficial to Sethe,[7] Denver is not pleased by his presence at first (she does, however, eventually realize his presence is better for her and her mom than the more welcomed presence of Beloved). Moreover, Paul D, Sethe, and Denver (and Beloved) are never really a family; when they begin to act like a family after the carnival, Beloved appears and begins to drive a wedge between the other three, to the point where Sethe considers the three women a stronger family without him. She thinks Paul D

resent[s] the children she had . . . [resents] sharing her with the girls. Hearing the three of them laughing at something he wasn't in on. The code they used among themselves that he could not break. Maybe even the time spent on their needs and not his. They were a family somehow and he was not the head of it. (*Beloved* 132)

The more important "traditional" patriarchal family we see in the novel—and one that functions to disprove Moynihan's claim that matriarchal tendencies lie at the heart of the problems of the "failed" African American youths—is that of the slave families. Sethe and Halle are "married" at Sweet Home, yet, as Hirsch points out in "Maternity and Rememory: Toni Morrison's *Beloved*," Sweet Home is full of distorted families since the whites are childless and the blacks cannot "own" their children (99). In fact, we see repeated instances that undermine the notion of family with respect to the slaves. Many were not allowed to marry at all or to marry a spouse of their own choice. Even if couples could marry, as Halle and Sethe did (although it was not a legal ceremony), they would not be sure they or their children would be able to remain together as a family:

[I]n all of Baby's life, as well as Sethe's own, men and women were moved around like checkers. Anybody Baby Suggs knew, let alone loved, who hadn't run off or been hanged, got rented out, loaned out, bought up, brought back, stored up, mortgaged, won, stolen or seized. . . . What she called the nastiness of life was the shock she had received upon learning that nobody stopped playing checkers just because the pieces included her children. (*Beloved* 23)

Many studies on slavery recognize its influence on family relationships. Hirsch claims slavery affects the notion of family, for if one cannot "possess" oneself or one's children, then what or how one feels about having one's children taken away is all the more difficult ("Maternal Narratives" 271). Carl D. Malmgren explains that in *Beloved*, slavery is the perverter of relations because it dehumanizes both sides of the relationships of self/other, master/slave (102).[8] Thus, while these families seem to be more traditional, Morrison's novel emphasizes the illusion upon which these families are founded as well as the way these families are, ultimately, as unstable as any dysfunctional, matriarchal family.

In fact, none of the more traditional "families" in the novel suggests a positive influence on younger generations or the self. When Stamp Paid is forced to submit to the repeated rapes of his wife, we see the psychological effects as well as his feelings of guilt and helplessness for being unable to do anything about the situation, a reflection, according to Trudier Harris, of the "psychologically warping system called slavery" (330). Because of the power system inherent in the institution of slavery, the "traditional" family was as ineffective in creating stability for its members as matriarchal families. In fact, the more traditional families in the novel at some point become nontraditional, simply because the notion of the patriarchal family presupposes one has the ability to marry, have children with one's spouse and raise one's children as well as provide and care for them—none of which was guaranteed to those living under the yoke of slavery. Even for those families allowed to stay together, if an opportunity to escape the bondage and oppression of slavery presented itself, whether by escaping or buying one's freedom, a slave could not afford to let it pass and would thus precipitate the separation of the family.

In these two novels, then, we see that the failure of the youth is not inherent in the family structure as the Moynihan report theorized, for both families—the "traditional" African American family, "dysfunctional" and matriarchal, and the "traditional" whitelike family, successful and patriarchal—end up with failed generations, with members who are not adapting to their situations or to society. Thus, it seems Morrison is not pointing a finger at the family, for if she were, we would see that there are no avenues of hope—all of us, no matter what kind of family we come from, would be doomed. The fact that both types of families can lead to failed youths cancels itself out—and society is left to blame. Once we look beyond the family structure as a debilitator of these younger generations, we see the underlying societal comments: the white society is rarely *seen* in either *Song of Solomon* or *Beloved*, yet it is constantly ostracizing the African Americans, making them feel as if they belong to a different class, as if they are inhuman, although they are conveniently judged by human standards when it suits the needs of those studying the family.

Song of Solomon is filled with incidents, some small, some extended, in which we see the African Americans excluded from society. When Reba wins a prize at Sears for being the half-millionth person to walk in the door, she is strangely stripped of her prize: "But they never did put my picture in the paper. . . . But they put the picture of the man who won second prize in. He won a war bond. He was white" (46). White society, then, makes the African American seem not to count—it will not see the African American as a part of society. Railroad Tommy also points out the differences between what a white citizen can have and what an African American can have:

And I'll tell you something else you not going to have. You not going to have no private coach with four red velvet chairs that swivel around in one place whenever you want em to. No. And you not going to have your own special toilet and your own special-made eight-foot bed either. And a valet and a cook and a secretary to travel with you and do everything you say . . . You [n]ever have five thousand dollars of cold cash money in your pocket and walk into a bank and tell the bank man you want such and such a house on such and such a street and he sell it to you. . . . And you not going to have a governor's mansion, or eight thousand acres of timber to sell . . . you never going to have four stars on your shirt front, or even three. And you not going to have no breakfast tray brought in to you early in the morning with a red rose on it and two warm crois-sants and a cup of hot chocolate. Nope. Never. (*Song* 59-60)

Throughout the novel, the men in the barbershop try to dispel notions of black and white. They fantasize that Winnie Ruth Judd, a white convicted murderer "who axed and dismembered her victims and stuffed them in trunks" (99), goes around the country killing other whites. This is the men's defense mechanism: while the rest of the coun-try—the whites, that is—screams "black" every time white blood is shed, the African American families were trying to find someone else to blame: "It was their way of explaining what they believed was white madness—crimes planned and executed in a truly lunatic manner against total strangers. Such murders could only be committed by a fellow lunatic of the race and Winnie Ruth Judd fit the description" (100). Unfortunately, these men knew that nearly every white murder resulted in a black indictment: "Amid the jokes, however, was a streak of unspo-ken terror. . . . Each man in that room knew he was subject to being picked up as he walked the street and whatever his proof of who he was and where he was at the time of the murder, he'd have a very uncomfortable time being questioned" (100-01). Not even the courts could protect the African Americans, we see in *Song of Solomon*, for the judicial system's treatment of African Americans is also far from being equal. As Guitar explains:

Where's the money, the state, the country to finance our justice? . . . Is there one courthouse in one city in the country where a jury would convict them? There are places right now where a Negro still can't testify against a white man. Where the judge, the jury, the court, are legally bound to ignore anything a Negro has to say. What that means is that a black man is a victim of a crime only when a white man says he is. (160-61)

The men in the barbershop have had to fight back—even if their method is crude and barbaric—because the white system refuses to treat them as anything but "other," as anything but guilty.[9]

One of the most disheartening comments white society makes in *Song of Solomon* occurs when Elizabeth Butler kills herself rather than live like Circe, an African American:

She killed herself rather than do the work I'd been doing all my life! . . . She saw the work I did all her days and *died*, you hear me, *died* rather than live like me. Now, what do you suppose she thought I was! . . . the way I lived and the work I did was so hateful to her she killed herself to keep from having to do it. (*Song* 24)

Miss Butler is the epitome of those who see something "different" in African Americans, something so different that she cannot bear to live as they do.

Like Miss Butler, the white society refuses to let African Americans escape the stereotypes they have been relegated to and, as important, denies and erases their heritage as well. The post office refuses to acknowledge Doctor Street and instead has "officially" designated the street Mains Avenue, even though the African Americans had named it before the postal service began delivering letters. But the white society controls the bureaucratic constructs and puts up signs saying the street "had always been and would always be known as Mains Avenue and not Doctor Street" (4). Likewise, Macon Dead and his father and son (both also Macon Dead) have had their own histories destroyed by white society. For when Macon's father registered with the Freedmen's Bureau, he was given the name Macon Dead because he said he was born in *Macon* and his father was *dead*. While the wife of the elder Macon likes the name because "it was new and would wipe out the past[,] Wipe it all out" (*Song* 54), it is precisely this erasure that keeps Milkman from finding his heritage for so long; he does not even know his ancestor's name —and thus, his own. So, in effect, Milkman does not know who he is. However, it is not always enough to know one's own name: that is, as long as the white society has the inclination—and power—to change a name, it has the power to deny and erase one's heritage, one's self. In "naming" Macon and Mains Street, then, white society has imposed its own constructs over those of the African Americans in the novel.

Gay Wilhentz, in uncovering the African traditions that function in *Song of Solomon*, argues that much of what we see in the novel reverts to slavery. Men would not have left their families (had to fly away) were it not for the institution of slavery: "In so visibly layering her novel, she directs us to the original message that has been censored, almost effaced, by the language of slavery, oppression, and hegemonic discourse" (73-74).[10] Similarly, the problems in *Beloved* stem from slavery, as many critics have recognized.[11] As Jean Wyatt argues, the novel persuades us to find fault with the institution which could make a woman see her child's death as preferable to a life under slavery: "The novel . . . present[s] the infanticide as the ultimate contradiction of mothering under slavery" (476)—a contradiction, perhaps, but also a logical result given that one's life and children were not one's own as long as one was a slave.

Just as in *Song of Solomon*, Morrison, in *Beloved*, suggests that white society's complicity in oppressing African Americans—while stemming from slavery—also goes beyond it. Dana Heller, in "Reconstructing Kin: Family, History, and Narrative in Toni Morrison's *Beloved*," explains that the "white" education forced on former slaves functioned as another form of enslavement, that while slavery was no longer present, blacks continued to face racial oppression in the form of "socially and morally sanctioned institutions of education and language" (114). Other instances suggest that the white society—although absent—is culpable in the oppression of African Americans. Harris points to the Sambo figure Denver sees at the Bodwins which, she argues, indicates the extent to which even abolitionists did not view blacks as social equals (337). While slavery had been abolished long before the events in the book take place, the novel makes it clear that the African Americans are not being treated as equals in society: "Eighteen seventy-four and white-folks were still on the loose. Whole towns wiped clean of Negroes; eighty-seven lynchings in one year alone in Kentucky; four colored schools burned to the ground; grown men whipped like children; children whipped like adults; black women raped by the crew; property taken, necks broken" (*Beloved* 180). As Stamp Paid's list acknowledges, white society was continuing to oppress the blacks, in a different form of slavery.

Morrison's novel points to the way the whites treated the African Americans, both during and after slavery. Their view that these people were no more than animals is emphasized in the many images used to depict the slaves from the whites' view: "Schoolteacher had chastised that nephew, telling him to think—just think—what would his own horse do if you beat it beyond the point of education. . . . see what happened when you overbeat creatures God had given you the responsibility of . . . you just can't mishandle creatures and expect success" (*Beloved* 149-50). Schoolteacher's views of the slaves suggest he equated them with animals; at times, in fact, he saw them as inferior to animals: "Unlike a snake or a bear, a dead nigger could not be skinned for profit and was not worth his own dead weight in coin" (148).

White society's attitude toward the former slaves is also apparent in Paul D's reaction to the newspaper clipping which details Sethe's crime:

Because there was no way in hell a black face could appear in a newspaper if the story was about something anybody wanted to hear. A whip of fear broke through the heart chambers as soon as you saw a Negro's face in a paper, since the face was not there because the person had a healthy baby, or outran a street mob. Nor was it there because the person had been killed, or maimed or caught or burned or jailed or whipped or evicted or stomped or raped or cheated, since that could hardly qualify as news in a newspaper. It would have to be something out of the ordinary—something whitepeople would find interesting, truly different, worth a few minutes of teeth sucking if not gasps. And it must have been hard to find news about Negroes worth the breath catch of a white citizen of Cincinnati. (155-56)

Paul D's disinclination to look at the article results from what he knows about the white's treatment of blacks in newspapers—this despite the fact that Paul D cannot read. While Sethe's "crime" seems to be the most horrific act in the novel, Morrison, in describing Sethe's fear that Beloved might leave, suggests otherwise:

[Beloved might leave] Leave before Sethe could make her realize that worse than that—far worse—was what Baby Suggs died of, what Ella knew, what Stamp saw and what made Paul D tremble. That anybody white could take your whole self for anything that came to mind. Not just work, kill or maim you, but dirty you. Dirty you so bad you couldn't like yourself anymore. Dirty you so bad you forgot who you were and couldn't think it up. (251)

Thus, at the heart of Sethe's actions lies the institution of slavery—its oppression and dehumanization of all of those who lost their human rights in the name of "progress."

While it may seem, then, that Morrison is undermining the patriarchal structure of the traditional, nuclear family, through Milkman's and Denver's growth we can see the issue is not that simple. Cooper explains how, by comparing his father's and his aunt's families, Milkman comes to find his identity (145-46). Smith takes this idea further to show how he learns from his past as well as his family: "In his ancestors' world, communal and mythical values prevail over individualism and materialism; when he adopts their assumptions in place of his own, he arrives at a more complete understanding of what his experience means" (281). Thus Milkman is held back in an environment that the Moynihan report suggested was necessary for the growth of youths. Once he becomes familiar with his aunt's family, he is able to search for the truth and the past he had previously shunned but which he now realizes is essential for his self-identity. Similarly, Denver is forced to leave 124 to provide for her mother and sister; the burden of the family falls on her. Because of this, Heller labels Denver the hero of the novel, not just because she saves her family but as important because she reestablishes the bond with the community that is necessary for the family to survive (115). Denver becomes withdrawn under the traditional family but is forced, under the matriarchal family, to leave the security of her home and make her way in the community while forging her mother's link to the community as well.

One cannot escape the images of slavery and its repercussions that haunt Morrison's novels, just as Beloved haunts Sethe's memory and her life. Hirsch, in discussing Bill Moyers's 1986 documentary on the Black family, reminds us of his depiction of slavery as the root of dysfunctional families ("Maternity" 95), just as Morrison's novels make clear. In Morrison's *Song of Solomon* and *Beloved*, the problems facing the younger generations are not a direct result of the family structure, be it matriarchal or patriarchal, but are instead, just like the problems within the families themselves, a repercussion of all that the African Americans were forced to endure as slaves and as supposedly free people. Indeed, Morrison's novels, rather than proving Moynihan's thesis that the African American families are a "tangle of pathology," extend the thesis derisively. While Moynihan and his supporters are busy disparaging the African American family, Toni Morrison's novels show us what really is in a "tangle of pathology"—a white society that oppresses the African Americans as if they are less than human and then blames them when they cannot mimic what the whites consider a standard, stable family. White society finds it difficult enough to have traditional, nuclear, stable families itself, and it is not weighed down with the legacy of oppressive circumstances which allowed African Americans no control of or freedom for themselves or their children—in short, no real family to speak of.

Notes

1. In the 1960s, at the time the Moynihan report was issued, Americans of African descent were known as Negroes, a label which has since evolved to blacks and most recently to African Americans. For consistency, I will refer to this group with the most recent term, except in direct quotes.

2. I am not saying that Toni Morrison was necessarily intentionally responding to Moynihan's report. However, it seems that, having been exposed to that criticism which it engendered, she could not help but be influenced by the findings of the report.

3. Gay Wilentz sees the Pilate/Reba/Hagar relationship as similar to an African village compound but, she argues, the constraints and realities of African American life deconstruct this: "For all her powers, Pilate is unable to bring her extended family back together as a force to confront racial oppression, nor is she able to save Hagar from the imposition of the white culture's definition of beauty after Hagar and Milkman's incestuous relationship ends in disaster" (67).

4. While he does keep from having sexual relations with Ruth, she had enticed him to her bed and was successful in getting pregnant with Milkman. When he tried to rid her of the reminder of the upper hand she gained, he also failed—thanks to Pilate, who helped Ruth keep her baby. Moreover, Ruth continues to flaunt her relationship with her father by visiting him in the graveyard. Despite these moments when Ruth does as she pleases, however, she is by no means the head of the family: she does not have Pilate's matriarchal strength and power.

5. Milkman is not the only "failed youth" to come from Macon's "normal" household. While Corinthians receives an education, she cannot get a job as anything other than a maid. When she does finally find a man, "she [is] ashamed of him" (195), and she will not consummate their relationship for fear her father will find out—yet she is forty-four years old. She ends up throwing her body over Porter's car, in a desperate attempt to hold on to her one chance to escape the Dead household. When her father discovers the affair, he "forbid[s] her to leave the house, [makes] her quit her job, evict[s] the man, garnish[es] his wages" (217). Corinthians is never allowed to live her own life—until she leaves the grasp of her father.

Magdalene called Lena, on the other hand, does not even succeed in doing half of what Corinthians has only barely managed to do. Rather, Magdalene called Lena stays home "because [she] was afraid of what he [her father] might do to Mama" (217). By the age of forty-five, she is still living at home, often drunk on sherry, bitter at the special treatment Milkman had always received.

6. Carl D. Malmgren, for example, argues that the novel suggests slavery is at the root of Sethe's actions but that she replicates the "awful logic" of it. The novel, he says, "finally holds Sethe responsible, insist[ing] that there had to be 'some other way'" (103-04).

7. Marianne Hirsch, in "Maternal Narratives: 'Cruel Enough to Stop the Blood,'" suggests that Sethe is only able to ponder the concepts of mother-hood—as well as selfhood—when Paul D is helping her (271). Similarly, Jean Wyatt sees Paul D as allowing Sethe to reclaim her past (479).

8. It seems, as well, that the novel also dehumanizes the mother/daughter relationship. For Sethe is willing to take her daughter's life just as Beloved is willing to drain the life from her mother in order to empower herself.

9. Barbara E. Cooper believes the hatred inherent in the actions of the Seven Days "perverts any sense of family" that the members have. She sees the Seven Days as "kill[ing] for families" (151) which of course puts yet another tailspin on Moynihan's findings.

10. Susan Willis makes a similar argument in "Eruptions of Funk: Histori-cizing Toni Morrison," where she posits "The end point of Morrison's journey is the starting point of [the] race's history in this country: slavery" (95).

11. Some of those who see slavery as the foundation of what happens in the novel are Malmgren, who sees slavery as the glue uniting the text (96); Martha Bayles, who finds it problematic that the system rather than the slave is blamed (4); Joycelyn K. Moody, who says Sethe serves as a condemnation of slavery which prohibits literacy and parenthood (638); and Dana Heller, who says contemporary family life is only part of the problem, that it can also be traced to racial oppression, historically and eonomically—to the institution of slavery (106).

Works Cited

Bayles, Martha. "Special Effects, Special Pleading." *New Criterion* 6.5 (1988): 34-40.

Billingsley, Andrew. *Black Families in White America.* Englewood Cliffs, NJ: Prentice-Hall, 1968.

Cooper, Barbara E. "Milkman's Search for Family in Toni Morrison's *Song of Solomon.*" *CLA Journal* 33.2 (1989): 145-56.

Demetrakopoulos, Stephanie A. "Maternal Bonds as Devourers of Women's Individuation in Toni Morrison's *Beloved.*" *African American Review* 26.1 (1992): 51-59.

Harris, Trudier. "Escaping Slavery But Not Its Images." *Toni Morrison: Critical Perspectives Past and Present.* Ed. Henry Louis Gates, Jr., and K.A. Appiah. New York: Amistad, 1993. 330-41.

Heller, Dana. "Reconstructing Kin: Family, History, and Narrative in Toni Morrison's *Beloved.*" *College Literature* 21.2 (1994): 105-17.

Hirsch, Marianne. "Maternal Narratives: Cruel Enough to Stop the Blood." *Toni Morrison: Critical Perspectives Past and Present.* Ed. Henry Louis Gates, Jr., and K. A. Appiah. New York: Amistad, 1993. 261-73.

——. "Maternity and Rememory: Toni Morrison's *Beloved.*" *Representations of Motherhood.* Ed. Donna Bassin, Margaret Hoeny, and Meryle Mahrer Kaplan. New Haven: Yale UP, 1994. 92-110.

Liscio, Lorraine. "*Beloved*'s Narrative: Writing Mother's Milk." *Tulsa Studies in Women's Literature* 11.1 (1992): 31-46.

Malmgren, Carl D. "Mixed Genres and the Logic of Slavery in Toni Morrison's *Beloved.*" *Critique* 36.2 (1995): 96-106.

Moody, Joycelyn K. "Ripping Away the Veil of Slavery: Literacy, Communal Love, and Self-Esteem in Three Slave Women's Narratives." *Black American Literature Forum* 24.4 (1990): 633-48.

Morrison, Toni. *Beloved.* New York: Plume-New American Library, 1987.

——. *Song of Solomon.* New York: New American Library, 1977.

Moynihan, Daniel Patrick. *The Negro Family: The Case For National Action.* Office of Planning and Research, 1965. Rpt. in *The Moynihan Report and the Politics of Controversy.* Ed. Lee Rainwater and William L. Yancey. Cambridge: M.I.T. P, 1967. 41-124.

Rainwater, Lee, and William L. Yancey. *The Moynihan Report and the Politics of Controversy.* Cambridge: M.I.T. P, 1967.

Scarpa, Giulia. "Narrative Possibilities at Play in Toni Morrison's *Beloved.*" *MELUS* 17.4 (1991-92): 91-103.

Smith, Valerie. "*Song of Solomon*: Continuities of Community." *Toni Morrison: Critical Perspectives Past and Present.* Ed. Henry Louis Gates, Jr., and K. A. Appiah. New York: Amistad, 1993. 274-83.

Wilentz, Gay. "Civilizations Underneath: African Heritage as Cultural Discourse in Toni Morrison's *Song of Solomon.*" *African American Review* 26.1 (1992): 61-75.

Willis, Susan. "Eruptions of Funk: Historicizing Toni Morrison." *Specifying.* Madison: U of Wisconsin P, 1987. 83-109.

Wyatt, Jean. "Giving Body to the Word: The Maternal Symbolic in Toni Morrison's *Beloved.*" *PMLA* 108.3 (1993): 474-88.

13

Pregnant with Possibilities:
Revising the Family Romance
in Stephen McCauley's *The Object of My Affection*

Paul M. Puccio

From its opening sentence, Stephen McCauley's *The Object of My Affection* (1987) challenges our assumptions about family and parenthood: "Nina and I had been living together in Brooklyn for over a year when she came home one afternoon, announced she was pregnant, tossed her briefcase to the floor and flopped down on the green vinyl sofa" (9). Because we (are meant to) assume that the narrator is, if not Nina's husband, at least her lover and the father of this forthcoming child, the ensuing dialogue, in which Nina complains that she already has weight problems and the narrator complains that they are out of catsup, shatters our expectations of parental behavior, and sounds, at best, absurd and, at worst, deeply callous. Right from the start, McCauley dismantles the family romance[1] and interrogates the presumably patent categories of "good mother" and "good father."

Only when George, the narrator, and Nina begin to discuss the possibility of their going out dancing, in order to get their minds off the baby, do we learn that they are not lovers, that George is an unlikely nominee for the father of Nina's child, and that while they live together, they do not "live together." George asks,

> "Disco or ballroom?" We did both styles, gracelessly.
> "Something noisy, I think."
> "Hetero or Homo?" We alternated, depending on who wanted to be noticed and who wanted to be left alone.
> "Homo," she said emphatically. "Definitely homo." (11)

However allusive this exchange, it establishes the idiosyncratic nature of Nina and George's ménage in somewhat less equivocal terms—they are roommates, and he is gay—and it explains, to some extent, George's detachment regarding Nina's announcement. Without any didactic

255

machinery, McCauley invites readers to give credence to this unorthodox relationship and to mistrust the more orthodox gender and family arrangements that provide the backdrop for Nina and George's narrative.

We will see that the dynamics of George and Nina's friendship are complex enough to allow the sort of misreadings that McCauley invites in these opening pages, but we also immediately learn that Nina's feelings about the actual father of her child are similarly ambiguous, if not ambivalent. When George asks Nina if her current lover, Howard, is the baby's father, and if she has shared her news with him, she replies:

> Of course he's "the father," George. Who else would be "the father"? You'd know if there was another candidate for "the father." But I don't tell him everything. I don't tell him every move I make. I don't report to Howard each time I go shopping at Key Food. (12)

The near-hysterical pitch of Nina's response betrays the muddle she is in. And for good reason. It turns out that Howard's best intentions are in perpetual conflict with his impulses: an attorney who specializes in defending underdogs, he attends pro-choice rallies, strenuously defends the rights of minority groups, and believes that the *New York Review of Books* is a "right-wing rag" (95). A man with a nurturing disposition who cooks elaborate meals for his friends, Howard nonetheless smothers Nina with attention and refers to her throughout the novel in culinary, vegetative, and otherwise inanimate terms of affection—such as "Pumpkin," "Daisy," and "Butterbean."[2] In spite of, perhaps because of, the sincerity and depth of his devotion, Howard threatens Nina's autonomy (even before she is pregnant) and this causes her misgivings over involving Howard, in any way, in her decisions regarding the baby. Nina's vehement resistance against even informing Howard of the baby's existence persists until George makes an accidental reference to Nina's "condition," which exacts an explanation of her elusiveness and the revelation of her guarded secret. Howard's response does not placate Nina's apprehensions: Howard gets protective, or as Nina puts it, "midwifey" (105), and expresses his hope that the baby will be a girl, exclaiming to Nina, "She'll be a munchkin, Munchkin" (107). At this point, Nina begins to avoid Howard, to terminate their relationship by default.

Over the course of the novel, Howard comes to understand the nature and depth of Nina's objections; he comes to see his own contradictions and how they compromise both Nina's selfhood and the kind of relationship they want to share. After several weeks of not seeing or talking with Nina, Howard admits to George that he understands Nina's decision to "cut [him] out of her life," however much this hurts him:

I'm too possessive. I'm too jealous. I'm a hypocrite. What I really want is to marry her and buy an apartment on the Upper West Side with her and raise our baby together. That's what's wrong between us. The first woman I meet who's strong and independent and has an opinion on everything under the sun, who'll always challenge me to a solid argument, who loves a good hearty meal, and what's my first thought? I want to make her my wife. I want to marry her and make her my wife the way my mother was my father's wife. His possession. There's no point in trying to kid myself or her anymore. I want the kind of relationship we're both ideologically opposed to. I'd want to get rid of me, too. (150-51)

Not only does this complicate Howard's character, offering insight and inviting compassion, it also reveals the inadequacy of a single-minded, not to say dogmatic, reading of gender stereotypes. While Howard may be possessive, he knows the faults inherent in such possessiveness; and while he may value personal relationships based on gender equality, he is not always capable of behaving according to that utopian vision. In Howard, ideology struggles against the social norms he has unconsciously assimilated all his life. This illustrates not only the inflexibility of gender stereotyping, but also its unassailability. Whatever Howard's political assessments of the roles of men and women in society and in the family, he simply cannot stop calling Nina "Munchkin"—a gesture that reflects and perpetuates a diminutive view of women. That Howard does not mean to do this makes it all the more insidious, frustrating, as we see, both to Nina and to Howard himself.

Recognizing this fundamental dead-end in her relationships with heterosexual men, Nina cannot help but impugn marriage, even while entertaining surprisingly few doubts about motherhood. And so, Nina resolves not to marry Howard (or any other man) and, instead, turns to George, proposing that he stay with her and be the baby's "father": "We can make this arrangement anything we want. We don't have to worry about getting stuck playing some prescribed roles the way Howard and I would" (85). This proposed arrangement envisions family without marriage, a child without a husband, personal relations between men and women without the rigidity of heterosexual norms, maternity without patriarchy. Yet, this paradigm is not woman-identified or even woman-centered; indeed, it might be called "heterosocial,"[3] based on a social bond between a man and a woman, but pointedly distinguished from a hetero*sexual* relationship. It embodies Nina's attempt to liberate herself and her child from the conventional expectations of the heterosexual family model—to guarantee, as much as possible, that her own selfhood will not be sacrificed to socially authorized behaviors and expectations, and that her child will experience, from an early age, radically revised standards of gender and family.

While Nina thoughtfully and deliberately constructs this "alternative" prototype of a family, on behalf of herself and her child, she does not fully grasp the implications of this arrangement for George. This invitation to reimagined parenthood scrambles George's outlook. It offers him much of what he wants in life—but not nearly enough. Having no luck meeting another man whom he likes, George sees his friendship with Nina as the most intimate relationship in his life, however incomplete that intimacy must be; on the other hand, as a gay man, he recognizes the inauthenticity of entering into a domestic partnership that would appear, to outsiders at least, as heterosexual. And yet, for George, who is a dedicated preschool teacher, the opportunity to raise a child is compelling, even if the child is Nina and Howard's.

This predicament, one might say, is pregnant with possibilities. McCauley establishes some of the inherent tensions in this situation, in part, through the interplay between the sentimental images of the traditional family and the modern narrative of Nina and George's anti-romance. For instance, George initially can only envision this family in a hopelessly nostalgic *mise en scène*:

I'd spent a fair amount of time fantasizing about helping Nina raise an infant. . . . It was all preposterous daydreaming: Nina and me strolling through Prospect Park pushing a stroller, bathing the baby in the kitchen sink, making a cozy bed for it in the top drawer of her bureau. (82-83)

Such one-dimensional icons of the mythic nuclear family collide with the uncertainties and ambiguities of George and Nina's actual circumstances. Even for a married heterosexual couple, these fantasies do not adequately embody the complexities and difficulties of parenthood and family, much less so for an unmarried woman and a gay man.

In opposition to George's Norman Rockwellesque daydreams, McCauley's depiction of Nina's proposal scene itself dismantles the paradigms of both romance and parenthood. Here Nina maps out her plan and invites George to be a part of it, while the two of them are riding the Octopus at Coney Island:

She told me that while she intended to have the baby, she didn't intend to become Howard's wife. She'd been married once and she knew the emotional complications of that racket, and she wasn't interested. And she'd lived with lovers . . . and it boiled down to the same thing in the end. She liked the way her life was going, she liked our living arrangement.

"What I mean, George," she yelled over the roar of the machinery, "is that I want us to keep living together." The tentacle swooped to the ground wildly and my stomach dropped. "I want you to help me raise the baby."

The bucket spun in a three hundred and sixty-degree turn and Nina was slammed against me in the corner of the seat, laughing hysterically. I laughed too, and then I looked her full in the face and said, "Are you out of your mind?" (82)

This scene functions as a metaphor for the precariousness of George and Nina's relationship, as well as the disorienting chaos of personal relations in contemporary America. George and Nina slam against one another in the bucket of the carnival ride just as their lives are thrown together more by circumstance and accident than by intention and desire; the dizzying motion of the Octopus parodies the instability of a modern urban culture characterized not only by its own state of flux (in politics, economics, aesthetic and social standards) but also by the constantly fluctuating perspectives it constructs of traditional and past cultures. In other words, like the bucket of the Octopus, contemporary life moves violently and furiously, all the while making it appear that everything around it is moving in just the same fashion. And the only responses are hilarity or terror—or both.

In this setting Nina declares her intentions: not so much a remedy for the world she lives in, but a feasible response to it. This re-envisioned family will, Nina presumes, liberate her from the conventional role of wife while still offering her the opportunity to be a mother; it will provide for her baby a more egalitarian model of gender roles and family expectations; and it will allow George to live his own life—a life that would include, but not be defined by, her and her baby. Rather than rescue the three of them from the carnival ride of contemporary life, Nina's solution would provide them with the means of coping with such a life. And that is, after all, what a functional family does.

Such a revised version of the family reflects (and develops from) George and Nina's friendship, which, resisting reductive descriptions and labels, offers them a profound, but sometimes puzzling, happiness. George tells us that he and Nina "loved each other and took care of each other and behaved a little like best friends, a little like brother and sister, and a little like very young and very tentative lovers." He describes their friendship as a "long and unconsummated courtship between two people with no expectations" (72). Indeed, it is their freedom from expectations that allows them to relate to one another as individuals, and not as players within a prescribed narrative of heterosexual behaviors and dynamics. The relationship has been successful for a full year before Nina's pregnancy, and she assumes that the addition of a baby would make no difference. One might say that *The Object of My Affection*, as its title suggests, is about the difference a baby makes.

Perhaps the most tenderly evocative emblem of George and Nina's "romance" is the ballroom dancing[4] they attempt at a decaying Arthur Murray dance studio, where a chain-smoking instructor fumbles with the tape machine and sings out the tempos for middle-aged Ginger-and-Freds: " 'Think of the dahnse as a three-minute love affair,' she'd say, posed with her eyes shut. Then she'd sail off into a solo demonstration, firmly held by her dream lover" (68). The pathos of the scene and the instructor suggests the urgent desire to create romance where it least likely exists. Wearing second-hand party clothes and prom dresses from the 1950s, George and Nina awkwardly stumble through waltzes and fox-trots—the worst dancers in the class—routinely breaking into hysterical sobbing before the end of the evening and then feeling such an emotional release that they return home, carefree and buoyant, purchase a quart of ice cream, and watch reruns of *The Mary Tyler Moore Show*, only to retire chastely to their own beds.

Once again, the narrative deconstructs a classic icon of the love affair, depicting not a traditional heterosexual romance but, instead, a self-conscious parody of such a romance. George and Nina appropriate the signs of an intimacy they do not embody; the result, at least at first, is a light-hearted counterfeit:

After the first few humiliating classes, the ritual of it began to appeal to me. Nina was rhapsodic. We went to the flea markets on Canal Street one weekend and picked up a bunch of flashy, ill-fitting outfits: puffy strapless prom gowns and open-toed high-heeled shoes for Nina; grossly baggy pleated pants and wide-shouldered sport jackets for me. We didn't dance any better in our new clothes, but we looked wonderful. (68)

While the middle-aged and retired couples at the dance studio assume them to be young lovers, George and Nina see themselves merely performing (and not too successfully) the gestures of young lovers. A further deconstructive turn, however, is the fact that this simulated heterosexual love affair actually offers George and Nina genuine affection, companionship, and synchronicity. Their "bad dancing" does not, at this point in their relationship, appear to reflect any serious asynchronicity of character; instead, there is such a mutuality in their moving "out of step" with one another that they end up being "in step."

Put another way, their celibate romance offers George and Nina an unconventional but authentic set of satisfactions. Two single people, unsuccessful with romantic attachments, they find in their friendship many of the pleasures and some of the fulfillment they might seek in lovers: good fun, domestic compatibility, companionship, honesty, warmth, support.[5] To become lovers, on the other hand, would make them into different people: Nina would no longer be the independent woman who has decided not to live with her lover, and George would no longer be the gay man he is. Sexual attraction and/or expression would not only be inauthentic, it would forbid the ease and openness on which their friendship is based. Indeed, as George tells us, it would shatter the very unconventionality of their relationship—invalidating their friendship, contradicting it, bankrupting it:

Sometimes, sometimes when we were sitting together in the living room late at night or sprawled in our respective rooms doing crossword puzzles and calling out questions to each other, I wanted to go to her and make love to her, make love to her in front of a fireplace or on an empty beach or in a canopy bed, in a dozen foolishly romantic and artificial settings. I wanted to make love to her with sweet words and tender looks and all the packaged images that have never in my life had anything to do with the genuine lustful passion I've felt. I wanted to feel closer to Nina than I sometimes did, to bring down what often felt like an enormous and invisible wall separating us. And still, I knew that if we ever did make love, it would be the act to consummate the end of our relationship and not the beginning of it. If we ever did make love, we'd be unable to go on with our dancing lessons and our cluttered life together, our safe celibate relationship. It wasn't really what either one of us wanted, and the fact that it never came up was one of the things that held us together. (240-41)

The "foolishly romantic and artificial" nature of George's fantasies involving Nina resonate with the same species of clichés that over-determine his daydreams of a nuclear family. In both cases, George references an American iconography that predates not only the period during which he and Nina live (the mid-1980s) but also the period of social and political turmoil that marked a turning point for American sexual standards (the mid-1960s). In a profoundly ironic way, George is nostalgic for an age that did not countenance pre-marital sex, single mothers, or gay people—an age that would have condemned both him and Nina for who they are and how they choose to live.

Despite George's tender evocation of this benighted past, we would be mistaken to interpret it as a longing for a return to a less sexually tolerant standard; George is *not* seeking a heterosexual romance and a traditional nuclear family as much as he is seeking the self-assurance—and, perhaps, the assumption of self-evident rightness—associated with heterosexual romance and the nuclear family. George is no reactionary; he merely fantasizes about a world where his romantic and sexual experiences, as well as the families he may create (or join), are not only tolerated but perceived as incontestable and positive parts of the social fabric. Anyone familiar with the social and political landscape of contemporary America can comprehend just how radical George's desires are, but McCauley's narrative goes further than to rehearse the plea for an acceptance of gay people and their lives into mainstream society. It suggests that this assumption of self-evident rightness, so complacently maintained by earlier generations and so strenuously bulwarked by current traditionalists, is not only no longer viable in the 1980s but is actually responsible, in part, for the massive social unrest regarding issues of gender, sexuality, and family. As we will later see, the depictions of more traditional families in this novel indicate both the models that George and Nina reject and the framework within which their own relationship and proposed family should be interrogated.

The arrangement of George and Nina's life together is transparently anything but simple.[6] While the inevitable sexual and emotional frustrations inherent in their relationship forecast its ultimate impossibility, it is Nina's pregnancy that marks the turning point in the "family romance" that they are co-writing: "a love affair can be wonderful but a courtship is far more enduring. And our courtship endured, right through the love affair [with Howard], until Nina became pregnant and raised the stakes somehow, tipped the delicate balance of our relationship" (74). If the mere fact of Nina's oncoming child has the capacity to tip the balance of her friendship with George because it would presumably solidify her relationship with Howard, Nina's decision to "terminate with" Howard and raise the baby with George, instead, tips the balance precariously in the opposite direction. At first, George demurs, maintaining that Nina loves Howard, that Howard would make a good father, and that she is afraid of commitment. Nina replies,

> "I'm not *afraid* to make a commitment to him, I simply don't *want* to."
> "Even though you love him?"
> "Who says I love him?"
> I was shocked. "Nina, come on."
> "Come on what? Come on what, George? What if I don't know? What if I truly don't know? Isn't there such a thing as not knowing?" (153)

Refuting all of the certainties guaranteed by conventional notions of romantic love, Nina insists on maintaining authority over her own life in the face of, indeed because of, her uncertainty.

Nina's assertion of independence (not only an independence from Howard and from the institution of marriage, but also from the narrative orthodoxies of heterosexual romantic love) partly constructs the postmodern discourse of the novel, but McCauley promptly overlays that discourse with the counterdiscourse of traditional romance itself. After George and Nina's conversation about Howard's meaning in her life, they take a walk in Prospect Park "with our arms around each other, watching the sun set behind Manhattan and looking over our shoulders for potential muggers" (153). Sitting in the Park, after dark, watching the yellow car lights circle the War Memorial arch, Nina admits to nervousness over George's approaching weekend away with an ex-boyfriend (Robert), but the two of them manufacture an illusion that eclipses her anxiety. Their shared fantasy reads like a scene in a 1940s Hollywood film romance:

> "We could be in Paris," I said, pointing to the towering arch. "That could be the Arc de Triomphe and we could be in Paris."
> "That could be the Louvre," she said, looking at the library.
> We sat in silence until it was dark and we could see the lights of Manhattan glittering in the distance, bright but unreal. Nina stood up and wrapped her shawl more tightly around her shoulders. (154)

The counterpoint of romance and reality in this scene sharpens the contrast between the normative elements of such a romantic scene and the actual circumstances of George and Nina's life at this moment.

The subsequent chain of events constitutes a series of ironic reversals: George and Robert go to Vermont for a romantic weekend in the country, but Robert proves to be so insufferable that George ends up going home with another man whom he meets in the bar at the inn where he and Robert are staying. But Paul, the "other man," proves to be much more than a one-night stand; in many ways he is the lynch-pin of the novel: for one thing, George and Paul prove to be compatible and companionable, and for another, it is because of Paul that George agrees to Nina's invitation to help her take care of her baby. Immediately upon meeting Paul, George discovers that he lives with his adopted son, a Salvadoran boy named Gabriel—a fact that fascinates and attracts George:

> "You're raising a child?" I asked. "By yourself?"
> "Well, friends help out sometimes, but it's mostly just Gabie and me."
> He said it tonelessly, as if it were of minimal interest, when, in fact, the mention of a child—from El Salvador, no less—instantly created a romantic aura around him that left me staring at him stunned and smitten. (174)

George's response is to tell Paul that he, too, has a child: that "the woman I live with is pregnant and . . . we're going to raise the baby together. . . . Sort of" (175). George's indecisions apparently dissolve in the presence of another gay father, a man at ease in a "family" that is necessarily unconventional. Paul seems to prove not only that a gay man can be a father, but, more broadly, that "family" is a more elastic structure than it is generally assumed to be. George admits, "If Nina had purposely set up a meeting with someone to try and convince me her plan wasn't totally harebrained, she couldn't have picked a better subject" (176).

Paul embodies what George might be, as well as providing depictions of fatherhood grounded in the realities of child-rearing, and dependent neither on mythologized images nor on a heterosexual family model. Paul describes parenting with candor and tenderness, a refreshing exception to the typically sentimental visions of angelic children and effortless child-rearing. In response to George's urgently asked "What's it like having a kid," Paul acknowledges (and invites George to acknowledge) the emotional complexity of the relationship:

Sometimes it's great, George. Most times it's great. Of course, every once in a while I wonder what I'm doing with a kid, and I forget why I wanted to adopt him in the first place. Usually around three in the afternoon when I'm working at home, my eyes are tired, and I need coffee or a nap. But everything seems wrong at three in the afternoon, and then Gabie comes home and I get caught up in loving him and taking care of him and I don't have time to wonder about it anymore. It's easy to love someone who needs you so much. (186)

With this testimonial in mind, George returns to Brooklyn and announces to Nina that he has finally decided to stay with her and help her with the baby—to settle into her proposed family.[7]

We cannot but question George's sudden decision to live with Nina just as he finally meets another man whom he very much likes and who very much likes him, not to mention someone with whom he shares a love of children. Blind to the possibility of a shared future with Paul and Gabriel, George can only see the disappointments and transience of his life—and Nina's proposed family offers him an alternative to that: "All that business . . . about you not having a lasting relationship or home or any of that . . ." George tells Nina, "That's my life story, too. I mean, here I am, almost pushing thirty and . . . I've never even owned a lint brush" (194). Seeking security, George perversely spies it in Nina's proposed family arrangement, which begins to sound (in George's language) like a Mutual Consolation Society.

Now parodying family life (just as they were parodying heterosexual romance), George and Nina are mistaken for, if not young marrieds, at least young parents: the furniture salesperson at Bloomingdales and their Arthur Murray dance instructor startle Nina by recognizing her as pregnant, and George by assuming that he is the father. However inaccurate this assumption, George finds comfort and solidity in his new role in the family that Nina is constructing:

I imagined a kind of permanence in my relationship with Nina, and sometimes, when I was polishing the surface of the new maple table or putting a folded stack of towels into the linen closet, I felt I was doing a reasonably good job of keeping house. I dutifully read through a couple of the baby books Nina loaned me, but frankly, nothing they had to say seemed addressed to me. They were mostly humorless tomes warning parents not to expect their infant to look like a human being for the first few months of life. There wasn't one book available on the role of the roommate of an unwed mother. (202)

The sheer obviousness of George's final remark does not render it pointless: there are no books available on the role of the roommate of an unwed mother because such a relationship is not part of the standard family romance. George and Nina would have to write their own book about this sort of family, and at least at this point in the narrative, one begins to suspect that *The Object of My Affection* might be that book.[8]

But the relative certainty regarding George and Nina's proposed family circle is shaken when Paul visits George in New York, with Gabriel and Molly, Paul's acerbic post-Communist mother, in town to protest the demolition of her low-income elderly housing. Once again in Paul's company, George begins to reveal, in spite of himself, signs of his own emotional muddle—a growing fondness for Paul and a reluctance to admit to it:

[Paul] stared at me for a second and said, "So anyway . . . it's great to see you again, George."

"Oh, I know," I said awkwardly, meaning it was nice to see him. (213)

The inaccessibility of George's feelings prevents him from acknowledging even a trace of desire for a committed relationship with Paul and Gabriel. Instead, the commitment he and Nina have espoused offers a safer arrangement for George to fall back on: with Nina, George can be mistaken for a husband or lover, as well as for a father, without ever actually saying so himself. Others can assume a traditional (or at least typical) family where none exists. And true emotional commitment becomes almost a moot point when the *appearance* of commitment is taken for its presence. This is not to say that George does not sincerely and deeply love Nina, but it is the love that a gay man has for the most important woman in his life, and while it may occasionally manifest what Evelyn Waugh, in *Brideshead Revisited*, calls the "bat's squeak of sexuality," sexual commitment rarely follows. George may consider courtship far more enduring than a love affair, but a courtship that is antithetical to consummation can hardly be expected to result in any sort of "marriage."

However appealing Nina's proposed family may be to George, we begin to see its inauthenticity for a man still searching for a satisfying (sexual) relationship with another man. During Paul's Thanksgiving visit, George experiences the tug of both emotional magnets: Paul and the possibility of a romantic relationship, and Nina and the possibility of a family. These two potential lives bump into each other when Nina returns to the apartment after George and Paul have been alone together for part of the afternoon. George responds to her appearance by frenetically dressing, inviting Nina into his bedroom, and struggling to make small-talk:

> "How was the lunch?" I asked Nina as she walked past my room.
> "Wonderful. Your mother's terrific, Paul," she called out.
> "You can go in and tell him," I said.
> "I want to lie down. I'm tired."
> "Do you want some popcorn?" I asked her, holding open the door.
> "Stop acting so weird," she whispered to me. "I just want to get off my feet."
> "Weird? Who's acting weird? I'm not acting weird."
> "Yes, you are," Paul said.
> "Thank you, Paul," Nina called out . . .
> Nina went off to her room and Paul sat up in bed staring at me with annoyance.
> "Nina does know we're not old college roommates, doesn't she?"
> "Of course," I said.
> "Then what was that routine all about?"
> "Nothing," I said. I listened for the sound of her bedroom door closing and then I took off my shirt and sat next to him on the bed, feeling distant and eager for him to leave. "I just don't want her to feel left out, that's all. She lives here, after all."
> "Right. And I'm visiting for the afternoon. So what's the problem?"
> "There's no problem," I said, but I still felt uneasy. (221)

It is almost as if George himself cannot distinguish between living with Nina and "living with Nina." In other words, he appears to regard the conventional heterosexual narrative, which he and Nina were initially parodying, as "the real thing"; George backs away from a relationship with both romantic and erotic components, swerving, instead, toward a facsimile romance and a facsimile nuclear family.

At this point, George seems destined to dissociate the romantic and the authentic; this is pointedly played out in a short scene between George and Paul that reprises an earlier one between George and Nina. The two men walk to Prospect Park and watch the traffic circle the War Memorial Arch:

> Paul put his arm around my shoulders in a friendly, familiar way. "Doesn't that remind you of the Arc de Triomphe, George?"
>
> "I don't know," I said. "I've never been to Paris."
>
> "Well, don't you think it looks like pictures you've seen of the Arc de Triomphe with cars going around it and the lights shining up on the stone?"
>
> "I hate to travel," I told him. He looked over at me with dismay, and I felt a kind of panic race through me. I was out of control and acting like a jerk. What if he got up then and just walked away into the Parisian twilight? "But it reminds me of the pictures I've seen of Paris, Paul. I tell that to Nina all the time." (222)

The repetition of this scenario self-consciously contrasts George's willingness to enter the romantic metaphor with Nina and his resistance to the same metaphor when articulated by Paul. Does his resistance stem from George's sense that "all the packaged images [of romantic love] . . . have never in my life had anything to do with the genuine lustful passion I've felt" (240-41)? In other words, is George simply incapable of allowing for romance in his sexual relationships—because the culture in which he lives has never permitted him the freedom to associate romance with sex? Does Paul, therefore, threaten to topple George's own internalized heterosexism? Or, does George dodge Paul's romantic gestures because he fears a commitment that might in fact make more demands than his relationship with Nina ever can? In other words, does George, consciously or otherwise, try to ward off a relationship that would allow him no emotional equivocation or ambiguity?

These emotional muddles reach a crisis point during George's Christmas visit with Paul and Gabriel. Throughout the week, George is unwilling to admit to his own happiness with Paul because that would mean not only acknowledging the depth of his feelings for Paul, but also confronting Paul's implied invitation for George to live with him; that one of Paul's friends needs a pre-school teacher for the school he is opening intensifies both the chances and risks involved in this invitation:

Toward the end of the week, a tense silence developed between Paul and me. Neither one of us was willing to talk about our relationship and it seemed inappropriate to talk about anything else. I didn't know what to say to him. I hated the thought of leaving, of going back to New York and saying goodbye to him and to Gabriel, but I couldn't bring myself to admit it aloud. Once you talk about something like that, you're done for. You sink into a swamp of responsibility you can never get out of. At least, if you don't mention your feelings, you can claim a misunderstanding later on when the demands start to hit the fan. And besides, there's no cold shower more effective than a long, serious discussion of love. Or whatever it was I felt for him. (259)

George realizes that with Paul he might make a serious commitment, not just to a lover but to a child and even to a community—a commitment to a relationship that would allow for no equivocation or ambiguity.

Certainly, the ambiguities of George and Nina's "courtship" initially protect them from confronting the inevitable complexities, not to say impossibilities, of their situation. Even Paul acutely asks, "Who's this marriage of yours pleasing? . . . How long do you think you're going to be satisfied with that?" (261). But we should query George's claim that "a love affair can be wonderful but a courtship is far more enduring" (74); the longevity of love affairs aside, a courtship cannot be "enduring" because, by definition, it is one chapter in the narrative of a romantic/erotic relationship. To remain fixed, if not trapped, in that chapter suggests stalled, even arrested, relations. At first, they are contented with such a suspended sexuality, but after George meets Paul, George and Nina's heterosocial relationship appears more transparently precarious, inadequate, and disabling. When they begin to confront and express their anger, confusion, and pain, we recognize (and we know that they recognize) the unavoidable tensions that result from their mock-romance.

Their frustrations pierce through the shields of romantic clichés quite appropriately during one of their dance lessons:

She . . . took my arm and started to lead me around the dance floor. . . .
    "You're leading," I said.
    "Someone has to."
    "I'm supposed to be the one leading."
    "Since when, Georgie?"
    "Since always, as far as I can tell," I whispered loudly. "You're such a very independent woman you dumped Howard as soon as you got the results of the pregnancy test. You couldn't wait to raise the baby on your own, but you dragged me into the scheme pretty quickly."

"*Dragged* you? . . . You're the one who came running back to me, begging to help with the baby . . . [Did you want to impress] the journalist with the Salvadoran kid? And while we're on the subject, why is he being dragged into this?"

"No one's dragging Paul anywhere."

"Thanksgiving, Christmas, why don't you just invite him to move in with us?"

"You're jealous again, Nina."

"You're right, I'm jealous again. You've got a boyfriend and I don't. Even though I'm pregnant I wouldn't mind having sex every once in a while" . . .

"It's not so fabulous that you have to be jealous about it."

"I'm not interested in the quality of your sex life, believe me, George."

"I wanted to help you with the baby because I love you." I held her tightly by the shoulders, away from me at arm's length. "I love you, Nina." (239)

Their attempted performance of traditional gender roles does not successfully mask the turmoil they face here (the dance instructor, troubled by their quarrel, sings out, in tempo with the music, "a *lit* tle sof ter, *keep* it sof ter . . ."), and George and Nina confront the limitations of a relationship whose lack of confinement they have hitherto celebrated. Once outside the dance studio, Nina explains: "This relationship is hard for me sometimes. . . . You don't disappoint me. And I didn't say I wanted to change anything. I didn't say it and I didn't mean it" (240). Although the contradictory impulses of ideology and desire do not damage Nina, as they might a less reflective person, they do distress her; she may be able to analyze and articulate the cross-currents of her feelings for George and Howard, but this does not assuage or simplify those feelings. Because Nina has chosen to redirect her life according to her own values and assumptions, she cannot expect conventional forms and practices to guide her conduct or her expectations. Even the structure of this particular emotional crisis—jealousy of one's gay roommate—does not have a prefabricated range of responses. In their relationship, as in their dancing, how can either of them determine what steps to take, let alone who is to "lead"?

The very thing that Nina most values in her relationship with George (the absence of a strictly hetero*sexual* intimacy) proves to have the greatest capacity to hurt her, and so the family model to which she is ideologically committed contains within it the potential for her own personal unhappiness. As in Howard's case, emotions prove wayward, recalcitrant, unwilling to conform to the theoretically sound frameworks that represent thoughtful and reasonable responses to the challenges of contemporary society. After all, a financially vulnerable young woman who wishes to preserve her independence and identity might intelligently turn to her gay roommate and suggest that, in defiance of the sexist and heterosexist paradigm of the nuclear family, they continue to share expenses and construct their own unconventional family for the child she bears. This single gay man, who works at a preschool and loves children might understandably agree to this suggestion, especially as he and his roommate are such good friends and enjoy a companionship that is at least as caring and compatible as many marriages.

George and Nina's attempt to rewrite the family romance may be somewhat over-determined, but it is rooted in a deeply human need for company and mutuality.[9] Moreover, McCauley brings their "experiment" into relief by contextualizing it among a series of "conventional" families that appear (or are described) throughout the novel. These family portraits reveal a variety of thwarted and alienated personal relations, some of them arguably capable of causing significant psychological or emotional damage. Against the backdrop of these family narratives, Nina's and George's pursuit of affection and commitment assumes both meaning and urgency.

Nina's experiences with her own family (and first marriage) account for her vehement desire to reframe personal relations in her life. Indeed, she explains that she came to study psychology because she had "been around nuts for so long" (61). On the top floor of the family's brick row home in Baltimore lived her Grandfather Borowski, who routinely threatened to throw himself off the roof if the family ever moved out of the house he had saved all his life to purchase. Nina's mother complained that Nina wasn't thin enough for a Hollywood film career, while her father obsessively joked that she had stolen her brothers' brains "through some mystical female powers": whenever she would play polkas on the accordion at family dinners, he would grumble, "if she'd been a boy she could have been an astronaut" (60). Her twin brothers took to drink, married, and moved out, but not far—into a two-family house within three blocks of Grandfather Borowski and his domain.

In order to "prove to her father she didn't intend to go off to college with the brains she'd stolen from her brothers," Nina worked in a factory for a short while—before eloping to Arizona with Thomas, the rebellious son of wealthy Washington liberals. When her husband became involved with a religious cult and killed her dog in a ritual sacrifice, Nina returned to Washington and informed her in-laws of their son's troubles; they responded by blaming Nina for their son's undoing, annulling their marriage, and paying her thirty thousand dollars to keep quiet. Nina's own family, in turn, accused her of botching her one chance at upward mobility. Suddenly a victim of dueling sets of family values, Nina left home and used the thirty thousand dollars to pay for college.

Her experiences chart a woman's attempts to escape from a prison of rigid gender stereotypes and claustrophobic family intimacy. In her early life, the family home iconographically represents the patriarchal structure of the social unit that delimits her conceptualizations of a future career and life. With her (paternal) grandfather at the top of the house, demanding the consolidation of the family under his roof, and her father jokingly antagonizing her for her ("masculine") intelligence, Nina might understandably assume that marriage would bring her, if not happiness then at least sane company. Instead, her husband and his family implicate her in their own narrative of rebellion and blame. Thomas's family is different only insofar as they have the available cash to maintain the imperturbable facade of family dignity and harmony: a nice quiet annulment, extensive deprogramming for Thomas, and a handsome bribe for Nina. Ironically, this money provides Nina with the means of rescuing herself from the prison of expectations that marriage and family have proven to be for her. Now pregnant, Nina is given another opportunity to assume a traditional role within a heterosexual paradigm; it is not surprising that she responds by redefining the role and toppling the paradigm.

Like Nina, George's early experiences with family (and romance) were troubling and discouraging; indeed, his sexuality appears to have caused at least as many problems as Nina's intelligence. Moreover, George faces analogous alienations—from his family because of his difference, and from lovers because of his desire for authentic connection. The pattern is established early, as it was for Nina. When his mother inferred that George (then in college) was gay, she amicably confronted him about it and George amicably admitted that, yes, "the person in California I was getting daily letters from was more than my friend" (62). The matter was then dropped. George was therefore surprised when, two days later, his brother Frank stopped talking to him and his father handed him a thousand dollars and told him he had two weeks to leave home. George first planned to use the money for a prolonged visit to California, but he was rebuffed by his friend's self-interested response, "Are you nuts? . . . What would my parents think? I've got to count on them for three more years of tuition, you know" (62).

With his first romance at an abrupt end and his family dispossessing him, George decides to leave everyone behind and take off for Boston; he is surprised when his mother responds, "Don't be ridiculous, dear, that's all blown over" (63). George discovers that his family is content as long as his sexuality remain invisible, unspeakable; as long as George's difference is neither conspicuous nor named, he is welcome to remain a part of the family. While George does not openly rebel against this plainly homophobic response, he is not unaware of either its personal or political meanings. Much later in the narrative, when George's mother remarks, "there's so much distance between us now. I wonder when it really happened that all this distance came between us," George reflects, "I could have told her the exact moment I thought it happened" (287). How could this experience of betrayal, rejection, and exclusion (though ending in a facade of indifference that was equally unkind) *not* irreparably readjust George's relations with his family. His initial reaction to his family's attitude toward his sexuality may appear to be impulsive and evasive, but, in fact, it foreshadows his arrangement with Nina and his future attempts to recreate the family: George goes to Boston anyway and stays with a friend at his "urban commune where people went to crash for a few days or weeks in varying stages of turmoil" (63). In this gesture, George turns to an "alternative" community, marking a break not only from his own family but from the nuclear-family structure itself.

This is not to suggest, however, that George displaces his family as conveniently as they have misplaced his sexual orientation. George's narrative is punctuated with telephone conversations with his mother— conversations that reveal their sometimes painfully awkward attempts to remain connected without ever openly addressing the facts of George's personal life. For instance, when George moves out of an apartment he was sharing with a lover, his mother's concern is cramped by her strenuous denial of George's homosexuality:

"So I guess it didn't work out living with that Joley friend of yours or whatever he called himself. Just tell me yes or no, George."

"Yes, it didn't work out. Thanks for asking, Ma."

"I'm sorry to hear it. I'm sure you'll find another . . . whatever. Just be careful what you're doing with all that disease business going on. You know what I mean, dear." (70-71)

"You know what I mean, dear" very craftily *both inscribes and erases* the facts of George's life; it allows his mother to admit to an awareness of his being gay without actually saying so. The identity of George's lover is washed out ("that Joley friend of yours or whatever he called himself"), and George's possible attempt to narrate his experience is silenced ("Just tell me yes or no").[10] His family may no longer demand that he leave home, but they continue to dismiss his experiences; his personal life suffers a banishment by silence. Tellingly, George's mother responds in the opposite fashion (inviting him to talk rather than insisting that he not) when he informs her that he has moved in with Nina:

"Maybe she'd be good for Frank [George's brother], unless you're doing something I would, honestly, be very interested in hearing about" (70). Her persistent preservation of a heterosexual norm reminds George of his marginalized position, not only vis-à-vis his own family but vis-à-vis the very paradigm that his family embodies, represents, and perpetuates.

This fact is nowhere made clearer than in the climactic scenes of *The Object of My Affection*, when George and a seven-month pregnant Nina visit his family for his brother Frank's wedding. It is here that traditional family structures collide with George and Nina's idiosyncratic circumstances—circumstances that, when brought into George's suburban family home,[11] appear not merely unconventional but in many respects subversive. For a wedding ceremony does not merely solemnize the marriage of two individual people; it solemnizes the entire institution of marriage, while entitling the newlyweds to kinds and degrees of social sanction otherwise unavailable to them as a couple. Quite obviously, neither George nor Nina has any place at this event—not so much because they are not married (or because George is not heterosexual) but because they are poised at a moment in their lives when they are making choices that dramatically and self-consciously replace, if not oppose, conventional heterosexual marriage.[12]

Not surprisingly, George's family is largely oblivious to these decisions—oblivious, indeed, to the fact that people might even make such decisions; after all, they have no reason to consider the political implications of marriage, the nuclear family, patriarchy, and heterosexuality more generally. Nina's one attempt to discuss Frank's wedding ends in blank incomprehension on Frank's part. Here he is explaining his fiancée's pet name:

"Cici's my name for her. Those are her initials. At least until tomorrow, right?"

"Then she's taking your name," Nina asked.

Frank was completely baffled. "Well, who else's name would she take? Richard Gere's?" He looked at me and laughed. "Right?"

"Some women do keep their own names when they get married," Nina told him.

"Well, some people get married in a barn,[13] Nina, but that's not my style. I mean, if she didn't want to take my name, why would she marry me?" (276-77)

Frank reveals an utter incapacity to imagine any assumptions regarding marriage other than his own thoroughly traditional ones. What McCauley demonstrates in the subsequent scenes is that this traditional view of marriage is not in itself so terrible; rather, culpability lies in the ruthless insistence that any assumptions not aligned with these traditions are suspect, indefensible, even inauthentic.

George's family displays this dogmatic attitude in their response to George and Nina's attendance at Frank's wedding. While his father remains oblivious to everything occurring around him—he has moved into a basement apartment in his family home and devotes all of his time to trying to master the Massachusetts State Lottery—George's brother and mother unashamedly announce their refusal to uncloset the gay son and his unmarried pregnant roommate. Initially, Frank has merely hinted to his fiancée that Nina is George's "girlfriend":

Your friends might be a bunch of open-minded liberals, who don't see anything odd in your life-style, but believe me, it wouldn't make for a romantic evening for me to uncork a bottle of wine and tell Cici my brother's a homosexual. She's a sweet kid. She's the kind of girl who probably wouldn't understand what the word means. (282)

But when Nina—noticeably pregnant—appears, George's mother and brother determine that they have no choice but to announce that George and Nina were secretly married; his mother explains, "Caroline's family is very religious, George . . . One of her aunts is a nun. . . . We can't just say you came to the wedding with a pregnant girlfriend. It would put you in a bad light" (283). When George argues for honesty and integrity, his mother prompts him to consider himself as an accomplice in this deception:

Let me point out that you're the one who lives with Nina and you're the one who brought her to this wedding. I can't tell you how delighted I was when I found out that you were bringing her. I assumed we'd quietly pass her off as your girlfriend. All I'd have to say is, "They're roommates," and shrug, and everyone would just chalk it up to living in the big city and I'd look like a good liberal parent to boot.

. . . You know, dear, you could have brought . . . well . . . you could have brought someone else to this wedding if you wanted to. It seems to me Frank and I aren't suggesting anything so far from the truth. You and Nina are proba- bly as intimate as your father and me. (286)

George admits, though only to himself at first, that his mother is right: "on the surface, the lie she and Frank had improvised wasn't such a long way from the life Nina and I were living. They were suggesting we play house for a few hours, which was exactly what we'd been doing for a year and a half" (288).

When this performance is demanded for the sake of propriety, George no longer perceives it as nostalgic amusement, but as falsehood: for while it is possible to understand George and Nina's ballroom dancing as a form of postmodern parody, there is, after all, as George himself admits, little significant difference between it and "Nina and me dancing across the floor of some suburban function hall with our arms around each other" (288). Both of these acts (allowing the other couples at their dance class to believe that they are a couple, allowing George's family to tell the wedding guests that they are a couple) efficiently capitulate to a patriarchal standard—injecting George and Nina into a narrative that does not accurately represent their lives. It is only after George's family attempts to coerce them into this narrative that George realizes the inauthenticity of it for himself and Nina:

there is a side to our relationship I've always considered fundamentally audacious. And it's this audacious side which, publicly anyway, has always pleased me the most. This fake marriage arrangement we were expected to make was draining the audacity out of our relationship in quarts and replacing it with a respectability I've never strived for or wanted. And somehow, the respectability made the whole relationship seem wrong. (296)

This reveals the conundrum of George and Nina's "romance": its audacity lay precisely in its appropriation of the signs of respectability. When George realizes that his family was planning not only to assert a literal reading of these signs to others but also to demand that George and Nina collude in that reading, he confronts the essential tyranny of respectability: the potential within any orthodox system for myopia, parochialism, and manipulative self-preservation. The comedy of these scenes is so brittle that we can see right through it to the underlying tragedy: a willingness on the part of George's family to misrepresent his relationship with Nina and to sacrifice his integrity in order to maintain appearances and avoid social rejection.

Suddenly, the novel's counterdiscourse of traditional (heterosexual) romance (constructed either as "audacity" or "respectability") appears to George as little more than a trap and a lie. This epiphany does not immediately catapult George into action, however. As if working out the original Freudian paradigm of the family romance, George must come to terms with his own parentage and inheritance in order to discover his true identity. This revisit to the family home does not merely help George understand who he *is not*, it also drives him to understand who he *is*. Just as George's mother (in her speech about his bringing Nina to the wedding) urges him to face the implications of his choice to "play house" with Nina, so George's brother proposes an analysis of their father that clarifies the terms of the choices still facing George:

Our father's a bachelor. He never should have married at all because he's a bachelor by nature. . . . Of course, in his day, there was no such thing as a bachelor, just like there was no such thing as divorce. Well, not really, anyway. But our father was a genuine single man. He never should have left the army. He was somebody when he was in the army, and now he's not. He's just a bachelor with a wife and a family he never knew what do with. . . . it probably isn't an inherited trait. You probably have to idolize your father to pick it up. You're not a bachelor, George. I can tell. That's why I think you should just go ahead and get married. (293)

George's response proclaims one of the novel's key ideas: " 'There are all kinds of marriages,' I said, but I doubted he'd know what I was talking about, and I wasn't so sure I did" (293). It is significant that this "message" includes both the politically confident statement *and* George's recognition both that his brother cannot likely comprehend the idea and that he himself still needs to grasp its full meaning. Resisting any polemical self-assurance, *The Object of My Affection* consistently depicts the difficulties not only in communicating challenges to the traditional marital and familiar paradigms but also in acting on those challenges.

Now acknowledging, at least to himself, that he is not a "bachelor" and that his life with Nina is essentially a dead-end relationship, George experiences his "dark night of the soul": he smokes a pack of cigarettes and reads *Johnny Tremain*, his favorite novel from his youth. With his lungs and eyes bruised from his smoking, and Nina snoring in the next bed, George cannot sleep; instead, he ponders his situation (with Nina, with Paul, and with their children) and how this encounter with his family illuminates the implications of the alternatives before him. At first, he inscribes himself and Nina into yet another mythical fantasy of the heterosexual family: "It occurred to me then that we could easily be Ozzie and Harriet chastely lying in our separate beds while the kids dozed next door dreaming of the Big Game tomorrow" (295). This reference is so transparently incongruous that it functions ironically, even deconstructively—a sign not only of what George and Nina are not, but also a sign of what George's family is not. These images of the "exemplary" nuclear family, oozing respectability and banality about equally, inadequately represent any family that George knows, least of all his own; living with other people (as the counterimage of the Octopus ride suggests) is a far more bumpy experience than Ozzie and Harriet ever dreamed of. As for George, faced with the choice between his unmarried roommate and her child, on the one hand, and a possible lover and his Salvadoran adopted son, on the other, nothing could pose a more hopeless *Baedeker* than a television situation-comedy from a period that resisted the empowerment of racial minorities, women, and gay people.

These events at his family's home move George to "light out" for a new emotional and social territory, to be true to himself and the people he will live with, including the child he will parent. A single realization clarifies the muddle in which he finds himself: "Had I thought to invite [Paul] to the wedding instead of making a career of avoiding his calls, I might have been able to make a stand for myself and avoid the impending disaster" (296). Confronting a crisis of authenticity, George phones Paul, apologizes for his evasiveness, and proclaims his willingness to move to Vermont to live with Paul and Gabriel. George chooses Paul's family over Nina's not because he loves Nina any less but because he loves her differently—because his "romance" with her is less viable than his connection with Paul: " . . . I was moving out after the baby was born. . . . I was abandoning our life together. Not abandoning her, but us and the idea of our relationship" (304). In order to explain this decision to Nina "with a note of finality and assurance, but [still being] . . . tender and loving, too," George arranges for them to stop on their way back to Brooklyn at an inn in Westerly, Rhode Island. When George announces that he has something to say, Nina responds with her own note of finality and assurance, and with more tenderness than we've seen her express for anyone in the novel:

We don't have to talk about it. I know what you want to tell me. . . I've probably known all along. I'm glad we tried it for a while . . . I guess, in the end, this isn't really what I wanted either. I love you, George. Maybe I love you because I know I can't have you. But maybe I just love you. (306)

And then, as the final gesture of their affection for one another, the conclusive and irreparable performance in the narrative of their romance, the ultimate event that both seals and unseals their relationship, George and Nina make love:

I took her hands [and] led her across the room. We stood beside the bed staring at each other cautiously, touching tentatively, knowing that in the morning when we got up everything would have changed between us and we would be farther apart than ever before. (306)

This is the final deconstructive twist to their romantic narrative: they dissolve their relationship with the act that typically consolidates (sexual) involvement; they reject the possibility of a family with the act that traditionally creates a family; they consummate a parting with the act that usually signals a beginning.[14]

Nevertheless, the final chapter of the novel does provide two beginnings, two new and apparently functional families: George is living with Paul and Gabriel in Vermont, and Nina and her new-born daughter Emily are living with Paul's mother Molly: "[Molly] needed a place to live and Nina needed a roommate. Nina wanted a mentor and Molly had found a protégée. Emily needed a grandmother" (311).[15] Nina continues to revise the family romance, extending the family out to someone not related by blood, but connected through a highly nontraditional relational chain. Moreover, Nina has not utterly excluded Howard from their lives: "Howard had started to come by the apartment, at her invitation, sometimes just to cook dinner and spend time with Emily and sometimes to stay over" (309).

These plot "resolutions," however, do not claim conventional narrative closure; indeed, both George and Nina articulate the open-endedness of their lives and the indeterminacy of the decisions they have made. Nina:

I'm happy with the way things are right now, George, believe it or not. I'm not sure what's going to happen, but right now I'm content. . . . Howard and I don't talk about the future much. I suppose we're both afraid to. I'm afraid he's going to start talking about moving in or getting married, and I imagine he's afraid I'm going to pull back again. Anyway, since Emily was born and you moved out, I haven't really wanted to make many plans. There'll be a showdown someday, I know. There always is. (313)

George:

I told her I was living quietly and contentedly in Vermont, I was learning a little Spanish, learning to cook, learning something about the stars. I enjoyed waking up to Paul in the morning and I was watching Gabriel grow. The summer was almost behind us now and the fall would be cool and bright. Did that add up to happiness? I didn't know. (314)

They do not presume to pass judgment on their own lives, the relationships they have chosen, or the families they have created. With a sensibility almost Forsterian in the breadth of its moral vision, McCauley demonstrates that human relations are too complicated to fathom with any certainty, and too fragile to harass with conventional expectations and assumptions. That these characters have found ways to be true to themselves and yet to live contentedly with others represents a triumph over the dislocating and disabling forces of contemporary society. Capturing both the violence of those forces and the urgent human need to oppose them, the novel's final image depicts George and Nina once again on the Octopus at Coney Island—swirling and revolving in the bucket of the amusement ride: "We must have stayed on the thing for twenty minutes, spinning in circles, getting tossed into the air, thrown against each other in a corner of the slick seat by some centrifugal force as inevitable as death and much stronger than love" (316). McCauley's closing words suggest the virtue (even the moral necessity) of *only connecting*—recognizing that the one thing we know for certain about other people is that we share a planet with them, and that we commit a crime against ourselves and one another if we deny our obligation to learn how to coexist not just peacefully but cooperatively. Of course, the novel, from start to finish, also reveals just how challenging and complex that obligation is.

When George first begins to confront the situation he and Nina are in, he ponders a single, suddenly important, word: "Motherhood. The word had a new, ominously personal meaning that made it sound heavy and alive, a word of power and complexity and several more syllables than I'd realized" (19). *The Object of My Affection* demonstrates that the same might be said of words such as "marriage" and "family," and that to deny them their power and complexity robs them of their challenges, their meanings, and their possibilities.

Notes

1. While the term "family romance" originates in Freud's notion of a neurotic fantasy regarding elevated parentage, I am using the term in the more broadly critical sense to indicate narratives that "designate identity in terms of relation to origin—be the origin literary, philosophical, sociological, religious, or historical" (van Boheemen ix). This essay argues that *The Object of My Affection* contains two "family romances": the parallel narratives of Nina's and George's constructions of revised families (that is, the accounts of Emily's and Gabriel's parentage), and the embedded narratives of traditional heterosexual marriage and nuclear family (the network of images of the conventional family, available in film, television, literature, and visual sources).

As this methodological statement suggests, I believe that this novel is illuminated by some of the theoretical paradigms of post-structuralism and post-modernism, as well as the more explicitly politicized frameworks established by Feminism and Gay Studies; however, I will refrain from depending on the language of these critical schools, in part due to my own suspicion of the clumsiness of this language, and in part due to McCauley's own wary attitude toward it. In his most recent novel, *The Man of the House* (1996), McCauley's narrator characterizes Gay Studies as "an academic pursuit that baffled me":

I always asked polite questions about [this] work, hoping for gossip on the sex lives of literary or historical figures, and was invariably treated instead to a lecture on power dynamics, images of sadomasochism and bondage, and gender identification in the novels of George Meredith and Jane Austen, or even, God forbid, in *Beowulf*—all delivered in a language that sounded only vaguely like English. (17)

In McCauley's fictions, human relations resist systematized thinking, even systems founded on notions of indeterminacy and unpredictability.

2. This split in Howard's attitudes sometimes manifests itself within a single scene or conversation, which highlights his frustrating self-contradictions. For instance, in the course of a phone conversation with George, Howard progressively asserts that "if more men would take responsibility for child care, we could balance out the ration of men and women lawyers in this country" while signing off by asking George to tell Nina "I think she's an Angel, a Brisket" (77).

3. I am forming this word to evoke the term "homosocial," as defined by Eve Sedgwick in *Between Men*: "'Homosocial' is a word occasionally used in history and the social sciences, where it describes social bonds between persons of the same sex; it is a neologism, obviously formed by analogy with 'homosexual,' and just as obviously meant to be distinguished from 'homosexual'" (1).

4. References to music from a nostalgically drawn American past provide the implied soundtrack for this novel: George and Nina and Howard repeatedly listen to Odetta and Connie Francis records on George's Webcor portable record player; George tells us that his brother Frank "always had the looks of a big-band singer from the forties" (275); and, of course, the title of the novel is also the title of a song written in 1934 by Pinky Tomlin, Coy Poe, and Jimmie Grier. The song appears in the films *Times Square Lady* (1935) and *The Fabulous Dorseys* (1947).

5. That George and Nina can appear to others as a conventional heterosexual couple is significant: performing awkward parodies of ballroom dances, walking arm in arm through Prospect Park, planning a Thanksgiving dinner for their friends are gestures that depend on the fact that they are a man and a woman. Their "romance" might also be said to collapse two conventional fictional narratives: the Hollywood film romance, which represents romantic love in dance sequences, long walks in the rain, and other intimacies that allude to but do not actually depict erotic attachment; and the buddy narrative, in which

two friends struggle to preserve their asexual relationship in the face of romantic entanglements that threaten to assume a greater importance in one or both of their lives. Within the same novel, these two narratives deconstruct one another, as the Hollywood romance functions within a rigidly heterosexual paradigm, and the buddy relationship within a strictly homosocial one. George and Nina, gay man and straight woman, ultimately cannot rely on either narrative for an accurate or useable model for their lives.

6. McCauley actually suggests that all human relationships are more demanding and more complicated than facile mainstream clichés allow: contemplating the wrinkles around his eyes, George reflects "the strain of cohabitation, of constantly being involved in the emotional disasters of roommates and lovers, was taking its toll on me and etching age into my skin" (117). The single characters in this novel (for example, George's friend Tim, or his ex-boyfriend Robert) appear to resist aging; they live cautious lives and scrupulously preserve emotional autonomy (Robert, for instance, is physically incapable of sleeping in bed with another person). McCauley makes it apparent, however, that such fastidiousness is tantamount to frigidity.

7. In line with George's tendency to conceptualize his relationship with Nina in heterosexual terms, he describes his return journey to New York (and Nina) in terms of romantic expectancy:

On the bus back to New York I sat staring out the windows, dazed by the trees flashing by and then by the gathering lights and buildings. I didn't think about much except Nina and what I was going to say when I told her I wanted to stay and help her with the baby. I felt a little as if I were going back to propose. I looked around the smoky insides of the bus and then out the window, and in one sudden break in the trees along the highway, I saw the entire skyline of Manhattan and gasped with a start of surprise. (188)

8. That this novel subverts narrative conventions as well as social ones suggests that it proposes a revised form for the family-saga, one that corresponds to the "new" families depicted here. Art, in this case, does not merely imitate life, it paves the way to different kinds of life.

9. Their attempts to reinvent the family also represent responses to distinctly modern facts of life: feminist value structures, gay liberation, AIDS, the necessity of double-income households, the need for child-care.

10. This exchange also nicely demonstrates how the unavailability of commonly acknowledged terms for gay experiences and relationships contributes to the erasure of those experiences and relationships from mainstream culture. "I'm sure you'll find another . . . whatever" indicates the absence of a term (acceptable to George's mother) to describe George's lover; the slippage into indeterminacy ("whatever") refuses Joley any authentic role in George's life.

The potential meaningfulness of a gay relationship is denied by this culturally determined unwillingness to articulate gay-ness in neutral terms.

11. Like Nina's family home, George's bears evident symbolic weight:

The house I grew up in was given to my parents for their wedding present by every member of the immediate family on both sides. My mother often said she would have preferred to start off her marriage in a small apartment where she didn't feel obliged to fill the empty bedrooms right away. As it was, I think certain relatives felt their present had been unappreciated when my mother produced only two kids. It wasn't a large house, but it was divided up into an incomprehensible number of small rooms on several disjointed levels. From the outside it looked like any other characterless suburban ranch house, but overnight guests had been known to lose their bearings on a 3 A.M. trip to the bathroom, wandering up and down the various tiny staircases. (278)

This house represents the expectations placed on George's own parents to produce a large and typical family, while also manifesting in its architectural eccentricities the muddles and confusions both experienced (and perpetuated) by George's family.

12. George himself identifies the opposition between Frank's wedding and his own comparatively closeted personal life:

I was jealous, admittedly, of all the attention and enthusiasm and gifts and forced gaiety about to be lavished on my brother for marrying some woman he'd known for a few months, while my relationships were a trial to have acknowledged, let alone celebrated. (274-75)

McCauley treats this distinction ironically, from start to finish: while George agonizes over his decision to move in with Paul, Frank admits that he is swiftly marrying Cici because "she's the first girl I've gone out with I'm maybe a little afraid of losing" (210); and this marriage, George discreetly tells us, does not last (301), despite the hopeful vows articulated and the rituals performed at Frank and Cici's church wedding.

13. No doubt, Frank would consider the house George eventually shares with Paul such a barn:

Paul's house . . . was a peculiar little cabin nestled into a grove of pine trees off the side of a rutted road. Aside from the bedroom, there was only a large square space sectioned off into living room and kitchen and study areas. Gabriel slept in a loft connected to the living room by a ladder. Paul had installed a fireman's pole for him to slide down, making the place seem even more like a playhouse. (181)

Significantly unlike George's family home, with its labyrinthine stairs and halls, Paul's house is architecturally "open," suggesting the sincerity and frankness possible there.

14. A similar structural reversal lies in the fact that the children in this narrative appear not as the end results of linear romantic/heterosexual relationships, but instead as the starting-points of variously defined intimate relations. The novel begins, we saw, with Nina's announcement of her pregnancy; with that established, the narrative flashes back to George's arrival in New York City, and the chain of events that led up to his meeting Nina and moving in with her. Mirroring this structure, George meets Gabriel in a flash-forward, after which the narrative backtracks to fill in the events of the night before, when George goes home with Paul. In both cases, the appearance (or announcement) of the child precedes and supersedes other details: Emily-in-utero and Gabriel are the pivotal figures in those scenes. We might even say that these children are the starting points for the families that develop over the course of the novel: Nina's woman-centered family (Molly, Nina, Emily), and George's male family (George, Paul, Gabriel).

15. The alliterative link between Molly and Emily resembles that between George and Gabriel. McCauley draws attention to this when Gabriel first meets George; at that moment, Gabriel announces, "George! That begins with a J. My name begins with a G. G-g-g-g-gabriel." George responds, "George begins with a G, too" (179). Though a minor subtlety in the story-telling, these pairings point not only to the inevitable adult-child relationships, but also to the parallelism between the two families.

Works Cited

Boheemen, Christine van. *The Novel as Family Romance: Language, Gender, and Authority from Fielding to Joyce*. Ithaca: Cornell UP, 1987.

McCauley, Stephen. *The Man of the House*. New York: Simon and Schuster, 1996.

——. *The Object of My Affection*. New York: Simon and Schuster, 1987.

Sedgwick, Eve Kosofsky. *Between Men: English Literature and Male Homosocial Desire*. New York: Columbia UP, 1985.

Contributors

Susan Allen Ford is professor of English and Writing Center Coordinator at Delta State University in Cleveland, Mississippi, where she teaches courses in composition, British literature, the English novel, and detective fiction. She has written on a variety of topics, both critical and pedagogical, including the novel of the Romantic period, Jane Austen, detective fiction, Southern women writers, as well as issues related to expanding the literary canon and pedagogy and practice in the Writing Center. Her essay springs from work done at two NEH Summer Seminars: Women and Men Poets in British Romanticism directed by Stuart Curran, and Social Change in Early Modern England and the Rise of the Novel directed by John Richetti.

Charlene E. Bunnell received her Ph.D. from the University of Delaware in 1995, specializing in eighteenth- and nineteenth-century English fiction. She is currently an adjunct professor at the University of Delaware and Widener University. Publications include an article on Mary Shelley's *Mathilda* in the *Keats-Shelley Journal* and an essay on Shelley's novels of manners in *Iconoclastic Departures: Mary Shelley After Frankenstein*. She has presented numerous conference papers at SAMLA, NEMLA, American Society for Eighteenth Century Studies, and Popular Culture.

Aleta F. Cane teaches at Framingham State College and Northeastern University, where she received her Ph.D. in June 1996. She has published articles on Gerard Manley Hopkins, Charlotte Perkins Gilman, and Sarah Josepha Hale. She is also the co-author, with Beth Shearer, of *Frankly Speaking: A Book for Caesarean Couples*.

Sheila Reitzel Foor received her Ph.D. in 1985 from The Ohio State University. She is now associate professor of English at Lincoln University in Pennsylvania where she has taught for twelve years; she also coordinates the department's English Education program. Author of *Dickens' Rhetoric* as well as numerous articles, Dr. Foor's interests include Victorian fiction and works by women of color.

286 Contributors

Hildegard Hoeller is a preceptor in the Expository Writing Program at Harvard University. Her work in American literature centers around a reassessment of realism and the sentimental tradition in nineteenth and twentieth-century American fiction. She is completing a book manuscript on Wharton's relationship to both of these traditions.

Elizabeth Mahn Nollen has taught composition and literature at West Chester University of Pennsylvania for thirteen years. Her scholarly interests include women's writing, Gothic fiction, and popular culture. She is currently co-writing a popular culture composition text for St. Martin's Press. Her publications include articles on Ann Radcliffe, Jane Austen, Charlotte Brontë, Thomas Hardy, Daphne Du Maurier, and Anne Tyler. She continues to be very active in the Popular Culture Association and NEMLA, where she has delivered numerous papers and chaired many panels. During the summers, Dr. Mahn Nollen teaches gifted, at-risk students from the Philadelphia School District.

D. Quentin Miller is an assistant professor of English at Gustavus Adolphus College in Saint Peter, Minnesota. His essay is related to his dissertation on John Updike and the Cold War. He has published articles on other twentieth-century American authors, such as Hemingway, Wharton, Tim O'Brien, and Bobbie Ann Mason, and he also writes fiction. He is currently working on a novel and on a number of academic projects.

Andrea O'Reilly Herrera teaches Victorian and multiethnic literature with a special concentration in colonial, postcolonial, and Diaspora literature and theory at the State University of New York College at Fredonia. She has published several scholarly articles on a variety of contemporary Latina/o and French authors and has recently completed her first novel. Currently she is working on a project that focuses on the Cuban Diaspora.

Wendy Perkins is an assistant professor of English at Prince George's Community College. She has published several articles on British and American authors and served as assistant editor of the *D. H. Lawrence Review* from 1991-94.

Paul M. Puccio is assistant professor of English at the University of Central Florida, Orlando. He has published on Victorian public school fiction, Stephen Sondheim, and pedagogical issues. His research interests include film and literature, Victorian/Edwardian literature and culture, and the literature of school and college experience.

Frank P. Riga is professor of English at Canisius College in Buffalo, New York, where he teaches children's literature, British Romantic writers, the Oxford Christians, and short fiction. He has co-authored, with Claude A. Prance, *Index to The London Magazine* and has published articles on St. Augustine, Mrs. Molesworth, George MacDonald, Rudyard Kipling, C. S. Lewis, and Jean Rhys. In his own little Christmas cottage industry, he has spoken and written on the Créche, the Magi, Santa Claus, and La Befana.

Michelle Pagni Stewart teaches literature and composition at California State University, San Bernardino. Her interests include Native American, African American and other ethnic literatures, children's literature, and short fiction. Currently she is studying the narrative structures of multiple narrator ethnic novels, and she has presented several conference papers in the last year exploring this interest.

Scott F. Stoddart is associate professor of Liberal Arts and the coordinator of Undergraduate Writing at Nova Southeastern University, where he teaches a variety of courses in American literature, film, and Popular Culture studies. He is the author of a number of articles on the work of Henry James, Stephen Sondheim, Stephen Crane and on a variety of pedagogical issues; he also has published on film adaptations of F. Scott Fitzgerald and Edith Wharton. Currently, he is writing *"The Master" of the House: Henry James and the Domestic Tradition.*

Maureen Thum teaches English and Honors at the University of Michigan-Flint. She is co-chair of the Language and Literature Section of the Michigan Academy and chair of the British Popular Culture Section of the Popular Culture Association. Dr. Thum has published articles on generic patterns and folk-motifs in *The Germanic Review*, the *Philological Quarterly, Milton Studies, Children's Literature Quarterly* and in the annual volume of the *Yale Children's Literature* journal.

Index

Abbott, Mary, 35
Ahearn, Kerry, 215
Allen, Elizabeth, 146
Ammons, Elizabeth, 8, 167, 181
Anderson, Benedict, 4, 26
Aries, Philippe, 32
Ash, Beth Sharon, 117
Auerbach, Nina, 74, 113
Austen, Jane, 3, 12, 280
  Northanger Abbey, 16
  Persuasion, 12

Bakhtin, Mikhail, 155
Balint, Alice, 191
Barbauld, Anna Laetitia, 26
Batchelor, John, 144
Bayles, Martha, 252
Baym, Nina, 116, 144
Becker, Elizabeth C., 76
Bellow, Saul
  The Adventures of Augie March,
    195, 198
Beowulf, 280
Berenson, William, 168
Betts, Doris, 217
Billingsley, Andrew, 238-39
Blades, John, 217
Blake, William, 33
Boheemen, Christine van, 279
Boone, Joseph Allen, 4, 17
Born, Daniel, 145
Bowstead, Diana, 27
Braddon, Mary Elizabeth
  Lady Audley's Secret, 13
Braxton, Joanne M., 75
"Britons Strike Home," 22, 27

Brontë, Charlotte, 5, 6
  Jane Eyre, 74
  Villette, 5, 55-72
Brontë, Emily, 12
  Wuthering Heights, 12
Browning, Elizabeth Barrett, 6, 79-94
  Aurora Leigh, 6, 79-94
Burke, Edmund
  *Reflections on the Revolution in
    France*, 16
Burnett, Frances Hodgson
  Little Lord Fauntleroy, 223
  The Secret Garden, 223, 231-32
Burney, Francis, 3
Butler, Marilyn, 16
Byron, Lord
  Don Juan, 52

Caird, Monica, 149, 150
Campbell, Thomas
  Gertrude of Wyoming, 52
Carby, Hazel, 69, 75
Chesterfield, Lord, 32
Chodorow, Nancy, 9, 183, 188, 191
Chopin, Kate
  The Awakening, 13, 195, 233
Clark-Beattie, Rosemary, 74
Coleridge, Samuel Taylor, 165
Colley, Linda, 15, 16
Cooper, Barbara E., 242, 250, 252
Cott, Nancy, 73, 74
Cowper, William, 71, 76
Craik, W. A., 75
Crosby, Christina, 74
Cunningham, Gail, 149
Curran, Stuart, 25

289